The public image of big business in America, 1880-1940

ALSO BY LOUIS GALAMBOS

COMPETITION AND COOPERATION: The
Emergence of a Modern Trade Association

AMERICAN BUSINESS HISTORY

THE CHANGING ECONOMIC ORDER: Readings in
American Business and Economic History
(co-editor, with Alfred D. Chandler, Jr., and
Stuart Bruchey)

The public image of big business in America, 1880-1940

A QUANTITATIVE STUDY IN SOCIAL CHANGE

Louis Galambos

WITH THE ASSISTANCE OF BARBARA BARROW SPENCE

THE JOHNS HOPKINS UNIVERSITY PRESS
BALTIMORE AND LONDON

The editors of three journals have kindly given permission to use in this book material previously published in the following articles: "AFL's Concept of Big Business: A Quantitative Study of Attitudes toward the Large Corporation, 1894–1931," *Journal of American History*, March 1971; "The Agrarian Image of the Large Corporation, 1879–1920: A Study in Social Accommodation," and (co-authored with Alfred D. Chandler, Jr.) "The Development of Large-Scale, Economic Organizations in Modern America," *Journal of Economic History*, September 1968 and March 1970, respectively; "The Emerging Organizational Synthesis in Modern American History," *Business History Review*, Autumn 1970.

Manufactured in the United States of America.

The Johns Hopkins University Press, Baltimore, Maryland 21218
The Johns Hopkins University Press Ltd., London

Library of Congress Catalog Card Number 75-11347
ISBN 0-8018-1635-1

Library of Congress Cataloging in Publication Data

Galambos, Louis.
 The public image of big business in America.

 Includes bibliographical references and index.
 1. Big business—United States—History. 2. Industry—Social aspects—United States—History. 3. United States—Social conditions. I. Spence, Barbara Barrow, joint author. II. Title.
HD2785.G34   338.6′44′0973   75-11347
ISBN 0-8018-1635-1

To Margaret,
   who reads the author better than
   most people read his books

CONTENTS

LIST OF TABLES

LIST OF FIGURES

ACKNOWLEDGMENTS

Custom dictates that one's wife and family make their appearance in the final paragraph of the acknowledgments. They wait off stage until you have thanked all of those who have given money, time, ideas, and other assorted services. I have never understood the rationale behind this tradition, unless it symbolizes the fact that our immediate families are more patient with us than our colleagues are. That alone, I think, warrants a break with custom. The contributions of an intelligent, discreet wife and understanding children are usually decisive—in my case, far more important than any other sources of support, whether economic, intellectual, or emotional. My wife, Margaret, put up with innumerable inconveniences, far beyond those that normally plague the spouse of a writing, and sometimes nonwriting, husband. I am deeply grateful for her help and for the assistance of my two daughters—Denise, who was Lisa in my last book, and Jennifer, who arrived in the midst of this project and thus thinks all historians earn their living with a desk calculator.

Most of us get by with the help of our friends as well as our family, and I am no exception to this rule. Foremost in providing support for this project were Alfred D. Chandler, Jr., and the Sloan Foundation. I initially launched this study under a grant the foundation made to the Center for the Study of Recent American History, under Chandler's direction, at the Johns Hopkins University. I am indebted to the foundation and its director, Arnold J. Zurcher, for the substantial aid they rendered and, in particular, for their willingness to free a great deal of my time from other academic duties. Over the years, Alfred Chandler's assistance was invaluable. He provided advice when I asked for it and economic support when I needed it—all the while giving me full rein to tailor my project as I saw fit. Especially helpful to me was the opportunity to exchange ideas with the world's foremost authority on corporate internal structures while I was studying big business's external relations.

My thanks also go to three universities: Rice, Rutgers, and the Johns Hopkins University. Rice tolerantly allowed me to disappear for extensive leaves and for long research trips, and when I was not adrift, the History Department and university officials extended every assistance the school could make available. My colleagues at Rice and at Rutgers and my students at both schools provided a critical audience for my ideas, but in this vein my special thanks must go to the participants in the seminars at Johns Hopkins. These sessions had an influence upon my work that can be fully appreciated only by those who have experienced this unique variety of intellectual combat. Between these gladiatorial contests, numerous administrators and colleagues at Johns Hopkins aided me in ways too numerous to list.

Other friends in Baltimore and elsewhere helped to coax this study ahead. The contribution of Barbara Barrow Spence was so important that her name has been included on the title page, and the precise nature of her efforts is described in chapter 2. Alan D. Anderson devised a computer program that yielded printouts intelligible even to my untutored eye, Mary Menefee made certain that the numbers they contained were correct, and John Spurbeck transformed my crude figures into the excellent graphs that appear in this book. Several typists labored over the manuscript, and I would like to thank Nellie Wahbe Barrett, Dolores Koheet, Marguerite Mareck, and Cecelia Pease, all of whom were tolerant and efficient. Many librarians also assisted me, and the courteous staff members at the library of the U.S. Department of Agriculture in Washington, D.C., were particularly helpful.

A number of persons read drafts of the manuscript and gave me their advice. Although I was occasionally stubborn enough to ignore their suggestions, I benefited greatly from the criticisms of Robert T. Hogan, Robert J. Brugger, Alfred D. Chandler, Jr., Robert M. Collins, David Herbert Donald, Jack P. Greene, John Higham, Richard Merritt, and Charles E. Neu. Finally, I would like to thank Gaston V. Rimlinger and Ferdinand Levy for leading me through the labyrinth of government grants; the grants, which are enumerated in chapter 2, note 42, would never have been available to me had I not received the expert counsel of these two academic entrepreneurs.

Even with all of this help, I could not entirely avoid mistakes, but I am fully responsible for the remaining errors. One problem in particular bothered me until I realized that it was generic to a history that combines a chronology based upon the pattern of the past (i.e., descriptive statistics) with an analysis of the process of social change or causation. With that in mind, I did not try to iron out this problem, realizing that the perceptive reader would quickly find it and understand it for what it was. Those scholars who take an interest in this sort of methodological question might also want to have a closer look at the annual percentages depicted in my various graphs, and they can write directly to me for a mimeographed copy of the data.

PART ONE. CONTEXT AND METHOD

1

THE LARGE-SCALE ORGANIZATION IN MODERN AMERICA

The single most significant phenomenon in modern American history is the emergence of giant, complex organizations. In the present day it is apparent that bureaucracies of one sort or another dominate our economic system, control the central features of our polity, and shape many of the important aspects of our culture. Most of the things that most of us do each day are either accomplished directly within this type of administrative network or are indirectly dependent upon the activities of one or more of the great modern organizations surrounding us. In recent years this situation seems to have made some Americans uneasy and others angry, but even the criticism of bureaucracy, the so-called establishment, or the military-industrial complex eventually finds expression in organizations that are themselves of great size and complexity. It would appear that we have become organization men and women, whether we like it or not.[1]

Since the late nineteenth century, big business has played a major role in our industrial economy. It has been the owners and professional managers of large firms who have made most of the vital decisions involving the production and distribution of our goods and services, who have for better or worse guided our progress in technology, who have determined the locus of economic activity in the nation. Their decisions have, of course, been influenced by a variety of considerations, including the growth of other large and powerful organizations. Sometimes these have been competing business firms. In many industries labor unions have achieved a measure of "countervailing power."[2] Increasingly, governmental agencies of awesome size and complexity have come to play a crucial role in the national economy.

Today large-scale political organizations perform functions which influence the daily decisions of most Americans. Federal bureaucracies promote technological change, gather taxes, regulate business behavior, administer welfare programs, and carry out activities ranging from defense to development, from environmental protection to education, from forestry to farming, and on through the alphabet. In 1970 the federal government alone accounted for more than one-fifth of our gross national product and employed almost three million persons in civilian jobs. One department, agriculture, provided employment for 116,012 persons—more than had worked for the entire government in 1881.[3] A similar, though less debated, expansion has taken place in state and local government; in New York, for instance, public expenditures in 1969 were about fifteen billion dollars and local government employees in the state numbered 879,000. At all levels of government, large numbers of people and great amounts of money are deployed by giant bureaucratic institutions.[4]

The tracks of these modern organizations can be followed into almost every facet of American life. In higher education the "multiversity" has invited the enmity of many (usually those most closely associated with it), but even their attacks testify to the powerful influence universities of this structure and size now exert in the academic world.[5] Similar changes have taken place among our churches: an elaborate hierarchy of national agencies has gradually emerged and acquired an important and growing role in the nation's religious life.[6] In the professions—from welfare work to engineering—the same distinct pattern can be seen.[7] In the modern era, power has come to be centered in new types of organizations, most of which are very large, complex in structure, and organized along bureaucratic lines.

This type of organization has certain distinct characteristics. As Max Weber pointed out, the formal attributes of the bureaucratic form of authority include a hierarchical structure in which power is allocated according to abstract rules. These rules or laws provide relatively precise definitions of authority and responsibility. Bureaucracies place emphasis on impersonal decisions made by a staff of experts filling positions which, theoretically at least, do not change when the personnel does. Men fill these positions on the basis of explicit technical qualifications, and in a normal career they advance in regular steps within the organization.[8] Weber explained both the origins of this style of formal organization and its final triumph in modern society in terms of efficiency: "Experience tends universally to show that the purely bureaucratic type of administration . . . is, from a purely technical point of view, capable of attaining the highest degree of efficiency and is in this sense formally the most rational known means of carrying out imperative control over human beings."[9]

In recent years a number of scholars have challenged Weber's emphasis upon efficiency and have also offered a variety of new ways to analyze bureaucracies. Some have focused on the web of personal relations and the structure of informal authority which persists even in supposedly impersonal organizations. In prisons, for example, an organizational chart may show that the guards give orders to the inmates; in reality the prisoners exercise considerable power over the guards—in an informal and extralegal way.[10] Other scholars have suggested that the flow of information within a bureaucracy may provide a more accurate guide to authority relationships than the explicit, legal relationships that Weber felt were so important. Whatever correctives students of bureaucracy have offered to Weber's model, however, they have continued to use many of the basic concepts of Weberian sociology and have also reaffirmed Weber's central vision of the rise of the bureaucratic organization as a crucial feature of modern society.[11]

This book is based on the major premise that historians as well as sociologists should acknowledge that the process of organizational change has had a more decisive influence on modern America than any other single phenomenon.[12] My purpose is not to test this premise. That will be the task of many historians writing articles and monographs that explore different aspects of bureaucratic development in the United States. The cumulative results of their work (and mine) will eventually indicate how influential bureaucratization was. For the present, however, all that one can do is pronounce this central assumption, study in detail particular patterns of organizational change, and work toward the goal of a general history. There are already signs that a broad historical synthesis along organizational lines is beginning to emerge.[13] But for the most part our recent history continues to be written from a different vantage point, one stressing the overriding significance of a special variety of political events. These are the elections, the legislative and judicial struggles, the political conflicts highlighted by the progressive or liberal approach to the past. The ribs of our history continue to be past politics, and even the severest critics of progressive history have not rejected this assumption. Now the time has come to do that. I am substituting a different point of view, one that centers about the large-scale organization and assumes that our political system, our economy, and our culture have experienced an organizational revolution in the past century.[14]

This book examines one facet of that revolution. My subject is the public response in America to the most powerful and rapidly growing form of bureaucracy, the large corporation. The objective is to determine how people, most of them middle-class citizens, perceived the rise of big business and how their perceptions changed over a period of three generations.[15] Insofar as their attitudes shifted, I try to find out what caused the changes that took place. My focus is largely on the first phase of organization-building in the United States, the years 1880 through 1930, when big business was all-powerful and all-important. I conclude with a chapter on the thirties, when government bureaucracies appear to have taken center stage, but I examine these political developments only to the extent that they influenced public attitudes toward the evolution of large-scale organizations in business. Here, then, is an extended essay in social perception—an examination of the origins of what might be called a corporate or bureaucratic culture. Given this subject, we must begin by describing the evolution of big business and by showing how this phenomenon was related to the major patterns of American organizational growth.

THE LARGE-SCALE ORGANIZATION IN MODERN AMERICA

II.   The rise of the large-scale organization in the United States began no earlier than the 1850s.[16] Even a brief examination confirms this choice of a starting point. In the colonial era some rather large joint stock companies were involved in the business of colonization; these organizations quickly gave way, however, to smaller groups and to individual efforts to cope with the frontier environment. It would appear that the problems of communication were too great, the need for flexibility and innovation too pressing, for the larger companies of the seventeenth and eighteenth centuries to survive. Poor transportation restricted the size of the colonial market, and limited markets imposed a constraint upon economic ventures, whether in commerce, agriculture, or manufacturing.[17] The political structure was almost as localized and fragmented as the economy, and the agencies of empire did little to counter the forces making for decentralization of power.[18]

These underlying conditions persisted with minor changes through the first half of the nineteenth century. Despite the creation of a nation state, despite advances in communications and transportation, despite the beginnings of industrialization, the scale of enterprise in America remained small. The adoption of a federated system and the widespread opposition to further centralization limited governmental growth at the national level. Even the Second Bank of the United States, a "monster corporation" in the eyes of its enemies, was a relatively small undertaking. Although the Second Bank maintained numerous branches around the country, they were never coordinated in a bureaucratic manner; and this lack of coordination, plus the bank's short life, prevented it from becoming a prototype for subsequent large-scale organizations.[19] The state canal administrations and the New England cotton textile mills were just as distinctly pre-bureaucratic.[20]

Around 1850, however, crucial changes in the transportation and communication systems produced a new kind of organization. The railroad began to integrate and round out the nation's transportation network, especially after the consolidation of the major east-west trunk lines. The resulting water and rail system, improved and extended in the following decades, laid the foundation for a truly national economy. Of equal importance was the telegraph, an invention that in the late forties and fifties made rapid, long-distance communication possible for the first time. These dual developments were the prime movers of organizational change in the modern era.

Between 1850 and 1880 a few organizations with a distinctly modern scope and style of operation emerged. Most impressive were the railroads, in part because of their size but also because of their bureaucratic mode of organization. The early trunk lines were capitalized at amounts dwarfing all previous ventures in the private sector of the economy: in 1855 the New York Central alone had over twenty-eight million dollars invested in road and equipment.[21] Extensive operations and a technological imperative for coordination fostered a series of experiments with more systematic forms of administration. The result was a prototype of the modern industrial corporation, a style of firm which by 1880 had most of the characteristics we associate with large-scale enterprise in the twentieth century.[22]

For our purposes, we will label this type of organization a primary bureaucracy—that is, a large and complex organization essentially concerned with the job of marshaling people and resources in order to produce goods or services. Secondary bureaucracies we will define as those organizations chiefly involved in coordinating the activities of, and communicating between, other organizations.[23] Examples of secondary bureaucracies included union federations, trade associations, and some government agencies. As late as 1880, however, there were hardly any notable secondary organizations at the national level, and the ones that did exist in the private sector—like the railroad freight pools and the National Labor Union—enjoyed only a fleeting existence.[24]

By 1880, in fact, the modern primary organizations were just beginning to get a secure foothold in America. There were hardly any private businesses to compare to the railroads. The Standard Oil Company grew fast, but not until 1882 did it change from a loose alliance of separate companies into a trust, and even then it took some years to consolidate the combine along bureaucratic lines.[25] The same could be said for Andrew Carnegie's iron and steel interests, which by 1880 had also reached substantial proportions.[26] Several national trade unions successfully weathered the severe depression of the 1870s, but these organizations and such early professional groups as the American Medical Association and the American Society of Civil Engineers were still isolated phenomena in a society oriented to local or regional affairs and to less formal styles of organization.[27]

Developments within the states in the years 1850–80 demand as much attention as events on the national level. State and local governments made important organizational innovations in the fields of education and mental health; a number of the states created regulatory agencies prefiguring the independent commissions that the federal government later established.[28] Unfortunately, we know less about these changes than we do about those which took place nationally, and it is hazardous even to guess whether bureaucratization within the states had a causal relationship with the subsequent organizational innovations in the national sphere. In the years following 1880, however, we are on firmer ground in asserting that the major thrust of organizational change came in bureaucracies operating across, not within, state lines.

III. Between 1880 and 1930 thousands of new primary organizations emerged at the national level, most of them in the private rather than the public sector.

Though many were business firms, many were not. During these years there was a tremendous expansion of professional organizations.[29] Although the American Society of Civil Engineers had been active since 1852, as late as 1879 ASCE and the American Institute of Mining Engineers (formed in 1871) were the only national engineering groups in the country. In 1880 the American Society of Mechanical Engineers joined them; two years later the stationary engineers formed an association; and by the end of the decade the electrical and naval engineers had also come together on the national level.[30] In the 1890s professional engineers organized five more groups, and during the following ten years the processes of differentiation and organizational innovation actually accelerated: the automotive engineers, the refrigerating engineers, and at least seven other groups found it necessary to organize their own separate associations. By the end of the 1920s, over thirty such organizations existed in the engineering profession alone, and an even larger number of state and local groups was arrayed beneath and around these associations.[31] By this time any action that would threaten or reward any substantial group of engineers was likely either to arouse a response from or actually originate in one or more of the professional associations. Before 1880 this had not been the case.

Engineering was only one of the many occupations experiencing this sort of organizational transformation. Similar patterns of development could be found in the academic disciplines, among social workers, doctors, and lawyers, as well as professional managers. Skilled laborers built a phalanx of new primary organizations, mostly craft unions, which were now able to survive major depressions and to control access to employment in a number of industries.[32] Among farmers the drive to organize on a nation-wide basis was temporarily diverted into third-party presidential politics, but after the defeat of William Jennings Bryan in 1896, farmers increasingly turned their energies to the job of building less dramatic organizations. Their success ultimately brought them influence far greater than that of the more colorful agrarian reformers of the late nineteenth century.[33]

Of all the new primary organizations that evolved in the fifty years after 1880, however, business firms clearly ran ahead of the field in terms of power, wealth, and degree of bureaucratization. At the beginning of this period only the larger railroads and a few manufacturing firms could be classified as modern corporations, and companies capitalized at five million dollars or more were a rare species. By 1929, a list of the five hundred or so largest industrial corporations—even if one left out the railroads—would include companies with assets ranging from around thirty-five million to almost two and a half billion dollars.[34] Some of these corporate giants had reached their awesome proportions simply by expanding their plants and reinvesting the earnings achieved through efficient production and distribu-

CONTEXT AND METHOD

tion; most, however, had arisen out of mergers between competing firms —that is, out of combinations that initially aimed at achieving market control and the profits of monopoly. While they all had to settle for something less than a complete or pure monopoly, many of the combines came close enough to inspire widespread public concern about the trust movement.[35]

These fears were understandable, for the trust or concentration movement effectively restructured the American economy. The most significant changes took place at the turn of the century, during a five year period (1898–1902) in which 2,653 separate firms disappeared via the merger route. There was a second round of mergers during the First World War and a third wave in the latter part of the 1920s.[36] By then giant corporations dominated most of the nation's leading industries, and the largest of these firms together owned a significant portion of the private property in America.[37] The family enterprise steadily gave way to the bureaucratized corporation. Although the families of great wealth lingered on and occasionally came to grips with the new age of organizations, control in most of the largest corporations gradually shifted to professional managers—men who brought to their tasks special skills and who built a career in the firm, not the family.[38]

For men of this breed the organizational changes we have been describing provided a new kind of frontier, a new path to success. Great financial rewards could be gained, along with power and prestige, if men—or women—could succeed in building an organization or consolidating one along bureaucratic lines. To us the improvement of communications within an organization may seem inherently less exciting than life on the frontier, but both jobs demanded a particular kind of innovative spirit and both offered to their respective generations an opportunity for upward mobility.[39] After 1880, there was certainly less room at the top of corporate society in the sense that few could expect to command the new organizations; by the same token, however, the path to this elevated position was actually wider, since the bureaucracies valued technical achievement more highly than the personal characteristics or family origins which had been so important in the early nineteenth century.[40] When the government informed Americans in 1890 that the old frontier was closed, a new one was thus already opening for those who could build, perfect, or administer a modern organization.

Many problems had to be solved. In most primary business organizations, combination was achieved quickly but the development of effective central controls took years to accomplish. The history of the Standard Oil Company is instructive. When John D. Rockefeller and his colleagues took their first steps toward control of the oil industry in the 1870s, they were content to reduce competition in refining without actually consolidating the several companies they ran. Gradually, they converted an "alliance" into a trust (1882) and then into a centralized bureaucracy, in which detailed information—often in the form of statistics—flowed upward to a series of committees which used the data to set policy for Standard's sprawling industrial empire. It was almost 1900, however, before Standard achieved thoroughgoing centralization.[41]

The need to centralize power along bureaucratic lines was not limited to the business corporation; it was, in fact, one of the three crucial problems that leaders of all of the primary bureaucracies faced. The top men in the professional associations, no less than the union officers in the national craft organizations, spent much of their energy ensuring that channels of communication operated effectively and that the prerogatives of the primary organizations were respected by their own members. Among unions, for example, the nationals fought intense and frequent battles against the very local unions that had joined together to create national bodies in the first place. Sometimes these difficulties were precipitated by questions of policy—on strikes, for instance; sometimes they centered about the problem of determining union membership. As early as 1870, the Bricklayers Union had acknowledged the need for a single set of rules on membership, particularly since the organization had to deal with the problem of expulsion. In the words of the union president: "The National Union should specify the offense that may be punishable by expulsion and guarantee to every member a fair and impartial trial, and the Executive of the National Union should be vested with the power to set aside the action of a union by which such punishment has been inflicted without a legal trial." Nevertheless, it was the 1890s before the union was able to solve this problem by establishing and enforcing a "Code of Crimes and Penalties." Power in matters of membership and of the purse was centralized only after a long struggle, and this type of conflict took place within all of the primary organizations during the years after 1880.[42]

A second major problem involved the definition and maintenance of optimal external boundaries. The Standard Oil combine initially concentrated on refining and transporting oil products, but demands for internal efficiency and external defense against competitors led Standard to expand. Like the Roman Empire, the oil trust kept seeing new threats on its frontiers. The corporation began to produce and transport its own crude oil and to market its own products. When the sources of crude and the markets for finished products were overseas, Standard became a multinational corporation with affiliates spread from Europe through Latin America and on to the Orient.[43] Similar, though less grandiose, problems faced the leaders of professional organizations: if they defined their boundaries too narrowly and limited their membership too drastically, their association could find itself threatened by rival organizations. Thus, in 1904 a group of technicians formed the American Society of Refrigerating Engineers, specifying that their members would be only those who "have accomplished important work in the refrigeration field or shall occupy an important executive position in the field." This requirement was stringent. Within a few years the result was a new group, the National Association of *Practical* Refrigerating Engineers, which could accommodate those turned away by the American Society.[44] One solution to this problem was simply to define the profession more loosely, but this too had a price; if entry to the organization was too easy, its members might suffer loss of both income and prestige. In the associations, industrial corporations, and national unions, expansion was also constrained by the ability of the organization to maintain effective communications with and controls over its constituent parts.

The third problem generic to this era of bureaucratization was that of maintaining contact with and power over the organization's external environment. Frequently this was expressed as a desire for stability or rationality—goals that were on the face of it quite unexceptional. Lurking behind these slogans, however, were the age-old questions of the distribution of power, wealth, and status, changed in the modern era only by the size, complexity, and bureaucratic nature of the contestants. Sometimes the call for stability actually reflected a desire to preserve the status quo, but often stability could only be achieved, it seemed, by rather drastic changes in society or some part of it. Hence, the business leaders who proclaimed themselves exponents of the traditional concept of individual competition could also seek stability even when the means they used to achieve that goal destroyed competition.[45] Unions, professional associations, and farm organizations all found themselves forced to exercise power in an effort to create the kind of environment best suited to their interests.

This task involved communication as well as control. The organizations needed a steady flow of information from their immediate surroundings if they were going to stabilize or—even better—manipulate their environments. They needed to know what other primary organizations were doing. Unwilling to leave their fates in the invisible hand of competition, the bureaucracies soon discovered that they could benefit from a measure of intergroup coordination. The result was the formation of a wide variety of secondary organizations. Among labor unions, for example, the American Federation of Labor was a secondary organization built on top of a foundation of national craft unions. The AFL sought to coordinate the work of the nationals; it also provided a clearing house for information and on occasion arbitrated disputes between the crafts.

As the AFL's history illustrates, one of the outstanding characteristics of the secondary organizations in the years before 1930 was their relative weakness. In wealth and power they lagged far behind the primary bureaucracies. The AFL's officers tried on many occasions to persuade the nationals to adopt certain policies, but aside from withholding support—a dangerous alternative—the Federation could do little to coerce its constituent craft unions.[46] The same relationship existed between corporations and the trade associations they organized; whether these associations were attempting to control prices and production or merely to formulate industry-wide political goals, the member companies kept a tight rein on cooperative activities.[47] Although the leaders of the primary bureaucracies wanted frequent communication and occasional coordination, they were unwilling to pay much for these goals when the price was their autonomy or the short-run self-interest of their basic organizations.

We have become accustomed recently to think of government as a coordinating mechanism, and during the years before 1930 some public bureaucracies attempted to perform this function. But they did so in a hesitant and half-hearted style. The regulatory agencies sought to discipline the behavior of individual primary organizations. The commissions tried to ensure that businesses adopted correct standards of organizational behavior in both their internal and external relations. Negative restraints were proclaimed and occasionally invoked. The government attempted, for example, to solve the boundary problem by setting limits for organizational growth through the antitrust policy. Federal power was attractive enough to persuade some businessmen (i.e., those who were serious about the need for coordination) actually to seek regulation; hence the creation of the Federal Reserve System in 1913.[48] The Fed was an exception, however, and most of the regulatory commissions were merely captured and neutralized by the businesses they sought to regulate.[49] Neither the public nor the private secondary bureaucracies provided effective central control to the imposing array of primary organizations that had arisen by the end of the 1920s.

IV. The Great Depression of the thirties exposed some of the weaknesses of this ill-coordinated system and launched a second phase in America's organizational revolution. Now the central innovations came in the coordinating-liaison units, particularly those in the public sector, and the changes that took place once again involved three major problems: the centralization of power; the definition and maintenance of optimal boundaries; and the preservation of control over the external environment. At first there was some attempt, under the National Recovery Administration, to absorb private secondary organizations into the government and vest them with coercive powers. After 1935, however, attention increasingly turned to public, not private, institutions.[50] Gradually, and often haphazardly, the federal government devised policies that sought to centralize control over aggregate demand in the economy and thus to guide development along selected paths. The evolution of these programs and their supporting institutions continues today: witness the wage-price guidelines of the 1960s

CONTEXT AND METHOD

and the wage-price controls of the 1970s. Power is slowly shifting from the primary to the secondary bureaucracies, essentially in response to the needs created by the new and uncoordinated system of powerful primary organizations that had developed in the years 1880–1930. In that sense it transcends partisan politics and the liberal-conservative terminology that contemporary observers have usually applied to these developments. For the same reason, the process is likely to continue regardless of which political party is in power or which leader sits in the White House.

Although they were less obvious than the innovations in public policy, important changes also took place within the primary bureaucracies during the years following 1930. For one thing, traditional concepts of organizational boundaries began to break down. Among unions the historical concept of "crafts" had operated as a constraint upon organizational growth long after the crafts themselves had become largely irrelevant to the tasks performed in most of the modern, technologically advanced industries. In the thirties and forties, however, new industrial unions abandoned the craft concept and succeeded in organizing workers in such major industries as automobiles and steel. These unions were not the first ones in America to look beyond the traditional crafts, nor was their growth wholly a function of their more flexible concept of unionism. They were, nevertheless, the first such organizations to become permanent elements in our industrial economy.[51]

Similar changes took place among business corporations. In previous years the concept of the "industry" had imposed a constraint upon the expectational horizons of corporate managers; a firm in the iron and steel industry or in copper production focused almost exclusively on that single product. While the company might begin to extract its own raw materials, transport them, and distribute its final products, all these operations were closely tied to the basic goal of making and marketing steel or copper. A few leading companies had begun to abandon this approach even before the 1930s; the result in the chemical and automobile industries was the diversified firm manufacturing and marketing a variety of different products. By the end of the 1940s, the diversified firm had become the rule rather than the exception among America's largest corporations.[52] More recently, the conglomerates have taken a further step in this direction, leaving behind even the restraint imposed by the idea of exploiting related technologies or similar distributing systems. Under current conditions, tradition no more limits the growth of the firm than does a national frontier.

As they expanded their boundaries along these new lines, the primary bureaucracies found it increasingly difficult to solve the other two problems generic to this age of organizations: they found it harder to control their internal operations and to stabilize their external environments. The three major problems facing the organizational entrepreneurs were thus closely interrelated, and once again Standard Oil provides an instructive example. By the early 1940s this giant firm had grown so large and had become so complex that its top officers could no longer remain in touch with all of its major operations; the company underwent two reorganizations aimed at improving its system of internal communications. In 1942, however, when Standard's president testified before a congressional committee, he revealed a lack of knowledge about his own company that even defensive duplicity could not explain.[53] The responses to these communication problems were varied. On occasion the organizational elite merely adopted new policies, but more often they introduced structural changes in the firm. Among large business corporations (including Standard Oil), decentralization became the most popular response to the demands imposed by diversification and by far-flung international operations.[54] Many professional associations followed a similar course, creating an elaborate system of regional divisions and standing functional committees which was supposed to keep the organization intact, meet the needs of a varied constituency, and avoid the loss of members to splinter groups. Important developments have thus taken place in the primary as well as the secondary bureaucracies during recent years.

Changes of this magnitude could hardly have taken place without influencing the attitudes and values that made up the national culture. Indeed, this organizational revolution appears to have forced Americans to adopt a new culture, one attuned to the needs of bureaucracy in an urban setting. In the past century, the individualistic orientation of an atomistic, competitive society has given way to an emphasis upon group or collective effort. It is large-scale organization, I think, which best explains the transition that David Riesman and others identified some years ago as a shift from inner- to other-direction. The other-directed man was, in their definition, in harmony with "a group milieu"; "at home everywhere and nowhere," he was "able to receive signals from far and near"—from many and changing sources. The other-directed man guided himself not by an independent code of behavior but by "elaborate equipment" that told him how others were reacting to what he did. "As against guilt-and-shame controls, though of course these survive, one prime psychological lever of the other-directed person is a diffuse *anxiety*. This control equipment, instead of being like a gyroscope, is like a radar." In the early 1950s Riesman and his colleagues felt that this type of character was "emerging in very recent years in the upper middle class of our larger cities."[55] I would argue to the contrary: the other-directed man was already working for Standard Oil in the 1890s. By the early 1900s, his values were displacing individualistic concepts, at least in the middle class.

Other, related cultural changes took place. Powerful bureaucracies demanded new types of followers, as well as leaders, and the United States

CONTEXT AND METHOD

eventually became the kind of society that could regularly provide the men and the values modern organizations needed. In the new bureaucratic order men tended to define their relationships to others in very specific terms, and they evaluated behavior in a relatively neutral, unemotional manner.[56] They applied standards that were more universalistic than those which had characterized the fragmented, particularistic, agrarian and small-town society that was being supplanted in the modern era.

What emerged in America was a new culture, a corporate culture, which included, I think, a new public image of the giant corporation. My focus in the following pages is upon that image and thus upon a single strand of the corporate culture; only by inference and by drawing heavily upon the work of others can I show how opinions of the giant firm were related to their cultural matrix. Chancy as that may be, the risks will be proportionate to the rewards if I can thereby place my subject in what I consider to be its proper historical context.

V.   Fortunately, earlier historians have told us a great deal about that context and about the public response to the rise of big business. Their various interpretations deserve careful attention. In the Marxian view of history, for instance, business combines played a central role in the class conflict that capitalism inevitably produced, a conflict centered upon real and vital economic issues. Attitudes were rooted in socioeconomic classes and in class interests. The large firm accelerated the process of capital accumulation leading to the "immiserization" of the working class and to the multiplication of the army of the unemployed.[57] As Marx explained: "The growing accumulation of capital implies its growing concentration. Thus grows the power of capital, the alienation of the conditions of social production personified in the capitalist from the real producers. Capital comes more and more to the fore as a social power. . . . The contradiction between the general social power into which capital develops, on the one hand, and the private power of the individual capitalists over these social conditions of production, on the other, becomes ever more irreconcilable, and yet contains the solution of the problem, because it implies at the same time the transformation of the conditions of production into general, common, social, conditions." Bourgeois, meliorative measures could not prevent the final resolution of capitalism's central contradiction through class warfare and the triumph of the proletariat.[58]

Joseph A. Schumpeter envisioned a different process of change with a somewhat similar result. Large firms, he felt, spurred technological progress and thus contributed to capitalism's economic success; but innovation and progress were accompanied by waves of destructive competition, which in turn fostered widespread discontent. Intellectuals channeled this dissatisfaction into reform movements that sought to prevent monopoly through antitrust proceedings and to control business through regulatory measures. Meanwhile, the large corporation itself changed, substituting administrators for entrepreneurs, and as a result it became less likely to innovate. Bureaucratization also supplanted the family firm and eventually eroded the social values that had sustained capitalism. The modern liberal state, the new attitudes, and the new style of giant firm were together choking off entrepreneurship and destroying the capitalist system. Socialism would ensue, Schumpeter said, from a peaceful evolutionary, not a violent revolutionary, process, and the large corporation would play a crucial role in that transformation.[59]

America's progressive or liberal historians offered a different perspective.[60] While they shared with Marx the assumption that real economic interests were the root cause of conflict between the trusts and society, liberal historians did not use the Marxian dialectic as a central feature in their interpretation of history, nor did they adopt Marx's vision of the triumph of the proletariat. Instead, they portrayed modern American history as a series of clashes between liberals and conservatives, with big business marching in the armies of the right wing. Liberal historians saw success, not subterfuge, in bourgeois reform. In their view, the Populist, Progressive, and New Deal reform movements provided effective political solutions to such problems as the concentration of economic power.[61] Like Schumpeter, they felt that intellectuals played a vital role in shaping public attitudes and thus in guiding political change; they gave more emphasis than Schumpeter did to liberal political leadership, and of course they did not see socialism as the inevitable product of reform.[62] Antitrust and regulatory measures, they concluded, broke up some combines and curbed the power of others; modern American history was a study in progress, and change was the product of creative political tensions. They saw opposition to the large corporation disappearing as government solved the trust problem.[63]

In recent years, many scholars examining America's response to the rise of big business have abandoned progressive concepts. Revisionists have discovered that large companies were not always the opponents of reform; instead of a monolithic "business community" they have found businessmen, large and small, arrayed in complex and changing coalitions which sometimes sought and sometimes opposed political change.[64] Some New Left historians have characterized the entire progressive movement at the national level as a product of efforts on the part of big business to establish through government regulation the stability and security that could not be achieved in the private sector.[65] The motives and behavior of reformers as well as those of businessmen have been reappraised. To the more conventional motives, such as direct economic and political interest, revisionists have added status anxiety, a longing for order, and a variety of irrational and nonrational desires. Cultural values have become almost as important in explaining man's behavior as market values once were.[66]

Revisionist and New Left historians alike have battered the central pillars of the progressive synthesis: the assumption of progress and the related premise that the good society was achieved largely through a process of creative political conflict. By looking beyond the passage of liberal legislation, by examining in some detail the manner in which, for instance, regulatory and antitrust measures actually worked, scholars have come to realize that progressive historians exaggerated the extent to which American society was reformed. Instead of change, many recent historians have found continuity to be the most outstanding aspect of the nation's history. Instead of conflict, they have asserted that consensus over basic values characterized the American past. Louis Hartz has concluded that Americans were, in fact, never very concerned about the trust movement and the manner in which large corporations concentrated economic and political power. To most Americans big business did not pose a real threat because the trusts and the people actually agreed on the basic goals of their society.[67]

While Richard Hofstadter was one of the founding fathers of consensus history, he broke with this tradition when he set forth his own ideas on the historical dimensions of America's antitrust movement. In his opinion, opposition to the trusts was widespread for a time and had substantial political impact. More recently, however, fear of big business seemed to have faded, particularly since World War II. The antitrust movement died, Hofstadter said, for a variety of reasons, including the excellent performance of the national economy after 1940, the "countervailing bigness" of labor unions and the government, and the country's actual experience with bigness—an experience that put to rest fears about continued concentration, technological decline, and opportunities for individual advancement. The post-World War II years saw the emergence of a new generation accustomed to bigness; these Americans were bent upon bureaucratic careers and interested in security. Meanwhile, Hofstadter said, the public had become aware that the small companies which often harbored right-wingers nevertheless frequently ran to the government for help.[68] As a result of these developments, Hofstadter concluded, most Americans had become placid about, if not actually pleased with, the role of the large corporation in our society.

Another eminent historian, Robert H. Wiebe, has used a different perspective and given us a different set of conclusions. In *The Search for Order*, Wiebe employed to good effect a brand of social equilibrium model. Eschewing the dynamic or long-run considerations that provided the foundations for the Marxist and Schumpeterian systems, Wiebe examined the more limited problem of how American society maintained, lost, and regained a sense of order in the nineteenth and early twentieth centuries. In his viewpoint, mid-nineteenth-century America consisted of a series of "island communities," each of which functioned as a largely autonomous social, economic, and political system. This stable order broke down as a result of rapid industrialization, urbanization, and immigration, leaving Americans from the seventies through the turn of the century searching for a new order. Then, the nation's "new middle class" of urban professionals and specialists provided organizations and values that restored equilibrium. The political phase of the new society was progressivism, but reform politics was only one part of the general transformation to a bureaucratic order.

By adopting an equilibrium model, Wiebe was able to provide an innovative interpretation of the role of big business in American society. As he saw it, business leaders were as confused as most other Americans in the late nineteenth century: "As shrewdly as some of them pursued the main chance, they were also trapped by the present, scurrying where they appeared to stalk."[69] When these "scurrying" businessmen formed large combines, many Americans condemned the trust movement, focusing on business all the animosities generated by the strains of a major social transformation. In the twentieth century, however, the trusts began to consolidate their operations and the bureaucratized corporation shared many values with the middle-class reformers who led the progressive movement in state and national politics. The managers of big business no less than the managers of reform sought a stable social order that stressed continuity, rationality, and centralization of authority. The climax of progressivism came in the 1920s when, as Wiebe explained, the new bureaucratic order rallied under the banner of the engineer-president, Herbert Hoover.[70] By this time most Americans accepted large enterprise in matters public and private as an essential element in their society.

The syntheses of Hofstadter, Wiebe, and others provide a variety of conflicting viewpoints on the public response to the rise of the large corporation. While my primary interest in the following chapters is in contrasting a liberal-progressive approach with an organizational-bureaucratic framework (of the Wiebe variety), all of the historical interpretations surveyed above generate useful questions. Were the trusts a source of intense politico-economic conflict? Or was the anti-monopoly movement only a slight symbolic ripple in a society largely characterized by social harmony? If in fact there was widespread concern about the trusts, did this unease follow class lines? Was it rooted in tangible economic interests? Or were Americans projecting onto the corporation the anxieties engendered by the breakdown of their traditional social order? If there was an antitrust movement, what were the roles of intellectuals and political leaders in molding opinion; when and why did the movement disappear? Was the acceptance of large-scale enterprise a post-World War II phenomenon, as

Hofstadter suggests, or was this shift in public attitudes fully developed by the 1920s, as Wiebe postulates?

My goal in the following pages is to provide answers to these and similar questions. The social theory that seems best suited to this task is an equilibrium model resembling the one Wiebe employed. Equilibrium in this mode of analysis does not mean stasis, the total absence of change; nor does it posit assumptions about the organic nature of social systems.[71] What equilibrium does mean is that there are patterns in human behavior, and that societies—whether large and complex nations or smaller social systems within a nation—can be analyzed in terms of the internal and external forces that act to maintain or disrupt those patterns. In dealing with the topic at hand, equilibrium can be defined as a situation in which public attitudes toward the large corporation are relatively stable and in which those attitudinal changes taking place are gradual or evolutionary. Sharp fluctuations in public thought will be taken as an indication of disequilibrium, regardless of what the evaluative content of the ideas was and regardless of the direction change takes.

While my approach is similar to Wiebe's, there are some important differences that should be clarified. Wiebe predicates a stable social order for the entire nation, using the sociological counterpart of what economists would call a general equilibrium model. Because I am focusing on the public response to the rise of only one type of modern organization, I am using the idea of equilibrium in a much more restricted sense; mine is the sociological version of the economist's partial equilibrium model. I hope that I have traded breadth for depth of analysis, particularly in the case of causal relations. I am as interested in the process as I am in the patterns of change (Wiebe's central concern). To study the forces that shaped attitudes, I will go below the level of the national society and analyze particular groups and their subcultures. I have, however, tried to examine each of these groups and each set of attitudes toward big business from the vantage point provided by the concept of social equilibrium.

All of the questions I have asked about the public response to big business can be translated into testable propositions that are compatible with an equilibrium analysis. If the consensus historians are correct, for example, I will find few signs of instability or disequilibrium, and hostility toward the corporation will emerge as a minor and fleeting phenomenon. If, however, group attitudes are found to be unstable and there are indications of conflict and deep hostility, it will be necessary to turn to one of the several conflict-centered explanations. The major factors shaping these opinions may be socioeconomic classes, as the Marxists would have it, and the long-run trend would thus be toward a sharpening of class differences and their related antagonisms. On the other hand, Hofstadter and the progressive

THE LARGE-SCALE ORGANIZATION IN MODERN AMERICA

historians have concluded that over the years these antagonisms disappeared. The social equilibrium framework is, I believe, broad enough and sufficiently neutral to encompass these varied hypotheses in addition to some of my own.[72]

I began this book with some tentative answers in mind for most of the questions I have raised. In the early years covered by this study, I expected to find a relatively stable set of attitudes about the large corporation in most, but not all, groups of middle-class Americans. Relations with the trusts would be neither entirely amicable nor homogeneous; farmers, for instance, seemed to me to be different from most other citizens, and I thought they were very angry at big business as early as the 1880s. For most other groups of Americans, however, I believed that unfavorable attitudes were balanced by favorable opinions, that values held in common throughout much of the society dampened discontent, and that above all, prosperity was a powerful and highly generalized force muffling conflicts of interest and stabilizing social relations.

These patterns were, I assumed, seriously disrupted by economic distress and by the continued spread of the concentration movement in the nineties. While the ensuing struggle became an important political issue, in my viewpoint the factors most responsible for instability and for the ultimate restoration of equilibrium were economic in nature. Economic change cut across the various groups and subcultures, providing the sort of generalized force that could restructure public opinion about big business. While income had different effects upon different groups, I did not feel that these differences could be analyzed in terms of socioeconomic classes. In that sense I began as a non-Marxist economic determinist, a historian who believed that income was the most powerful sanction in American social relations. This has not been a very popular position in recent years, but my suspicion was that many historians had swapped accuracy for subtlety in their quest for intellectually pleasing explanations of human behavior.

While economic factors were paramount, my initial assumption was that organizational change itself ranked second in importance as a factor shaping group attitudes toward big business. I felt that the most influential organizational developments would be those taking place within the groups antagonized by the emergence of big business; new elites and new organizations would provide either the reality or the semblance of countervailing power. I also thought that new organizations such as the professional associations that developed around the turn of the century promulgated values which blended easily with the bureaucratic point-of-view (à la Wiebe) in the business system.[73] I expected to locate some of these changes among the primary bureaucracies, others among the secondary organizations that stood between the groups and the giant corporation. Gradual changes in the

CONTEXT AND METHOD

large firm itself might also have influenced public attitudes, although I thought Americans probably perceived these changes in a number of different ways.

Ranking third in importance were the political factors which at times fostered conflict and at other times made for a decline in hostility toward the corporation. My hypothesis was that progressive historians had greatly exaggerated the impact of political reform movements and that at best one could give only a tertiary role to the antitrust and regulatory measures that had so tightly gripped the attention of liberal and revisionist scholars. While anticipating that reform politics would be more influential in some groups than others, I was doubtful that political events or political leadership would provide a sufficient explanation of the changing opinions in any substantial part of the middle class. Similarly, I suspected that both the progressive historians and Schumpeter had grossly overstated the role of intellectuals. Ideas and values seemed important to me, but only to the extent that all actions are infused with ideas and values, not because the ideas could be traced back to some leading intellectual. I thought that most of the behavior which interested me could probably be explained without ever once mentioning Lester Frank Ward, Richard T. Ely, or, for that matter, even John Dewey.

In varying mixtures these political, organizational, and economic factors made for accommodation, for a new equilibrium in the relations between major groups in America and the giant firm. This was a long term, gradual, and uneven process of change; it was one that I thought was probably completed for major groups in society during the 1920s. By that time the corporate culture was, I felt, securely planted among the middle classes in America. At the end of that decade, however, I knew that the stock market crash and the Great Depression created new tensions and an air of crisis. I was baffled by the 1930s, uncertain and unwilling to formulate a clear hypothesis about the impact of economic distress and New Deal politics on the public image of the giant corporation. Here my own assumptions trapped me. On the one hand it was only reasonable to believe that depression in the thirties would arouse anger at big business just as unemployment and declining income had done in the nineties. On the other hand, I was aware that Franklin D. Roosevelt's attempt to revive the antitrust movement in the latter part of the decade had not been very successful. So I decided to proceed, without providing that part of my study with a guiding hypothesis. By that time, however, I was already long on hypotheses and short on the evidence that would enable me to test my ideas and those of the other interpretations reviewed. I found it useful to develop a particular kind of quantitative data to serve that purpose; the origins and the nature of my evidence are explained in the next chapter.

2

RESEARCH TECHNIQUE: CONTENT ANALYSIS
DESCRIBED AND DEBATED

Only a few years ago an American historian embarking on a study of long-run shifts in public attitudes toward big business would probably have considered a prologue on research techniques unnecessary. Questions of methodology were treated in the historical manuals and were presumably understood by all graduates of the better doctoral programs. The basic rules were simple. One selected a subject which, preferably, had not been studied before, looked at all (or at least as much as possible) of the relevant source material, arrived at certain conclusions, and then cited in the footnotes as many of the sources as convention required and the publisher allowed. A practiced hand could flip through a set of these footnotes and decide in a few moments whether the research was substantial enough to yield results worthy of serious consideration.

Of late, however, a series of challenges has undermined the profession's sense of community and shaken the historian's confidence that he can speak for the past. In part the critique has focused on traditional research techniques; questions have even been raised about the philosophy of history, a subject that most American historians had long judged to be at best irrelevant to their trade.[1] The present chapter on methodology and its implications can be seen, then, as a testament to this new insecurity and the introspection it breeds.

In economic history, where change has been most pronounced, the challenge has come from scholars trained in economics. The economists have insisted that, among other things, hypotheses should be stated with precision and should be formally tested, preferably with quantitative data. Many of the spokesmen for this "new economic history" have also substituted explicit (for implicit) models of human behavior and frequently have expressed the relationships among the variables in these models in the language of mathematics. Some have grounded their new methods in the "covering-law" theory of history, a philosophy which equates explanation in the sciences and in history and which directs historians to the task of testing general propositions (or covering laws) about past human behavior. The results in this particular branch of history can with justice be labeled a revolution—a behavioral revolution which has significantly raised the standards of proof and the quality of analysis in economic history.[2]

One of the less favorable by-products of the revolution has been, however, an emphasis on those aspects of the past which best lend themselves to quantitative expression. Investment rates, foreign trade, railroad and canal construction, population changes, gross national product: all provide rich and attractive statistics. By contrast, most features of the institutional environment—patterns of thought as well as formal organizations—have been described in non-quantitative terms; all too often the result has been that economic historians have ignored these factors, held them constant, or left them in the unexplained and ignominious residue.[3] We have, therefore, a lopsided brand of history in which the institutional setting of economic activity has received far too little attention.

Recently some economists as well as historians have recognized this problem and have sought to right the balance. One response has been to use traditional historical techniques while merely giving more emphasis to institutional subjects.[4] Another reaction has involved the use of behavioral methodology to explore institutional problems.[5] Despite the claims of the covering-law theorists and of their archenemies in the historicist school, there seems little reason to select one course over the other on purely logical grounds. Both approaches will doubtless improve our knowledge of the past; each will generate a particular blend of hypotheses and data; each will encounter special problems and limitations. Indeed, the recent experiences in economic history strongly suggest that in the long run the profession will be best served by a tolerant combination of these two differing methodologies and their related philosophies.

My own choice was to apply systematic, behavioral techniques to the study of past attitudes toward the large corporation. Previous studies of the public response to the rise of big business—and, for that matter, most historical studies of public attitudes on any issue—had not used these techniques. An investment in a more systematic approach seemed warranted if only because research on this subject had been so unsystematic. Even among economic historians the standards of proof where public attitudes are concerned are relatively low. One of the leading new economic historians, a scholar who is meticulous in his appraisal of the statistical data on the gross national product, can thus briefly summarize what Americans, presumably all of them, of the Gilded Age thought. Certain ideas, he says, were "an integral part of the popular thought." To support his conclusion he cites a book written by Sir S. Morton Peto, *Resources and Prospects of America*, and two magazine articles. While "the dominant opinion at the close of the Gilded Age" may indeed have been what the author says it was, the reader has virtually no indication of how he reached this conclusion about the attitudes of some sixty million people.[6]

RESEARCH TECHNIQUE

Institutional historians cannot afford to gloat over this example, however; their record is not much more impressive. All too often a few convenient quotations from prominent journals or newspapers have sufficed as evidence for American opinion on one issue or another. The *New York Times* has been a convenient source for citations, in part, perhaps, because it is indexed. Foreign observers, including of course James Bryce and the omniscient de Tocqueville, have provided generations of historians with evidence about American attitudes. Autobiographies have yielded appropriate quotations, and some scholars have synchronized their own education with the singular observations of Henry Adams. Even when historians have dealt with the opinions of smaller groups—the business community, for instance—they have given little explicit attention to methodological problems. How, exactly, can these attitudes best be studied? What constitutes a valid sample of the ideas prevalent in any such group? What conclusions can be drawn with a reasonable measure of confidence from the evidence derived in historical research?

Fortunately, a few scholars have been worrying about these problems. Lee Benson, for example, offers "An Approach to the Scientific Study of Past Public Opinion" focusing exclusively upon opinions about political issues.[7] Benson's critique of previous work in this field is useful, but his conclusion that voting behavior provides the best guide to past opinions leaves my own project without an attractive alternative to the traditional methodology. While big business was frequently an issue in political campaigns, the large corporation was never the only issue at stake. Unless one is willing to lean upon roll call votes in the legislatures, another approach seems called for by this particular problem. In another pathbreaking book, Ernest R. May analyzes the role of elite groups in shaping opinions about foreign policy. May isolates a group of "probable opinion leaders" and then describes the factors influencing their concepts of American diplomacy.[8] While this approach is rewarding in May's case, his technique would be almost impossible to apply to my question. There was no readily identifiable elite group with regard to the trust question, and even if there had been, it would have been almost impossible to systematically analyze the changes in the factors influencing the elite (or elites) over a period of sixty years. May's technique seems better suited to the study of particular kinds of discrete policy decisions than it does to the analysis of long-run shifts in public attitudes toward institutions like the large corporation.

Political scientist Richard Merritt's application of content analysis to the study of communication patterns in pre-Revolutionary America offers a more appealing alternative. Merritt examines the symbols in colonial newspapers, a source that also plays an important, although secondary, role in May's study. Merritt uses the newspapers as indicators of public opinion so he can develop quantitative data about long-run shifts in attitudes; he then uses his data to test various hypotheses about the revolutionary experience in America.[9] His volume suggests that content analysis of newspapers and journals provides an approach particularly well suited to my problem. Sources like these are abundant for the period 1880 through 1940, and many publications devoted substantial attention to the rise of big business. Content analysis provides a systematic means of studying these sources, and its use might avoid some of the problems outlined by Benson and May.

II.   The main thrust of the work in content analysis has involved a search for systematic means of analyzing the verbal symbols that appear in a society's public documents. Several content analysis projects have, like Merritt's, attempted to give quantitative expression to the patterns of symbol usage as a means for inferring their underlying structure of ideas.[10] Many of the questions asked have been political in nature, although there have been significant exceptions to this rule.[11]

Content analysis has tempted the dedicated behavioralist by promising to transform the study of the cultural components of society from an impressionistic art into a policy science. Through this technique it is possible, for instance, to convert the soft and particularistic information in a newspaper's editorials into hard data with universal properties. There was—and perhaps still is—hope that the categories employed to "catch" the information would ultimately be so well understood, so widely and easily applicable, that one could achieve a high degree of replication. Then experiments could be duplicated, and the resulting hypotheses could be tested under something resembling controlled conditions. These goals were reflected in most of the content analysis projects in political science during the 1940s and 1950s.

The content analysis studies of political scientists exerted a substantial influence upon the design of the present project, even though the major objectives here were those of history, not those of a policy science. My goal, in other words, was not the creation of a model that would have predictive qualities; my interest was in achieving a better understanding of the past.[12] Two general characteristics of the project reflect this difference. First, I was more interested than most social scientists would have been in capturing the particularistic properties of my subject matter—that is, the properties associated with a time, a place, and special groups of persons. The question was one of degree and could conveniently be expressed as a position on a continuum or scale ranging from a highly particularistic (historicist) to a highly universalistic (covering-law) orientation. While my interest in systematic research pushed me away from traditional historians and the related historicist philosophy, I stopped short of the position occupied by ardent behavioralists and devotees of covering-law theory.[13] A second characteristic involved replication. In brief, I was willing to sacrifice some part of this goal when it seemed to interfere unduly with my desire to capture important characteristics of the material being studied. This problem arose, for instance, when I decided to record implicit, not merely explicit, expressions of opinion about big business; this choice introduced a subjective element that necessarily increased the error term and made it less likely that others could easily reproduce my results.[14] Had my dedication been to science and not merely to a more systematic brand of history, this and other decisions would probably have been different. But perhaps the best way to illustrate this point is to examine the details of the research technique and the publications that my research assistant and I analyzed.

III. A critical problem in any content analysis project is the selection of the materials to be studied. In this case a variety of considerations shaped this process. I wanted to concentrate primarily on images of big business which had currency in that broad stratum of society usually known as the middle class. My focus was largely upon persons who owned property or felt they soon would, who were white, who were literate, and who possessed some skill or special ability. While they were skilled, they were not virtuosos. While they could read, they were certainly not intellectuals. While they owned or aspired to own property, they were neither *rentiers* nor a wealthy economic elite. In all these regards they were a distinctly middle class.

My subject was one element in a middle culture, or to be more precise, a set of middle cultures. They were cultures in the anthropological, not the commonsense, use of the term: my concern was not with art, taste, and manners but with shared patterns of verbal symbols transmitting ideas, beliefs, and values.[15] These cultures were middle in their relationship to the class defined above, but they were also middling in terms of their degree of sophistication. My choice of subjects was dictated by the fact that we already know a great deal about the intellectual's response to big business, but we know very little about the extent to which his ideas penetrated other, larger strata of society. The decision not to search into the culture of the lower classes was based on expediency; in reality we know even less about the history of the lower class in America than we do about the bourgeoisie, but I decided to tackle the easier task first.

Within the middle class, I selected some broad but well defined occupational categories: farmers, organized laborers, and professional men. By using occupational categories I was able to analyze relationships between attitudes and changes in the political, social, or economic standing of a group, and also to compare the images of big business circulating in three different branches of the middle cultures—among blue-collar workers as well as white, among employers and the self-employed as well as wage earners. In part, too, these groups were chosen because the existing historical literature offered a substantial body of data and hypotheses about their attitudes. Consistent with my interest in the external response to big business instead of its self-image, none of the groups—with the possible exception of some professionals—were part of the business or managerial elite that controlled large national enterprises. Finally, these three groups together constituted a significant and influential portion of middle America, and for that matter of the total American population, during the years under study.

Next, it was necessary to decide which journals to examine. The decision to use occupational categories eliminated those newspapers and magazines addressed to a highly variegated audience. Among the occupational journals, I favored those which had a relatively long publishing history. They had to include some discussion of big business, and the content had to be framed in terms that were not entirely technical. Journals with a substantial subscription rate received preference on the assumption that some relationship existed between circulation and support for the publication's ideas—although I was unwilling to accept the idea that there was a simple one-to-one relationship between the number of subscriptions and the number of opinions a paper represented.

In dealing with the farmers, I concentrated upon two substantial subgroups, those in the South and those in the Midwest.[16] For the South during the years 1879 through 1935, I used *Southern Cultivator*, which was published in Georgia and had a circulation of 35,000 copies in 1890 and 50,000 in 1906; these were impressive figures for this type of publication and for this period.[17] Most of the readers were in Georgia, Alabama, Mississippi, and the Carolinas, and judging from the contents of the paper, most of the subscribers were involved in cotton farming to some extent. In 1935 another journal absorbed the *Southern Cultivator*, and for the years 1935–1940 I turned to the *Progressive Farmer*, a monthly publication with an even higher subscription rate. Each issue of the *Progressive Farmer* appeared in five different editions, and I selected the Georgia-Alabama-Florida edition, since it was most comparable to *Southern Cultivator*.

In the Midwest I chose *Farmers' Review* for the 1880s and early 1890s. This paper, published in Chicago, had a circulation (in 1880 and again in 1890) of around 25,000. Most of these subscribers were in the Middle West, but the journal had readers scattered about a large area ranging through the Dakotas and as far south as Texas.[18] In the 1890s *Farmers' Review* began to change in several ways, and I began to suspect that the paper was increasingly out of touch with midwestern farm attitudes. Both the editor and the owner of the journal were officers in a savings and loan company, and this connection, along with their insensitivity to the numerous and active farm organizations with which I was familiar, convinced me that *Farmers' Review*

RESEARCH TECHNIQUE

was a less reliable proxy for agrarian opinions than it had been during the eighties. Accordingly, I shifted to *Wallaces' Farmer* (1895–1932), a journal published in Iowa and directed primarily at corn and hog producers.[19] *Wallaces' Farmer* was a prosperous family enterprise whose editorial staff provided the government with two secretaries of agriculture (Henry C., 1921–1924; Henry A., 1933–1940) and a vice president (Henry A., 1941–1945).[20] I was satisfied that the paper was more closely attuned to farm attitudes in this part of the country than *Farmers' Review* was, but in studying the 1930s I became concerned that the editors might be identified too closely with the policies of the Roosevelt administration. I then turned to *Nebraska Farmer* (1933–1940), a monthly publication that emphasized wheat farming as well as the production of corn and hogs.[21]

Each of these farm papers had its own bias, but all of them had certain characteristics in common. The papers agreed in advocating systematic, rational, businesslike farming. They directed themselves at the literate, white farmers who either owned or felt they deserved to own their farms. Politically, the papers were relatively moderate—relative, that is, to the several tides of agrarian discontent which swept over America during these years. Although the editors were certainly not immune to pressures from the left, they normally resisted extreme ideas presented from any quarter. While most of the editors claimed at some time or another to be nonpolitical, the papers all expressed political opinions, and they all projected attitudes toward the nation's major economic institutions, including big business.

With an eye to the similarities of the farm journals, I spliced the data from them together in order to have two sets of figures reflecting farm opinion in the South and Midwest over a sixty-two-year period. Of course the figures were only indicators, not direct measures, of the images of big business which had currency among these two subgroups. The results were not a direct expression of the subscribers' opinions. Although the editors of the papers were influenced by their subscribers' attitudes, these sources yielded a proxy once removed from the farmers themselves. When I further combined the data from these two subgroups and talked about agrarian attitudes in general, the indicator was twice removed from the farmers' own perspectives.

By using the agrarian journals as a source of farm opinions I did not mean to imply that the editors were merely neutral or passive conduits for the ideas of others. The editors shaped the flow of information, in this case the composite image of big business. The papers were one of several institutions handling and channeling agrarian attitudes, and, using an approach similar to that of Ernest R. May's, one could study the role of the publications as formulators of public opinion. While I found some opportunities to touch upon this subject, the primary goal throughout was to examine the papers as a source of images, not as opinion leaders.

CONTEXT AND METHOD

The editorial role in shaping attitudes was of greater consequence in the labor publications. In this case it was necessary to focus upon that portion of the labor force organized in unions. Sadly, the unorganized laborers seldom left any substantial historical record, at least not of the sort which would yield data comparable to that from the farm journals. Using publications tied to a particular organization magnified the risk that the images reflected in them would be heavily influenced by the dominant groups, by even a very small elite, within the union. This was true even though letters to the editor were a source of numerous items in the labor papers. However, since I found no practical alternative to the union publications, I could only acknowledge that their characteristics were somewhat different than those of the farm papers.

The *National Labor Tribune* (1880–1915) was one of the three labor journals studied. In 1880, the *Tribune*, published in Pittsburgh, was the official organ of the Amalgamated Association of Iron and Steel Workers and of the Window Glass Artisans' National Association. During the early eighties, however, the Tribune's orientation was somewhat diffuse, and the editors printed items on many different unions, including the Knights of Labor. They devoted some attention to most of the major industries in the Pittsburgh area, especially coal, coke, iron, transportation, steel, and glass. In following years the *Tribune* continued to report on these and other industries, but its ties to the Amalgamated Association and to the American Federation of Labor became stronger and its focus narrower. These ties were not broken until the early 1900s, when the Amalgamated Association began to publish its own journal in competition with the *Tribune*. For a time the *Tribune* supported the Sons of Vulcan, a puddler's union, and the United Mine Workers of America. After 1915, however, the paper's allegiance shifted more drastically: while proclaiming itself an "official organ of the American Workmen," it became in reality a spokesman for the employer's interests.[22]

To supplement and then to replace the *Tribune*, I used the *American Federationist* for the years 1894–1940. This journal was the official voice of the American Federation of Labor and enjoyed a much larger circulation than the *Tribune*. The *Federationist* was more general, more abstract, and more sophisticated than the *Tribune*. The AFL paper never wavered in its devotion to the goal of strengthening craft unionism. While local and detailed information of the sort published by the *Tribune* appeared in the *Federationist*, the editors concentrated primarily on general problems affecting many members of this diverse federation of national craft unions.[23]

Since the *Federationist* usually seemed to exclude the radical opinion that had—at least indirectly—influenced the agrarian periodicals, I decided to include the official publication of the Industrial Workers of the World. *Solidarity* (1910–30) was an anomaly, differing from the trade union

RESEARCH TECHNIQUE

journals in many regards. The IWW's commitment to a socialist ideology shaped almost every aspect of the paper's content. It was more concerned with politics, national and international, than were either of the trade union publications, but in fact particular events of any type made little impress upon the image of big business projected by its pages. I could not have included *Solidarity* on the basis of circulation: while precise subscription figures do not exist, its list was so small that the editors commented in 1915 on the loss of 63 subscribers and hoped in 1922 to increase the circulation to 25,000.[24] This goal eluded them, and three years later they observed that the circulation was at its lowest ebb.[25] *Solidarity* was the only journal used which did not address itself to an element of the middle class. In terms of property, income, and status, its clientele was probably lower class. By any standard other than intellectual sophistication, *Solidarity* provided contrasting instead of complementary data.

With the exception of *Solidarity*, the labor publications yielded information on the images of the large corporation current among organized, skilled craftsmen. The data came from the moderate wing of the labor movement (moderate insofar as issues political or economic were concerned), and the point of view was predominantly that of the American Federation of Labor. As with the farm papers, one could use the results of the content analysis only as an approximate indicator of attitudes prevalent in a larger group—in this case, the members of the AFL. With similar qualifications, I combined the figures from the three papers into an indicator for the attitudes of all organized workers.

For similar information about the viewpoints of professional men, I turned to the publications directed at two subgroups: engineers and Protestant clergymen. In part the choice of subgroups (one might just as well have selected lawyers or doctors) was dictated by the availability of journals that would provide the information I needed for the years 1880 through 1940. Additionally, it was no small consideration that three publications could be used to cover the entire period. More important, these choices enabled me to compare a profession that was apparently achieving greater status, engineers, with the clergy, a subgroup seemingly experiencing a decline in prestige.

From among the many publications addressed to engineers, I selected a New York journal, *Engineering News* (1880–1940). It touched upon many different types of engineering (especially in the 1880s and 1890s), but its primary concerns were building and construction work. In the latter part of the nineteenth century the problems of railroad construction and operation figured prominently in the magazine. Later, road building and utilities became more important. If one excludes from consideration such magazines as *Popular Science*, *Engineering News* was one of the largest journals in the profession.[26] While its content was highly technical, the editors and contributors made frequent comments upon a variety of economic issues, including questions posed by the rise of big business.

It was impossible to find an exact counterpart to *Engineering News* for the Protestant clergymen. One could not study the journals with the strongest professional orientation, those of the theological seminaries, because none of them touched upon questions of economic and political import frequently enough to justify a lengthy examination through content analysis. Fortunately, the official church papers did, and I picked one of these, the *Congregationalist*, despite the fact that it was written for both lay members and the clergy. I decided that this paper could be used because it was written to a very substantial extent by the clergy and also because clergymen formed a large portion of the readers. Indeed, some members of the church complained that the paper was published by and for the clergy, not the lay members of the church.[27] Nevertheless, this publication was not entirely equivalent to *Engineering News* as a professional journal.

The choice of a denomination also presented special problems. After some consideration I settled upon the Congregational church, even though its clergy and total membership were not very large. The decision was dictated largely by the need to have sufficient material to analyze. As Henry F. May's work indicates, the Congregational church was in the vanguard of the liberal or social gospel movement, and, as a result, its official paper discussed the trust problem at some length.[28] Employing this journal meant, however, that my data on clergymen would come from the left side of their political spectrum. All of the other publications—except *Solidarity*, of course—were more moderate and were closer to the center position within their particular group or subgroup. This special qualification should be kept in mind when analyzing the data drawn from *Congregationalist* (1880-1934) and its successor, *Advance* (1934-40).[29] These were the only journals used to provide information on the Congregational clergy's view of big business and on the attitudes of Protestant clergymen in general. As was the case with the farmers and laborers, the subgroup data for clergymen and engineers were added together to give me a proxy for the opinions of professional men during the years 1880-1940.

The church papers, engineering journal, labor and farm publications yielded an awesomely large body of information on the American image of the large corporation, but of course these sources excluded many persons from consideration. Black Americans were ignored. The immigrant was discussed in the papers under study, but he was usually neither the writer nor the reader of that record. The unorganized, the inarticulate, the unskilled, the downtrodden—for the most part, their attitudes were not examined. Future historians who study them will, I hope, find the material that this project has gathered from middle American cultures useful for comparative purposes. To judge the quality of that material and of my conclusions,

RESEARCH TECHNIQUE

however, the reader must understand the content analysis procedure that was used in this study.

IV. We examined all of the journals in the same manner, reading each of the issues selected in its entirety (only advertisements, fiction, poems, and jokes were excluded).[30] It was necessary to cover the entire paper because occupational journals in the latter part of the nineteenth century were unsophisticated and their contents often undifferentiated. The contrast between an editorial and a news story was barely recognized, let alone respected. In the farm publications, for instance, at the end of a long and painfully detailed article on fertilizer, the reader would find the author's moral: "Use Manure and beat the Fertilizer Trust!" Regardless of one's opinion of calcareous (or, for that matter, noncalcareous) fertilizer, it seemed essential to capture this and similar conclusions about big business. Our subject was thus the total image projected by the journals in their news coverage and letters to the editor, as well as editorials and signed articles.

In the issues read we recorded information on each separate item which mentioned big business. An item was defined as any separate article, editorial, letter, or news story, and all such items were counted as equal, regardless of their length. Thus, the lengthy editorial that appears later in this section counted as one item, equal in that regard to a one-line filler on the trust question. Coverage was limited to selections that mentioned the largest firms in mining, manufacturing, and transportation, thus eliminating financial institutions and agricultural businesses. All railroads were assumed to be big business, regardless of their actual size.[31] When companies other than railroads were mentioned by name, we used the following standards: for the years 1880–1909, we included any firm that had assets or capitalization of five million dollars or more; the cutoff point for the years 1910–18 was raised to ten million dollars in order to yield a list of around 500 such companies. For the period 1919–28, the limit was raised to twenty million dollars; it was set at forty million dollars for the years 1929–40, for similar reasons. We could not apply these standards to many of the items because the discussions were framed in general terms, and as long as the content indicated that the author was talking about big business, the item was included. Using these standards of selection, we collected data on almost 9000 separate items, an average of 147 items for each year covered by the project. About 2400 of these selections came from the farm papers, 3000 from the professional journals, and 3500 from the labor publications (see table 2-1).

We recorded the information from each of these items on a standard form that included a number of separate categories, and since this was the step in the research which actually converted the data into quantitative form,

CONTEXT AND METHOD

it deserves a full explanation. (Figure 2-1 is a sample score sheet.) Perhaps the simplest way to explain how this was done is to list the categories in order, along with some brief account of what each involved. First came a set of bookkeeping entries that merely enabled us to locate and identify the items. These included the journal's code number and a page number (1), and the date of issue (2); then, we made a notation to indicate whether the selection was a news story (3), an editorial (4), a letter to the editor (5), or some other type of article (6). Later, I used this information to isolate the major sources of data and opinion within the various journals and in some cases to analyze that part of the publication providing new images of the large corporation.

The next category, the single most important one used, called for an appraisal of the attitude toward big business projected by the entire item (7). There were only four possibilities: on balance, the selection could be favorable to big business, unfavorable, neutral, or ambivalent (that is, with an equal division between favorable and unfavorable remarks). In practice, we reached this conclusion after we had broken down the image of big business into a variety of specific aspects (categories 13 through 53); each of these separate aspects was judged to be favorable, unfavorable, neutral, or ambivalent, and we normally totaled them to arrive at the overall attitude of the item.[32]

In deciding whether an editorial, article, or letter conveyed a favorable or unfavorable appraisal of the large corporation, we considered both implicit and explicit judgments. An editorial in a labor journal claiming that a particular firm refused to negotiate with the union or fired union men was considered to be inherently unfavorable to big business. We drew this conclusion even though the editor did not explicitly state that he opposed the action.[33] This introduced a subjective element into our work. Although we made a substantial effort to be systematic about these decisions in order to preserve the comparability of the different sets of data, some of our choices were admittedly like a referee's judgment on a charging foul in basketball. As every fan knows, the marginal cases leave behind a faint taste of doubt. Fortunately, only a small number of our decisions were this difficult, and we were satisfied that by evaluating implicit judgments we were adding to our data an important part of the image of big business as it appeared in these journals.[34]

We also indicated the origins of an item (8), that is, what prompted its appearance in the paper.[35] In some instances it was clearly the action of a court or legislature which aroused comment. Frequently, activity by a business firm itself stimulated discussion. Often the meetings of labor, farm, or professional organizations were the occasion for an editorial or article mentioning the large corporation. These data provided a partial view of the sources of attitudes within each of the groups and enabled me to comment

RESEARCH TECHNIQUE

upon the patterns of communication between the groups and their environment.

In addition to analyzing what stirred up comment, I wanted to know what kinds of big businesses were of greatest concern to each of the groups. With that in mind, we recorded the specific companies mentioned (9), the industries (10), and the businessmen (11). The industries were later sorted into what are called two-digit groups (according to the government's Standard Industrial Classification index), which is merely a means of putting related industries into larger groupings on a systematic basis.[36] Thus, the two-digit group for the manufacture of transportation equipment (number 37, hence the two-digit label) encompassed several related industries, including the production of motor vehicles, aircraft, and locomotives. On the basis of this information, I was able to compare the patterns of attention characteristic of farmers, laborers, and professional men, and to analyze changes in these patterns over several decades.

Only one part of the project involved the kind of word count that has been used in other content analysis projects. We listed all of the nouns, other than proper names, used in the article to refer to big business (12). All of the words were later categorized as "pejorative"—for example, *hog, serpent,* and *trust*—or as "non-pejorative"—for instance, *company, firm,* and *business.* This provided information on long-run shifts in what could be called the vocabulary of the antitrust movement; to the extent that this vocabulary was related to values and modes of orientation in the general society, these data opened a window on the relationships between each of these groups and the broader reaches of American culture in the modern period.[37]

TABLE 2-1. Total number of items scored

	Name of Journal	Dates Used	Number of big-business-related items
Farm	*Southern Cultivator*	1879–1935	466
	Progressive Farmer	1936–1940	21
	Farmers' Review	1879–1894	657
	Wallaces' Farmer	1895–1932	1,203
	Nebraska Farmer	1933–1940	55
Labor	*National Labor Tribune*	1880–1915	1,812
	American Federationist	1894–1940	1,290
	Solidarity	1910–1930	413
Professional	*Engineering News*	1880–1940	2,407
	Congregationalist	1880–1934	595
	Advance	1934–1940	57
Total			8,976

CONTEXT AND METHOD

In categories 13 through 53, we broke down the image of big business into more specific elements, labeling each as favorable, unfavorable, neutral, or ambivalent. One group of aspects consisted of the economic characteristics of the large firm. An item might mention that big business was efficient (13) or inefficient (14), that it enhanced the economic opportunities of individuals outside the firm (15) or diminished those opportunities (16). The large corporation could contribute to the general wealth (17)—of the nation, a region, state or locality—or it might not contribute (18). The concentration movement could be pictured as a natural (19) or an unnatural phenomenon (20), and comments could be made on the giant firm's general economic power (21), financial or "money" power (22), and price policies (23).[38]

Other economic categories included discrimination or nondiscrimination between customers (24); products and services (25); credit (26), purchasing (27), and wage-hour policies (28); the control of the company, whether by owners or managers (29); the business's general bureaucratic attributes (30); its impersonal or personalized authority (31); and its use of rationalistic standards (32). The supervision exercised by the company could arouse comment (33), as could the extent to which it enhanced (34) or diminished (35) its employees' opportunities. The tasks of the workers could be meaningful and rewarding (36) or meaningless and unrewarding (37); an item could remark upon the speed of operations in the plant (38), or upon the degree of safety involved in the work (39). In the final four categories, we scored references to the existence or expansion of big business (40 a); labor relations (40 b); corporate financial practices (40 c); and any miscellaneous economic characteristics or functions which could not be squeezed into the previous slots (40 d).

A second general grouping of specific characteristics were those which touched upon the social, cultural, or status-related aspects of big business. Thus, an item might refer to corporate influence on the rank order of status groups (41), the determinants of status (42), or the status of a particular person (43). Business could be associated with an elite group (44) (for instance, new business leaders), or the article could mention other miscellaneous social factors (45), such as the large firm's impact upon community values. These were the only categories that we used to capture the social dimension of the corporate image, and as should be apparent, these slots were neither as numerous nor as detailed as those used in the previous section on economic characteristics. As it turned out, however, a more detailed breakdown of the data was unnecessary because social considerations proved to be relatively unimportant to all but one of the groups studied.

The political facets of the large corporation were substantially more important and made up the third set of characteristics in our standard form. Each of the separate political categories mentioned—as was the case with the

RESEARCH TECHNIQUE

economic and social aspects—was scored as favorable, unfavorable, neutral, or ambivalent. An item might refer to big business's general relations to politics (46), political values (47), or political power (48). The techniques of political action—bribery or publicity campaigns, for example—could be discussed (49), and business might be portrayed as independent of (50) or dependent upon (51) political assistance. An article could bring up business's immediate political objectives (52), the large firm's violation of or conformance to the law (53 a), its cooperation with the government or lack of it (53 b), and, finally, any miscellaneous involvement with the political system which could not be placed in the previous categories (53 c).

This completed our breakdown of the image of big business into a set of constituent concepts, each of which bore an evaluative label. After the data were totaled and percentages were figured for each respective journal, we had what could be called an aggregate, annual profile of big business as it was seen by the readers of each of these occupational journals. The single most important figure for my analysis was the percentage of the items which were favorable, unfavorable, neutral, and ambivalent. It was, I felt, this series which indicated most clearly whether the groups were becoming more or less hostile toward big business between 1880 and 1940.

In addition to the information on the large corporation's profile, we recorded any responses or reactions to such firms which an item presented in a favorable light. In some cases unionization was suggested as a solution to the trust problem. Some journals felt that individual responses such as better farming were preferable. Other papers looked to the government for help. We recorded these data in a style similar to that used for the image of big business, that is, by breaking the information down into a limited number of discrete categories. We indicated whether the response or solution discussed was in the past (54), the present (55), or the future (56). In some cases a selection called for individual action (e.g., better farming) (57), or some variety of private collective activity, perhaps through a trade union or the Grange (58). When public collective action, that is, the government, was invoked, the item could merely approve of a political response (59) without specifying the branch or level of government involved. On the other hand, an article or letter could specify action at the level of the state (60) or federal governments (61). In addition to the above, we had the inevitable miscellaneous slot (62) for those responses that had not somehow been anticipated. When the figures drawn from these score sheets were added together and converted into annual percentages, they provided a set of quantitative proxies for changing group concepts of a proper solution to the trust problem. This information offered an insight into some of the factors reducing tensions between the various groups and the corporation.

Recording the suggested solutions to the trust problem was the last step in our formal content analysis procedure, but it may be presumptuous at this point to assume that the reader not already familiar with this technique can visualize how the process actually worked. Those who can are advised to skip to the next section (V) of this chapter. Those who cannot will perhaps benefit from an example. The following editorial appeared in *Engineering News* in 1926:

Combinations and Holding Companies

Significant during the year has been the changing attitude of the federal government toward business combinations. The Supreme Court decisions in the maple flooring and the cement cases were accepted by the Department of Justice as indicating a more lenient view toward the trade association. Superficially these decisions and the administration viewpoint have been considered as approving combinations which during the years of the Sherman and Clayton Act prosecutions were distinctly illegal. In reality all they did was to approve a more liberal interpretation of the rights of a given industry to collect and distribute its production and sales statistics, on the theory that production based on full information will approximate a prospective consumption and will therefore tend to common trade efficiency. Industries, however, have been warned that this is not license to combine in restraint of trade and that the criterion of legality will continue to be the undue extension of this restraint. More ominous in its prospect than the occasional belief of business that the way is now opening to that illegal combining which once was known as the trust is the growing tendency of big business of every form toward the holding company, with its usual concomitant of the non-voting common stock issue. Every sign points to the belief on the part of the financier, and his sinister adviser the corporation lawyer, that in the holding company is being developed the machinery which is at once legal, safe, and profitable for the fortunate few. Insofar as the public utilities are concerned there is much to be said for the technical efficiency of the holding company. It concentrates management in intelligent and trained experts, it reduces overhead and it pools purchases and, during successful operation at least, it rewards the consumer in reduced rates. But against this it sets up a non-resident directorate out of touch with the consumer and it rests real control in an impersonal financial entity most difficult of supervision by the public. Even the most bigoted private ownership advocate realized that the only answer to privileged monopoly is public control. Any legal device which tends to destroy that control is doomed. It requires no prescience to predict that the next few years will see a growing effort on the part of the people to check the financial operators who are moving so fast toward the accumulation of the highly profitable voting shares in large and diversified holding companies, the capital for which is furnished by stock and bondholders who have no voice in management and indeed in many cases only a depreciated equity in the over capitalized property.[39]

We recorded the information in the article as follows (see figure 2-1 for a copy of the score sheet): (1) 31 (the paper's code number), p. 50; (2) vol. 96, no. 2 (January 14, 1926). This was our "footnote" to the item, and we also checked category 4 to indicate that the selection was an editorial. The general image of big business was unfavorable, so category 7 was scored *U*; when the image was broken down into its constituent elements (see below), a

RESEARCH TECHNIQUE

FIGURE 2-1. Sample score sheet.

1) *31, p. 50*
2) *Vol. 96, No. 2 (January 14, 1926)*
3)
4) *"Combinations and Holding Companies"*
5)
6)
7) *U*
8) *federal, general—federal attitude toward bb*
9)
10)
11)
12) *company, 5*
   trust
   big business
   monopoly
   corporation

ECONOMIC RELATIONSHIPS

13) *F—"Insofar as the public*
   utilities are concerned there is much to be
   said for the technical efficiency of the
   holding company."
14)
15)
16)
17)
18)
19)
20)
21)
22) *U—"the financier, and his sinister*
   adviser the corporation lawyer", also, see 31
23) *F—holding companies often*
   mean reduced rates to consumers because
   of greater operational efficiency
24)
25)
26)
27) *F—the pooling of purchases*
   which holding companies can do
28)
29) *U—the holding company*
   "concentrates management in intelligent and
   trained experts" (F); "But against this it
   sets up a non-resident directorate" (U);
   non-voting common stock (U)
30)
31) *U—the holding co. "rests real"*
   control in an impersonal financial entity
   most difficult of supervision by the public."
32)
33)
34)
35)

36)
37)
38)
39)
40) *U—(exis) "the growing tendency of big*
   business of every form toward the holding
   company"

   U—(financial) the holding co. is very
   profitable, but only to the "fortunate few"—
   the implication is that it has been created as
   a device for wealth accumulation, that the
   profits are too large and unjust; over-
   capitalization

STATUS RELATIONSHIPS

41)
42)
43)
44)
45)

POLITICAL RELATIONSHIPS

46)
47)
48)
49)
50)
51)
52)
53) *U—(evades law) illegal trusts of the past;*
   the holding co. is a "legal device" which
   evades the spirit, though not the letter
   of the law

SOLUTIONS OR RESPONSES

54)
55)
56) *X*
57)

58)

59)
60)

61) *F—"Even the most bigoted private owner-*
   ship advocate realizes that the only answer
   to privileged monopoly is public control."
   [The item does not specify federal control,
   but this is implied by the first paragraph.]

62)

CONTEXT AND METHOD

total of six of these aspects were negative and three were favorable. On balance, then, we judged the editorial to be negative, a conclusion that confirmed our first impression. Various actions by the federal government appear to have given rise to the editorial, and this was listed as (8) federal, general (the latter because both the executive and judicial branches were involved and we could not specify which one actually aroused the editor's attention).

Next, we did the word count, noting merely the nouns which were used. These included: [holding] company (five times); trust (once); big business (once); monopoly (once); and corporation (once). Two of these words, trust and monopoly, were classified as manifestly pejorative, while the rest were non-pejorative. As the reader may have noticed, words in the first five sentences were not tabulated, because they refer to loose combinations, in this case trade associations, and not to big business.

Under the economic characteristics of the large firm, we marked the following categories. The editor approves of the "technical efficiency" of the holding company, the manner in which "it reduces overhead" and cuts costs, so we scored (13) *F*. On the other hand, these companies are associated with financiers of an unsavory nature, "financial operators" who are in league with that "sinister adviser the corporation lawyer"; hence, category 22 was scored *U*. Counterpoints to this negative evaluation come in the statements that combination results in lower prices and that pooling of purchases is one of the specific means of achieving lower rates (categories 23 and 27—favorable). Here the reader should be alert to the fact that purchasing policies were marked in a separate category (27), while reduction of overhead was not; since there was no separate and specific category for the latter, we placed it under the general concept of efficiency (13). In this and other ways, the nature of the categories obviously influenced the results of the content analysis, a subject that receives further discussion in the final section of this chapter.

The editorial also touches upon management/ownership, the controlling factors in the corporation. The holding company "concentrates management in intelligent and trained experts," a point which has strong appeal for the editor and no doubt for the readers of an engineering journal. Nevertheless, the editor adds two negative remarks. The management is "a nonresident directorate," and this type of control is only "profitable for the fortunate few." In our final evaluation we thus marked (29) *U*. Once again, technique shaped the results. Three bits of information were combined; on the computer card all that appeared was the final score, (29) *U*. One particular piece of data—the favorable concept of expert management—was sacrificed in the process of quantification.

Other economic aspects include the reference to "an impersonal financial entity" (31 scored *U*), and a remark that the trend toward

RESEARCH TECHNIQUE

combination is "ominous" (40 a scored *U*). The editor also frowns upon some of the financial practices of the holding companies, specifically overcapitalization and the use of non-voting common stock (40 c scored *U*).

While this item does not touch upon the social dimensions of the giant firm, the editor comments upon one political characteristic. The trusts of earlier days were, he says, clearly illegal, and even though the modern combines stay within the letter of the law, they violate the spirit of the law and create a threat to the public (53 a scored *U*).

The editorial offers a solution to the problem of combines. In the near future (56), the people will attempt to establish "public control" of the companies, and relying upon the editor's previous references to the national government, we concluded that he means federal regulation (61).

This is how the information in one editorial was translated into categories lending themselves to quantitative expression. The data from this score sheet were then transferred to computer cards and the figures from all of the items produced by one journal in one year were combined in order to yield totals and percentages for each of the separate categories. These are the constituent elements in the time series described and interpreted in the subsequent chapters of this book.

As should be clear by this point, content analysis was an intensive, time-consuming technique, and it was of course absolutely essential to sample the selected materials. The first set of papers we examined were the agrarian journals, and we began by using all of the issues appearing in the months of January and July.[40] Since most of the papers were initially monthlies and the issues were relatively short, we were able to read and analyze this very large sample. When we reached those years when the papers began to appear on a weekly basis, and the issues in some cases became much longer, this sample size proved to be too cumbersome. Determined to complete the project within five or six years, we tested with satisfactory results the effect of a change in sample size, and from that point on we used only the first issue to appear in the months of January and July.[41] This was the sample used in our analysis of the agrarian journals after 1920 and in our study of all of the other papers. While the statistical tests generated confidence in the sample, the reader deserves a warning. The project was designed to produce data that could be used to interpret long-run trends of large proportions, and partly for this reason the figures in the subsequent chapters are frequently grouped for five- and six-year periods. As a rule of thumb, it seems prudent to ignore fluctuations of less than ten percentage points for any one year.

V. To my mind, however, the major problems of my research technique were not related to the use of samples; in reality all historians use samples whether they accept the fact or not. Late in the week, after working on editorials like the one reprinted above, I usually worried about other problems. A major difficulty—one that was inescapable—was the maintenance of strict and unvarying rules about what information went into each category and about the exact manner in which the categories were labeled favorable, unfavorable, neutral, or ambivalent. It was impossible to eliminate variance or "drift" (or, as my research assistant called it, the "devilfish") entirely in the application of these rules. I could have reduced the variance in two ways: by making the categories smaller and more specific, and by recording only explicit (not implicit) judgments of big business. But both of these decisions, particularly the latter, would have sacrificed a significant part of the content of the journals. Editors and other contributors often find it unnecessary to print explicit judgments; knowing their readers, they convey meaning in more effective and less obtrusive ways.

Indeed, the writers and their prose styles were complex, and at the beginning of the project I was not prepared for the infinite number of slight variations on what, from the point of view of my interests, were marginal selections. Before this experiment with content analysis, I had never realized that the English language allowed for so many subtle shifts in meaning. I soon came to see that in my previous, non-quantitative research I had simply ignored most of these variations, skimming over the surface of the material until I had found a particularly strong and explicit statement of opinion. Now, however, I found it necessary to analyze all of the content of the journals, and that task was exhausting and difficult.

This experience demonstrated to me that content analysis, like any other research technique, has certain inherent limitations. Using the kinds of sources I studied, a project could only be entirely systematic (or scientific, if you prefer) if the researcher was willing to employ very minute, specific categories to catch the information. For the historian, who is normally interested in complex and long-run processes of change, this kind of category imposes a significant constraint upon his ability to reach general conclusions. Only by accepting an inordinately narrow definition of his hypotheses could he hope to satisfy fully the demands of both science and history. Because of this problem, content analysis is best suited for dealing with relatively unsophisticated materials. Even though I examined occupational journals drawn from what I felt was a middle-class culture, the contents were complex and subtle enough to make systematic analysis difficult. My own experience indicates that for this part of society, content analysis is extremely useful, but that traditional methods will continue to be best suited for research on the products of the intellectual elite.

Content analysis was also expensive in terms of money and time. In dollars and cents the cost of systematic research was high, and the project could not have been completed without substantial support from private foundations and government agencies.[42] Even more crucial to me was the expenditure of time. The hours spent sorting out small, marginal items could have been invested in different ways, and time was also one of the factors limiting me to the study of only three occupational groups.

My final cause for concern was the extent to which dedication to system had sacrificed the particular, the time- and place-rooted qualities of my data. By turning each bit of information into a statistic, I was assured comparability of the data; figures from different journals and different years could certainly be compared. But the danger was that the analysis of dots on an x-y axis would become an end in itself, and I felt that if I or my readers forgot that behind these figures were letters and articles written and read by individuals in a special setting, then I would have lost touch with my original goal, the writing of history.

Fortunately, Friday's anxiety about content analysis always gave way before Monday's optimism. As the week began I would recognize that in fact I had struck a reasonable balance between the particular and the universal—the right balance, at least, given my goal of achieving a systematic, long-run analysis of the changing image of big business in America. My concessions to the particular qualities of my data included numerous quotations that I hoped would breathe some life into a volume filled with trend lines and tables. Along the way, I had managed to include few individuals, but I had been able to deal with specific groups and with such formal organizations as the American Federation of Labor and the Farm Bureau Federation. It seemed, then, that I had in fact fallen exactly where I wanted to be, between two extreme positions, and that my task was that of meshing the concerns and procedures of traditional narrative history with those of modern social science (or behavioralism). This was no small undertaking, and each reader can judge for himself whether I succeeded or not.

In my positivist phase I could recognize that while we had not driven away the "devilfish," entirely eliminating drift, the project was far more systematic than most previous historical studies of changing images. Despite the large number of subjective judgments that we made, we were able to reproduce our own results with a high degree of accuracy. Furthermore, we could measure and analyze our ability to achieve replication under these conditions. By the standards of present-day survey research, this project certainly leaves room for improvement in technique; by the standards of existing work on similar problems by historians, the errors in our technique are not very important.

While the statistical data was expensive, the cost did not seem out of line with the benefits of quantification. Content analysis provided information that heretofore had not been available to historians. Using that data, I was able to test a variety of hypotheses about an important, long-term process of change in modern America. The statistics enabled me to analyze some of the elements in this process in ways that would have been extremely difficult, perhaps impossible, if I had been using the traditional sources and techniques.

My answer to the inevitable question is: yes, if I were starting this project over, I would again use content analysis. With the advantage of hindsight, I could eliminate some of my mistakes, and I still retain certain fundamental reservations about this research technique. My goals and general research design would, however, remain unchanged. But before judging this subjective conclusion, the reader should examine the evidence and analyses offered in the following chapters.

PART TWO. FIRST GENERATION: A STUDY IN THE SOURCES OF CONFLICT

3

AN UNEASY EQUILIBRIUM, 1879-1892

Between 1879 and 1892, Americans seemed determined to leave nothing in their society unchanged. As we saw in chapter 1, the combination movement that had already reshaped the nation's rail system began in these years to spawn similar primary bureaucracies in manufacturing and distribution. These innovations in organization took place against an economic background which itself was in constant flux. The rapid economic growth of the years immediately before the Civil War continued, multiplying the nation's wealth and pushing per capita income to new heights.[1] Abundant land and natural resources contributed to this latest surge in the economy—as they had, for that matter, since the founding of the colonies. An expanding transportation system, the railroad in particular, also spurred growth, as did a factory system which was steadily replacing the shop as the primary source of manufactured goods. What was most outstanding about the American experience during these years, however, was not some single innovation but the multiplicity of changes, large and small, which were taking place in almost every sector of the economy and every part of the country.

The South, traditionally agricultural, shared the mixed blessings of economic change with the industrial North, the Midwest, and the West. By the 1880s southern farming had begun to recover from the effects of the war and the end of the slave labor system; sharecropping now replaced the plantation in the production of such staple crops as cotton. Meanwhile, the railroad had redefined the regional patterns of distribution, making Atlanta, Georgia, the commercial capital of a "New South." Factories accompanied the railroad, and the new textile industry that sprang up in the Piedmont region of the Southeast soon challenged New England's supremacy in the manufacture of cotton yarn and cloth. Changes of similar magnitude were taking place in the Northeast, the Midwest, and the West, in the distribution as well as the production of goods, in the sources of labor as well as the uses of land.[2] Speculation in real estate was—as it is today—the common denominator of American development.[3]

Rapid growth produced problems as well as profits for America. Cyclical fluctuations in the rate of economic activity meant insecurity for everyone, but it was most acute for the urban laborer, who could not fall back on the land for sustenance. While the farmer may have suffered less, he often found himself simultaneously producing larger crops and going deeper into debt. During the mid-eighties businessmen felt just as hard-pressed when demand dropped off, prices fell, and competition for markets intensified.

In an effort to cope with these problems, laborers, farmers, professional men, and businessmen all experimented with new forms of organizations, but the very act of experimentation caused strains; some were created by the problems of adjustment within the group, others by the struggle against opposing organizations. Among workers, for example, the growth of labor unions in the eighties and early nineties was punctuated with strife between rival organizations and power struggles inside the groups themselves, in addition to the familiar battles with employers and hostile public officials.[4] So marked were these signs of social disorientation that Robert Wiebe has labeled late nineteenth-century America a "distended society" in which an earlier system of isolated local and regional communities had broken down without being replaced by a stable alternative. Americans were, says Wiebe, engaged in a long and initially frustrating "search for order."[5]

Certainly new and demanding conditions were forcing many Americans to change their lives. In the emerging industrial system the machine was eroding the boundaries of, and in some cases destroying the demand for, the traditional crafts. Where this happened skilled labor lost some of its market value as well as its social significance. Agrarians also found it difficult to accept a new age in which the factory was replacing the farm as the nation's primary source of wealth. In the cities the professional men—who seemed to have all of the advantages of modern life in the farmers' eyes—faced their own special problems. All too often their professions received neither the respect nor the financial rewards that their members felt they deserved. The cities themselves were swollen with newcomers from southern Europe; urban governments were often corrupt. Immigration appeared to many to threaten not only life within the cities but the national culture itself, and in 1884 a church paper nervously asked what would happen "if, some day, the Mongol, Sclav, and the Latin elements in this country should combine against the Celt."[6] In light of these tensions in the cities, in the factories, and on the farms, one would naturally expect to find that the trust movement and the related changes taking place in their society disturbed middle-class Americans.

II. Yet, when we examine the group images of the large corporation, we find that among professional engineers, for example, there was little hostility toward big business during these years (figure 3-1). The engineer had a predominantly neutral image of big business and often lauded corporate accomplishments.[7] These attitudes were extremely stable through the entire thirteen-year period (see Appendix). For the engineer there was apparently no search for order; he already had a clear notion about how society should be ordered and he accepted the fact that large-scale organizations would play an important role in industrial America.

During the late eighties his confidence in these conclusions was shaken slightly, and he became, for a few years, somewhat more critical of the corporation. Briefly, negative and positive attitudes were evenly balanced. The reason the engineer had these doubts is partly explained by looking at the characteristics of the large company that he stressed, as well as those he ignored. He framed his image primarily in economic terms. Between 89 and 100 percent of the times he discussed big business he touched upon its economic functions (table 3-1). In the late eighties three specific economic characteristics received far more attention than any others. In rank order they were: the management or ownership of the company, its products and services, and, finally, its existence or expansion. Two of these were primarily internal matters; only products and services touched in an immediate sense upon corporate relations with its several publics—with those, for instance, who met the giant corporation in the marketplace and experienced its power firsthand. Missing was any concern about the firm's price policies or about anything connected with the labor force, either inside or outside the company. The traumatic labor struggles of the eighties have excited later generations of historians, but to the professional engineers of that time they were a minor problem.

Nor did the socio-political dimensions of the corporation arouse the engineer. He was actually oblivious to the social or cultural aspects of the large firm—its impact upon status systems, for example, failed to interest him despite the fact that his own status was increasingly dependent upon businesses such as these. While the political affairs of the corporation attracted his attention fairly often, almost all of his comments on charters, government contracts, and railroad land grants were neutral. Matters of practical, not political, economy drew his criticism, and it is there that we must look for the sources of his discontent.

When he discussed the economic features of big business, he talked most often about the railroads. In the eighties this was where the action was for professional engineers; construction and maintenance on the nation's railroads provided a major source of employment for the readers of *Engineering News*, and the paper fed this interest by surveying transportation developments throughout the entire United States and other countries as well. Running a poor second to the railroad was the production of primary metals, which included the railroad-related iron and steel industry. Only eight different industries were even mentioned during the years 1880-86, but the engineer was attentive to the spreading concentration

FIGURE 3-1. The engineer's evaluation of big business, 1880-1892. The annual percentages represent the proportion of items in *Engineering News* reflecting each attitude. For an explanation of my methodology, see chapter 2.*

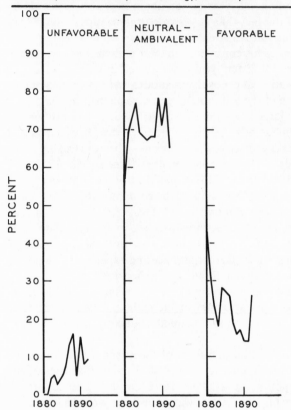

movement; in the next six years he discussed the activities of big business in twelve major industries, and those in the second, third, and fourth places received more consideration than they had before. Still, the railroad and closely related industries continued to dominate the engineer's image of large enterprise in the late eighties.

In the various economic functions of the railroad industry, the engineer found one particular flaw that aroused his anger. He could hardly complain about employment opportunities when a great boom in railroad construction between 1886 and 1892 was producing over forty thousand miles of new track.[8] Nor did these professional men worry much about the public debate over railroad regulation by the Interstate Commerce Commission (estab-

*Those readers who are interested in the annual percentages depicted in figure 3-1 (and in all of the subsequent graphs) can write directly to the author for a mimeographed copy of the data.

FIRST GENERATION

lished in 1887). Their concern was stirred by a more prosaic fact: the growing number of railroad accidents. Many of these events took place under circumstances that forced the engineers to consider the inherent tension between their roles as professional technicians and as employees of private firms. The accidents raised questions about the quality of railroad management and the services the lines provided. Private profit and professional engineering seemed to the technicians—as they did later to Thorstein Veblen—to be in conflict.[9] When a bridge collapsed, *Engineering News* noted that "the obstinate refusal of a prominent railroad line to attach any importance to alleged defects in one of their structures would seem incredible if it were not well known that such is frequently the case. . . . Nor has it been at all uncommon in the past for the recommendations of a too stringent engineer to be quietly shelved, and he along with them."[10] Even the best railroad lines could, it was suggested, improve their "operating methods," and the worst were said to be guilty of dishonesty as well as incompetence.[11] Following one serious accident, a letter to the editor observed: "The officers of the company which owned this bridge swore, year after year, in their annual reports to the State authorities that all their bridges were examined

TABLE 3-1. The engineer's image of big business, 1880-1892

Aspects of big business mentioned[a]	1880–1886			1887–1892		
	High year	Low year	Mean[b]	High year	Low year	Mean[b]
Economic	100%	93%	98%	100%	89%	96%
Political	23	7	16	21	8	13
Social	6	0	1	1	0	less than 1

Leading characteristics of big business (in rank order)	1) Existence or expansion 2) Management or ownership 3) Products or services	1) Management or ownership 2) Products or services 3) Existence or expansion
Leading industries mentioned	1) Railroad transportation (40)[c] 2) Primary metals (33) 3) Communications (48)	1) Railroad transportation (40) 2) Transportation equipment (37) 3) Local passenger transportation (41)

SOURCE: *Engineering News.* For an explanation of my methodology, see chapter 2.
[a]These figures show what percentage of the articles mentioned each aspect; the columns can total more than 100% because a single article could mention one, two, or all three.
[b]Mean of the annual percentages.
[c]In this and subsequent tables, the industries are categorized according to the *Standard Industrial Classification Manual* published by the Executive Office of the President, Bureau of the Budget (Washington, D.C., 1957); the number appearing after each industry indicates its two-digit group.

AN UNEASY EQUILIBRIUM, 1879-1892

every 30 days, and that these examinations were analytical and made by a competent person. Moreover they also swore that all their bridges and trestles were provided with guard rails, but you will find no trace of any in the photograph [as was indeed the case]."[12] Where safety was involved, American management was said to be inferior to the English, and furthermore, "the American railway engineer labors at a disadvantage in not possessing the money and authority of the English engineer."[13]

The engineer's professional ideology was the primary force shaping his image of big business.[14] This ideology was a belief system which assured that on most issues his outlook would be neutral. Normally he was more interested in determining what, exactly, the situation was than in deciding what, in any general fashion, the situation meant.[15] When he did evaluate corporate behavior, his moral yardstick was provided by a group which thought of itself as highly rationalistic, dedicated to system and to science, and restricted in its judgment to those areas of life which the engineer encountered in either his formal education or professional experience, especially in the latter. All men and their institutions (except perhaps the profession itself) were entitled to an empirical test; achievement, that is, performance of the task at hand, determined quality, not inherent or inherited characteristics. The ideology dictated a single standard whether its adherents were judging men, bridges, or giant railroad combines.[16]

In the 1880s the engineer's opinion of the combines was stable, in part because this ideology was firmly implanted. The organizational base was provided by an association which had been active for three decades, and by journals like *Engineering News*, which regularly clarified, updated, and reiterated the engineer's catechism. As new publications and new associations emerged, it was frequently necessary to reconsider the nature of the profession.[17] But these internal problems do not seem to have radically changed the major concepts in a professional point of view which was already cast in what appears to us as a modern—that is, twentieth-century—pattern of thought.

While the engineer's ideology helped to assure that his response to the concentration movement would be unemotional and consistent, professionalism also gave him a form of tunnel vision. Many important aspects of the giant firm were blocked from his view, including the great power and wealth being amassed by these combines. Broad questions of public policy toward such aggregations crept only occasionally into sight. In 1890 he considered the general trend toward monopoly in city utilities and the problems of the New York transit system in particular.[18] At times he mentioned other trusts, but he saw a far different business system from the one that angered Henry George and Richard T. Ely. *Engineering News* mentioned Standard Oil, the prototype of the modern corporation and the object of severe attack from public officials and publicists, only twice in the years 1880 through 1892.[19] The creation of the Interstate Commerce

Commission produced only a brief ripple of concern, and in 1890, when the Sherman Act was passed, the engineer was worried more about railroad accidents than about the antitrust movement.[20]

Even though the engineer would doubtless have insisted that his judgments were entirely objective, his outlook was full of class overtones. He saw corporate enterprise from the top, seldom considering the thousands who worked for the combines or the millions who paid for their products; he was content instead to ponder the behavior of the select few who guided these business giants. America's business leaders should pay more heed to their technical staffs, he concluded, but on balance the strengths of management outweighed its weaknesses.[21] He certainly felt that the rights of property should be curtailed as little as possible and that business self-regulation was preferable to federal control, even in the vital matter of railroad accidents.[22]

The impact of a class-tinctured, professional ideology could be seen in the ease with which the corporation redeemed itself in the early nineties. Concerned about the accidents and doubtless prodded by the threat of regulatory legislation, railroad lines began to install more safety equipment.[23] The engineer was pleased to see the companies displaying a progressive attitude, although frequently the new equipment was not ordered until a severe accident had left dead and injured passengers and employees strewn about the tracks.[24] Despite the fact that the railway death toll continued to climb in the early nineties, the engineer found solace in the knowledge that the companies involved were adopting the best equipment available.[25] Thus ended his brief cycle of discontent.

III. In many ways the Congregational minister's perception of the revolutionary organizational changes taking place in business resembled that of the engineer. Both groups of professional men looked upon the trust movement with considerable equanimity; their image of the firm consisted primarily of neutral-ambivalent symbols (figure 3–2), and their opinions remained relatively stable during the years 1880–92 (see Appendix). Both engineers and ministers saw more to like than to dislike in the behavior of big business, although the balance shifted slightly against the corporation in the latter part of the decade. The clergy also stressed several of the same characteristics of the large firm that were uppermost in the engineers' minds. To the minister the trusts were largely an economic phenomenon, and he gave particular attention to their managers and to their products and services (table 3–2). Political considerations were of secondary importance, but they still received much more attention than did the social aspects of corporate enterprise.

In part these similarities were a function of class alignment. Perched as they were (and saw themselves to be) in the upper branches of the middle class, the minister and the engineer gazed at private enterprise from the top

FIGURE 3-2. The Congregational clergy's evaluation of big business, 1880-1892. The annual percentages represent the proportion of items in *Congregationalist* reflecting each attitude.

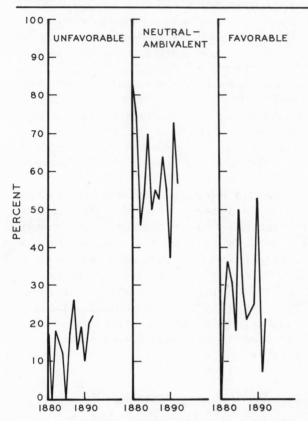

down. The clergyman found much to say about the nation's railroad leaders and industrial titans, some of whom heard their sermons in Congregational churches, others in less prestigious surroundings. For the minister, the large firm was fleshed out, given personality and a locus of personal responsibility, by the actions of its top managers. While a number of these moguls were, to the clerical mind, socially irresponsible, their property rights were seldom challenged much more seriously in the pages of the *Congregationalist* than they were in *Engineering News*.

There was also an ideological side to the clerical view of the trusts, but in the clergyman's case the ideology did not stem from his professional organizations. Unlike the engineer, the clergyman was touched by an ideology that originated outside the profession and only gradually and partially filtered into his church. While the engineer's belief system narrowed

FIRST GENERATION

his vision to those aspects of the environment touching in obvious ways upon his professional interests, the ideology that influenced the clergyman actually pulled his attention away from the pulpit and his immediate congregation. The ideology in this case was the brand of modern liberalism which, after it had penetrated the Protestant church in America, became known as the social gospel.

Scholars have thoroughly examined the origins and impact of the social gospel, and we need only pause momentarily to review some of its major outlines.[26] According to its foremost historian, the social gospel began largely as a reaction to two post-Civil War problems: the spread of urban slums and the increase in violent labor-management struggles. To some Protestant leaders these outgrowths of industrialism seemed to demand government intervention (in varying degrees) where laissez-faire had failed. These spokesmen concluded that it was the duty of Protestants to assume responsibility for guiding society through this political and social transformation. In the eighties, R. Heber Newton, an Episcopal minister and one of the leaders of "progressive social Christianity," advocated such moderate measures as taxation reform and regulation of monopolies. His pleas were seconded from a Congregational pulpit by Washington Gladden, and a muffled echo of their voices was heard in the *Congregationalist*.[27]

TABLE 3-2.   The Congregational clergy's image of big business, 1880-1892

Aspects of big business mentioned	1880–1886			1887–1892		
	High year	Low year	Mean	High year	Low year	Mean
Economic	100%	82%	94%	100%	84%	90%
Political	22	0	13	32	12	23
Social	17	0	4	12	0	5
Leading characteristics of big business	1) Products or services 2) Management or ownership 3) Existence or expansion; Miscellaneous political activities			1) Management or ownership 2) Products or services 3) Existence or expansion		
Leading industries mentioned	1) Railroad transportation (40) 2) Local passenger transportation (41) 3) Communications (48)			1) Railroad transportation (40) 2) Petroleum refining (29) 3) Electric-gas-sanitary services (49)		

SOURCE: *Congregationalist*.
NOTE: If multiple entries follow one number, the categories were tied.

AN UNEASY EQUILIBRIUM, 1879-1892

The most convenient place to study the intersection of this liberal ideology and the minister's class bias is in the basic values that underlay his religious philosophy.[28] One of these was a brand of individualism that the Congregational minister shared with many Americans.[29] In this case class interests and the reform impulse coalesced to generate fear that the trust movement would someday squeeze out the small, independent businessman. In the early eighties, the clergy identified big business with only five major industries; in the years 1887–92 that number doubled, and the *Congregationalist* concluded: "If the trust plan of business is to prevail it means that it is a good thing for combinations of capital to absorb one by one the industries into which men, in the pursuit of natural right, have deemed it best to enter to obtain a livelihood; that a man is worth more to himself and his country as a salaried employé of a great corporation . . . than in the independent exercise of his abilities as a producer of wealth."[30]

While the Protestant minister was critical of the trusts, his interest in the "natural right" of the individual also led him to respect those men of accomplishment who successfully ran the country's large firms. Corporate management drew more positive remarks from *Congregationalist* than did any other aspect of big business. "What a complicated creation a great railroad is," the paper exclaimed, "and what exceptional ability and care are required to run one."[31] The clergyman valued achievement, even in its crudest material form, and big business scored impressive marks for its contributions to America's progress. "The railroads touch the business world in its every artery," the minister commented. "For where the railroads prosper, business generally is good."[32] From Kansas City he observed that the area's "background network of rails connecting with every corner of the continent, make up a marvellous picture of American energy and progress."[33] He applauded industrial combines for their efficiency, and in the same year that the Sherman Antitrust Act was passed enthusiastically praised the trusts for their ability to "avoid the ruin which always results from unbridled competition."[34]

Balanced against an appreciation of these accomplishments was a growing concern about corporate irresponsibility. Achievement, like sin, was ultimately a personal matter, and the Protestant minister had a deep concern for the responsibilities of man to man, of man to country, and of man to God. These responsibilities were as diffuse as they were essential. Men were obligated to one another in ways that went far beyond what their contractual relations might specify. These obligations, filtered through a class perspective, often became a form of noblesse oblige. The clergyman expected those men of "exceptional ability" who ran giant corporations to be even more responsible than others, and he noted that all too often they ignored their duties—especially when they went to battle with labor. *Congregationalist* attacked those "vast combinations of capital" which were insensitive to the problems they created for their workers as well as for the general public.[35] The paper applauded when the New York railroad commissioner stopped a "lock-out" by the elevated railways and, while maintaining some reservations about trade unions, the journal frequently blamed business for inciting labor-management strife.[36] It also charged corporations with irresponsible political behavior. The railroads maintained a powerful lobby that corrupted legislators with free passes; corporations continually asked for "fresh legislation" that benefited the companies, not the public.[37] Firms like the New Haven Railroad frequently behaved as if they stood above the law. In 1891 a judge acquitted the officers of the company on the charge that they had created a hazard by heating passenger cars with stoves. He released Chauncey Depew, president of the New Haven and a notable citizen, despite the fact that Depew was "morally to blame."[38] Other rail lines invited the clergyman's criticism by violating the Sabbath: "The roads which have invariably on hand some job for Sunday are the roads with jaded men and frequent catastrophes. The roads which allow derailed and demolished cars in ghastly piles to lie along their embankments because Sunday is a convenient day to gather them up, find that day, at length, too brief for their convenience."[39]

Still, when big business and its leaders met the diffuse obligations that the clergy had in mind, the *Congregationalist* was quick to confer its approval. Acts of philanthropy aroused numerous favorable comments, and in 1890 the Congregational minister was particularly pleased to see that the New York Central Railroad had provided "five handsome structures . . . devoted to their employees as places of rest and centers of educative, refining and Christian influences. Such generous consideration for workmen goes far toward disproving the common saying 'that corporations have no souls.' "[40] Harmony in labor-management relations invited similar praise, and by 1892 the clergy had decided that "working men are coming also to appreciate more the value of enterprises supported by large amounts of capital and managed by able and experienced men, as insuring permanent employment and stability of wages."[41]

Dedication to social harmony maintained by a diffuse sense of responsibility, to individualism, and to achievement made the Protestant minister sensitive to a broader range of events than was the engineer. When the corporation became involved in social conflict, the clergyman was invariably aroused. The violent and newsworthy strike would almost certainly stir his concern. In that sense, his image of the corporation was inherently less stable than that of the engineer, because equilibrium depended primarily upon the absence of a particular class of events which usually took place far beyond the reach of the profession. Furthermore, these events were a normal product of two cyclical phenomena generic to modern industrial societies: fluctuations in the rate of economic activity and impulses of liberal reform.

The downturn of the business cycle almost inevitably bred conflict in the centers of industry. Labor unions, able to win concessions from employers during good times, were defeated and frequently destroyed in the midst of depression.[42] Unorganized workers often walked off the job over wage cuts, longer hours, and changes in working conditions only to find themselves replaced by strikebreakers who then received protection from company detectives and local police. The result was industrial strife that made the Protestant minister reflect anew upon the social responsibility of the large corporation.

Reform movements had somewhat similar results. In the late eighties, for instance, when railroad regulation was a subject of concern, the *Congregationalist* published economist Richard T. Ely's fiery attack on the businessmen who had amassed "such accumulations of capital in corporations as the world has never before seen" and who were guilty of "scandalous mismanagement of railways."[43] While the paper's editorial comments were more moderate than Ely's, the incident revealed that reform movements had the potential to be an important factor in shaping the clergyman's image of the corporation.[44]

In the early nineties, however, neither economic conflict nor political reform produced events that would grate against clerical values and disrupt in any significant way the clergyman's rather placid view of the trust movement. The economy was in fact booming, wages were increasing, jobs were plentiful, and strikes were at least no more frequent or troublesome than they had been in recent years. The strongest reform efforts were those with which he felt the least affinity in class terms, the Populist movements in the South and West. As a result, his opinion of the nation's largest business firms remained stable and relatively conservative through 1892.

IV. In the early 1880s, similar attitudes prevailed among southern farmers. The antimonopoly crusade had yet to march through the cotton country, and the farmer's concept of the large corporation was surprisingly favorable (figure 3–3). To him big business was primarily the railroad, and he saw much that he liked in the performance of his region's recently improved rail system (table 3–3). The railroad gave "access" to new farming regions and made such specialty crops as fruits profitable for the first time; as one booster proudly proclaimed: "This country . . . is all aglow with factories, mills, churches, schools and prospective railroads."[45] The farmer was touched by the New South spirit, a brand of regionalism evident in the widespread efforts to encourage manufacturing in the southern Piedmont. He was pleased to see that the railroads taught men how to use tools, doubling the amount of work they could do, furnishing "a partial remedy for want of books."[46] He praised the men who directed the transportation companies for their "brains and energy"; and when these businessmen went so far as to run their own farms in addition to their corporations, the farmer felt that they demonstrated to the world that they had a "practical eye" to go with their "business acumen."[47] This judgment was reinforced by the fact that railroad officials often had the wisdom to give reduced rates to farmers who were attending agricultural conventions.[48]

In these respects southern farm attitudes seemed to resemble those of professional men, but there were important differences between these groups that became evident in the latter part of the decade. While farmers had a conception of their social role, they were not committed to a professional ideology in the way that engineers were. The agrarian concepts were less specific and were not anchored in professional organizations of the sort which institutionalized the engineer's image of himself and his relationship to the large firm. Instead, a variety of different organizations with differing programs and opinions vied for the farmer's support. As a result, his opinions were more volatile than the engineer's (see Appendix), and he was open to the influence of a wider range of events.

A class-related difference also existed between the attitudes of the farmer and those of the professional men. The southern farmer looked at big business and at its leaders from a lower rung on the class ladder, from a self-assessed position somewhere between the professional men above him and the common laborers below. He was uneasy about his status, concerned that others regarded his occupation as "degrading," and he plaintively called upon his peers to "realize that their vocation is just as honorable, just as ennobling and elevating as any other."[49] He resented the "expressed reproach that, in many places, attaches to being a farmer—'only a farmer.' "[50] When, in the latter part of the decade, the trusts and railroad combines angered him, he began to state his ideas in explicitly class-related terms, to see himself, for instance, as oppressed by "class legislation."[51] As this happened, his middle-class concern for property rights began to give way to his desire for new forms of regulation that would curb the power of business.

In these years the cotton farmer could not look upon big business with the kind of detachment that characterized the clergyman. Although *Southern Cultivator* sometimes commented upon the corporation's dealings with third parties—with labor unions, for example—the paper was almost exclusively concerned with those aspects of big business directly touching, or appearing to touch, the farmer's interests. On infrequent occasions, these interests were social or cultural (see table 3-3), as they were in 1887 when monopoly was linked with the fact that farmers could no longer "command a decent respect."[52] More often, the cotton farmer saw the combines threaten-

AN UNEASY EQUILIBRIUM, 1879-1892

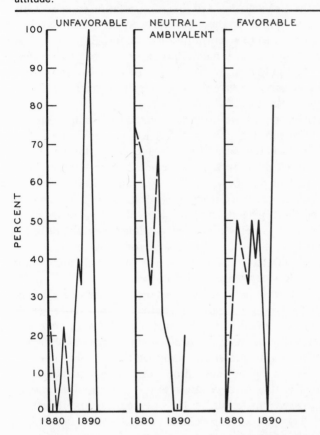

FIGURE 3-3. **The southern farmer's evaluation of big business, 1879-1892.** The annual percentages represent the proportion of items in *Southern Cultivator* reflecting each attitude.

ing his political position, stealing, through "class legislation," the few dollars that he had wrung from the soil. In 1890, when his anger at the trusts reached its peak, 40 percent of the items in *Southern Cultivator* touched upon the political involvement of the trusts—and all portrayed this activity in extremely negative terms.[53] The tariff took money away from farmers and made millionaires in the North: "Protection fixes the price of axes and not competition." The tariff on British iron and steel made equipment more expensive, taxing "heavily the daily consumption of sixty million souls."[54] Big business even exploited the courts, which the people paid for with their taxes, by taking advantage of the convict labor system. In 1890 there was a sense of crisis, of desperation, in *Southern Cultivator*, and while the journal continued to discuss peaceful reform it also concluded "that the masses are reduced to a helplessness that is without remedy outside of revolution."[55]

FIRST GENERATION

Even in the pivotal years around 1890, however, the central thrust of the southern farmer's critique was aimed at the economic depredations of big business. The corporation was, in his eyes, primarily an economic entity that he saw as "oppressive monopoly," the "favored few," the "cormorants, trusts and combinations."[56] He emphasized the general economic power that these "unholy combinations" had come to possess: they used their power to destroy the "legitimate laws of trade as regulated by the laws of supply and demand"; they sought to "rivet the fetters of vassalage upon us and our posterity."[57] Not satisfied with the immense power they already held, the trusts were spreading, threatening soon to control all industries and to charge prices that would "plunder" the poor farmers.[58] "The times 'run riot' with the spirit of insatiate greed, fattening upon the toil and hard earnings of others, and the end is not yet."[59]

As this rhetoric suggests, one source of disequilibrium and extreme hostility was the southern farmer's declining economic situation. By the late 1870s he had managed to solve the labor problem stemming from the war and the end of slavery; total cotton production exceeded the records set in the best ante-bellum years, and during the period 1879–92 he continued to increase the acreage planted in cotton. The results were a heartening increase in output and a disheartening fall in prices. The average price he received for a pound of cotton was 10.2 cents in the years 1879–86 and only 9.2 cents in the following six years.[60] The impact of lower prices was felt most severely in the states to the east of the Mississippi River, where farmers were gradually being forced to use larger amounts of commercial fertilizers to keep up their

TABLE 3-3. The southern farmer's image of big business, 1879-1892

Aspects of big business mentioned	1879–1886			1887–1892		
	High year	Low year	Mean	High year	Low year	Mean
Economic	100%	83%	92%	100%	70%	89%
Political	21	0	10	40	0	22
Social	11	0	2	10	0	3

Leading characteristics of big business	1) Products or services 2) Contributions to general wealth; Management or ownership	1) Prices 2) Existence or expansion 3) Economic power; Management or ownership

Leading industries mentioned	1) Railroad transportation (40) 2) Food processing (20) 3) Machinery—nonelectrical (35)	1) Railroad transportation (40) 2) Fabric products (23) 3) Food processing (20)

SOURCE: *Southern Cultivator*.

AN UNEASY EQUILIBRIUM, 1879-1892

production and gross income.[61] The new acreage being brought into production was primarily in Texas and Oklahoma, and western crops from new and fertile soils created the same problems for the Alabama grower that he had once created for the farmer of South Carolina.[62]

These short-run economic concerns help explain the cotton farmer's mounting anger at the trusts and transportation companies. There was a calculating and thoroughly rational dimension to his response. He indeed faced serious economic problems which were exacerbated to the extent that industrial combines and great railroad systems influenced the prices of the goods he purchased and the crops he sold. He focused most of his attention on the railroads, on the companies that sold him bagging for his cotton bales, and on the firms that processed farm products (see table 3-3). He knew that, in the long run, political measures favoring these large corporations would probably spur regional economic expansion to his personal benefit, and except during the peak years of the crisis, *Southern Cultivator* continued to discuss the developmental facet of the large corporation.[63] But, in the short run, political measures had to be paid for by the people, most notably the farmers; and in 1890 it appeared that they might not last long enough to enjoy the blessings of economic growth. Threatened, the farmers turned on the "combinations of capital" and the "corporate power" which had yoked them with oppressive systems of "finance and taxation."[64]

At best, however, economic interest provides only a partial explanation of the southern farmer's shifting opinion of big business. Correlations between cotton prices and the annual figures on attitudes substantiate this conclusion. The statistical tests indicate a significant and positive relationship between the prices the farmer received and his tendency to discuss the trusts in a neutral vein; on the other hand, the same tests do not yield significant results for the attitudes we are most interested in explaining, that is, the negative evaluations that increased so sharply in the late 1880s. In 1889, when the percentage of unfavorable opinions was higher than before, cotton prices were slightly above the level of the previous four years; in 1890, the price of the southern staple again increased by a small amount, while opposition to the concentration movement reached its peak. Gross farm income from cotton and cottonseed (in constant dollars) was also higher in 1890 than it had been in the preceding years.[65] While the cotton farmer (especially if he lived east of the Mississippi) was trapped in a painful cost-price squeeze, his economic plight alone does not provide an adequate explanation of his growing animosity toward the trusts. His response was clearly out of proportion to his direct involvement with big business or to the changes taking place in his economic fortunes.

The anxiety grounded in economic interests was, in his case, bound up with a general sense of social disorganization. He lashed out in one direction and then another, searching for targets. Although he had previously ignored the political power of big business, the southern farmer in 1890 repeatedly attacked such corporate chicanery—only to abandon this as a major issue two years later. His image of the trusts had a variety of irrational or nonrational facets.[66] As we have seen, he was upset about his declining status, and in his mind monopoly was vaguely associated with the farmer's inability to "command a decent respect."[67] These fears were linked with the threatened breakdown of the family farm. His children were leaving the farm—the center of "the real, the good and the true"—in order to live in the city, where the good was "encrusted with vanity and pretense and false theories and ideas." They left in part because the educational institutions that the farmer himself supported gave them "a dislike for agriculture" and led "the young to believe that the only place where their education can be of service is in the city." His entire way of life seemed to be under attack, and he recognized that "the power to preserve social purity, to perpetuate Christian faith in simplicity, to guard liberty, to resist oppression of monopoly, and to avert the march of communism, must be the conservative character product of the independent and happy rural home."[68] When he saw his happy home collapse, when monopoly grew apace and his "manhood" was threatened with "utter destruction," the farmer found a scapegoat in the large corporation. Like a lightning rod, the trust attracted social discontent (whatever its source) and added it to the animosity bred by real economic grievances.[69]

Some restraint is called for, however, lest we load the poor farmer with a historical reputation he does not deserve. This, I think, is what Richard Hofstadter did in his brilliant analysis of the tawdry aspects of late-nineteenth-century agrarian reform.[70] Obviously, my evidence partially sustains Hofstadter's treatment of the irrational features of the farm movement in the 1880s and 1890s, just as it supports Robert Wiebe's more restrained picture of farmers searching for order and finding it in the past.[71] But I find many strands of Hofstadter's critique questionable. While it was not the subject of my content analysis, I was attentive to the farmer's view of other groups in America, particularly immigrants and Jews.[72] My evidence suggested that farmers in both the South and Midwest were occasionally guilty of nativism and of anti-Semitism (especially the former), but that these attitudes were not a prominent part of agrarian thought and were certainly shared throughout the middle classes in these years. Every callous remark that a southern farmer made about opening the "flood gate" to foreigners who were "nihilists or socialists" could be paired with a similar observation by the engineer or the clergyman who was worried about "the constant inflow of ignorant immigrants. . . ."[73] If the midwestern farmer was hostile toward "foreigners, large numbers of whom can neither speak nor read our language," his feelings were echoed by the skilled craftsman who felt that the public would surely blame employers for bringing in immigrant strikebreakers or, as the worker described it, "vomiting on them these hungry Hungarians."[74] Through the entire period covered by this study (1880–1940) there was only the slightest evidence of anti-Semitism, and it was not the sole property of any group.[75] Instead of attacking Jews or Hungarians, the southern farmer made big business the target for his animosities, a choice indicating that, while he felt oppressed and was often confused about the source of his discontent, his reactions to a changing environment were not devoid of reason.

His attitudes were very unstable, however (see Appendix), and organizational changes were in part responsible for this aspect of agrarian thought. As mentioned above, a wide variety of different organizations stressing varied roles and values competed for the farmer's allegiance. To one side was the Grange, which had changed over the years but still gave special emphasis to the farmer as head of the family and voluntary member of a fraternal order; on the other hand, there were the agricultural colleges and the government experiment stations, which saw the farmer as an individual producer and economic man.[76] There were numerous other farm clubs and societies, and in the late eighties the Farmers' Alliance spread through the southern states. This group pictured the farmer as an involuntary member of an oppressed class and called upon him to seek joint, not individual, solutions to his problems. Like a magnifying glass drawing rays of light together on one point, the Farmers' Alliance focused the discontents of the southern farmer on the trusts and on the need for political action against the farmer's corporate enemies. In that sense, it heightened feelings and contributed substantially to the peak period of discontent with big business occurring about 1890. Hesitant at first, *Southern Cultivator* had by that time opened its pages and its editorial heart to the Farmers' Alliance and to its concept of the farmer; it was then that the paper mounted its "holy crusade against an army of extortionists," against the "oppressive" combines which "cripple your industries, rob labor of its bread and toil of its earnings."[77]

In the next two years, however, the tide of antitrust feeling subsided. The single organization that had done the most to channel agrarian discontent proved itself to be unstable; cooperatives organized by the Farmers' Alliance failed, and the familiar venture into third-party politics forced the cotton farmer to make yet another difficult transition in thought and action. Meanwhile, fair-seeming victories encouraged optimism and dampened emotions that the organization had helped to fire. In 1890 farm-supported candidates won elections in a number of southern states and in Washington the Congress passed the Sherman Antitrust Act. Even though the politicians backed by agrarian reformers were often more conservative in office than they had been in the campaign, and even though the antitrust act was discussed more often than it was enforced, the southern farmer seems to have been convinced that significant progress had been made toward solving the trust problem.[78] The fact that such insubstantial accomplishments could

FIRST GENERATION

quiet reform demands lends further support to the view that the nonrational components in this cycle of antitrust sentiment were relatively important. The vaguely worded Sherman Antitrust Act provided an appropriate response to the cotton farmer's vaguely defined anxieties. With the Farmers' Alliance losing its appeal and with some putative victories over big business salving his wounds, the cotton farmer stopped worrying about monopoly —at least for a brief time.

V.   The midwestern farmer's image of the corporation resembled that of the cotton farmer in several ways. In the North, farm attitudes were unstable in the eighties (see Appendix), with the period of greatest opposition to the large corporation falling in the first half of the decade (figure 3-4). In the next few years the farmer became less concerned about the trust movement, and by 1888 he was far more likely to praise than to condemn big business. These favorable attitudes quickly gave way, however, to a second (somewhat milder) cycle of increased hostility occurring around 1890 and 1891. Whether he grew corn or cotton, the farmer looked upon the corporation as primarily an economic institution, but an economic institution with important political functions (table 3-4); he was concerned about the prices these companies charged as well as their products and services. Normally, when he said "big business" or "the corporation," he really meant the railroad, which from 1879 through 1892 remained his leading subject of concern. Around 1890 he began to see the trust movement spreading to a wider range of industries, but he still paid less attention to these producers than he did to the rail companies that carried his corn, pork, beef, or wheat to the Chicago markets and from there to the eastern seaboard.

It was the railroad which most often appealed to the midwestern farmer's instinct for boosterism. Both in 1882 when he was very upset with big business and in 1888 when he was not, the midwesterner saw that the railroad was the vital link between his fields and "the markets of the world." It provided the key to "rapid settlement," hence to greater land values, for him and his fellow agrarians.[79] His appreciation of these visible signs of progress varied considerably over the years—as figure 3-4 illustrates—but he, like his southern counterpart, seldom ignored for any length of time the relationship between corporate enterprise and economic growth.

In the Midwest, as in the South, big business was at times a focal point for animosity it had not really earned. The corn and hog producer was beginning to worry about the young boys and girls who were fleeing the pleasures of rural life to take their chances in the threatening environment of the city. He warned them that the city lad was "by the tyrannous rules of the labor organizations . . . practically shut off from all chances to learn a trade. The farmer's boy can learn things on the farm which will serve him better in

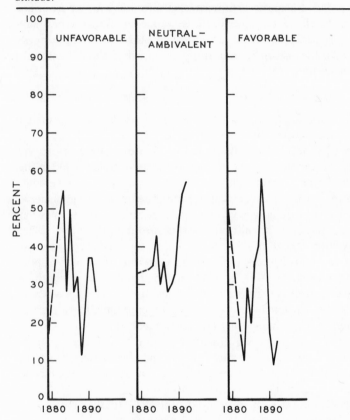

FIGURE 3-4. The midwestern farmer's evaluation of big business, 1879-1892. The annual percentages represent the proportion of items in *Farmers' Review* reflecting each attitude.

getting a start in life than a trade does the city boy."[80] He wanted to keep the "high-spirited" boys in the country so that they could "build it up to the position of respectability and influence which belongs to it." They were the ones who, if properly educated, "would fight the battles of agriculture against the lawyer and merchant and railroad, in commerce and in legislation."[81] As these remarks suggest, his unrest about the family was closely linked with a sense of declining status and on occasion the two fears coalesced around the issue of big business.

The nonrational component in midwestern farm thought became strongest in the early nineties when the farmer was becoming anxious about the broader aspects of the concentration movement. Now he began to see trusts on every side of him; here was the sugar combine, and there a monopoly in the manufacture of cereal, of asbestos, of paper, tobacco, and

FIRST GENERATION

soap. There was even a rumor that "New York and London capitalists are planning an extensive drug store trust."[82] On occasion these new combines posed a direct threat to midwestern agrarian interests, as they did when trusts were organized in food processing, in the production of harvesting equipment or barbed wire.[83] But the corn grower was no more imperiled by the drug store syndicate than he was by the combination in cotton duck, and one can only conclude that the trusts were attracting some anxieties which were both social and economic in nature but which had very little direct relationship to the large corporation itself.[84]

Midwesterners were as sensitive as southerners to class relationships and had equal reason to be confused about the farmer's role in society. Country men frequently saw themselves as part of the "far wost [sic] oppressed class of men in the United States."[85] The midwestern farmer gazed upward at the "dangerous rich classes who have accumulated enormous wealth" and hoped fervently that others would recognize that the complexity of agricultural production "elevates the farmer above any mere mechanic."[86] Farm organizations of every sort addressed themselves to his problems, but they seldom agreed upon the course that the farmer should follow or the specific role that he should play. From one side he heard the call for cooperatives, from another the need for scientific farming, for lower tariffs, for cheaper money, for price fixing.[87] Perhaps the only point of agreement among all of these organizations, from the Alliance to the agricultural colleges, was their belief that the midwestern farmer had to change his way of life in order to improve his economic fortunes.

TABLE 3-4.   The midwestern farmer's image of big business, 1879-1892

Aspects of big business mentioned	1879-1886			1887-1892		
	High year	Low year	Mean	High year	Low year	Mean
Economic	100%	79%	92%	98%	86%	92%
Political	26	17	22	28	7	17
Social	5	0	1	0	0	0
Leading characteristics of big business	1) Prices			1) Prices		
	2) Products or services			2) Products or services		
	3) Existence or expansion			3) Existence or expansion		
Leading industries mentioned	1) Railroad transportation (40)			1) Railroad transportation (40)		
	2) Primary metals (33)			2) Food processing (20)		
	3) Communications (48)			3) Textile mill products (22); Primary metals (33); Communications (48)		

SOURCE: *Farmers' Review.*

AN UNEASY EQUILIBRIUM, 1879-1892

While northern and southern attitudes and problems were similar in these regards, there were significant differences between the regions. For one thing, the midwestern farmer's response to the large corporation was on balance more rational than that of the cotton farmer and was characterized more by careful calculation than by a sense of indirection and disorganization. Midwestern attitudes were more stable; this was true of both the level of unfavorable opinions and the major aspects of big business that the farmer stressed. He kept his eye fixed throughout on prices, products and services, and on the establishment or expansion of the corporation. His interests were also more specific than those of the southerner. After all, the northern farmer had more direct experience with large firms, and especially with the railroad; the effects of this experience could be seen clearly in the major cycle of 1879 through 1888.[88] His opinions at this time were closely attuned to short-run changes in his economic situation and in particular to railroad freight rates. When rates were high in the early eighties, the farmer was angry at "freight monopolies."[89] He felt that he was "plagued with high transportation rates," and where there was no competition from water routes he was forced to pay "extortionate rail rates."[90] "Suppose the canals and navigable streams were owned by the Goulds and Vanderbilts! Such a state of things can hardly be conceived," he said. "And yet where is the real difference between owning a navigable stream or a canal and a line of railroad?"[91] As one farmer proclaimed in a letter to the editor: "The Northwestern railroad company controls all of this section of country, and they grind the farmer down to nothing. Farmers are owned body and bones by that tyrant corporation."[92]

In the farmer's viewpoint, the rail kings and other tyrants exploited the government to shore up their monopolies. In the early eighties, corporate dependence upon political favors ran a close second to price policies as a source of complaint.[93] There was evidence of a pre-industrial concept of monopoly as a product of political preference. The farmer objected to railroad land grants, to "the exactions of patent monopolists, to unfair taxes and to all varieties of 'class laws' "; large firms, he said, "have found in too many cases willing tools in the judiciary, in municipal governments, in state legislatures, and even in the halls of our national legislatures."[94] Since they were "soulless," the corporations were "troubled by no scruples as to methods when the rights of the common people stand in the way of their greed for gain."[95]

In the mid-eighties the midwestern farmer began to change his mind about the tyrant corporations. Unfavorable attitudes dwindled, and he found frequent opportunities to praise the large companies which provided him with goods and services. This was true despite the fact that farm income remained relatively low and prices for his commodities were far below the level of 1882.[96] The dynamic factor in this case was freight rates. Competition among the major rail systems brought rates tumbling down, and the farmer soon responded to this pleasant although fortuitous development.[97] By 1886 there was not (in this sample) a single negative remark about freight charges, and by 1888 the agrarian attitude toward big business consisted primarily of positive evaluations.[98]

While political measures had an impact upon the farmer's vision of the corporation, my evidence indicates that reform legislation was less important than a highly specific economic variable. In 1887 the farmer supported passage of the Interstate Commerce Bill, although he doubted that it would pass because "congress is owned, body, soul and breeches by the railroad corporations"; when, to his surprise, the Senate passed the measure, he was pleased with the idea that a federal commission might now eliminate "monopolistic injustice."[99] Three years later the Sherman Antitrust Act won his approval, just as state antitrust laws did, and he expressed some hope "that the trusts will be able to find no pretext or plan by which to evade these just laws."[100] But lower freight charges had, in fact, dampened his hostility toward the railroads long before the ICC was established, and the Sherman Antitrust Act exerted, in the short run at least, a negligible influence upon his general attitude toward big business. He remained suspicious about political solutions even after the passage of reform legislation, and in 1892, while he was not unusually agitated, he was still concerned about the burgeoning power of those "combines" and "soulless corporations" which the Sherman Act allegedly curbed.[101] His anxieties were not all rational, as we have seen, but his was primarily an interest-oriented equilibrium dominated by highly specific issues, most of which were economic in nature.

VI.   On the trust issue the skilled laborer more nearly agreed with the midwestern farmer than he did with either the clergyman or engineer. In the early 1880s the worker was already agitated about big business; unfavorable viewpoints far outweighed positive opinions (figure 3–5). During the period 1880–86, the average level of negative attitudes in the *National Labor Tribune* was over 40 percent, while only 11 percent of the items stressed positive aspects of the large firm.[102] The corporation the craftsman saw was primarily an economic institution; it was above all an organization touching his vital interests as an employer and as a producer of goods and services (table 3–5). He also gave substantial attention to the growth of the large firm. For the skilled laborer, the trusts were not a distant phenomenon, associated with nebulous Wall Street bankers or international cartels. He focused rather narrowly on the businesses which were bread and butter concerns: for the Western Pennsylvania craftsman these were transportation, primary metals (especially iron and steel), and coal mining.

When the skilled worker complained, it was often about the way these companies dealt with their employees and with labor unions or about the firm's policies on wages and hours.[103] Strikes and lockouts were fertile

FIGURE 3-5. The skilled worker's evaluation of big business, 1880-1892. The annual percentages represent the proportion of items in *National Labor Tribune* reflecting each attitude.

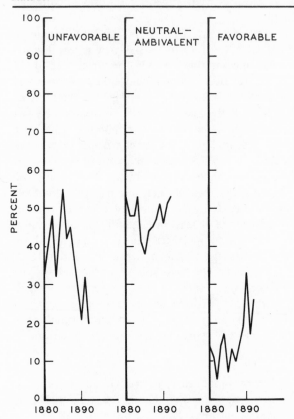

ground for growing discontent. In 1881, he watched helplessly while "one firm with great wealth, made . . . by the men who have been demanding some of their rights as to wages and terms of labor, . . . expended money in buying up property on which the strikers have been in camp, that the men may be ordered off the premises."[104] In the coke regions that year there were "nearly ten thousand human beings struggling bravely with a few huge and ruthless corporations, which have by their cunning and oppression become immensely wealthy and powerful, and which are mercilessly pressing their iron heels on the neck of labor." The coke firms were, he said, "not all as inhuman as the Clay Frick Company, but Clay Frick will either force the others to his cruel policy or they will be driven out of the coke business."[105] Scabs, government troops, blacklisting, private armies, and lockouts—the weapons capital used to keep its employees working for "pauper compensation"—all of these earned the worker's repeated condemnation.[106]

FIRST GENERATION

The craftsman was also deeply concerned about the large firm's involvement in politics. Corporations, in his view, exploited their alliance with the government in order to defeat his organizations. He complained about the "public lands donated to monopolies" and about the way in which "the profits of toil and commerce are gathered up through the manipulations of law by monopolies."[107] There was in his image of the corporation a substantial residue of the traditional, pre-industrial concept of monopoly achieved through governmental sanction.[108] "It is," he said, "the rule and policy of the money power and allied monopolies to control and rob the laborer of his just reward, keeping him constantly on the verge of pauperism in order that through political power the suffrage of the workers may be wielded . . . for the benefit of those who rob him; as the more closely the laboring man can be kept to a state of pauperism, the more easily is he controlled, as the underfed man will not mature a sufficient mental force to assert his political independence." Congress was "dumb as an oyster at the command of the monopoly which happened to be in control."[109]

The craftsman's mentality contained a strain of class consciousness that impinged on his image of the corporation much as class perspectives did on the outlook of the farmer. The laborer was aware of the gulf between himself and the "monied aristocracy."[110] He sensed, furthermore, that the gulf was widening and that class differences were becoming more pronounced. "The man who worked with his hands was a hundred years ago regarded as the peer of any other citizen—now it is rather fashionable to look upon the workman's garb patronizingly, and the wearer as an inferior, not only to 'his nobs' who has money, but to the better dressed class. . . . We do not mean to intimate that any decent workingman is hurt by such

TABLE 3-5.   The skilled worker's image of big business, 1880-1892

Aspects of big business mentioned	1880–1886			1887–1892		
	High year	Low year	Mean	High year	Low year	Mean
Economic	96%	80%	90%	100%	93%	97%
Political	26	16	22	18	8	13
Social	5	0	2	7	0	2
Leading characteristics of big business	1) Labor relations 2) Products or services 3) Existence or expansion			1) Products or services 2) Labor relations 3) Wages and hours		
Leading industries mentioned	1) Railroad transportation (40) 2) Primary metals (33) 3) Coal mining (11–12)			1) Railroad transportation (40) 2) Primary metals (33) 3) Coal mining (11–12)		

SOURCE: *National Labor Tribune.*

AN UNEASY EQUILIBRIUM, 1879-1892

snobocracy; what we assert is that the growth of this class proves that the country has not been living up to the principles upon which the republic is based." Members of the "snobocracy" and the "railroad aristocrats" were out of reach of the "tin bucket brigade," and the worker decided that "the era of a workingman class and a capitalist class is before the citizens. . . . The fact is it seems pretty well under way now."[111]

Despite such class antagonisms, the worker gradually changed his mind about big business. In the late 1880s he became less angry about the trusts and more inclined to stress the positive contributions of the large company. He did not lose his awareness of class differences; it was just that highly specific economic and organizational developments became more important in shaping his attitudes. A substantial part of the change was related to his new appraisal of the political situation. It was not that he began to look with favor on the trust's political activities; almost anything that a large firm did in the political realm invited criticism. The craftsman simply found fewer opportunities to mention politics at all. No longer was he particularly worried about the corporation's need for political assistance, its power in the government, or the nefarious techniques businessmen employed to influence public officials. At the same time he started to reappraise the economic activities of big business, finding substantially less to criticize and some things that even invited praise. Leading the list of favorable characteristics in the years 1887–92 were corporate products and services, wage-hour policies, and labor relations. Poor service on the railroads, wage cuts, and strikes still earned criticism, but in the years following 1886 the craftsman devoted more and more attention to the excellent products of such companies as the Baldwin Locomotive Works, to favorable wage scales like those of Carnegie, Phipps & Company, and to such innovations in labor policies as those adopted by the Illinois Steel Company. When Illinois Steel put aside a special building for the recreation and education of its employees, the skilled worker happily acknowledged that the president of that firm had thereby established himself as an excellent manager, a man "well grounded in business principles."[112]

These new attitudes were primarily rooted in the craftsman's improving economic situation. The general prosperity of these years and, in particular, the increase in railroad construction between 1886 and 1892 were all-important to the economy of western Pennsylvania. The three industries of greatest concern to the *Tribune*'s readers were railroads, iron and steel, and coal mining, all of which shared in the economic upturn of the late eighties and early nineties. As real hourly wages went up, animosity toward the corporation ebbed and positive opinions increased.[113] In 1890 and again in 1892, favorable evaluations actually outweighed criticism in the pages of the *National Labor Tribune*.

Organizational developments also helped shape the worker's new image of big business. One of the products of prosperity was an increase in membership and bargaining power for the region's trade unions and particularly for the Amalgamated Association of Iron, Tin and Steel Workers. By 1891, there were 24,000 members in the Amalgamated Association, and the union was one of the strongest trade groups in the country.[114] The Knights of Labor, with its diverse and reform-oriented program, was rapidly fading, while the new American Federation of Labor was gaining strength; as reform unionism gave way to pure and simple trade unionism, the skilled worker focused more of his attention on the economic and less on the political facets of his corporate employers.[115] Trade unions such as the Amalgamated Association institutionalized a relatively narrow concept of the craftsman's role, and as the Association gathered strength—a strength symbolized in 1889 by its victory at Carnegie's Homestead plant—the union directly and indirectly shaped the laborer's attitudes toward big business. In this case, organizational change worked hand in hand with increasing income to mold a new and more favorable image of the corporation.

The strength of the craft unions in the Pittsburgh region also helps to explain the relative stability and the rational quality of the skilled worker's attitudes. In contrast to either group of farmers, the laborer was not given to sudden shifts in mood (see Appendix). He kept his attention focused on those industries with which he was directly involved as an employee, and while occasionally concerned about his status, the state of the nation, or the ominous influence of the distant money powers, he normally worried about more immediate, tangible problems. There is little evidence in his attitude of social disorganization or disorder, of scapegoating or lightning-rod effects. He was manifestly prejudiced against Hungarians, against Italians, against Blacks—against, in fact, any group threatening his job and income; but these threats were not imaginary and the worker was not paranoid—he repeatedly saw such groups break strikes and take his job at the large corporation's plants.[116] Neither irrational emotions nor political reform measures had much effect on him. He was not very interested in railroad regulation or in the Sherman Antitrust Act, and he sometimes expressed skepticism about the efficacy of any kind of political restraint on business.[117]

In the early nineties the craftsman was relatively satisfied with his situation: jobs were plentiful, wages were high, and his trade unions were growing in membership and bargaining power.[118] In the summer of 1892 there were some disquieting rumors about events at Andrew Carnegie's Homestead mills, where it was reported that one hundred men had been dismissed, that a new fence had been built, and that Pinkerton detectives had been hired. But Carnegie had been so cooperative with the unions that these stories were hard to believe. The working man was in fact full of praise for Carnegie, whom he had for several years looked up to as "the father of Allegheny manufacturing" and "the real iron king of the known world."[119] His attitudes toward king Carnegie and toward big business in general were favorable and stable, held in balance by a blend of economic and organizational factors that the laborer had reason to hope would remain unchanged for years to come.

VII. The mechanic's outlook on the trust question thus differed from that of the midwestern farmer, just as the perspective of the midwesterner differed from that of the cotton grower, the clergy from that of the professional engineer. The opinions of each group were rooted in its distinctive occupation, its awareness of social class and status, its economic fortunes, its belief system and values, and its relationship to political authority. Organizational development was fundamentally important but different in each group. In this sense there was no American response to the rise of big business, no single overriding pattern cutting across all of the middle cultures. There were, instead, varieties of thought: in the terms of our analysis, various systems of equilibria. We can now array these systems, define them in terms of the major variables that shaped attitudes, and in the course of doing that look for parameters that will enable us to see more clearly the common elements in two or more of the groups.

One such element was the extent to which the groups had firsthand experience with the large corporation. Using this standard we can group together midwestern farmers, organized laborers, and engineers. All had direct and extensive contact with big business, and those experiences certainly helped form their views of the trust movement. All three of these groups were concerned about business activities directly affecting their interests. These activities, largely but not entirely economic in nature, normally involved specific functions of the corporation rather than its general relationship to society.

Direct experience with big business produced a high degree of hostility in two of the groups, midwestern farmers and laborers, although by the early nineties both were less angry than they had been in the previous decade. The major variable shaping the farmer's image of the large firm was the level of freight rates charged by the railroads carrying agricultural products to market; an equally specific determinant, fluctuations in real wages, molded the laborer's vision. By the early nineties wages were higher than they had been and freight rates were lower, so both groups found fewer opportunities to attack monopolies.

There were, of course, some important differences between the patterns of thought characteristic of these two groups; specifically, the farmer's ideas were less stable and slightly more diffuse than those of the craftsman. For the most part this difference can be traced to contrasts in income and in the organizations which served the two groups. The midwestern farmer's economic problems were more serious and prolonged than those of the craftsman, and the organizational base of the occupation was less stable. The skilled worker's concept of his role and his position in society came to center about strong trade unions that provided him with a measure of confidence that the farmer seldom enjoyed. The corn and hog producer was confronted with complex and rapidly changing organizations, each of which offered him a different concept of his position in society. Perhaps the only common aspect of these diverse organizations was their tendency to define that role in sweeping terms that involved a life style and not a mere occupation.

The farmer saw the trusts through a broad window, while the engineer looked at the same subject through an ideological peephole. Narrowing the engineer's perception was a professional ideology institutionalized in strong and stable organizations, buttressed by the values of his particular class. This ideology and its related concept of the engineer's social role left him concerned with only a few facets of the corporation, and in none of these areas did big business threaten the vital interests of either his profession or his class. When for a brief time he became slightly perturbed about the large firm, the source of his hostility was a highly specific form of business behavior that seemed to challenge his professional expertise. All it took to quiet his fears, however, was the avowed desire of business to seek self-reform. By 1892, the engineer was again certain that all was well in the realm of giant enterprise.

Neither the clergy nor southern farmers had such extensive firsthand contacts with big business, and the results could be seen in their attitudes toward the concentration movement. In the case of the Congregational minister, class values favoring the large firm were balanced against a growing commitment to the social gospel; the variable tipping the balance one way or the other was the number of attention-capturing, conflict-producing events, especially the violent struggles which occurred between labor and management in the eighties. The appearance of disorder forced the clergy to question the moral quality of the large firm and its leaders. Fortunately for the trusts, however, the prosperity of the early nineties lowered the potential for economic conflict and shifted the balance in the clergy's mind from social reform to social class.

While the cotton farmer encountered big business face to face more often than did the clergy, his direct involvement was substantially less than that of the other three groups. As a result, his perception of the large firm was often framed in abstract terms and was unusually responsive to general changes in his own political, economic, and social situations. Concerned about his political and economic plight, his status, and the sanctity of his family, he began to look to the Farmers' Alliance for leadership, and this organization focused his animosity on monopoly in all its forms. The trust became a lightning rod that attracted the anxiety produced by his sense of social disorganization. Class antagonism increased his anguish, but his consciousness of class was no more stable than his sense of the farmer's role in society. His feelings were vulnerable to symbolic political action like the passage of the Sherman Antitrust Act; by 1892, when he had sensed political victory and had begun to abandon the Alliance, he was no more worried about the trusts than the clergy were.

From the vantage point provided by these several categories of equilibria, we can reexamine the economic, political, and organizational variables that different historians have stressed as the primary determinants of change. Clearly, results to this point support the hypothesis that economic factors were the single most important influence on attitudes toward big business. But already ambiguities have emerged, and the need for a more complex analysis has become apparent. In some instances the economic interests involved were highly specific, as they were with laborers and midwestern farmers; in other cases interest meant group income or even economic conflicts far removed from the group itself. The classical version of economic man as a maximizing machine is not enough; we must employ objective measures of economic interest—whether specific or general—in a context that includes a far more complex combination of variables.

One of these essential complexities is a set of social or cultural factors which deserves to be ranked along with the economic, organizational, and political forces that historians have emphasized. All of the groups manifested a sense of their social class. While none of the shifts in attitude could be understood wholly in class terms, none could be analyzed fairly without taking class concepts into consideration. The same can be said for value systems, a cultural phenomenon which exerted an important influence on middle-class perceptions of the trust movement. We can lump together values and class concepts in a single category called (for want of a better term) the social variable. This factor was less important than economic and organizational changes in guiding middle-class attitudes, but, on the other hand, social elements were clearly more influential than was the political system during the years 1880 through 1892.

Throughout most of the middle cultures in these years men were not yet prepared to throw their established values overboard and search for new normative standards, for what Robert Wiebe has called a new social order. The professional engineer was already devoted to modern, corporate values—he stressed the role of group activity, the need to control emotions and remain neutral, the necessity of universal standards and highly specific definitions of responsibility. The other occupational groups were dedicated to more traditional values, and for the most part they seemed to feel that these values still deserved their allegiance. Individualism or self-orientation was still firmly planted in the national character, and Americans continued to measure men and events in terms of material and visible achievements.[120] As befitted a rural and small-town country, relationships between men remained diffuse—that is, they involved a wide variety of unspecified

FIRST GENERATION

obligations—and emotions were freely, frequently, and strongly expressed.[121] For the most part, the standards applied to people's behavior were tailored to suit the particular needs of the family, the locality, and the region; and these particularistic values were encased in the basic premises that the universe was God-centered and the laws governing its operation were immutable.[122] Though under challenge in the early nineties, these values continued to provide a sheet anchor for a nation coping with the strains of rapid industrialization and urban growth.

The organizational setting, which had a close relationship to the social variable, ranks just below economic change as a determinant of middle-culture images of big business. Among some of the groups, the organizations that institutionalized group norms were stable and were a source of substantial consensus within the group. Some organizations provided their members with countervailing power; others offered an appropriate ideology. Where the organizational base of the occupation changed frequently, the group was left uncertain about its own position in society and its evaluation of the emerging giants of the business world. This was the case with both groups of farmers, but especially with those in the South.

Political developments could certainly not be ignored, but for the period between 1879 and 1892 they had a less decisive influence than did economic, organizational, and social variables. All of the groups recognized (in different degrees) that the corporation was a political creature both shaping and shaped by the government. All of the groups discussed regulatory measures and the antitrust issue. Farmers in particular were sensitive to reform movements and interested in state and national legislation aimed at curbing the power of business. But in all of the groups except southern farmers, other factors seem to have had a more significant effect on attitudes. The Interstate Commerce Act of 1887 provides a good example. I expected to find agrarian hostility toward the railroads and other corporations reaching a peak in 1887 and 1888 and declining as the ICC became active. Instead, the level of unfavorable opinions in the Midwest fell off sharply after 1885, and in the South, farmers were not particularly upset about big business as late as 1888. This evidence calls into question certain elements of the progressive concept of this important act and indeed seems to support the revisionist and New Left contentions that the businessmen who shipped goods by rail and the railroads themselves were the major combatants in the drive for railroad regulation.[123] While my figures touch upon only one aspect of this problem, the data are clearly more consistent with these newer interpretations than they are with the liberal concept of reform legislation riding in on a wave of public protest.

Some light can also be thrown on the relations between public opinion and the passage in 1890 of the Sherman Antitrust Act. Historians have long been perplexed about the extent of public interest in the trust question, some of them concluding that there was a ground swell of antitrust sentiment in the late eighties and others deciding that most Americans were unconcerned about the concentration movement.[124] My results indicate that in the middle cultures, at least, public antagonism toward the large firm was not at a fever pitch in the latter part of the decade but that on balance there was more opposition to the trusts than there had been in the early eighties. In three of the five groups studied, the percentage of negative attitudes increased in the later period, with the most pronounced change taking place among southern farmers. If the legislators calculated that a vague measure would relieve some of the tensions accumulating around the trust issue and mollify that part of the public which was aroused, my study suggests that they were excellent judges of their constituents' frame of mind.[125] Even though the Sherman Antitrust Act was not enforced (and the ICC had already proven to be ineffective), hostility toward big business had declined markedly by 1892.

As late as 1892, few signs indicated that the concentration movement would produce a major crisis in America's middle cultures. In only one of the groups studied—southern farmers—was there substantial evidence of social disorganization. While northern farmers began in the late eighties to react to big business in a somewhat similar fashion, their attitudes were still much more rational and balanced than those of the cotton grower. Taking all of the groups into consideration, the picture that emerges is one of a stable social order which was still successfully coping with the strains of change.

The equilibrium of the early nineties was, however, neither universal nor entirely secure. Threatening it, for one thing, was the continued spread of the merger movement; at every level of the middle class, attention focused on "trustification" and the growth of the existing combines in transportation and manufacturing. Some Americans were willing to settle for the status quo, but even they were uneasy about the further growth of monopoly. As long as the economy continued its upward course, however, prosperity muffled the fears of the middle class.

FIRST GENERATION

4

CRISIS, 1893-1901

In 1893 a panic in the stock market sent the prices of industrial and railroad securities plummeting, and the nationwide depression that followed the crash abruptly detoured America's long climb toward a more prosperous tomorrow. Some contemporary observers identified Wall Street as the source of their misfortune. They linked the crash in market values with financial chicanery and that, in turn, with the widespread unemployment, lower earnings, and declining output that troubled the nation. To others, the depression was the inevitable product of laws as immutable as the biblical prophecy that lean years would follow fat or the socialist prediction that industrial capitalism would perforce encounter deepening economic crises. Less holistic commentators blamed particular government policies, the tariff and monetary programs especially, for the nationwide depression.[1]

Whatever their analyses of its causes, most Americans were touched in some way by the depression. Economic distress cut across class and regional lines. Many farmers were pinched between the fixed costs of their mortgages and the falling prices of their crops. Even those laborers with the greatest skills found their wages reduced and their plants running part time, if they ran at all. An abrupt decline in railroad construction hurt engineers as well as laborers, and the clergy could worry about the falling contributions for church work if they chose not to be disturbed about the decline in their personal incomes.[2] Economic distress multiplied the mounting strains of social change. Whether trying to find progress and security in the move from the country to the city, attempting to preserve the family farm, or seeking to establish a profession, build a permanent union, or protect a body of theology from the inroads of science, Americans in the mid-nineties began to sense that they might fail. Instead of betterment and stability, they were faced with economic collapse, an air of panic, and the clear signs of heightened conflict throughout the nation.

The political system both reflected and contributed to the growing sense of crisis. Agrarian discontent spawned a third party movement that reached formidable proportions in the mid-nineties. The populist revolt also gave America a new political leader, William Jennings Bryan, who dramatized the division between those who were wealthy and those who were poor, between those who loaned money and those who borrowed it, between those who wielded power and those who felt powerless. Bryan's unsuccessful campaign in 1896 contributed to a major realignment in party strength, the first such change since the 1850s.[3] Under the banner of William McKinley, the Republican party marched into the twentieth century securely established as the majority party in national politics. In the polity, as in the economy and, for that matter, in society as a whole, the nineties was a decade of dramatic transition, and the effects of these changes could be seen in the public image of the large corporation.

II. The depression forced the Congregational clergyman to reconsider the merits of large enterprise and the quality of the men who controlled the country's great firms. While the minister's connections with big business were more remote than those of the laborer or the engineer, the clergyman had adequate evidence on the trust question. His church paper frequently mentioned big business, most often when commenting on a wide variety of meetings and conventions of both church and secular organizations (see "Leading sources" in table 4-1). The organizations involved ranged from the International Railway Congress to the University of Michigan, from the Maine to the Northern Pacific Congregational conferences. Even the convention in 1900 of the American Economic Association prompted consideration of the new style of industrial organization which had "made competition a thing of the past" in many branches of the economy.[4] The depressed condition of that economy frequently brought the trust issue to mind in the mid-nineties, and throughout the period 1893–1901 other publications—including books and articles—often stirred up controversy about the concentration movement. The *Congregationalist* gave the minister a window opening on the upper reaches of intellectual life in America. Here he could share the ideas emanating from more sophisticated thinkers, from those intellectuals who wrote books on *Social Facts and Fancies* or on *Industrial Freedom.*[5] In this sense the scope of his thinking was relatively broad, and his ideas were in part shaped by concepts flowing from the kind of intellectual elite emphasized in the progressive view of modern American history.[6]

In the mid-nineties the ideas the minister received from these and other sources increased the tension between his class values and his moderate liberal ideology, between his support on the one hand for material achievement and his desire on the other for social harmony. He was angered to hear of the bankruptcies of major railroad systems and industrial combines, problems which "sadly impaired our national credit at home and abroad." All too often the financial plight of these companies could be traced to "individual dishonesty" on the part of management.[7] Business leaders grossly inflated the capitalization of their firms and then found it difficult to pay dividends on their watered stock.[8] The result was a "crash" bringing down the "financial magnates" but injuring innocent parties as well.[9] Corporate dishonesty spilled over from the marketplace into government; many of the moguls who faced bankruptcy in the depression were the same men who had built their business empires "by superior wiles and by the dexterous use of courts and bribed legislatures and in disregard of law."[10]

This sort of businessman showed no more respect for his employees than he did for the law, and the clergyman was vexed. The depression precipitated a series of bitter struggles between labor and management. The Pullman strike of 1894 was most upsetting, and disturbing conflicts involving the street railways occurred in Brooklyn and Philadelphia. The minister looked with dismay on the disorder accompanying strikes and lockouts. Big business, he felt, should not hire armies of mercenaries to defend its property; nor should giant transportation companies allow controversies with labor to interfere with the service they owed to the public. In the clergyman's highly personalized view of labor-management strife, the central problem was one of individual morality: when the managers and owners of large corporations failed to recognize their responsibilities to their workers and the public, the result was social disharmony and often dangerous conflict.

Events such as these rubbed against the clergy's values. The result was a cycle of anticorporate sentiment (figure 4-1). As neutral imagery gave way, the percentage of unfavorable items in the *Congregationalist* climbed higher during the depression than it had ever been before. The leading symbol of big business in the years after 1893 was the Pullman Company, and labor relations became for the first time one of the salient aspects of the large corporation (table 4-1). While the clergy's attitudes were not especially unstable (see Appendix) during the nineties, subtle qualitative and quantitative changes took place as economic troubles fueled a new sense of concern about "corporation greed" and "corporate abuses of monopoly."[11]

In the struggle between liberal and class values, however, the ultimate victor in the nineties was social class rather than the social gospel. While the Congregational minister was increasingly critical of big business, he remained throughout a vocal defender of the rights of property, including the property of big business. During the violent Pullman strike, for instance, he seldom doubted that the primary power to direct the nation's railroads should remain in the hands of private owners and managers; he applauded when "federal strength" was used to break the strike: the "highest welfare of the public," he concluded, "is dependent upon the continuous flow of life through the arteries of trade—the railroads."[12] While often sympathetic to the employees of such giant corporations as the Pullman Company, he remained suspicious about "the interference of labor associations," and in retrospect he decided that "the country feels that those great strikes [of 1894]

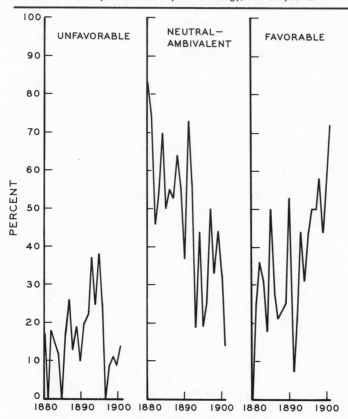

were not altogether justified, and is satisfied with the manner of suppressing the accompanying lawlessness."[13]

All the clergyman demanded from management was a proper concern for the welfare of corporate employees, and he saw little reason to be critical when concern blended into social control. After all, he was himself interested in eliminating such problems as excessive drinking on the part of the lower classes and he recognized a similar impulse in the tightly regulated "model city" that George M. Pullman had provided for his workers: "Strange as it may be, labor as such does not seem to take kindly to Mr. Pullman's model city. It matters not that the streets are always clean, that they are well lighted, that the lawns are fresh and closely shaved, that sanitary arrangements are perfect, that an elegant library is at the disposal of every laborer at a nominal price. The fact that there are no saloons within the corporate limits of the place—that every one living there must submit to certain

FIRST GENERATION

conditions promotive of the general good—has by many been complained of from the first as an infringement on personal liberty. . . . There has been a sort of feeling that Pullman ought to furnish all the advantages of a model city without requiring anything of the laborer in return."[14] Power exercised from above, by the social class with which the clergyman identified, was acceptable when the goal was a modern city on a hill, a town free of trash and the temptations of alcohol.[15]

TABLE 4-1. The Congregational clergy's image of big business, 1893-1901

Aspects of big business mentioned[a]	1893-1896			1897-1901		
	High year	Low year	Mean[b]	High year	Low year	Mean[b]
Economic	100%	88%	96%	100%	78%	91%
Political	31	0	22	21	8	12
Social	12	0	4	14	0	5
Leading characteristics of big business	1) Management or ownership 2) Labor relations 3) Financial practices			1) Management or ownership 2) Financial practices 3) Products or services		
Leading industries mentioned	1) Railroad transportation (40)[c] 2) Food processing (20); Local passenger transportation (41)			1) Railroad transportation (40) 2) Primary metals (33); Local passenger transportation (41)		
Leading firms mentioned[d]	1893-1901 1) Pullman 2) Boston & Albany Railroad 3) Three railroads tied					
Leading sources of items on big business[e]	1) Meetings and conventions 2) Economic conditions 3) Other publications					

SOURCE: *Congregationalist.* For an explanation of my methodology, see chapter 2. Similar data for the previous period are in table 3-2.
NOTE: If multiple entries follow one number, the categories were tied.
[a] These figures show what percentage of the articles mentioned each aspect; the columns can total more than 100% because a single article could mention one, two, or all three.
[b] Mean of the annual percentages.
[c] The number appearing after each industry indicates its two-digit group in the *Standard Industrial Classification Manual.*
[d] For 1880-92, these were: the Chicago, Burlington and Quincy Railroad; the New York Central Railroad; and the Illinois Central Railroad, which tied with the Union Pacific.
[e] For 1880-92, these were: Meetings and conventions; and Action taken by big business, which tied with Action taken by labor.

Class concepts can be seen in other aspects of the Congregational minister's shifting image of the large firm. While he was frequently critical of corporate performance in the area of labor relations, in the years 1893–96 he actually found more opportunities to complain about financial practices influencing thousands of owners of stocks and bonds than he did about labor policies affecting millions of workers.[16] And while he addressed himself to these problems, he also found more and more that he liked about the modern style of industrial firm. In the nineties the percentage of favorable items in *Congregationalist* increased sharply. At no time, in fact, did negative evaluations exceed favorable comments. The Protestant minister continued, throughout the depression, to respect the administrative skills of the men who ran large companies, using them as a measuring rod for the accomplishments of others. He observed: "the management of the business affairs of a great city like Boston involves plans and expenditures which require abilities in administration equal to the demands of the very largest corporations in the country."[17] Material achievement continued to win his applause. He felt that national economic progress was to a considerable extent dependent upon "the vast railroad industry" and he approved of corporate mergers when they appeared to embody a plan for local and regional economic development.[18]

These positive themes in the clergy's image of the corporation became ever stronger as the economy pulled out of the depression in the late nineties. The financial affairs of big business—recently a sore point with the minister —invited strong praise in the years 1897–1901. The increasing value of railroad securities seemed to put the entire stock market in a bullish mood; while the Congregational minister was skeptical about "the wild desire of the public to speculate" in these shares, he now acknowledged that speculation was the price the country had to pay for "vast enterprises" and for the "great changes which cannot be made without great risks."[19] Although lurking in Wall Street were "men who exploit the public," he used these villains (much as an attractive person sometimes uses an ugly friend) to underscore the sound management of such companies as the Boston and Albany and Vanderbilt's New York Central.[20]

To this point at least the social gospel had not penetrated very deeply. Traces of liberal ideology could still be found in the prosperous years 1900 and 1901; wedged in the midst of a series of eulogies prompted by the philanthropy of J. P. Morgan, G. F. Swift and other assorted titans, there were some harsh words about the men who sought "to aggrandize themselves through dishonesty shielded under corporate, syndicated power."[21] By the turn of the century, however, criticism in this vein was a distinctly minor theme. The Congregational minister was optimistic about the new age of large-scale organizations; his sense of social class and pleasure with material progress overwhelmed his liberal ideology.

FIRST GENERATION

In the clergyman's view, good businessmen knew how to make money and also how to spend it. The philanthropy of John D. Rockefeller and Andrew Carnegie drew frequent praise from the Congregational minister, and the memory of Homestead, where Carnegie's men had crushed the union, was washed from the pastorly mind by a flood of Carnegie libraries.[22] As the *Congregationalist* wryly observed: "College presidents warn their outgoing students in Baccalaureate addresses against the dangers of commercialism and the perils of devoting themselves to the pursuit of wealth, and in the same addresses they announce with pride large gifts from wealthy men to their institutions. Harvard, Yale, Chicago and other universities rejoice in gifts reaching into the millions from Rockefeller, Morgan, [and] the Vanderbilts." If the magnates had good motives and used their wealth properly, the church spokesman could see no danger "in developing the material resources of the country and amassing wealth" along the way.[23]

While the Congregational church might itself benefit from acts of philanthropy, there is no evidence that direct economic interest explained the changes that took place in the clergyman's attitude toward the trusts. Indeed, during the early years of the depression, when he was becoming more antagonistic toward big business, the Congregational minister actually experienced an increase in real income. In the mid-nineties prices dropped while his salary remained relatively stable.[24] Later, as prosperity returned, the minister suffered a loss in purchasing power; but if he was concerned about his real income, he was not inclined to focus his anxiety on the concentration movement. He became ever more pleased with the "harmonious action" of big business.[25] By 1901, when his real income stood at the lowest point it had reached in a decade, he rejoiced at the sight of business leaders who displayed "a Christian conception of the mutual duties of laborer and capitalist." He concluded that "the combinations of labor and of capital, which are so prominent a feature of the time, are signs of progress and not of decay."[26]

No longer, it would appear, was he worried about the small businessmen who were being squeezed out by trustification. By 1901 this theme—so important before the depression—had disappeared. In the midst of the greatest merger movement in American history, the Protestant clergyman looked on combination as a sign of "progress." He was now less concerned about the loss of opportunity accompanying the transition to large-scale enterprise, and his dedication to individualism was qualified; he had begun, in fact, to "trade in" one of the values that had long been a central feature of his outlook and that of most of his fellow citizens. The nineties marked only the first hesitant and partial step toward a new, group-oriented perspective. But the transition was as important as it was incomplete. The sequences of depression and prosperity, of conflict followed by combination, seemed to have convinced the clergyman that, while sin was still an individual matter, achievement was fated to be a corporate phenomenon in the twentieth century.

III. Equally significant changes took place in the outlook of the southern farmer during the nineties. Initially the depression appears to have unsettled agrarian attitudes, leaving the farmer almost as angry about the trust movement as he had been in 1890 (figure 4-2). It is impossible in this case to specify the effects of the depression with any precision because we do not have data on attitudes for the years 1893-95; but it seems likely that the continued decline in cotton prices in part explains the southern farmer's increased hostility toward the "tyranny" of the trusts. The Sherman Act, he now felt, was a "dead letter" because the men charged with enforcing the law were conniving with the "trust octopus." Nor had railroad regulation provided the farmer with any relief from oppressive rates; he condemned "Pierepont [sic] Morgan and his monster railroad trust" and, to make the problem more specific, he calculated that the railroads took "an average of $9,251.66 2/3 per month out of the pockets of the farmers of Floyd county, Georgia."[27]

In this and similar ways, southern attitudes were much the same as they had been in the previous cycle of antitrust sentiment (which had peaked in 1890). There was in the cotton farmer's outlook some evidence of a general sense of social disorganization, and his opinions were characterized by a high degree of disequilibrium (see Appendix).[28] He continued to fear such distant and abstract enemies as the "great money syndicates" that sought to reduce the American people to "a nation of serfs."[29] He was still anxious about the collapse of the family farm. Some young people, he felt, were driven away from agriculture by hearing only the negative aspects of a calling which was in reality "the most natural, most healthful and one of the most honorable of all occupations." He suggested that his peers would do well to "so present its bright side to our young people that they will not only be induced, but be anxious to stay upon the farm."[30] His repeated efforts to shore up the family farm by proclaiming the virtues of agriculture reflected considerable uneasiness on his part about the farmer's status; he worried that the farmer did not count for enough, that agriculture was "considered a menial vocation by the masses of the people," and that "there are men who think any 'clod-hopper' can be a farmer. Let them try it [he righteously proclaimed] and they will find that in farming, as in all business, there is a bottom as well as a top to the ladder."[31] Frequently he vented his emotions on the city, which he saw as the center of "savagery and shiftlessness."[32] In these regards the cotton farmer's outlook appears to have remained much as it was before the depression and the 1896 climax of the populist movement.

Nonetheless, some important changes took place in the late nineties as his ideas about big business began to stabilize. For one thing, he was less

FIRST GENERATION

inclined than he had been before 1896 to mingle general fears about his family and his status with more specific concerns about monopoly. He was beginning to lose some of that millenary fervor that had led him to see reality divided into two warring camps and had allowed him to focus all of his varied anxieties on the visible, corporate enemy of country people. Rethinking his relationship to big business, he emphasized a range of problems which were directly and obviously associated with his economic interests. Increasingly, his attention centered on two specific issues: the large firm's products and services, and the prices these corporations charged their farm customers (table 4-2). He had of course mentioned these aspects of big business before, but they now became his major concerns and were to remain central features of his particular concept of the large firm for years to come.[33] The pattern of southern farm thought which was emerging in the late nineties was a brand of interest-oriented equilibrium shorn of many of the symbols of social disorganization which had been evident in previous years.

The cotton farmer's new attitude—narrower and less open to calls for all-embracing class conflict—was reflected in the industries he associated with big business and with which he was most concerned. The railroad led the list (table 4-2), followed by food processing, chemicals, and the manufacture of nonelectrical machinery. The cotton farmer encountered these industries face to face in the marketplace when he shipped his products or bought supplies, when he sold the livestock that southerners were beginning to produce in greater quantities, and when he bought fertilizer and farm equipment. These industries had been on his mind before, as he had attacked the trusts or commented on the progress of the New South. But in the late nineties his attention centered on those industries that would occupy a crucial role in southern attitudes throughout the entire next generation. The cotton farmer's opinion of the corporation thus began to stabilize around a new set of norms. Even when the southern farmer criticized the trusts, the nature of his charges changed in ways which indicated that he was moving toward new concepts of his own role in society and his relationship to those major institutions (such as big business) having some influence on his life.

The painful defeat of agrarian reform in the election of 1896 contributed to this transition in thought. Once again it is necessary to acknowledge that the absence of data for the years 1893-95 handicaps analysis, but we can nevertheless find in the available figures the outlines of a long-run learning process partly related to populism. One aspect of that process was of course the simple experience of defeat, a negative sanction that "taught" the farmer to look somewhere other than politics for a solution to his problems. More important, to my mind, was the manner in which fusion and the Republican victory in 1896 disrupted agrarian organizations and thus weakened the influence of institutions that had for some years exerted a powerful influence on southern farm attitudes.[34] Judging from both the information presented in the previous chapter and the figures offered here, the abstract

FIGURE 4-2. The southern farmer's evaluation of big business, 1879-1901. The annual percentages represent the proportion of items in *Southern Cultivator* reflecting each attitude.

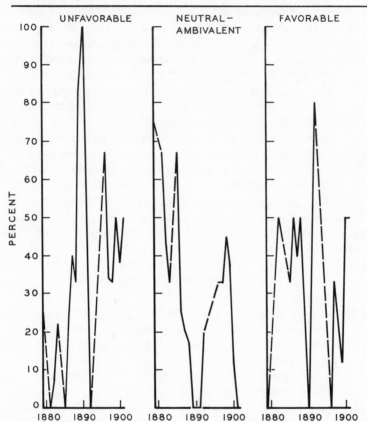

southern farmer with whom we are dealing was not a hardcore agrarian radical from beginning to end; he came to populism late, left it early, and even during the peak years of the farm movement he seems never to have been fully committed to the Farmers' Alliance or to any other reform organization or ideology. Starting in the late eighties, however, organizations like the Alliance had exerted a growing influence on his thought, an influence which increased his antagonism toward big business by adding to the dictates of short-run economic and political self-interest a sense of general social chaos; the upheaval in his life, the farmer came to feel, could be traced to his enemies in business and government.

In the late nineties radical organizations were withering; their poor leadership and shaky finances, along with the nature of their strongest supporters, made these farm organizations inherently unstable and likely to decline even in the absence of a serious political setback. The defeat of Bryan

FIRST GENERATION

accelerated their collapse, suddenly depriving the more moderate farmer of institutions capable of focusing his anxieties on a few primary opponents. As he observed regretfully, "the Farmers Alliance and the Grange were genuine efforts to get the farmers together, but they have largely failed; their objects were good and they wrought some good results, but in spite of this they have waned."[35] As they did, they left behind a farmer with a less complex, less ambitious, and narrower outlook on his role in society and his relationship to big business; this outlook was a residue in the sense that it had existed in the years before 1893 when it had been subordinated to the themes accentuated by the more radical organizations. As the radical groups and their ideas "waned," the southern farmer began to look to new kinds of organizations which would be "less liable to get into politics" and which would in the bargain be "less expensive and more instructive."[36]

TABLE 4-2. The southern farmer's image of big business, 1896-1901

Aspects of big business mentioned	High year	1896-1901 Low year	Mean
Economic	100%	78%	94%
Political	33	12	22
Social	0	0	0

Leading characteristics of big business	1) Products or services 2) Prices 3) Existence or expansion
Leading industries mentioned	1) Railroad transportation (40) 2) Food processing (20); Chemicals (28) 3) Machinery—nonelectrical (35)
Leading firms mentioned[a]	1) Central of Georgia Railroad 2) Southern Railroad (These were the only companies mentioned more than once)
Leading sources of items on big business[b]	1) Other publications 2) Letters to the editor 3) Meetings and conventions

SOURCE: *Southern Cultivator*. Lacking data from a southern farm journal for the years 1893-95, I combined the figures from 1896 with those for the following years. Similar data for the previous period are in table 3-3.
[a]The top firm, 1879-92, was the Georgia Railroad; only four other companies were mentioned more than once, and they included two railroads (the Central and the East Tennessee, Virginia and Georgia), the Southern Express, and McCormick Harvesters.
[b]The leading sources during the years 1879-92 were: Meetings and conventions; Other publications; and Letters to the editor.

CRISIS, 1893-1901

One sees the immediate effects of organizational change on the agrarian image of big business in the data on the leading sources of articles in *Southern Cultivator* (table 4–2). Before 1893, meetings and conventions had prompted more such discussions than any other single source (see note b, table 4–2); resolutions passed by the Farmers' Alliance and meetings of the Grange had kept the farmer's eyes focused on the trust question. These and a variety of lesser organizations (or to be more precise, bodies less well known to historians), ranging from the American Poultry Association to the East Tennessee Farmer's Convention, had not allowed the cotton grower to forget that his economic and political fortunes, sometimes even his manhood and his family life, were in the hands of the "cormorants, trusts and combinations."[37] By the late nineties, some of these organizations had become less active, others had disbanded, and the farmer was taking less note of organized activity of any sort.

During these years other publications became the leading stimulant to discussions of big business, and here too there is evidence that the farmer's outlook was narrowing. Both before and after 1893, the journals that *Southern Cultivator* drew upon for ideas and excerpts were most often farm papers like *National Farm and Fireside*, the *Farm Trade Journal*, and *Rural New York*. But in the years prior to the depression, the paper had also tapped a variety of nonfarm publications from the South and even the Northeast—the *New Orleans Picayune* and the *Atlanta Constitution* appeared alongside the *Boston Post* and the *New York Sun*. In the period 1896–1901, the array of papers which provided comments on big business became considerably narrower and the farmer's purview more ingrown, more likely to depend upon another agrarian journal for information than upon an urban newspaper or a magazine with a national reputation.

As this new pattern of farm thought coalesced, the southern image of the corporation at first remained primarily negative. Not yet could the farmer open his billfold and find some visible assurance that he might survive. As recovery began in 1897 and 1898, cotton prices lagged behind the rest of the economy.[38] Gross income (in constant dollars) from cotton and cottonseed was actually lower in 1898 than it had been in 1890 and 1891. In 1900, however, prices for the leading southern staple suddenly jumped from 6.6 cents a pound to 9.3 cents, and gross income in cotton farming was higher that year than it had been for the past two decades. During the following year, prices dipped slightly (to 8.1 cents), but farm income in the South remained far above the depths it had reached in the worst years of the depression.[39]

The southern farmer displaced some of the good feeling that higher income created onto the large corporation. Now he was particularly pleased with the products and services of the larger firms because, as he saw it, such corporations as the Swift Fertilizer Company were "reliable."[40] When you ordered something from the "big firms," you could be certain you would get what you wanted.[41] While the farmer could still drum up some anger when he thought about the fact that the trusts affected legislation and controlled "too many Senators," he was now willing to concede that the economic activities of the largest companies deserved more praise than condemnation and that in reality there were some important functions—for instance, opening "markets in foreign lands"—which only large combines could perform.[42] In both 1900 and 1901, in the midst of the great merger movement, the level of favorable opinions toward large enterprise was high, and the trend toward a more positive image of the corporation was to continue in the years ahead.[43] Southern farm attitudes had changed decisively during this second cycle of the antitrust movement; a new equilibrium emerged from a special blend of political, organizational, and above all, economic changes—a series of developments which by 1901 had already given the cotton farmer a narrower and more stable vision of his role in America's corporate economy.[44]

IV. The depression and the political struggles of the nineties were traumatic experiences for the midwestern farmer. He confronted the corporation firsthand and recognized that his economic fortunes were to a great extent dependent upon the performance of the country's largest businesses. This familiarity nourished a mounting anger at "unnatural monopolies," "railroad extortion," and "the encroachments of corporate power."[45] Agrarian attitudes were extremely unstable—far more so than they had been in the eighties.[46] By the measure we have adopted (M.D.), the degree of disequilibrium was greater in the nineties than it had been previously and was higher in fact that it would be until the 1930s.[47] Through the end of the decade the midwestern farmer was unusually hostile toward big business (figure 4-3). He found hardly any facets of business behavior which deserved a neutral label, let alone a favorable opinion. He could not afford to be impartial when he faced the "invisible empire" of "corporate wealth," an opponent "more powerful than those who wear the crown and wield the sceptre; more powerful than those who sit in presidential or gubernatorial chairs or who occupy the seats in senates, congress or legislature."[48] In the corn and hog country, sentiments like these reached an all-time peak in the 1890s.

When a historian sees that farmers traced their troubles to an "invisible empire" whose "power is felt rather than seen" and pictured their enemy as about "to suck into its maw everything between the Mississippi River and the Atlantic ocean north of the Ohio river," he can hardly help but conclude that agrarian attitudes in that time and place were to some extent irrational.[49] Sprinkled throughout the farmer's discourse on the trust question were the symbols of social crisis, accompanied by a new sense that the nation

FIGURE 4-3. The midwestern farmer's evaluation of big business, 1879-1901. The annual percentages represent the proportion of items in *Farmers' Review* and *Wallaces' Farmer* reflecting each attitude.

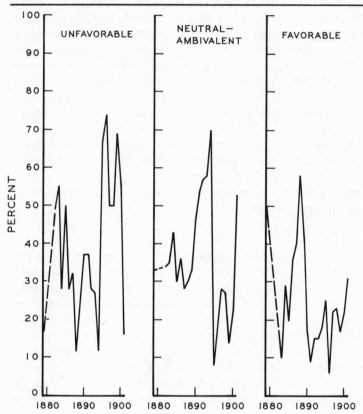

was girding itself for an all-encompassing final conflict between the forces of good and the forces of evil. Now there was doubt whether even the hoeman, backbone of the nation, could "hold in leash the magnates of the invisible empire."[50] The farmer's position was being weakened in part because his sons and daughters were catching "town fever" and deserting their happy rural homes.[51] "The plague spot of American civilization," he concluded, "is in the cities and one of the curses of railroad combinations is that by special rates they build up great cities."[52] Uneasy as he was about his family's future and his status, the midwestern farmer was capable of projecting his anxieties (whatever their source) onto the "railroad combinations" and the "trust octopus."[53]

Under severe pressure, the farmer at times saw his entire social class and its moral standards threatened by combinations and by corporate

FIRST GENERATION

corruption. In the cities the middle class was disappearing as a result of a trust movement that left behind only the few rich and the many poor: "The only middle class we will have shortly outside of the farm is the army of employees whose wages will depend largely on the will of large corporations governed by a corporation conscience."[54] The "few rich" of the "best society" were, in the farmer's eyes, an "aristocracy" posing a threat to "public morality"[55] and corrupting officials with "social honors." By the farmer's standards, "the fellows that Christ drove out of the temple were saints" compared with trust organizers who built churches and endowed colleges with funds "sweated out of the laborer on one hand and filched out of the pocket of the consumer on the other."[56] Even when the activities of the tycoons fell within the limits set by "the ordinary code of morals," they could not measure up to "that higher code which men in their hearts recognize."[57] These social and class considerations multiplied the anxieties that more material considerations of political economy generated in the nineties.

One of our problems is estimating the relative importance of these sources of antitrust fervor: were midwestern farmers responding primarily to general changes in their social situation, changes that in fact had only a tenuous relationship to big business, or were they reacting for the most part to perceived threats to their immediate political and economic interests? Illustrative evidence can be produced to support either side: remarks reflecting status anxiety (concern, for example, that the farmer was portrayed as "uncouth, ill-dressed, ill-mannered") can be paired with notably precise attacks on railroad rate discrimination, corporate political power, or the implications of the beef combine's destruction of smaller competitors.[58] One recourse is to determine the salience of the two categories of issues simply on the basis of the frequency with which they were mentioned; the evidence then indicates that emotional or nonrational considerations were still a minor theme in a pattern of thought dominated by the same sort of politico-economic calculations that had figured so heavily in midwestern farm thought before 1893.

The farmer was concerned about big business's political influence and, in particular, about the manner in which business had achieved its political power. The leading issue was the political techniques the combines used to manipulate all branches of the government—local, state, and national. When the farmer saw "great corporations working together without regard to party and unblushingly buying newspapers . . . for the purpose of electing men to office who will sell their positions, who can go in poor and come out rich," he began "to wonder whether or not the Republic will continue."[59] He knew that for years "the policy of the railroads had been to seduce and debauch public men who had a reputation as antimonopolists."[60] The companies' tactics succeeded often enough to leave him doubtful that even "the intelligent, independent, clear-headed, honest-hearted, right-thinking farmer" would be able to defend successfully "the liberties of the American people."[61]

While the Populist crusade and the election of 1896 had an effect on the farmer's perception of these political issues, such dramatic events at the national level had less influence on agrarian attitudes than one might have expected. Although the election year witnessed a sharp increase in concern about the political activities of big business, the midwesterner was even more aroused by this subject in 1899 than he had been three years before.[62] As table 4-3 shows, the average amount of attention directed at business's political affairs was slightly lower in the years 1893-96 than in the five years

TABLE 4-3. The midwestern farmer's image of big business, 1893-1901

Aspects of big business mentioned	1893-1896			1897-1901		
	High year	Low year	Mean	High year	Low year	Mean
Economic	98%	90%	94%	100%	86%	92%
Political	35	6	18	48	8	22
Social	8	0	2	17	0	5

Leading characteristics of big business	1) Prices 2) Existence or expansion 3) Products or services	1) Prices 2) Existence or expansion 3) Products or services; Financial practices

Leading industries mentioned	1) Railroad transportation (40) 2) Food processing (20) 3) Primary metals (33)	1) Railroad transportation (40) 2) Food processing (20) 3) Primary metals (33)

Leading firms mentioned[a]	1) Chicago, Rock Island and Pacific Railroad 2) Chicago, Great Western Railroad 3) Armour; Pullman	1) Swift 2) Chicago and Northwestern Railroad 3) Armour

Leading sources of items on big business[b]	1893-1901 1) Meetings and conventions 2) Action taken by big business 3) Other publications	

SOURCE: *Farmers' Review* and *Wallaces' Farmer*. Similar data for the previous period are in table 3-4.

[a]The top firms, 1879-86, were: Illinois Central Railroad, tied with Chicago and Northwestern Railroad; and the Chicago, Rock Island and Pacific Railroad. The leaders, 1887-92, were: Chicago, Burlington and Quincy Railroad; and Armour, tied with Northern Pacific Railroad.

[b]The leading sources, 1879-92, were: Letters to the editor; Meetings and conventions; and Action taken by big business.

FIRST GENERATION

following. The information on leading sources (also in table 4-3) lends further support to this conclusion. Political institutions at the federal level were not a major stimulant to discussions of the trust problem, and, in fact, state politics was slightly more effective than national politics in channeling agrarian attitudes on this question.[63] Judging merely from the data in table 4-3, one is forced to conclude that the elaborate networks of farm organizations and publications exercised a more substantial influence on opinions among this generation of farmers than did presidential politics.[64]

Channeling agrarian attitudes were an unpretentious lot of organizations and publications, hardly the stuff of history on a grand scale. They included state agricultural societies, stock breeder's organizations, an occasional chautauqua, and the meetings of such national groups as the American Live Stock Feeders' and Breeders' Association and the National Association of Co-Operative Mutual Insurance Companies. The newspapers and magazines contributing ideas about big business were also a homely array, ranging from the *Des Moines Register* to *Farming World* and the *Breeders' Gazette*. On occasion an article from the *Chicago Tribune* or the *New York Telegram* penetrated to this level of the middle cultures, but normally the farmer's attention focused on the state and local level, his horizons bounded by the poultry show and the stockmen's convention. While these organizations and papers brought news from the world beyond Des Moines and even beyond Chicago, they usually kept the farmer's eyes fixed on those local and regional problems which were immediate and pressing for his occupation; they helped ensure that his concern would be with his short-run economic situation and that economic determinants would continue to be the primary factors shaping his attitude toward the trusts.

Above all else, the prices charged by big business angered the midwestern farmer (see table 4-3).[65] In the years before 1893, as we have seen, the railroads had cut rates so substantially that the farmer had stopped complaining about freight charges and discrimination. During the depression of the nineties, however, the farmer began once more to attack the railroads for "extortion." Even though rates (i.e., revenue per ton mile) continued to drift downward, the farmer now said the roads were "taking one half the crop as pay for marketing the other half."[66] Nor did he limit his assault to the railroads; he was not about to "forget that manufacturers, merchants and capitalists have laid their plans to see that they get all there is in our crop this season, large as it may be, and for this purpose through combinations have raised the price of everything we have to buy."[67]

When he was not complaining about prices, the corn and hog raiser was lamenting the spread of the general merger movement or the growth of some particularly obnoxious combine.[68] When Standard Oil opened a new wholesale supply depot, he had a chance to "observe the practical working of one of the worst, if not the worst, monopolies in the United States"; when a combination of some thirty railroads was being discussed, he recognized a scheme "to fix rates for all time to come on transportation between sea board cities and the Mississippi River."[69] As the merger movement was reaching its peak, *Wallaces' Farmer* ran an entire series on the "Trusts and How to Deal with Them," and by the end of the decade there was fear in the corn belt that eastern capitalists were about to launch a combine of combines, the ultimate "king trust."[70]

While the farmer was thus capable of conjuring up some highly abstract enemies, he lavished most of his animosity on those industries and firms with which he had direct economic relationships. When he said *corporation*, he usually meant the railroad, and if not, he was probably talking about the meat packers (see table 4-3). The specific firms which attracted most of his attention in the years 1893-96 were transportation companies or packers, and the same was true (although the particular companies changed) in the latter part of the decade. These were the corporations and the industries that seemed to have the most direct influence on his income either as buyers of farm products—e.g., Swift and Armour—or as sellers who provided him with a vital service.

The farmer was angry at these trusts and transportation companies, and the key variable shaping his attitudes was purely and simply income. Whether measured in current or constant dollars, the income of the corn and hog man suffered a sharp decline after 1893; the prices of the commodities he produced dropped precipitously in 1894 and had not recovered their predepression level as late as 1900.[71] Correlations between the figures on gross income and the annual data on favorable and unfavorable attitudes substantiate the conclusion that as farm income went, so went the antitrust movement in the Midwest.[72]

The statistics for 1900 and 1901 are of special significance. The midwestern farmer did not at this time suddenly abandon his self-image as a middle-class citizen, backbone of the nation, nor did he stop worrying about the sinful cities and the collapse of his family farm. What did suddenly change was his economic situation and, with it, his opinion of big business. In these two years prices and income shot upward, and by 1901, the farmer was directing more praise than condemnation at the trusts. He had never completely ignored the positive contributions of big business, even when farm prices had been at their low point in 1896 and 1897. The railroad, he had then acknowledged, was absolutely vital to the economic success of the country's farm regions.[73] Before 1901, however, this positive theme had been overshadowed by his fierce attack on those "great organizations of capital" that were attempting to "rob the public." But as his own economic fortunes improved, the farmer apparently forgot about the public and decided that there was much to be said in behalf of men like Philip D.

Armour who were creating "a new era in the business life of America."[74] By 1901, when J. P. Morgan organized the nation's first billion-dollar combine, the midwestern farmer was actually more placid about trustification than was the professional engineer.

V. The engineer's attitudes were, however, far more stable than those of the farmer. Neither the wave of rail and industrial consolidations at the turn of the century nor the depression preceding them were able to dent in any significant fashion the engineer's calm outlook on big business (figure 4-4). Unlike the cotton farmer, the engineer was pleased with the prices charged by the country's largest combines.[75] Unlike the minister, he was not particularly upset when some of these companies ran into financial difficulties; there was for him no morality play in the bankruptcies that jarred Wall Street after 1893.[76]

Although normally uninterested in labor relations, the engineer was unable to ignore completely the tumult of the 1894 Pullman strike.[77] Clearly his sympathies were more closely aligned with the social class owning the roads than with the class of men who were striking. Irresponsible strikers caused derailments and wrecks and labor organizations possessed, in his view, "a power and a solidarity which are dangerously underestimated by too many men in positions of authority." Most of the railway employees were, he felt, "law-abiding and honest citizens. . . . But in these matters the radical minority is apt to take the lead, while the conservative majority stifles its convictions and follows with blind obedience the leaders. Further, in every such conflict of capital and labor, there are unfortunately too many firebrands from the semi-criminal classes, who will seize the opportunity to destroy property and commit violence of every sort."[78] Property rights were all-important to the engineer. In fact, he divided everyone connected with American railroads into "men of high and low degree," and he left little doubt about the class with which he identified.[79]

The engineer's special blend of professional ideology and class consciousness withstood the impact of the depression, promising that the most outstanding characteristics of his image of big business would continue to be stability and neutrality. Judging from the figures in the Appendix (i.e., the mean deviation), the nineties was not a period of disequilibrium; there were changes, as we shall see, but the pace of change was slow and the major dimensions of the engineering mentality were stable.[80] The engineer continued to pay more attention to the products and services of the large firm and to its managers than he did to any other facets of business activity (table 4-4). He was most interested in the same three industries that had been of greatest concern to him before 1893, and all three were either directly or indirectly involved in transportation. Even the specific firms he talked about

FIGURE 4-4. **The engineer's evaluation of big business, 1880-1901.** The annual percentages represent the proportion of items in *Engineering News* reflecting each attitude.

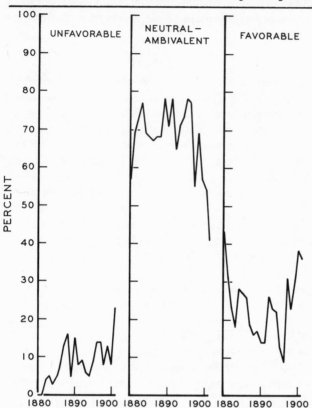

most frequently changed less than one might have expected during a period of major reorganization in the transportation and industrial sectors of the economy. Other Americans might have been worried about Standard Oil or the sugar trust, but the engineer kept his eyes fixed on the Pennsylvania Railroad, a company he considered more important than any other large enterprise in America.

His ideas about big business flowed down a narrow valley, bounded on one side by the hard rock of his direct experience with the large firm and guided on the other by his professional organizations and technical journals. When he commented on the large corporation, his remarks most often stemmed directly from something business itself had done (see the category "Leading sources" in table 4-4), from making "extensive improvements," to conducting experiments with a new type of motor car, to reorganizing the company's administration.[81] Meetings and conventions were the next most important source of ideas, followed by books and articles published in newspapers and in other magazines. The meetings included those of a variety of different organizations, but almost all were of some form of professional group directly involved with engineering. They included local associations such as the Civil Engineers Club of Cleveland, regional groups along the lines of the Engineering Association of the South, and most often the national organizations of the mechanical and civil engineers, the railway master mechanics, or the master car builders.[82] The publications that interested him were also largely technical and professional in their orientation; on rare occasions he might garner some useful idea from the *Pittsburgh*

TABLE 4-4. The engineer's image of big business, 1893-1901

Aspects of big business mentioned	1893-1896			1897-1901		
	High year	Low year	Mean	High year	Low year	Mean
Economic	100%	93%	96%	96%	91%	95%
Political	25	7	16	30	8	18
Social	0	0	0	0	0	0
Leading characteristics of big business	1) Products or services 2) Management or ownership 3) Miscellaneous political activities			1) Products or services 2) Management or ownership 3) Miscellaneous political activities		
Leading industries mentioned	1) Railroad transportation (40) 2) Transportation equipment (37) 3) Local passenger transportation (41)			1) Railroad transportation (40) 2) Local passenger transportation (41) 3) Transportation equipment (37)		
Leading firms mentioned[a]	1) Pennsylvania Railroad 2) Chicago, Burlington and Quincy Railroad; Westinghouse			1) Pennsylvania Railroad 2) Baltimore & Ohio Railroad 3) Chicago, Burlington and Quincy Railroad; General Electric		
Leading sources of items on big business[b]	1893-1901 1) Action taken by big business 2) Meetings and conventions 3) Other publications					

SOURCE: *Engineering News*. Similar data for the previous period are in table 3-1.
[a] The top three firms, 1880-86, were: Baltimore & Ohio Railroad, tied with Pennsylvania Railroad; Northern Pacific Railroad. For the years 1887-92, the leaders were: Pennsylvania Railroad; Baltimore & Ohio Railroad; Northern Pacific Railroad.
[b] For the 1880-92 period, these were: Action taken by big business; Meetings and conventions, tied with Other publications.

CRISIS, 1893-1901

Times, the *Buffalo Express*, or even the *North American Review*, but normally his cultural exchanges were with the *Railway Age*, the *Engineer*, and the *Yearbook of Railway Literature*. These sources reinforced professional attitudes and helped to preserve his particular concept of the engineer's role. Unless big business abruptly turned on itself, unless the engineering associations suddenly decided that technology was less important than social equity, unless the editors of technical journals hastily adopted a broader view of their mission, the engineer was unlikely to abandon any of the major elements in his outlook on large-scale enterprise.

The changes that took place in the engineer's image of the corporation were thus minor transitions in an otherwise stable pattern of thought, and the job of isolating and explaining these new developments is like handicapping a snails' race—small differences matter a great deal. One such difference can be seen in the balance between negative and favorable evaluations of the large firm. Although the engineer never became as upset about the trusts as did the farmers and skilled craftsmen, in the mid-nineties there was a brief period in which he was more likely to condemn than to praise the corporation (figure 4–5). By this particular measure, in fact, he was more agitated about the problem of big business in 1896 than at any other time in the entire sixty-one year timespan covered by this study. If, instead of these figures, we use the same percentages employed for the other groups, 1901 stands out as the peak year in this cycle of anticorporate sentiment (and also the peak year, 1880–1940). In either case, the years 1893 through 1901 deserve special attention, and it would appear that not even the professionally minded technician was entirely impervious to the important transitions taking place in American society during this pivotal decade.

Indeed, the depression and the merger movement prompted some anxious consideration of the kinds of opportunities the future held for the engineer. When railroads were combined, he observed, and "thousands of miles come under one head, one man can, and does, decide such questions for a large portion of the United States just as well as for a road 100 miles long. The result is that there has been a very great diminution in the number of engineers employed per mile of road and a great increase in the number of assistants compared to that of chief engineers, and that there are a large number of engineers in subordinate positions such as chainmen, rodmen, draftsmen, etc., for whom there may be little or no chance of promotion; and there are many who must occupy practically the same positions all their lives, as there are very few men above them to whose positions they can hope to succeed." Even those who reached the lofty position of chief engineer could expect to find their role in the enterprise diminished, as they would no longer actually build things—they would decide what kinds of equipment and supplies to purchase and then the specialists would direct the construction.[83] On occasion the engineer looked back with nostalgia on the boom

FIRST GENERATION

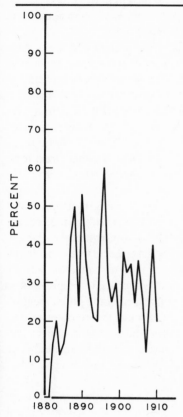

times of "rapid railway extension," those predepression days when "good and reliable men" had been "scarce . . . in proportion to the demand."[84] His own prospects seemed reduced, and he pondered "the list of high operating officers of the railroads of the United States," wondering why "there are very few indeed taken from the engineering profession."[85]

As these remarks suggest, the engineer's opinion of big business could be influenced—at least in minor ways—by changes in his economic fortunes. During the first years of the depression, his income (in both current and constant dollars) continued to increase; in the middle of the decade, however, his annual income began to level off, and as economic recovery began his salary increases failed to keep pace with the rate of inflation.[86] In 1900 and 1901, his income was lower in terms of purchasing power than it had been in 1898. Significant correlations between income data and the

CRISIS, 1893-1901

figures on favorable attitudes substantiate the conclusion that economic variables were, in part, responsible for the changes taking place in the engineer's image of the large corporation.[87] The engineer found fewer opportunities in the nineties to laud the corporate managers who controlled his salary and his chances for advancement within the firm.[88]

Another change in engineering attitudes can be traced in large part to the new economic setting of the nineties, although in this case the relationship was less direct and personal. As the construction of new railroad lines waned, various urban-centered projects became more important as a source of employment for the professional engineer.[89] Thus, city and suburban transportation systems assumed new significance for the engineer in the years following 1892 (see "Leading industries" in table 4-4). Since local transportation ventures brought private enterprise into intimate relations with urban governments, the engineer also became more interested in the political dimension of big business. He now began to express growing concern about the dishonesty that all too often characterized these undertakings.[90] Some years before Lincoln Steffens published his muckraking articles on urban corruption, the engineer was taking note of the shameful collusion between city officials and assorted tycoons; one such episode was considered by *Engineering News* to be "as pitiful a case of juggling with an official trust as has been made in many a day by men above the grade of pot-house politicians." The commissioners were "mere puppets of some power behind the throne."[91] On occasion the engineer looked beyond the confines of the city or state to raise broad political questions about, for instance, the relationship between tariff protection and the trusts.[92] But normally he directed his critique of political economy at the problems closest to his immediate professional interests.

A third development in the engineer's image of the large firm involved a new concern on his part with the overall efficiency of large-scale enterprise. In this case his conclusions as late as 1901 were overwhelmingly favorable to big business.[93] Farmers and laborers might attack the sugar trust for raising the price of an essential commodity, but the engineer found comfort in the fact that the combine kept all of its machinery in operation and thus reduced its "maintenance account."[94] While new combinations in the railroad industry angered other citizens, the technician smiled at the news that the roads were responding to "the demand for greater economy in the movement of a traffic that has grown and multiplied year by year."[95]

The immediate source of this new interest seems to have been the large firm itself. There was, of course, a growing enthusiasm for efficiency and scientific management in the professional organizations, and as Samuel Haber and Samuel P. Hays have shown, that enthusiasm existed far beyond the world of the professional engineer.[96] But this phenomenon belonged to the twentieth century, and in the nineties the engineer was responding largely to developments within the large corporation. In the railroad industry, for instance, the mergers of the nineties followed on the heels of a long period of declining rates, leaving management newly concerned with the need to lower costs through more efficient operations. Much of the railroad construction that took place in these years was aimed more at improving existing lines than at extending service into new areas. The engineer reacted to these efforts, and for the most part his response was praise for his employers.[97] This was one issue on which the principles of engineering and the principles of business seemed to yield the same results. Later, when his interest in efficiency became even stronger, the engineer would have some second thoughts about the effectiveness of the largest firms, but in the years 1897–1901 he was convinced that big business was doing a good job of improving its internal operations.

Changes in engineering attitudes toward the corporation were thus primarily a result of economic and organizational factors and, to a lesser extent, political developments. Lower income and depression conditions sparked a more critical attitude toward the large firm as an employer. A basic shift in economic opportunities drew the engineer's attention to urban projects and hence to the problem of corrupt city governments acting in collusion with big business. At the same time, however, many of the country's largest firms won praise for their efforts to operate more efficiently. While the engineer's ideology and class values ensured that the major outlines of his concept of the corporation would remain stable, these three themes represented important changes and each would continue to be important in the years to come. In that restricted sense the nineties witnessed a significant transition in the engineer's attitudes toward the giant firm.

VI.   The engineer and the Iowa farmer thus convinced themselves that big business presented no threat to their vital interests, but the skilled craftsman who worked around Pittsburgh could not. The steel trust and other combines had a crucial impact on his life. If not employed in one of the trust's mills, he probably worked for another large corporation that regularly encountered U.S. Steel in the marketplace. The steel trust came to symbolize for him the forces of change in modern industry, forces transforming the role of the skilled worker and threatening the labor organizations designed to protect his craft. To understand how the worker responded to these changes, however, we must first look back to the early nineties, to the months immediately preceding the depression.

At that time the rumors circulating about Andrew Carnegie's Homestead mills had proven to be completely and unfortunately true: the "iron king of the known world" had armed to fight the Amalgamated Association of Iron, Tin, and Steel Workers and to free his plants entirely of union influence.[98] The ensuing strike was brutal, and while both sides suffered as a result of this struggle, union losses were most obvious, immediate, and overwhelming.[99] After Carnegie had defeated craft organizations in the most progressive iron and steel plants in the nation, the outlook for trade unionism in this vital industry was at best poor. In the difficult months that followed, the skilled worker was reminded again and again of that "painful contest," "the most noted labor conflict of modern times."[100] There were trials for the men charged with criminal action in the strike, and Carnegie was linked with a "style of terrorism" which was "part and parcel of ring political methods."[101] His philanthropy invited scorn from the workers: "When the Carnegie Steel Company twelve-hour men are done with the day's labor of course they will feel keen in pursuit of knowledge and the cultivation of the beautiful, hence will rush to the Carnegie libraries."[102]

The harsh defeat at Homestead was followed by the depression, with its inevitable rounds of wage cuts, layoffs, and new strikes. As the skilled worker surveyed the railroad, iron and steel, and coal industries, he saw little that was encouraging for the future of trade unionism; when he reflected on the industrial giants dominating these vital industries—whether the Carnegie enterprise or Jones and Laughlin or the Pullman Company—the outlook seemed gloomy both for the craftsman and for his organizations (see table 4–5).[103] In 1894 during the violent Pullman strike he witnessed the victory of a company engaged in "coldblooded tyranny" imposing "a system of gouge and fraud upon its employees."[104] A few months later, when he could "still hear the groan of oppression and poverty from the town of Pullman," he saw the "coal barons," the "brutal vultures" who monopolized the industry, hire "midnight assassins" to defeat the workers and deprive them of "time, light of day and the means to clothe and educate their families."[105]

Nor did the economic recovery of the late nineties bring the worker any immediate relief. Even though good times dampened labor-management strife and pushed up wages, prosperity could not heal the wounds of the Amalgamated Association. The leading union in the area was still weak and growing weaker, just when the merger movement in transportation and in manufacturing was reaching boom proportions. The craftsman was uncertain what the implications of these latest mergers were for him; he watched closely as new combines emerged among the manufacturers of tools, wire, nails, thread, silver products, tin, paper, tobacco, and food. On occasion he grumbled about paying tribute to trusts that underpaid their employees and overcharged customers for products "of universal use, such as sugar, oil, thread, and, shall we say, whiskey . . ."; at times he became extremely angry, as he did when one of the new corporations shut down its smaller and less efficient plants, depriving many skilled craftsmen of their jobs. In these circumstances he might conclude that the men had "to combine together closer than ever or else the . . . 'combine' will get the best of us." But tighter combination seemed to be a more realistic goal for the monopolists than it was for their employees.

FIRST GENERATION

The worker was disturbed with big business but uncertain of exactly what he should do, and his opinions were unstable throughout the nineties (figure 4–6). By our measure (M.D.), the nineties were the years of maximum disequilibrium in the opinions of those workers who read the *National Labor Tribune*. No longer were the fluctuations in the worker's image of the large firm closely keyed to changes in his real income, as they had been in the eighties.[106] No longer could he feel assured that prosperity would undo the damage wrought to his major union by the previous years of depression. He was, in Robert H. Wiebe's terms, searching for order, for a new orientation that would include a new way of conceiving his relationship to the giant firms surrounding him.

His complaints about these companies fell into an interesting and revealing pattern.[107] His major objection during the years from 1893 to 1901 was to corporate labor relations, followed by expressions of dissatisfaction with the policies on wages and hours. During the years 1893–96, he also frequently lamented business's dependence on help from the government —especially in the form of injunctions—and he often criticized corporate management. In the following five years, his third- and fourth-ranking complaints shifted as the merger movement got underway: now he grew worried about the general economic power of the combines and about the mere fact of trustification.[108] Missing, however, was one of the central problems he faced in the nineties—that is, the displacement of skilled workers that occurred as corporations mechanized their operations. He frequently discussed the improvements large concerns were making in their plants, and he was well aware that following a merger, a combine normally shifted production from its less efficient to its more efficient locations.[109] But the relationship between mechanization and the traditional crafts rarely received much attention—despite the threat technological advances posed to his security.[110] His failure to discuss mechanization reflected, I believe, his powerlessness as an individual to fight the machine and his inability to organize effective craft unions.[111]

Confused and threatened, the skilled worker began to look elsewhere for support; he began, in fact, to look to the companies themselves for protection.[112] When this happened, his image of big business began to stabilize around a new set of norms. Equilibrium in this instance was a product of resignation, of acceptance of his inability to achieve countervailing power through unionization.[113] The hopes of 1892 had been dashed, and by 1901 the craftsman had adopted a new outlook on the corporation and a new concept of his own role in the emerging system of industrial giants.

In that year the stability of this new perspective was tested when J. P. Morgan successfully organized the United States Steel Corporation. This combine was enormous, held a strategic role in the national economy, and was all-important to the readers of the *Tribune*. The first remarks about the

CRISIS, 1893–1901

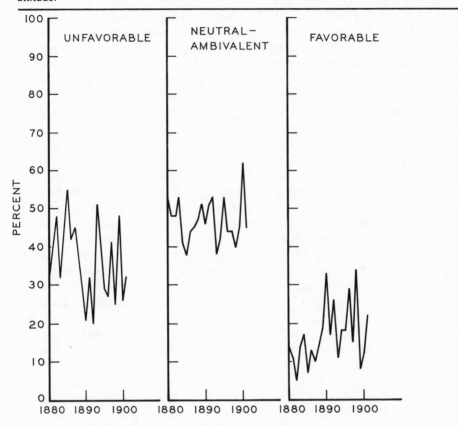

FIGURE 4-6. The skilled worker's evaluation of big business, 1880-1901. The annual percentages represent the proportion of items in *National Labor Tribune* reflecting each attitude.

steel trust appeared in April 1900, when a rumor circulated that the combination of leading sheet steel producers was "only a forerunner for a still greater one" which would bring together companies making a wide variety of iron and steel products.[114] A few months later this story surfaced again, but the paper cited "a well-known industrial authority" who had concluded that insofar as industrial combines were concerned, the "virtual limit of consolidation" had been reached.[115] Expert authority sold at a sharp discount in February 1901, however, after U.S. Steel brought together under one corporation most of the major producers in the iron and steel industry, including the enormous Carnegie interests.

The skilled craftsman kept a wary eye on the trust's every move. At first his responses were mixed; he seemed unable to decide what, exactly, would come of the combine and the men it employed. On the one hand there was ground for optimism when one of the corporation's leading officers asserted that the company would yield "benefits" to its workers, including "stock distributed to deserving employees."[116] If the trust could in fact stabilize conditions in the industry, that too might benefit the workers. On the other hand there was good reason to fear a "master" combine composed of mills which were, for the most part, nonunion. It was unclear how Morgan and his managers would treat labor organizations, but initially they made no effort to bring all of their plants under one rule.[117] Through the early summer of 1901, the worker still had mixed feelings about the corporation.

In subsequent months his attitudes changed in two distinct phases. In the fall of 1901, when the Amalgamated Association began a protracted and losing battle with the Morgan interests, the skilled laborer found much to criticize in "the moneyed power," the "soulless barons" who used "hunger

TABLE 4-5. The skilled worker's image of big business, 1893-1901

Aspects of big business mentioned	1893-1896			1897-1901		
	High year	Low year	Mean	High year	Low year	Mean
Economic	100%	93%	96%	99%	92%	96%
Political	18	16	17	20	7	13
Social	2	0	1	4	0	1

Leading characteristics of big business	1) Labor relations 2) Products or services 3) Wages and hours	1) Existence or expansion 2) Labor relations 3) Wages and hours
Leading industries mentioned	1) Railroad transportation (40) 2) Primary metals (33) 3) Coal mining (11-12)	1) Primary metals (33) 2) Railroad transportation (40) 3) Coal mining (11-12)
Leading firms mentioned[a]	1) Carnegie Iron & Steel 2) Illinois Steel 3) Jones & Laughlin	1) American Tin Plate 2) Carnegie Iron & Steel 3) National Steel

Leading sources of items on big business[b]	1893-1901 1) Action taken by big business 2) Other publications 3) Letters to the editor

SOURCE: *National Labor Tribune*. Similar data for the previous period are in table 3-5.
[a] In the early eighties, the top firms were: Jones & Laughlin; Baltimore & Ohio Railroad, tied with the Pennsylvania Railroad. During the period 1887-92, they included: Carnegie Iron & Steel; Pennsylvania Railroad; Reading Railroad, tied with Pennsylvania Steel.
[b] Before 1893, these were: Action taken by big business, tied with Other publications; Letters to the editor.

and privation" to break the workers' resistance (figure 4–7).[118] But surprisingly, this hostility soon gave way; by January 1902, the worker's appraisal of the steel trust and of big business in general was once again primarily neutral, with negative viewpoints at a distinctly lower level. While he still bestowed more criticism than praise on large enterprise, he was apparently resigned to a situation in which neither he nor his trade organizations could realistically expect to change the balance of power. His new outlook on the trusts had thus proven to be relatively stable under unique and trying conditions.

VII. Other workers—favored with stronger unions and more stable crafts —looked upon giant enterprise from a markedly different perspective. The readers of *American Federationist* saw an extremely negative portrait of the trust movement (figure 4–8), and during the depression of the nineties, the Federation's members appear to have been even more upset with big business than were farmers in either the South or Midwest.[119] The AFL member focused his discontent on two highly specific issues: labor relations and wages and hours (table 4–6).[120] He found opportunities to criticize big business when the Northern Pacific Railroad cut wages (but not the salaries of its receivers), when Andrew Carnegie used "the arbitrary power of discharge from employment," when men requesting a wage increase were locked out of their shops, when a traction company used "methods of coercion and intimidation, discharge and blacklist," and when laborers were "penned behind Pullman's . . . silent walls."[121] The combination movement—that is, "the forced aggregation of capital into monopolies and syndicates"—earned condemnation, as did "the railroad kings who now command the courts to enforce reduction of wages."[122]

His attitude was consistently negative through the depression and the late nineties. In the years 1894–96, he directed most of his attention toward four major industries: railroads, iron and steel, food processing, and the manufacture of tobacco products. After 1896, the top four industries on the list remained the same, with only a slight change in rank order. The specific firms attracting most of his animosity varied from year to year, as strikes and lockouts drew his attention from one corporate enemy to another; but throughout the nineties the leading irritant was and continued to be James B. Duke's American Tobacco Company. Duke's "scab cigars" upset the AFL member even more than the nonunion biscuits manufactured by U.S. Baking or the coal that came from Rockefeller's government-defended Colorado mines.[123] In these regards, his concept of the corporation remained stable through the latter part of the decade.

There was a class dimension to his thought, and occasionally his discussion of big business revealed signs of a general sense of social disorder.

FIGURE 4-7. **The skilled worker's evaluation of big business, 1900-1901, by months.** The percentages represent the proportion of items in *National Labor Tribune* reflecting each attitude. Dates pertaining to the formation of United States Steel are noted.

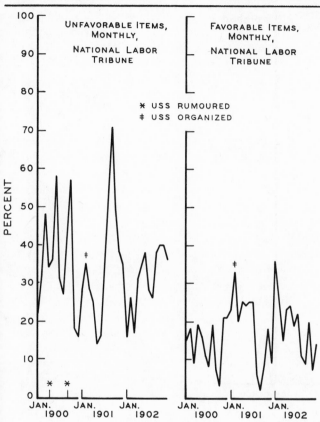

Sometimes he was anxious about his status. He condemned "the upper class" and the government which brought "the scum to the top" of American society.[124] He was aware that the distinguished citizens who paid for the pews in the country's churches were also the people who were responsible for the terrible working conditions in the Chicago stockyards.[125] In his mind "millionaire corporations" were linked with high society and both were in turn associated with opposition to trade unionism.[126]

On balance, however, these aspects of the organized worker's concept of big business were distinctly minor themes in an outlook dominated by specific material considerations. One of these was income, and the high correlation between earnings and attitudes in the nineties emphasizes the difference between this group of craftsmen and those who read the *National Labor Tribune*.[127] The latter were dismayed by the problems facing their

FIGURE 4-8. The AFL's evaluation of big business, 1894-1901. The annual percentages represent the proportion of items in *American Federationist* reflecting each attitude.

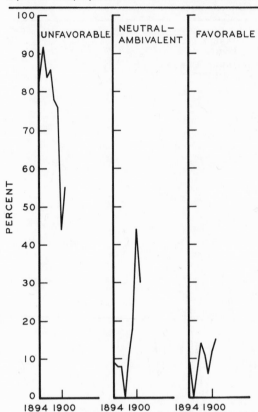

leading unions, while the former remained fixed on a steady course directed at the exclusive goal of immediate, material gains to be achieved through craft unionism. The major sources of ideas for the AFL member were internal to the trade union movement: they were letters (usually organizer's reports) to the editor, and accounts of actions taken by labor groups, normally either the Federation itself or an affiliated union (see table 4-6).[128] His was a narrow outlook, and he was open to the influence of only a few, highly specific variables—one of which was income. Not until the very end of the decade, when his wages began to increase sharply, did he begin to relax his aggressive stance toward the trusts, and even then he traded negative evaluations for neutral, not favorable, opinions.[129]

A second factor contributing to a change of opinion at the turn of the century was the AFL's great increase in membership.[130] As the federated organizations achieved greater support and bargaining power, they found

FIRST GENERATION

that their relations with the trusts improved. The telegraphers discovered that they could now adjust their grievances with the railroads; the freight handlers at last forced James J. Hill's Northern Pacific to yield to their demands; and the machinists who worked for the National Enameling and Stamping Company were able to win the nine-hour day.[131] Giant combines such as these appeared to the AFL member to be making less use of political muscle, and he found fewer opportunities to condemn injunctions, the militia, and "the charlatans and demogogues of hired monopoly."[132] He still had serious reservations about "the tremendous powers" of U.S. Steel and other "concentrated monopolies," but by 1901 his antagonism toward big business was no longer as firmly rooted as it had been during the depression.[133] He was beginning to waver, and his attitude toward the trusts would remain unstable for a number of years while he debated the relative merits of large enterprise.

TABLE 4-6. The AFL's image of big business, 1894-1901

Aspects of big business mentioned	1894-1896			1897-1901		
	High year	Low year	Mean	High year	Low year	Mean
Economic	100%	83%	91%	100%	88%	98%
Political	42	16	32	35	5	17
Social	13	0	6	7	0	2

Leading characteristics of big business	1) Labor relations 2) Wages and hours 3) Existence or expansion; Dependence on political assistance	1) Labor relations 2) Wages and hours 3) Existence or expansion; Dependence on political assistance
Leading industries mentioned	1) Railroad transportation (40) 2) Primary metals (33) 3) Food processing (20) 4) Tobacco manufacturing (21)	1) Railroad transportation (40) 2) Food processing (20) 3) Primary metals (33) 4) Tobacco manufacturing (21)
Leading firms mentioned	1) American Tobacco 2) American Biscuit; George Ehret	1) American Tobacco 2) U.S. Baking; Bunker Hill & Sullivan Mining

Leading sources of items on big business	1893-1901 1) Letters to the editor 2) Action taken by labor 3) Other publications

SOURCE: *American Federationist.*

CRISIS, 1893-1901

VIII. By 1901 an entire generation of Americans had acquired distinctive attitudes toward big business. Each of the occupational groups studied—indeed, each of the subgroups—had reacted to the trust movement in a different manner. Economic, organizational, and political interests had shaped these attitudes, as had values, ideologies, and a sense of class alignment. Despite differences, there were some patterns of thought common to all or at least most of the groups studied: most had become increasingly perturbed about the trusts; all had seen the combination movement spread to a wider range of major industries; all had changed their concept of the corporation in some significant way. The most general pattern that emerges is one of mounting hostility, as images of the giant firm among the middle cultures became more negative, reaching a peak in the depression of the mid-nineties (figure 4-9).[134] Neutral attitudes gave way as Americans vented their anger against the trusts and syndicates that were remaking the structure of the industrial economy.

The only qualifying factor in this picture of emerging conflict and crisis was the extent to which most of the middle classes continued—even in the depression—to look with favor on certain of the material accomplishments of big business. Favorable attitudes were thus far more stable than negative opinions. For this reason, we must bow slightly to the consensus school of history even though, for this generation, our major theme is mounting hostility toward the corporation.[135] During the worst years of the depression, middle-class Americans had some praise for the products and services of big business and for its contributions to the country's wealth, and these opinions provided an important foundation upon which subsequent generations would build a culture which found the modern corporation an acceptable—although not always praiseworthy—institution.

In the nineties, however, most middle-class citizens were still opposed to the combination movement, and all of our evidence indicates that this decade witnessed a major crisis in American life. Many scholars have found evidence indicating important shifts in thought during the nineties, but all too often their arguments are met with opposition from historians who hold that similar changes were taking place before 1890.[136] The problem, of course, is to find what was normative for the society—or in this case the middle classes—and content analysis data is particularly well suited to answer this kind of question. We can conclude that while there was evidence of disequilibrium and some signs of social disorder in the eighties, the changes taking place after 1890 represented a far more significant turning point for the middle class. Supporting this conclusion are the data on disequilibrium, the high level of hostility expressed toward the large firm, and the substantial changes that took place in the content of the several group images. By these measures the nineties emerge as a decade of social turmoil and dramatic cultural transition.

FIRST GENERATION

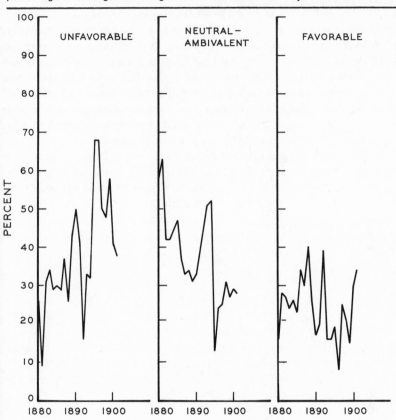

FIGURE 4-9. American middle-class evaluations of big business, 1880-1901. The annual percentages are weighted averages of the data from all of the journals. See note 134, chapter 4.

Even at this point in the study, we can reexamine and begin to sort out some of the major historical syntheses discussed in the first chapter. We have already seen that consensus history provides a useful concept, but not an acceptable synthesis, and the same might be said for the progressive and Schumpeterian frameworks. Neither is useful without first performing major surgery on their analyses. From both the progressive and Schumpeterian syntheses one must remove the intellectuals as a major causal factor; in only one subgroup—the clergy—do they appear to have had an important effect upon attitudes. Similarly, political leadership and the political system in general appear to have been less important in shaping this generation's ideas about the trusts than liberal historians have concluded. Indeed, political variables *in toto* had less impact on opinions than did social factors. We found abundant evidence of class concepts and these ideas colored middle-class perceptions of the trusts, much as a Marxist historian would

CRISIS, 1893-1901

have it. Class opinions were more malleable than Marxian analysis suggests, but along with occupational-group values, they exerted a significant effect upon the public image of the great corporation.

We can also use the Marxian emphasis on the underlying economic situation as the major force shaping attitudes in society. Clearly, economic factors influenced the changing patterns of group imagery more decisively than any other general class of variables. Equally clear is the conclusion that these economic factors were varied and complex and should only be studied within their organizational context. The organizations providing their members with power and sustaining (or failing to support) role concepts, ideologies, and value systems had an important impact upon attitudes. For this first generation, organizational factors were second only to economic forces as a determinant of public opinion. The interaction between economy and organization was crucial in molding the first generation's hostile reaction to the emergence of the modern corporation.

PART THREE. SECOND GENERATION: A STUDY IN THE PROCESS OF ACCOMMODATION

5

THE PROGRESSIVE CYCLE, 1902-1914

By 1901 the United States was a powerful, wealthy nation, and the generation of Americans coming of age in the early years of the twentieth century experienced a period of prosperity lasting through the end of the First World War. In 1903 and again in 1907, panics in the stock market triggered recessions, and in 1913-14 the economy appeared to be sagging into a full-scale depression comparable to those of the seventies and nineties. But the downturns of 1903 and 1907 were short-lived, and the combination of war orders from Europe and demand from countries previously supplied by European producers pulled the economy out of its 1914 slump.[1] At home, new and fast-growing urban markets generated demand for a variety of consumer goods; city-building—urban and interurban transportation systems, for example—spurred the market for producer's goods and helped to keep the economy growing.[2] As a result, an entire generation of Americans, including those farmers, laborers, and professional men who are the focus of this study, lived through a unique and prolonged era of prosperity. This experience had a significant impact upon their responses to organizational change and upon their image of the giant corporation. By the end of the war there were clear signs that big business and a new set of bureaucratic values were winning a secure place in the culture of middle-class America.

The breadth of this cultural transition reflected the fact that organizational change during these years was not limited to the realm of big business. Throughout America people devised new ways to cooperate and compete by forming or refurbishing large-scale, complex organizations. As highly organized activity became more common, values appropriate to a bureaucratic setting began to exert greater influence within the middle cultures. Norms that had characterized professional engineers since the eighties now spread gradually and unevenly through the middle class, providing it with new standards by which to judge giant enterprise.

Few scholars have seen these changes in values, their related organizational developments, or, for that matter, American prosperity as the most significant features of the years 1902-14; instead, they have labeled this period "the era of progressive reform." To the liberal historian writing about these years (and to many of his academic opponents), the transition in values could be crammed into the progressive framework as a cause of the reform impulse, and one could understand organization-building either as a political dilemma (i.e., the trust problem) or as a governmental solution (i.e., the Federal Trade Commission).[3]

But prosperity posed a tougher problem. How could one explain the rise of a nationwide reform movement in such a flourishing nation? While the agrarian reformers of the previous century could be linked to the falling prices of farm commodities, the men and women who joined progressive ranks and supported Theodore Roosevelt and Woodrow Wilson were clearly not motivated by direct economic need. They were rather well-to-do people living through a time of plenty. Why, then, did they behave as they did? The answers provided by earlier historians were varied, but they all seemed to have one thing in common: they provided weak, unsatisfactory explanations of the behavior of progressives. The liberal historian embraced a crucial paradox: on the one hand, he portrayed conservatives and their cohorts as men who performed in accordance with a simple calculation of their short-run economic interests; on the other hand, he pictured intellectuals, reform politicians, and other liberals as men who seldom gave self-interest a thought. If indeed the motives of these citizens were so unalike, it was striking that the progressive historians had no adequate explanation of these differences.

This weakness in progressive history attracted the attention of Richard Hofstadter and other revisionists, who refused to believe that any group in society could have been entirely disinterested, motivated only by a concern for others and the good society. Hofstadter's explanation for reform in the midst of prosperity was "status anxiety" or, in its later form, "cultural politics." The reformers, he said, were driven by a desire to protect or to regain status in a society that was leaving them behind; instead of a political struggle over material interests, "status politics" involved "the clash of various projective rationalizations arising from status aspirations, and other personal motives."[4] Hofstadter's sophisticated analysis appealed to many historians, and while subsequent studies have raised serious doubts about the status concept, the debate over motivation continues, with much of the discussion centering upon questions which Hofstadter raised.[5]

This chapter will touch upon these questions, but we cannot allow them to monopolize our attention entirely. There are other tasks to perform, and one of these is to explore in some detail the relationships between the public image of big business, politics, prosperity, organizational change, and social values. Along the way, we must arrive at some rough measure of the relative importance of these factors as causal agents and use our conclusions in turn to test the general hypotheses presented in the previous chapters. Perhaps the best way to begin is by examining the aggregate data in order to acquire a sense of the context in which these several causal forces operated.

SECOND GENERATION

II. Judging merely from the percentages arrayed in figure 5–1, a substantial residue of animosity toward corporate enterprise existed at the beginning of the national phase of progressivism. The favorable economic conditions and relaxation of political tensions that had occurred in the latter part of the decade had not completely dissipated the extreme hostility of the nineties; in 1902 negative opinions were still twice as prevalent as favorable concepts of the corporation. Between the first and second generations a measure of continuity existed. To the extent that these preexisting patterns of thought were inherited by a national reform movement, the problem of causation—of accounting for the origins of progressivism in an era of affluence —grows more manageable. Americans were already incensed at the trusts, their feelings rooted in the experiences of the less prosperous nineties. Although government antitrust policy was dormant when Theodore Roosevelt took office, antitrust opinions were widespread. The middle classes awaited a leader who could effectively express their feelings and shepherd their anxieties into the valley of national politics.

Our problems of explanation are also reduced to the extent that opposition to big business during the progressive era was less intense (figure 5–1) than it had been during the mid-nineties. In the peak phase of the progressive cycle (1905–6), the level of hostility was lower than it had been in 1895–96, and we can start our inquiry by rejecting the idea that antitrust sentiment "reached its climax . . . in 1906 and 1907."[6] The figures on equilibrium (M.D.) suggest a similar conclusion. During the years 1902–14, attitudes on the trust issue were far more stable than they had been during the previous decade.[7] There were two brief periods (1905/7 through 1906/8; and 1912/14 through the first years of the war) in which the public image of the large corporation was in flux; but from the vantage point of our comparative data, attitudes in the progressive era were stabilizing, and change itself was becoming more gradual and evolutionary. Seen in this light, reform and prosperity no longer seem to be such incompatible bedfellows; one would expect to associate moderation with good times and find opinions stabilizing around new norms in the years following a severe depression. What emerges is a version of progressivism which, in its broader outlines, closely resembles Robert H. Wiebe's description of a movement "founded in stability," seeking not to destroy but "to adapt an existing order" in ways restoring cohesion to society.[8]

Restoration along liberal lines nevertheless involved some important changes in America, and aggregate data on the public image of big business enable us to diminish the problem of explanation but not to eliminate it entirely. While change in the progressive years was gradual, change did take place. While there was an element of continuity with the 1890s, there was in the early 1900s a new cycle of increasing animosity toward the large

FIGURE 5-1. American middle-class evaluations of big business, 1880-1914. The annual percentages are weighted averages of the data from all of the journals. See note 134, chapter 4.

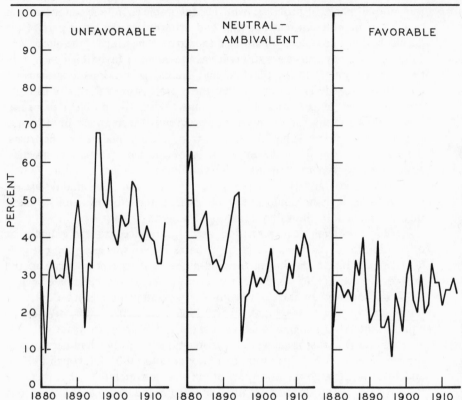

corporation, a phenomenon that demands analysis. While less hostility was expressed in these years than in the nineties, antitrust opinions were more salient in the early 1900s than they had ever been before 1895 or than they would ever be in subsequent years. To account for this cycle of antitrust sentiment, we must look behind the aggregate figures and find how political developments, prosperity, organizational change, and social factors influenced attitudes in each of our occupational groups.

III. Of all the groups studied, the Protestant clergy were the most responsive to reform politics. Changes in their image of the corporation can be explained largely in terms drawn from progressive history. The minister was attentive to presidential leadership, and Theodore Roosevelt frequently inspired the clergyman to reflect on the implications of the trust movement. The *Congregationalist* voiced its approval when the president condemned "those combinations of capital and labor which during recent years have assumed the attitude of monopoly as over against fair trade and have defied the State to curb their power."[9] In the Congregational minister's opinion, Roosevelt did more than any of his predecessors to control monopoly, and the clergyman was especially pleased with T.R.'s efforts to bring railroad rates under control and to counter the beef trust with a meat inspection law.[10] Before 1902, presidents had seldom had any substantial impact on his opinions about big business. During the progressive era, however, the actions of the federal executives became a major stimulant to discourse on the trust question (see table 5-1).[11]

Other sources of ideas on antitrust were the intellectual elite and the publications that filtered liberal ideology down to a broader, less knowledgeable audience.[12] The Congregational minister's relationship to this strata of society conformed quite well to the progressive vision (and to that of Joseph A. Schumpeter) of a society in which the intellectuals spurred political change. From such liberal intellectuals as Washington Gladden (*The New Idolatry*), the clergyman learned that some of the money given to missionary colleges was tainted by its association with John D. Rockefeller's "questionable business methods."[13] From Henry George (*The Menace of Privilege*), the minister heard about "the means by which men have acquired vast wealth and the use they have made of it," including successful efforts at "controlling legislation" as well as the "university and pulpit."[14] President Lowell of Harvard taught him that "large corporations and trusts . . . employ managers who are as indifferent to the conditions existing under them as were the merciless overseers in Ireland."[15] Frequently such liberal criticism of the corporation flowed to the clergyman by way of middle-class magazines like the *North American Review*. In the pages of the *Review* he discovered that the "repute of the [legal] profession" was endangered when lawyers rendered their services to the trusts.[16] *Everybody's* told him "how big business has seemed to influence decisions of the courts"; and *Lippincott's* broadened and strengthened this charge by explaining that giant corporations were contributing to the "corruption of the state."[17] The clergy was more open to the influence of these publications and of elite intellectuals than were any of the other groups in the middle cultures. To the Protestant minister men of ideas mattered, and their ideology had a significant influence on his image of the corporation; for him the progressive cycle of antitrust sentiment was in part a direct product of the ideas of systematic thinkers.

Effective intellectual and political leadership thus aroused a group of citizens who had become rather complacent about the corporation. As late as 1902 the clergyman's opinion of big business was framed in overwhelmingly friendly terms (figure 5-2). At that time he seldom had anything critical or even neutral to say on this subject. He was pleased, for instance,

THE PROGRESSIVE CYCLE, 1902-1914

when the Vanderbilts graciously paid half a million dollars to the depositors in a Tacoma (Washington) bank that had failed while under the guidance of their cousins. The Vanderbilts, he said, were under no obligation to pay: "Those who declare that accumulation of wealth mean[s] moral degeneracy will please take notice."[18] When Theodore Roosevelt and the intellectual critics of the corporation began to fuel the antitrust movement, however, the minister became less certain about the consequences of accumulation. At first he argued with himself, matching the good side of business behavior against the bad; out of one eye he saw the moguls "grasping for more power and wealth," but out of the other he saw John D. Rockefeller, Jr., conducting "his now famous Bible class."[19] Throughout Roosevelt's second term the minister alternately condemned monopoly and embraced the monopolist, but on balance he still found more to praise than to punish in the realm of corporate affairs.

FIGURE 5-2. **The Congregational clergy's evaluation of big business, 1880-1914.** The annual percentages represent the proportion of items in *Congregationalist* reflecting each attitude. For an explanation of my methodology, see chapter 2.

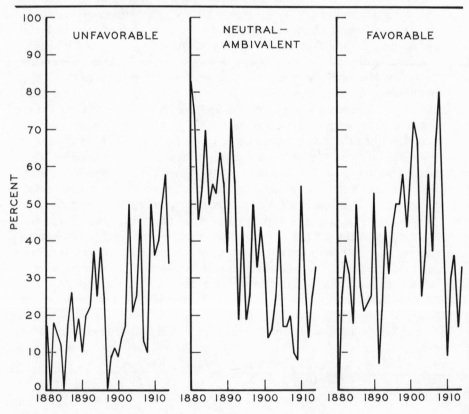

SECOND GENERATION

TABLE 5-1. The Congregational clergy's image of big business, 1902–1914

Aspects of big business mentioned[a]	1902–1908			1909–1914		
	High year	Low year	Mean[b]	High year	Low year	Mean[b]
Economic	100%	67%	88%	100%	86%	91%
Political	42	0	17	50	10	27
Social	33	0	16	20	0	11

Leading characteristics of big business	1) Products or services 2) Management or ownership 3) Miscellaneous social aspects	1) Management or ownership 2) Existence or expansion 3) Products or services
Leading industries mentioned	1) Railroad transportation (40)[c] 2) Local passenger transportation (41) 3) Food processing (20)	1) Railroad transportation (40) 2) Food processing (20) 3) Water transportation (44)

Leading firms mentioned[d]	1902–1914
	1) Pennsylvania Railroad 2) Standard Oil 3) New York, New Haven & Hartford Railroad

Leading sources of items on big business	1) Meetings and conventions 2) Federal executive action 3) Other publications
Leading solutions or responses[e]	1) Federal action[f] (61%) 2) State action (16%) 3) Private collective action (15%)

SOURCE: *Congregationalist*. For an explanation of my methodology, see chapter 2. Similar data for the previous periods are in tables 3-2 and 4-1.

NOTE: If multiple entries follow one number, the categories were tied.

[a]These figures show what percentage of the articles mentioned each aspect; the columns can total more than 100% because a single article could mention one, two, or all three.

[b]Mean of the annual percentages.

[c]The number appearing after each industry indicates its two-digit group in the *Standard Industrial Classification Manual.*

[d]Specific firms were mentioned so seldom that I did not feel I could use the figures for sub-periods 1902–8 and 1909–14.

[e]Comparable data for the years 1880–92 were: Federal action (37%); Private collective action (28%); Individual action (20%). The leading solutions for 1893–1901 were: Federal action (53%); State action (20%); Private collective action (10%).

[f]Also includes general references to an unspecified governmental response or solution.

THE PROGRESSIVE CYCLE, 1902–1914

After 1908 this balance broke down and the social gospel triumphed over the dictates of social class. Personal philanthropy seemed to wear thin. The clergyman was no longer certain that giant corporations were supplying the public with reliable goods and services or were furthering the growth of the economy. Government assaults on the trusts wore away at his class allegiance until he finally became a frank opponent of corporate management. His interests followed public policy (instead of leading it): after the beef trust and Standard Oil came under attack, he focused more of his attention on their respective industries. During these years only the Pennsylvania Railroad earned more of his concern than the Standard Oil combine.[20] He was certain in 1909 that William Howard Taft's election ensured "a serious effort to bring corporations under federal control," and he echoed Taft's pronouncement that monopolies had to be regulated in the public's interest. The combines had powers that had "grown too great to be intrusted to the selfish decisions of a few."[21]

From this flurry of reform activity emerged some evidence suggesting that the clergyman was anxious about his status and might be displacing that anxiety onto the trusts and their leaders. In one instance a lurid murder case provided comments not merely on individual sin but also on the general economic conditions that gave rise to such personal tragedies; the case was "symbolical of conditions that always exist in great centers of populations, or in nations where wealth is suddenly acquired by those without character to use it." The minister left little doubt that he looked upon this situation from afar—not just in the literal, geographical sense, but economically and socially as well; he could be grateful, however, for the insight it offered him into "the social conditions which exist in some of our newer great centers of wealth and commercialism." He was now able "to understand, as never before perhaps, 'the moral anemia of the newly rich,' of whom Pittsburg has many."[22]

Such remarks reflected anxiety about being left in the backwash of industrial society, but despite this evidence, the results of my study do not sustain Hofstadter's argument that status anxiety was a prime cause of reform sentiment in the progressive era. Instead, the data point to the conclusion that after 1901 (as before) the clergyman was provoked chiefly by events placing big business and the culture it promoted in conflict with his basic values. He was extremely concerned, for instance, about the social implications of the concentration movement, in large part because he saw a direct relationship between the behavior of the elite and general social norms. When business leaders misbehaved they set a bad example, particularly for the young. Conditions had been bad enough in the days of Jay Gould and Jim Fiske, in the era of "the individual highwayman," but after 1900 there was even more to fear because "public robbery had been incorporated."[23] Shrugging off corporate propaganda, the minister recog-

SECOND GENERATION

nized and lamented the fact that "great businesses are built up by methods which violate the laws both of God and man, and Christians are often partners in them."[24] All too often the monopolists were able to conceal their wrongdoing behind the legal facade of the firm: "Nothing has been more baneful in our recent social development than differentiations between what men do as officials of corporations and what they may do as private individuals."[25] The Protestant minister's response to this aspect of trustification provides an excellent example of what Hofstadter himself called "cultural [as opposed to status] politics," that is, political behavior which centered about "questions of faith and morals, tone and style."[26]

The responsibility for restoring faith and righting the moral stance of big business rested primarily with the federal government. Only Washington, the Congregational minister now felt, could solve the trust problem (see "Leading solutions" in table 5–1). During the 1880s he had only occasionally reflected on solutions to the difficulties giant corporations created, and when he had thought about it, he had favored private almost as often as public action. In the nineties he had become more concerned with responses to the trusts and had given increasing attention to governmental restraints, especially those imposed at the federal level.[27] During the progressive years, these trends continued, reaching a peak in the period 1909–14; by that time almost 90 percent of the solutions he considered were in the domain of the national government. The states could not meet the challenge of the giant firm, the clergyman recognized, any more than the individual could. In the emerging corporate society the minister felt that business would "have to work under government, not over it."[28] Realizing that history could not be reversed and that large enterprise was here to stay, he was determined to curb business's power. By 1913 he had concluded that only the federal government could perform this task.

When the government appeared to assert itself the clergyman was pleased, and by 1914 his anger at industrial combines was beginning to subside. The antitrust suits of previous years had consistently won his favor, as had new federal statutes ostensibly directed against corporations that were "defying the State with impunity."[29] He had opposed government ownership of monopolies and remained certain that "collectivism" was "impossible and dangerous."[30] But moderate, liberal "trust regulations" and the work of such independent regulatory commissions as the ICC had gradually convinced him that America's future was not imperiled by the concentration movement. He was especially happy when the government directed its fire at company officials—individuals—and not just at the corporation; then he felt reassured, pleased with the knowledge that it was no longer possible in America to distinguish "between what men do as officials of corporations and what they may do as private individuals."[31] Political reform in this "progressive" style was thus the variable best

THE PROGRESSIVE CYCLE, 1902-1914

explaining the major patterns of change in the clergyman's image of the giant corporation between 1902 and the outbreak of the First World War. Crucial, as well, was the interaction between the political and social variables—that is, between reform and the clergyman's basic values.

IV. Liberal politics had a similar although less decisive impact upon the attitudes of midwestern farmers. Here too there was a cycle of increasing hostility toward the trusts, a cycle roughly corresponding with the national phase of the progressive movement (figure 5-3). The farmer was receptive to liberal policies that promised to curb powerful business corporations. In 1902 he already saw more to dislike in the trusts and giant railroad companies than did the clergy, and even though agrarian anticorporate sentiment was far below the levels of the depression years, the farmer by the early 1900s had only learned to tolerate big business, not to like it. He acknowledged that large enterprise made positive contributions to American society; indeed, throughout the progressive era his opinion of corporate accomplishments remained stable.[32] But at neither the beginning nor the end of the progressive cycle did the farmer find more to like than to dislike about the corporation.[33]

In part the midwestern farmer's frame of mind was a heritage from the nineties and populism, but socialization cannot account for the sharp increase in negative viewpoints in the farm belt after 1903.[34] The farmer, it would appear, was responsive to political leadership and activity centering around what were ostensibly reform issues. For instance, there was a substantial increase in the percentage of the items which appeared in *Wallaces' Farmer* as a direct result of some form of political action. While no single branch of the government, state or national, stirred up enough commentary to rank among the three leading sources in table 5-2, all of the varieties of political behavior combined accounted for almost one-fourth of the articles dealing with the trust and railroad questions.[35] In the farmer's view, Theodore Roosevelt was making a sincere effort to control big business and to leash that "small group of purse-proud and arrogant plutocrats" who dominated corporate affairs.[36] The president's head was "entirely level" and his policies "set a higher standard on morals."[37] The midwestern farmer was also alert to the actions of Congress and the courts, of his state legislative and executive officials, and of regulatory commissions, both state and national; frequently the letters he sent to the editor of *Wallaces' Farmer* reflected his sensitivity to the politics of reform.[38]

While attentive to political leadership, he was largely oblivious to that ideologically oriented intellectual elite that was an important element in shaping the attitudes of the Congregational minister. The farmer did not give much attention to the *North American Review* or to the latest publications of Washington Gladden or Richard T. Ely. Walter Lippmann and Herbert

Croly toiled away largely unnoticed by a farmer who paid little heed even to the sensational revelations of the muckrakers.[39] He could on occasion steal a glance at viewpoints gathered from the *New York Herald*, the *United States Investor* ("one of the leading financial journals of the country"), and even the *London Express*.[40] But his culture was attuned primarily to ideas current in homelier sources: in Iowa newspapers, for instance, and agrarian journals like the *Crop Reporter* and the *Live Stock Report*.[41]

In explaining the origins of this cycle of antitrust opinion, the historian can safely ignore John Dewey and can relegate to a minor role such nonrational patterns of motivation as anxiety about status and animosity toward the city. As we have already seen, before 1902 there was some evidence that farmers were focusing upon the corporation their concern about a broad range of social issues; this lightning-rod effect, while never a major cause of discontent with big business, had become more evident in the nineties than in the eighties—and this trend continued through the progressive years.[42] The farmer usually expressed these anxieties by referring to the threat that big business posed to fundamental American values: "The moral effect [of railroad rebates] is even worse than the financial. We American farmers pride ourselves on our manhood, on our independence, on our ability to pay as we go. We are not cabbies, nor waiters at a hotel table, nor even porters on a Pullman car. We scorn to receive bribes, or to sell our votes, or to be treated as underlings, yet how much better is the moral position of the merchant or shipper who solicits rebates? It is not a good sign when individuals and communities feel that their well being depends on a rate which if given to themselves means prosperity, but, if given to the other fellow means . . . ruin to themselves. This is not the soil out of which grows a vigorous, robust manhood."[43] No nation could remain great "unless it remained morally great," and American morality was endangered by the trusts and "railroad magnates."[44]

These remarks—and others—reflect a degree of anxiety about the farmer's own position in America. To bemoan the high social standing of the robber barons was to admit a touch of envy, and to deny being "cabbies" and "waiters" was to betray a suspicion that one's foot had somehow slipped off a middle rung of the ladder of status. The corn-belt farmer was also deeply bothered by the breakdown of the family farm, and on occasion he even linked this directly with the rise of big business.[45] These subconscious motives heightened his anger at the trusts and powerful railroad systems, giving his political rhetoric a chiliastic tone. But it would be a gross distortion of the data to conclude that these emotional elements were of primary importance among farmers during the progressive years. Compared to their rational, politico-economic interests, social concerns continued to play a minor role in this phase of the agrarian movement, just as they had during the turbulent nineties.

THE PROGRESSIVE CYCLE, 1902-1914

FIGURE 5-3. The midwestern farmer's evaluation of big business, 1879-1914. The annual percentages represent the proportion of items in *Farmers' Review* and *Wallaces' Farmer* reflecting each attitude.

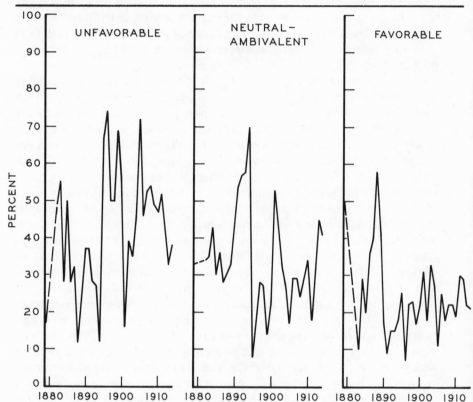

Although in 1887 the farmer had not been unusually concerned about railroad regulation, in the progressive years no subject was more central to his interests. He was determined to bring railroad rates under effective government control. Prices and price discrimination were the two aspects of railroad operations drawing most of his fire; he repeatedly complained about excessive freight and passenger rates and condemned "discrimination in favor of certain persons and places."[46] The places were large cities. The persons were those men of great wealth who controlled corporate empires in transportation and manufacturing: did George III, he asked, "ever exercise a more regal authority than does King Morgan or King Rockefeller now?"[47]

The midwesterner reflected at great length on the intimate relations between these new kings of business and public officials. Previous efforts at regulation had failed; the progressive campaign was meeting strong opposition. The problem, he decided, was in Washington, D.C., where there were

SECOND GENERATION

too many "Congressmen who had been sleeping comfortably in corporation beds."[48] The combines often controlled the press (although certainly not the farm papers!), and the railroads used free passes to influence political conventions and legislatures. Washington was filled with "oily-tongued lobbyists" and was "heavily charged with the microbes of plutocracy."[49] When Congress actually did pass the Hepburn Act in 1906—leaving out of the bill the one provision the "oily-tongued lobbyists" most desired—the

TABLE 5-2. The midwestern farmer's image of big business, 1902–1914

Aspects of big business mentioned	1902–1908			1909–1914		
	High year	Low year	Mean	High year	Low year	Mean
Economic	97%	89%	92%	96%	81%	88%
Political	52	18	32	33	11	22
Social	13	3	7	6	0	3

Leading characteristics of big business	1) Prices 2) Products or services 3) Financial practices	1) Products or services 2) Prices 3) Management or ownership
Leading industries mentioned	1) Railroad transportation (40) 2) Food processing (20) 3) Primary metals (33)	1) Railroad transportation (40) 2) Food processing (20) 3) Primary metals (33)
Leading firms mentioned	1) Standard Oil; Armour 2) Chicago, Burlington and Quincy Railroad	1) Chicago, Burlington and Quincy Railroad 2) Chicago and Northwestern Railroad 3) Chicago, Milwaukee and St. Paul Railroad

Leading sources of items on big business	1902–1914 1) Letters to the editor 2) Meetings and conventions 3) Economic conditions
Leading solutions or responses[a]	1) Federal action (36%) 2) Individual action (18%) 3) Private collective action (16%)

SOURCE: *Wallaces' Farmer*. Similar data for the previous periods are in tables 3–4 and 4–3.
NOTE: If multiple entries follow one number, the categories were tied.
[a] The comparable data for the years 1879–92 were: Federal action (33%); Individual action (32%); State action (19%). The leading solutions, 1893–1901, were: Individual action (36%); State action (23%); Federal action (17%).

THE PROGRESSIVE CYCLE, 1902–1914

farmer applauded his victory but watched nervously to see if President Roosevelt would appoint "clean-cut, upright, able men" to the ICC, men "who will enforce the law without fear or favor."[50]

Public policy was of vital importance because the farmer was convinced that only the federal government could handle the trust and railroad problems (see "Leading solutions" in table 5-2). In previous years he had still frequently expressed a desire for individual remedies; he had wanted, for instance, to beat the corporation with "better farming." In the progressive era this hope began to melt away. Instead, the farmer looked to the Hepburn Act of 1906 and the Mann-Elkins Act of 1910 to bring railroad rates under control.[51] These two measures were of overriding significance to the farmer —no other policy attracted so much of his attention or elicited so much approval. He was also pleased with the Meat Inspection Act of 1906—even though he acknowledged that it would drive small packing houses out of business—and he enjoyed the occasional sight of giant corporations under indictment for violating the antitrust laws.[52] At first he seemed to think that the trusts could not "live a single year" unless they were "given some special advantage in the way of freight rates," but he later came to the conclusion that direct action under the antitrust laws was necessary against such companies as Standard Oil and the leading meat packers. In the tobacco industry, he decided, "the remedy lies in the breaking up by the government of the tobacco trust."[53]

As the reform bandwagon got well under way, the farmer's attitudes began to stabilize, and in 1912–14 his hostility toward big business started to wane.[54] The antitrust suit against Standard Oil provides an excellent example of how this process of accommodation worked. The farmer had not been particularly interested in the oil combine before 1900, when the company was actually acquiring its near monopoly of the industry and was under severe attack in the press and in the state courts. After 1900, however, President Roosevelt had turned Standard Oil into an important negative symbol and had launched a highly visible attack on the firm. The farmer responded by making the company a leading subject of discussion (see "Leading firms" in table 5-2). While the Supreme Court decision in 1911 ordering the company's dissolution actually did very little to change the structure of the highly concentrated oil industry, the farmer believed that Rockefeller was defeated in court and the trust problem in oil thus solved. After 1911, the farmer seldom mentioned either Standard or the oil industry. New federal regulatory measures—in some cases more substantive than the highly symbolic antitrust laws—produced similar results.[55] Public policy was not the sole cause of the decline in antitrust sentiment after 1911, but among midwestern farmers it was the single most important factor contributing to a more neutral image of big business.

SECOND GENERATION

V.   The politics of reform had some impact upon the attitudes of all of the other groups studied, but in each instance the political system appears not to have provided the major variables shaping their image of the corporation. While professional engineers were more vulnerable as a group to political influence at this time than was organized labor or the southern farmer, professional interests and a particular brand of ideology continued to dominate their opinions. The engineer's discussions of the "public service corporations," that is, the railroads, utilities, and urban transportation systems, ignored many of the questions that were close to the hearts of reformers—questions of unemployment and social welfare, of labor relations, and of competition and individual opportunity. The engineer's major concern was the railroads; he simply wanted them to operate efficiently without imposing undue hardships on anyone. Acknowledging, in 1905, that the lines discriminated in favor of large customers, the engineer thought it was "within the power of many railroad officers to cause large losses to the property owners of communities, towns and cities, merely by their control over the freight rates enjoyed by competing commercial cities." All too often these officers were contemptuous of the law, and recent publications, including a "lurid exposé by Mr. Thos. W. Lawson" and a report by the Bureau of Corporations, had alerted the public to their dishonesty. The engineer concluded that "the rank and file of intelligent business and professional men throughout the country, with a more thorough understanding of the situation than 'the man in the street,' and a greater appreciation of the difficulties in the way of action, are no less firmly of the opinion that action of some sort should be taken."[56]

The engineer reached a similar conclusion when public service companies at the state and local level encountered difficulties. In 1903 he admitted that service on the Chicago transit system was so poor that an investigation was justified; a few years later, he saw that the problem had grown more serious and that it involved gas, electricity, water, and telephone companies, as well as street railways. Corruption, he found, was "more or less prevalent," and there was a "seamy side of corporate management." Still, the solution did not rest in the "monstrous absurdity" of competition or in municipal ownership.[57] The answer was private ownership with regulation. By 1912 numerous reform measures along this line had been adopted and the engineer felt that both this problem and the railroad question were being solved efficiently. Corporate leaders no longer had a "public be damned" attitude, he said, and limited government regulation had clearly provided a proper solution.[58]

While the political system influenced the engineer's attitudes, nonpolitical considerations weighed much more heavily on his mind. He was far more likely to talk about self-reform of business than to discuss regulation; his reflections on the corporation were provoked most often by the businesses themselves and not by politicians, either liberal or conservative (see table 5–4). He was primarily attracted by the same types of issues that had dominated his discourse since 1880, that is, issues touching directly upon his professional interests. In that sense, his image of big business was largely beyond the reach of progressive politics.

This was even truer for the organized laborer, who was much more sensitive to economic and organizational developments than he was to politics. Few of the articles on big business appearing in either the *National Labor Tribune* or the *American Federationist* were a direct product of political activity, and few suggested that the trust problem should be solved by the government (see tables 5–5 and 5–6). To some extent, the worker was uncertain that there really was a trust problem; he was actually pleased when the combines seemed to be stabilizing prices. U.S. Steel, he noted with approval, was impervious to "merely ordinary depressions": "For a great share of this healthful stability, credit is generally given to the United States Steel Corporation. This is one regard in which concentration of management in the industries does not work an injury to the public."[59] For the skilled craftsman the years 1902–14 were important, but not because of progressive reform, and the government was not responsible for the significant changes that took place in both the worker's situation and his image of the large corporation.

The southern farmer was equally insensitive to liberal politics. He was aware of the politico-economic problems that obsessed his midwestern counterpart; Roosevelt's investigation of the packing houses left him bemoaning the fact that he was putting his "money out to help swell the millions of the Beef Trust."[60] Later, he objected to the meat inspection system, which he thought was unsuccessful because of collusion between the packers and government officials: "Laws are made to punish small offenders. The great are beyond its reach. These Chicago packers feel too strongly entrenched and think they can with equal ease, run over the government and the people."[61] But the cotton farmer's solution to this problem was, typically, to call for less, not more, government intervention and to combat the trusts by talking about the establishment of rival packing houses in the South. The evidence from this study indicates that politics had a distinctly minor role in shaping the southern agrarian image of large enterprise during the early years of the twentieth century.

Perhaps the most general conclusion that one can draw from this mixed bag of results is that in studying the period from 1902 through 1914 historians can neither abandon the liberal synthesis nor embrace it without serious reservations. For two of the groups included in our sample of the middle cultures, the antitrust cycle of this era was primarily a political phenomenon, both in its origins and in its decline. In one instance there was significant interaction between political and social variables, that is, between reform and the clergyman's values. The other groups were less responsive to political leadership and public policy, but none was totally inattentive to the main currents of change in American government. It is only when we attempt to explain the major developments in their concepts of the large corporation that the liberal framework proves inadequate. Then we must look elsewhere, to economic, organizational, and social phenomena concurrent with the progressive movement but themselves largely apolitical.

VI. The group that came closest to providing a purely economic man was the southern farmer. As we saw in the previous chapter, the cotton farmer had in the late nineties begun to develop a new outlook on big business. While he still complained about the depredations of the trusts, he had begun to acknowledge more frequently the positive contributions large corporations made to the South in general and to agriculture in particular. While his image of the large firm had occasionally included some references to corporate involvement in politics, he had increasingly stressed the economic functions of big business. While he had not forgotten that he belonged to a social class or that the family farm was threatened (as was his standing in American society), he had begun to dissociate these problems from the rise of corporate enterprise in transportation and manufacturing.

These patterns of farm thought extended through the progressive era. The cotton farmer continued to focus most of his attention on two highly specific aspects of the large firm: its products and services, and the prices it charged its farm customers (table 5-3). He was interested in the industries that had been his leading concerns before 1902: railroads, food processing, and chemicals. The railroads—especially the Southern Company system —were the chief means of transporting his products to market and his supplies to the farm, but they also provided him with a variety of other miscellaneous services. The Southern promoted the improvement of highways, for instance, with a "Good Roads Train" that traveled through the South building specimen roads.[62] The farmer had a strong interest in the condition of his highways and was pleased with the railroad publicity campaign. The food processers—most prominently Armour and Swift —were building new plants in the South and, along with such chemical firms as the Virginia-Carolina Company, were selling the farmer increasing amounts of fertilizer. Thus his pattern of attention was fairly stable, centering on subjects of direct economic interest to him, and he was highly sensitive to changes in his economic fortunes.

Change came rapidly when, in the early 1900s, the southern farmer experienced a sudden increase in income. Between 1902 and 1903 the price of cotton jumped from 8 to 11 cents a pound. Gross farm income (in current dollars) from cotton and cottonseed went up by more than 20%, and during

FIGURE 5-4. **The southern farmer's evaluation of big business, 1879-1914.** The annual percentages represent the proportion of items in *Southern Cultivator* reflecting each attitude.

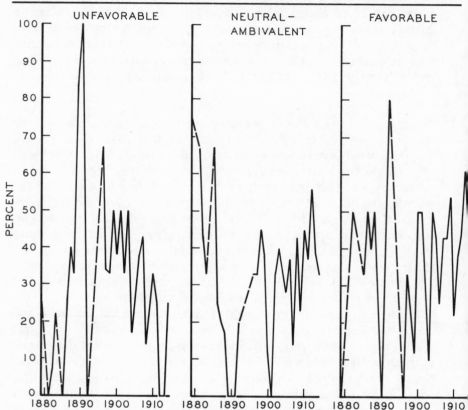

the following year, with prices holding steady, the South produced its largest cotton crop since the Civil War (12.72 million bales); gross income jumped to $704,000,000, an increase of 27% in one year. Even if one reduces these figures to constant dollars by taking into account the general inflation in prices, it is clear that the cotton farmer's economic situation had improved to an unusual degree. The average gross income for the years 1902–14 was 77% higher than it had been during the previous six years.[63]

This heavy flood of dollars washed away the agrarian enthusiasm for antitrust just as President Roosevelt was launching his career as a "trust buster." As late as 1903, the cotton farmer was still highly critical of corporate combines, pointing out that they made "immense profits," were guilty of "unjust discrimination," and were under the leadership of "soulless men."[64] In the next few years, however, his attitudes mellowed and his criticism gave way to praise (figure 5-4). The suggestion that income was the

SECOND GENERATION

major variable producing this change is substantiated by the statistical data: the coefficient of correlation between gross income (current dollars) and the percentage of unfavorable attitudes was –.57 for the years 1902–14.[65] In this second important phase in the process of accommodation between the cotton farmer and the corporation, the correlation between income and attitudes as well as the specific nature of the changes in opinion indicate that it was economic factors which were most influential in converting negative imagery into neutral and favorable evaluations.

TABLE 5-3. The southern farmer's image of big business, 1902-1914

Aspects of big business mentioned	1902–1908			1909–1914		
	High year	Low year	Mean	High year	Low year	Mean
Economic	100%	86%	98%	100%	89%	98%
Political	17	0	9	25	0	8
Social	14	0	4	8	0	1

Leading characteristics of big business	1) Products or services 2) Prices 3) Management or ownership	1) Products or services; Prices 2) Enhances individual's opportunities; Enhances the general wealth

Leading industries mentioned	1) Railroad transportation (40) 2) Food processing (20); Chemicals (28)	1) Railroad transportation (40) 2) Food processing (20) 3) Chemicals (28)

Leading firms mentioned	1902–1914
	1) Southern Railroad 2) Armour 3) Virginia-Carolina Chemical; Swift

Leading sources of items on big business	1) Letters to the editor 2) Meetings and conventions 3) Other publications; Action taken by big business

Leading solutions or responses[a]	1) Individual action (61%) 2) Federal action (31%) 3) Private collective action (7%)

SOURCE: *Southern Cultivator.* Similar data for previous periods are in tables 3–3 and 4–2.

[a] Comparable data for the years 1879–92 were: Private collective action (43%); Federal action (17%); Individual action (15%), tied with State action (15%). The leading solutions for 1896–1901 were: Individual action (43%); Federal action (18%); Private collective action (12%).

THE PROGRESSIVE CYCLE, 1902-1914

Most of the southern farmer's good will was directed at the residual benefits of big business. The cotton grower acknowledged that his range of opportunities broadened when the railroad lines gave him access to new markets and when they encouraged their "patrons to do good farming."[66] Further, as the large packing firms moved into the South, they promoted a more diversified agriculture. It also pleased him when "the International Harvester Company of America established the I.H.C. Service Bureau. Already it has done much work of real value. The object of the Bureau is the promotion of agricultural education, and a co-operation which will tend to raise the whole tone of farm life."[67] Often the entire region—not merely the individual farmer—benefited. One contributor to *Southern Cultivator* delighted in the thought that a large packing firm might open a branch in his home state of Georgia; it would, he guessed, "double the value of the cattle in the state or add nearly $10,000,000 to the value of farm property."[68] In the farmer's universe these figures were astronomical and they reflected a contagious sense of regional progress, an atmosphere charged with high prices and high farm income. By the years 1912–14, the cotton farmer was five times more likely to stress these positive characteristics of large enterprise than to stress high freight rates or discrimination by trusts.[69] The farmer completely depoliticized the corporation. No longer did he see the political dimension of big business or discuss any public policies aimed at curbing the power of the trusts. In fact, he no longer felt compelled to reflect on any kind of response to the large firm, because he no longer felt that a problem existed. Prosperity had legitimated the new order.

VII. While none of the other groups offered as unmistakable a portrait of economic man, all were to some degree responsive to economic change. Engineers were at times nervous about their income and opportunities for advancement within the giant firm. One of them complained that even brakemen and clerks frequently did better than civil engineers: "So far as chances for promotion are concerned any young man of ability certainly makes a mistake to enter the engineering department of a railroad." Frequently, he suggested, this policy on promotions was responsible for costly mistakes in construction.[70] Another engineer proclaimed that there were "but two classes of technical men who make a success in a railroad career, men of extraordinary ability, and men considerably above ordinary ability who have a 'pull.' All others would do much better in other lines of their profession."[71] The editor of *Engineering News* also felt that this was a problem, and he later answered a correspondent by explaining that income and status in society were closely linked: "It is only human nature to set a low value on that which costs us little. In order that the public shall properly appreciate the value of engineering service, it is necessary that the compensation of engineers shall be put upon a proper plane."[72] Substantial correlations between income data and attitudes support these quotations, and together they indicate that changes in his salary and his economic opportunities were coloring the engineer's image of the corporation.[73]

Specific material considerations also influenced the attitudes of organized laborers. For neither group of craftsmen—those who read the *National Labor Tribune* and those who subscribed to the *American Federationist* —did the statistical correlations indicate that income, pure and simple, had a significant impact upon the worker's opinion of big business between 1902 and 1914. At that level of aggregation (and abstraction), one could reject the hypothesis that economic factors shaped the laborer's attitudes. By penetrating a bit more deeply, however, we can see several noteworthy relationships. The wage and hour policies of the trusts had been leading subjects of concern on the part of labor in the nineties, and they continued to be a major subject of discussion among skilled craftsmen after the turn of the century (see tables 4-5 and 4-6). He still had occasions to complain. He pointed out that the very same "trusts by which the output of industry is controlled, and prices arbitrarily set" were the companies which cut their employees' wages; after the Carnegie Steel Company reduced wages, he lamented that "the men have never in the history of the steel industry been asked to work for such a pittance."[74] But balanced against these critiques was his favorable reaction when U.S. Steel gave its workers "the largest voluntary increase ever known in [the] wages of 100,000 men."[75] More and more often he found opportunities to praise the giant firm for this aspect of its performance. As early as 1900, the AFL member began to change his mind on this subject, but the crucial turning point came with the cycle of inflation-deflation centering around 1907. During and after the panic, the trade unionist looked with greater interest and mounting favor at corporate wages and hours. Every year from 1907 through 1912, one-half or more of the references to wages and hours in the *American Federationist* were either favorable or neutral; by 1910, only 17 percent were negative in tone. When the business cycle turned down, the craftsman discovered, the larger firms were slower to cut wages than were their smaller rivals. He was willing to trade the questionable benefits of competition for the stability that he now associated with the concentration movement.

As this change in attitude took place, the craftsman's attention also began to shift to a new range of industries. In the early 1900s he had associated big business for the most part with the same industries upon which the previous generation had concentrated: these included the railroads, tobacco manufacturing, and food processing. During the second phase of the progressive era, however, only the railroad remained among the leaders (see table 5-6). The other industries most prominent in his viewpoint were primary metals and petroleum refining. Here were the sort of industries that were least dependent upon skilled labor, but by the same token, the were the industries that could afford to offer their employees higher wage and other related benefits. By 1914 the laborer had only begun to work ou in his mind the implications this transition had for him and for his trade union. In the years ahead, a changing economy would continue to force him to take account of industries that were distinctly modern in their technology and that presented a unique situation to the craftsmen.

Even the midwestern farmer was influenced by his changing economic situation, although in his case the economic factors were tightly linked with politics. The most important turning point in his attitudes was not 1907 but 1911; with the passage in the previous year of the Mann-Elkins Act, the ICC seemed at last to have the statutory power that it needed to regulate the railroads. Events in the next four years—a period immortalized in the parity formula—bore out the accuracy of this appraisal.[76] While railroad rate: leveled off, farm income from corn and hogs increased.[77] Even when the gross income data (for corn and hogs) is converted to constant dollars, the years 1910-14 emerge as a period of unusual prosperity for the midwestern farmer.[78] Profits seem to have functioned as a positive sanction for political reform, abating the farmer's fears about the railroad combines and industrial monopolies that for so long had drawn his bitterest condemnation.

Farmers, professional men, and craftsmen were thus all touched by economic forces, but each in slightly different ways and with somewhat different results. For the southern farmer, a simple increase in income converted his assault on the trusts into praise of big business. The engineer worried about his income and job opportunities in the giant firm. Skilled craftsmen learned to associate the large corporation with stability of wages and hours, while the midwestern farmer's improved income acted as a complement to the political reforms that were decisive in reshaping his image of the corporation. In these several ways, economic forces worked to alter middle culture opinions about the giant firms that were coming to dominate America's industrial economy.

VIII. Intertwined with these economic developments were organizational phenomena that exerted an important influence upon middle-class attitudes. The engineer's response to large enterprise, for example, continued to be primarily a product of his professional associations—the ideology they proclaimed, the role concept they reinforced, the values they represented. Next to the actions of business itself, these professional organizations were the most important stimulus to discussions of the large corporation (table 5-4).[79] The organizations' programs and committee reports encompassed a wide range of technical subjects, from standard specifications for box cars to improvements in General Electric machines, from techniques for building concrete culverts to methods of testing steel pipes.[80] On occasion the topics were less technical, touching for instance on the general tendency of reform movements to be "carried to extremes" and on "the advantages of a general partnership and common co-operation" as a mode of "industrial organization."[81] In either case, however, the professional organizations charted a fixed course toward highly specific goals, avoided affective responses, and stressed material achievement to the exclusion of all other standards.

The engineer's emphasis on achievement and progress was reflected in what he considered the major problem of big business in the progressive era: inefficiency. In his profession there was a cycle of antitrust sentiment peaking around 1901 (figure 5–5); judging from the balance between positive and negative judgments of the trusts, this subdued wave of hostility did not begin to ebb until 1909. While the engineer was perturbed at this time by the "public service corporations," the single most prominent subject of debate was the efficiency, or lack of it, of the giant corporation.[82] Many railroads were unable to effectively handle the cars belonging to other lines. It was difficult to obtain "harmonious action on the part of the officers of the several roads," and since each insisted on using his own technique, the system militated against "exact uniformity in practice."[83] As a result, the service provided in the vital rail center of Chicago was lamentably poor. In a more general vein, the engineer condemned those "large corporations, in whose business something of the same inefficiency and red tape are to be found that are popularly supposed to belong only to government business."[84]

On the other side of the ledger, the engineer gave some large firms special accolades for "economical production" and "convenient adaptations of time and labor-saving devices." He complimented one such producer for pressing others to adopt similar techniques and thus working "a wonderful influence" that reverberated through the entire economy.[85] The engineer saw many examples of cost cutting techniques, innovations in plant layout, and successful administration, all of which deserved praise; and while these laudable practices overshadowed the instances of poor corporate management, he continued to debate the issue vigorously through the first decade of the twentieth century.

Professional interests dictated the focal points of the engineer's discussion and its outcome. He did not usually worry about inefficiency in all sectors of the economy, but concentrated on those industries and those specific companies giving him a job, selling him a product, or offering a technological or administrative technique he might adopt (table 5–4). He talked about railroads and urban transit systems, about steel mills, and about Westinghouse and General Electric. When he concluded that big business posed problems, he looked increasingly to self-reform for solutions. From 1880 through 1902, he had slowly changed his mind about whether the concentration movement presented a sufficient threat to justify some kind of

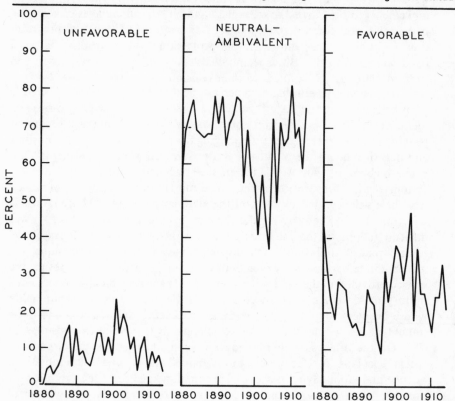

FIGURE 5-5. The engineer's evaluation of big business, 1880-1914. The annual per centages represent the proportion of items in *Engineering News* reflecting each attitude

public or private action; by 1902 he was more convinced than ever that something had to be done. But the "something" did not normally involve the federal or state governments; he gave far more emphasis to individual action by business itself. The efficiency dilemma would thus be resolved in a kind of bootstrap operation in which inefficient firms, perhaps with some gentle prodding from the engineering associations and journals, would mend their ways.

Around 1910 the engineer began to feel that self-reform had worked. Big business, he thought, could no longer be charged with inefficiency. Large firms were responding to the demands for standardization.[86] To the remaining critics of the corporation he now pointed out that "only operations on a large scale and backed by abundant capital can conserve raw material"; even the belabored railroads, he said, handled "a volume of traffic which would be impossible in any other country."[87] In cases where isolated examples of

SECOND GENERATION

unsystematic operations persisted, he was convinced that the firms involved were already taking steps to eliminate their problems. After 1911 he assumed that the country's great combines were the picture of industrial efficiency. The engineer's attitudes had stabilized. His new equilibrium was dictated primarily by his organizational context, and by the ideas emanating from both his professional associations and the great business bureaucracies which employed him.

TABLE 5-4. The engineer's image of big business, 1902-1914

Aspects of big business mentioned	1902-1908			1909-1914		
	High year	Low year	Mean	High year	Low year	Mean
Economic	100%	97%	98%	98%	94%	97%
Political	19	0	10	24	10	16
Social	0	0	0	2	0	less than 1

Leading characteristics of big business	1) Products or services 2) Management or ownership 3) Efficiency	1) Management or ownership 2) Products or services 3) Miscellaneous political activities
Leading industries mentioned	1) Railroad transportation (40) 2) Local passenger transportation (41) 3) Primary metals (33); Electrical machinery (36)	1) Railroad transportation (40) 2) Electric-gas-sanitary services (49) 3) Primary metals (33)
Leading firms mentioned	1) Pennsylvania Railroad 2) Westinghouse 3) General Electric	1) Pennsylvania Railroad 2) Baltimore & Ohio Railroad 3) Westinghouse

Leading sources of items on big business	1902-1914 1) Action taken by big business 2) Meetings and conventions 3) Letters to the editor
Leading solutions or responses[a]	1) Individual action (45%) 2) Federal action (26%) 3) State action (20%)

SOURCE: *Engineering News.* Similar data for previous periods are in tables 3-1 and 4-4.
[a] Comparable data for the years 1880-92 were: State action (31%); Federal action (29%); Individual action (27%). The leading solutions for 1893-1901 were: Individual action (34%); State action (33%); Federal action (23%).

THE PROGRESSIVE CYCLE, 1902-1914

IX. During these years a similar array of organizations began to develop in agriculture, particularly in the Midwest. They were not nearly as influential as reform politics, but they nevertheless had some impact on the farmer's opinion of big business. The most prominent of the new organizations, the county agent system, gave rise to the Farm Bureaus, which later formed the National Farm Bureau Federation.[88] Colleges and state universities also instituted new programs involving the farmer. All of these organizations stressed a new set of values and a new concept of the farmer's role in society. They emphasized the need for collective (as opposed to individual) action, for systematic and rational (as opposed to traditional) techniques, for a narrow and specific (as opposed to a diffuse) definition of the farmer's relationship to his environment. These institutions, their values, and their role concepts began to make themselves felt among midwestern farmers in the last few years of the progressive era. They complemented the political and economic forces already dissipating antitrust sentiment among corn belt farmers. In future years their relative influence was to grow and spread from the Midwest into the South and throughout the nation's agricultural regions.

X. For the skilled craftsman, organizational developments were the primary forces molding his opinion of big business. In his case organizational phenomena were closely intertwined with the economic factors we have previously discussed. On the eve of the progressive era, some skilled workers (represented in this sample by the readers of the *National Labor Tribune*) had been unable to create strong and lasting trade unions that could deal effectively with the country's largest firms. As a consequence, the worker had begun to shift some of his allegiance from his trade organization to the business itself, and by 1902 his new orientation and correspondingly new image of the large firm had stabilized. He continued to stress virtually the same aspects of big business that had occupied most of his attention before 1900 (compare table 5-5 in this chapter with table 4-5 in the previous chapter). He kept his eye fixed on the same basic industries. He talked most of the time about a few leading firms, either the companies he had concentrated on before the turn of the century or the combines that had absorbed them. His discussion of this subject was, as before, stimulated largely by the activities of the businesses involved or by articles appearing in other publications. In 1902, for example, these publications ranged from the *New York Journal of Commerce* to West Virginia's *Wheeling News* and back to the *Iron Trade Review*.[89]

From such sources, the craftsman sketched a portrait of big business drawn largely in neutral gray, with negative tones outweighing positive touches by an insignificant margin (figure 5-6). He had not entirely abandoned the mistrust of the corporation that had characterized the previous generation. The sore point was labor relations. The craftsman watched unhappily while the Amalgamated Association of Iron, Steel and Tin Workers bargained away its control over output per man in the tinplate industry; he condemned the blacklist, lockouts, and the use of scabs; he denounced George Baer, who led the employers in the anthracite strike of 1902, as one of the country's "incendiary labor baiters."[90] While there were occasions when the laborer saw "the men and management . . . dwelling in peace and harmony," he most often felt himself surrounded by "gigantic trusts which oppress labor."[91]

Most other characteristics of the corporation were, however, painted in more favorable hues. As we have already observed, the craftsman was impressed by corporate wage and hour policies, pleased with trust products and services, and complimentary about the quality of the nation's business leaders. Trust management, he said, took in men "who show brains and activity."[92]

He became less certain about the intelligence of the trust magnates when U.S. Steel and the other major firms in the iron and steel industry crushed the Amalgamated Association (1910) and, while proclaiming an "open shop," closed their doors to trade unionism.[93] In the aftermath of this strike the workers became as uncertain of themselves as did the *National Labor Tribune*. The trusts, preventing their employees from exercising their "lawful rights and privileges," posed a threat to American republican institutions.[94] On the other hand, there was "welcome news to the men" when large orders provided more jobs.[95] Deprived of strong union leadership and confronted by contradictory experiences, the worker was ambivalent about the trusts. Giant firms paid him well and then fired him when he got older; they alternately employed him and oppressed him. In the last years before the First World War, the laborer's image of the corporation was almost as unstable as it had been in the 1890s.

The AFL member had a different experience with trade unionism and, consequently, had a different opinion of the trusts. During approximately the same years in which the combination movement in industry reached its peak, Federation unions were gathering in hundreds of thousands of new supporters. Total 1897 membership has been estimated at 272,100; by 1904, affiliated unions included 1,681,800 workers.[96] This phenomenal expansion put the Federation in a more secure position; its leaders could at last worry less about survival and more about achieving the organization's material goals. The increase in membership and in bargaining power was an essential precondition of the attitudinal changes that took place in the following years (see figure 5-7).

Before a process of accommodation could begin, however, big business had to justify itself to the worker in certain specific ways. Corporate wage and hour schedules and labor relations policies headed the list. Union-

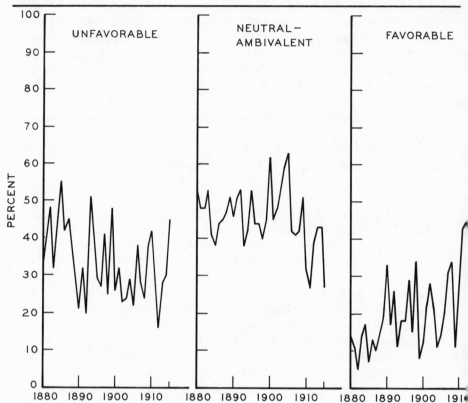

FIGURE 5-6. The skilled worker's evaluation of big business, 1880-1915. The annual percentages represent the proportion of items in *National Labor Tribune* reflecting each attitude.

corporate relationships were to the AFL member the salient aspect of the large company; he knew that as an individual he was powerless to deal with the corporation, and he felt that neither federal nor state governments would provide him with a first line of resistance (table 5–6). He almost invariably looked to his trade union and its direct dealings with business as the best means of improving corporate labor relations. Improvement was needed, and through 1906 he had little that was positive to say on this subject. The craftsman complained when giant firms refused to bargain with the unions or dealt unfairly with union members. But after 1906, his attitude began to mellow. From 1909 through 1913, in fact, there was no single year in which negative remarks in *American Federationist* outweighed the combined total of favorable and neutral references to labor relations. Although he was still quick to criticize business resistance to union demands, the worker found more and more instances in which large employers were meeting his

SECOND GENERATION

needs, compromising after disagreements arose, and even negotiating in good faith.[97] After one railroad began to deal with the union, he cheerily reported from Virginia that "everything is working in harmony, and the men are endeavoring to prove daily that unionism is good for the employer as well as the men."[98]

The development of two prominent secondary organizations that advocated extreme positions on organized labor probably encouraged the

TABLE 5-5. The skilled worker's image of big business, 1902-1915

Aspects of big business mentioned	1902-1908			1909-1915		
	High year	Low year	Mean	High year	Low year	Mean
Economic	100%	92%	96%	100%	87%	94%
Political	18	0	8	45	10	20
Social	2	0	1	14	0	6
Leading characteristics of big business	1) Labor relations 2) Wages and hours 3) Management or ownership			1) Labor relations 2) Wages and hours 3) Products or services		
Leading industries mentioned	1) Primary metals (33) 2) Railroad transportation (40) 3) Coal mining (11-12)			1) Primary metals (33) 2) Railroad transportation (40) 3) Coal mining (11-12)		
Leading firms mentioned	1) U.S. Steel 2) Republic Iron & Steel 3) Carnegie Iron & Steel[a]			1) U.S. Steel 2) Republic Iron & Steel 3) Carnegie Iron & Steel		
Leading sources of items on big business	1902-1915 1) Action taken by big business 2) Other publications 3) Action taken by labor					
Leading solutions or responses[b]	1) Private collective action (46%) 2) Federal action (30%) 3) State action (11%)					

SOURCE: *National Labor Tribune*. Similar data for previous periods are in tables 3-5 and 4-5.

[a] In this and a few other instances in which a company was absorbed in a merger but clearly retained its separate identity, we continued to list the firm under its established name.

[b] Comparable data for the years 1880-92 were: Private collective action (45%); Federal action (24%); State action (14%). Leading solutions for the period 1893-1901 were: Private collective action (47%); Federal action (28%); State action (14%).

THE PROGRESSIVE CYCLE, 1902-1914

FIGURE 5-7. The AFL's evaluation of big business, 1894-1914. The annual percentages represent the proportion of items in *American Federationist* reflecting each attitude.

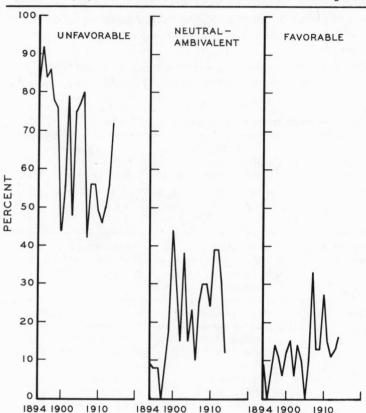

AFL member to favor large over small businesses. The National Association of Manufacturers, speaking mainly for small and middle-sized businesses, enjoyed a substantial increase in strength after 1903, when the association began to crusade against organized labor. It soon became the leading national spokesman against unions.[99] At the other pole stood the National Civic Federation, speaking the language of compromise and "convinced that modern industry needed organized labor if serious social tensions were to be averted."[100] Composed primarily of businessmen associated with large corporations, the Civic Federation received notable support from conservative trade unions like the AFL, whose president in fact was a prominent member.[101] These two secondary organizations worked like a carrot and a stick, the Civic Federation tugging and NAM driving the union member toward conciliation with corporate bigness.

SECOND GENERATION

More important, however, was the actual performance of the large firm. No amount of persuasive rhetoric, even from the Civic Federation, could offset the impression the union man received from his daily experience with big business. Greatly broadening that experience was the information flowing into the Federation headquarters and into the pages of the union paper from a network of organizers spread from Connecticut to California, from Michigan to Texas; they tersely reported what was happening

TABLE 5-6. The AFL's image of big business, 1902-1914

Aspects of big business mentioned	1902-1908			1909-1914		
	High year	Low year	Mean	High year	Low year	Mean
Economic	100%	90%	96%	100%	85%	94%
Political	30	0	16	33	17	27
Social	0	0	0	6	0	2
Leading characteristics of big business	1) Labor relations 2) Wages and hours 3) Existence or expansion			1) Labor relations 2) Wages and hours 3) Existence or expansion; Diminishes individual's opportunities		
Leading industries mentioned	1) Railroad transportation (40) 2) Tobacco manufacturing (21) 3) Food processing (20)			1) Railroad transportation (40) 2) Primary metals (33) 3) Petroleum refining (29)		
Leading firms mentioned	1) American Tobacco 2) National Biscuit 3) Continental Tobacco			1) Standard Oil 2) Southern Railroad 3) Pennsylvania Railroad		
Leading sources of items on big business	1902-1914 1) Letters to the editor[a] 2) Action taken by labor 3) Other publications					
Leading solutions or responses[b]	1902-1908 1) Private collective action (79%) 2) Federal action (15%) 3) State action (5%)			1909-1914 1) Private collective action (63%) 2) Federal action (27%) 3) State action (9%)		

SOURCE: *American Federationist.* Similar data for the previous period are in table 4-6.
[a]Most of these letters were organizer's reports from the field.
[b]Comparable figures for the years 1894-1901 were: Private collective action (68%); Federal action (22%); State action (4%).

THE PROGRESSIVE CYCLE, 1902-1914

to the union in their locale, and their letters constituted the skilled workman's single most important source of information on the large firm (table 5–6). Reading the *American Federationist*, he learned that "the new steel bridge for the Southern Pacific Railroad will be constructed by union labor"; then, stifling his optimism, came a report that in New York organized labor was "apathetic in the railroad shops," while in Michigan boilermakers had still not won a strike that had lasted for a full three years.[102] The record of union-corporation relations in the progressive era was checkered with this sort of contradictory information.

As a result, in the years immediately preceding the First World War the skilled craftsman in the AFL was less upset with big business than he had been in the nineties but more hostile than were either farmers or professional men. He still saw very little in the world of corporate giants to elicit his unqualified approval. When a recession in 1913–14 hardened management resistance to union demands, his anger quickly mounted. He saw armed force used to break the streetcar strikes in New York and Indianapolis; he saw "corporation government" in Colorado placing the state militia at the beck and call of Standard Oil.[103] What resulted was a substantial degree of disequilibrium and renewed hostility, as the worker felt pressure from the "greedy, conscienceless trusts" on one side and from a rival labor organization, the Industrial Workers of the World, on the other.[104]

XI. The IWW member viewed America's prewar industrial society from a radically different organizational and ideological position, and his image of big business should help to put into perspective the trade unionist's attitudes and opinions in the rest of the middle cultures. The socialist worker saw virtually nothing that could win his approval in the behavior of the large corporation (figure 5–8). During the years 1910 through 1914, only 5 percent of the articles in *Solidarity* were favorable to big business; and while a slightly higher percentage (13%) were neutral, most treated the trusts with an antipathy matched only by the hatred directed at "Gompers and his crowd."[105] Karl Marx had clearly labeled capitalistic combines, themselves the inevitable product of industrialization, as the most formidable enemy of the proletariat, and America's experience seemed to confirm the Marxian vision. What else could the radical worker conclude when he surveyed the performance of "the powerful, unscrupulous and merciless steel trust," or the "meager earnings" of the coal workers, or "the growing army of unemployed"?[106]

Over the long run the radical worker's image of the trusts was almost as stable as the engineer's despite the fact that the IWW was in a far less secure position than the engineering associations.[107] In a sense, this comparison is unfair because the radical worker's organizational context actually reached far beyond the IWW and its immediate national environment to encompass a worldwide socialist movement. This movement, with its roots spread widely and deeply in the Western industrial nations, buttressed an ideology powerful enough itself to make up for some of the shortcomings of the Industrial Workers of the World. While the IWW was as flimsy as the radical farm organizations of the 1890s, the laborer had in Marxism the sort of intellectual framework that the agrarian radicals had never been able to develop. Such ideology insulated the socialist from many of the forces that were reshaping trade union opinions in the progressive era.

Too much should not be made, however, of the contrast between the craft unionist and the radical laborer. Labor historians, especially those in the Commons school of interpretation, have taken great pains to explain why American labor rejected socialism and embraced the pragmatic, craft-oriented philosophy of the AFL.[108] More recently, students of consensus have stressed anew the un-American character of socialism and the delusions of its economic diagnosis.[109] While some scholars have sympathized with the IWW, even friendly historians have acknowledged the wide gulf that existed between the class-conscious radicals and middle-class Americans.[110]

The data from this study suggests, however, that on the trust question one could easily exaggerate the distance between the radical worker and the middle class, including the trade unionists perched in its lower echelons. As far as this single issue was concerned, one cannot help but be impressed by the similarities between the IWW's view and that of the more conservative unions. While the radical looked on the trusts with great disfavor, his hostility was almost matched by that of the Federation craftsman in the years 1894 through 1906. Similarities outweigh differences in the characteristics of the trusts that the two groups stressed (compare table 5–7 with tables 5–5 and 5–6). While the socialist was more worried about the general aspects of corporate economic power than was the AFL member, this problem was one that the *National Labor Tribune* had brought up repeatedly during the great merger movement at the turn of the century. The radical was perturbed about much the same industries as was the skilled laborer, although the socialist tended not to focus as much of his attention on one industry as did the conservative unionist. The firms mentioned most often by these two laborers were virtually the same, and both emphasized support for the union as the best solution to the trust problem. In the radical's case, of course, that solution meant the hope of a socialist future, but in the pages of *Solidarity*, and in *American Federationist* as well, there was much more consideration of means than ends, of the intermediate objective of strengthening the organization for its next battle with the trusts.

One might well argue that my content analysis technique is simply too crude to catch the vital differences between radicals and conservatives, but even after taking this limitation into account there seem to be grounds for

THE PROGRESSIVE CYCLE, 1902-1914

FIGURE 5-8. The radical worker's evaluation of big business, 1910-1914. The annual percentages represent the proportion of items in *Solidarity* reflecting each attitude.

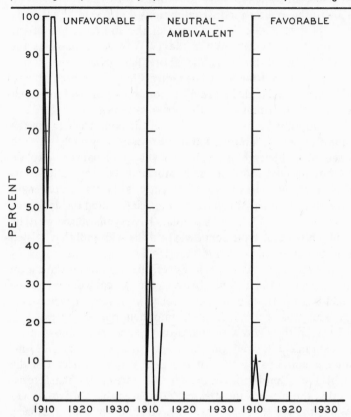

concluding that historians have stressed unduly the differences between these two groups. Viewed from outside the restrictive Commons school of interpretation, the two images of the corporation appear to be more alike than different. This is especially true if one compares the socialist attitudes of 1910–14 with those of the AFL craft unionist in the years 1894–1906. This comparison suggests that the spirit of radicalism was stronger in the AFL than either its contemporary leaders or subsequent historians have wanted to admit.

Insofar as the trust question was concerned, socialists were on the edge of, but not outside, the mainstream of America's middle cultures. Socialism offered an alternative that, with some tailoring and cosmetic work, might well have gathered strong support in the middle class, especially during the years 1893–1910. A full analysis of the failure to reap this harvest would

SECOND GENERATION

150

carry us too far afield, but we can see at least one problem that the socialist faced. For some groups the major phenomena shaping attitudes were political; for others, they were economic; for still others, organizational and social variables were extremely influential. What was needed in this situation were vague, many-faceted organizations, political ideologies, and symbols. The socialist offered instead a logical, clear, and, by its own definition, complete ideology and supporting cast of organizations, a combination which failed to capitalize on the widespread animosity produced by the rise of the trusts. After 1910, as antitrust sentiment declined, the radical was faced with a harsh choice: he could either adjust his ideology to fit this new situation or lose the opportunity to gain wider support—at least in the foreseeable future. As this study indicates, the radical worker preserved intact the Marxist system, leaving most Americans to settle their differences with big business in a more conservative way.

TABLE 5-7. The radical worker's image of big business, 1910-1914

Aspects of big business mentioned	1910–1914		
	High year	Low year	Mean
Economic	100%	86%	93%
Political	38	11	25
Social	7	0	3

Leading characteristics of big business	1) Labor relations 2) Wages and hours 3) General economic power
Leading industries mentioned	1) Primary metals (33) 2) Railroad transportation (40) 3) Food processing (20)
Leading firms mentioned	1) U.S. Steel 2) Southern Pacific Railroad; Carnegie Iron & Steel[a]; American Tobacco
Leading sources of items on big business	1) Other publications 2) Action taken by labor 3) Meetings and conventions
Leading solutions or responses	1) Private collective action (88%) 2) Federal action (8%) 3) State action (3%)

SOURCE: *Solidarity*.
[a] In this and a few other instances in which a company was absorbed in a merger but clearly retained its separate identity, we continued to list the firm under its established name.

THE PROGRESSIVE CYCLE, 1902-1914

XII. In the progressive period, social variables were less influential than political, organizational, or economic forces, but social factors nonetheless had a manifest impact upon attitudes toward the trusts. A sense of social class had a significant effect upon opinions in two of the occupational groups. Among the clergy and the engineers, both of whom were professional men in the upper range of the middle classes, attitudinal changes followed a distinctive pattern. Our concern here is with the relationship between favorable and unfavorable imagery over time. In both groups a cycle of increasing hostility toward big business was accompanied by a rise in the percentage of favorable opinions (figure 5-9). Among engineers and the clergy as well, this process of polarization began in the mid-nineties and extended through the early years of the progressive era. The groups were debating with themselves

FIGURE 5-9. **Professional men's evaluations of big business, 1890-1910.** The annual percentages represent the proportion of items in *Engineering News* and *Congregationalist* reflecting each attitude.

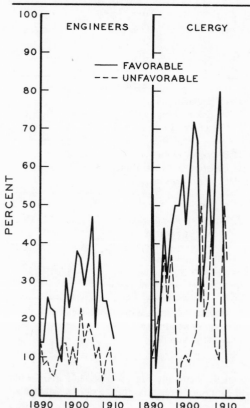

SECOND GENERATION

the merits of the new order of large-scale organizations, were finding every day more problems upon which to ruminate, but were at the same time finding even more merits in the corporation to satisfy their sense of class alignment with big business and its leaders. In their initial stages the two debates were similar, but they had markedly different results. The engineer resolved in favor of the large firm while the clergyman turned against his own social class and came down on the side of the social gospel. Whatever the outcome, the pattern of polarization which characterized the professional men was unique to their strata of the middle cultures and was, I think, a distinctively upper-middle-class phenomenon.

Changes in social values also had a visible impact upon the attitudes of most middle-class Americans. As bureaucracy spread, more and more people became enamored of rationalization, system, and control; the traditional emphasis on individualism and competition began to wane. Frequently the new values were reflected in a desire to emulate the large business corporation. The Congregational minister recognized that "in an age when tests of efficiency are being applied to many industrial enterprises it is not surprising but rather to be expected that organized Christianity should be subjected to similar scrutiny."[111] He acknowledged that "the trend of the time is away from independence and toward centralization, union and federation."[112] Similar sentiments were expressed by farmers and by organized laborers, as they too found values attuned to the organizational revolution increasingly attractive.

One product of these values and their related corporate culture was a new way of talking about large-scale organizations, including those in business. During the progressive era, the language of antitrust changed significantly. In the 1880s and 1890s, middle-class Americans had frequently expressed their ideas about big business in emotion-laden, affective language (see figure 5–10 and table 5–8). The midwestern farmer claimed the trusts were "oppressive," "extortionate," and "tyrannical."[113] The laborer condemned the "damnable Pinkerton system" employed by the "plutocracy" and described the businessman as a "modern savage" and a "robber baron." Even *Congregationalist* frequently called upon strong pejoratives to express its distaste for the tycoons and their trusts. In the early twentieth century, however, the language of antitrust began to mellow. Such labels as *octopus, hog*, and *outlaw* were traded in for neutral expressions: *firm, company*, or *business*. In each group the watershed came at a slightly different time. For midwestern farmers the peak use of pejoratives came in 1899, and a decisive transformation in the style of language began in 1913; for the AFL the two comparable dates were 1903 and 1912; in *National Labor Tribune* they were 1908 and 1912; in *Congregationalist*, 1901 and 1913. Between 1899 and 1913, then, the basic mode of talking and thinking about large-scale organizations shifted as affective language gave way before a new and more neutral style of

THE PROGRESSIVE CYCLE, 1902–1914

discourse. In a sense, all of the groups became more like the engineers had been since 1880. The new language reflected, I think, a broad transition in values—a transformation sometimes linked to politics (as with the clergy) but more often related to organizational developments themselves. This shift in culture cut across class lines and in the long run had the effect of dampening antitrust sentiment. While Americans dreaded the "octopus" and hated the "robber baron," they were inclined to be less intense—even when they expressed disfavor—about the corporation and the corporate executive.

The new cultural setting thus had effects similar to those of reform politics. As liberal historians have claimed, however, political factors were the most influential determinants of attitude in the years 1902–14. The clergyman and the midwestern farmer were especially responsive to political leadership and increasingly interested in governmental solutions to

FIGURE 5-10. Percentage of pejoratives used in reference to big business, 1879-1914. See table 5-8.

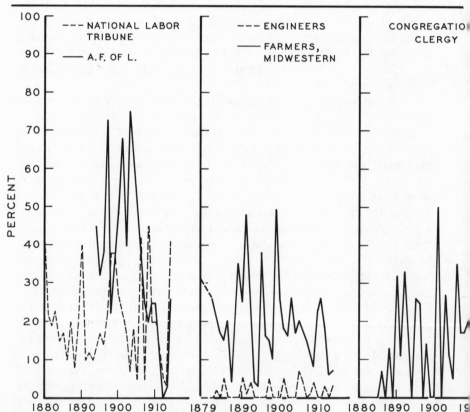

SECOND GENERATION

TABLE 5-8. Percentage of pejoratives used in reference to big business, 1879-1914

Year	Farmers,[a] Midwest	Laborers, National Labor Tribune	Laborers, AFL	Congregational clergy	Engineers
1879	31				
1880		43		0	0
1881		22		0	0
1882	26	19		0	0
1883	21	23		0	2
1884	17	15		0	0
1885	15	17		0	5
1886	20	10		7	0
1887	4	20		0	0
1888	23	8		13	0
1889	35	19		0	0
1890	25	40		32	5
1891	48	10		11	1
1892	24	12		33	4
1893	4	10		20	0
1894	3	14	45	0	0
1895	38	17	32	26	0
1896	16	14	38	25	0
1897	15	22	73	0	5
1898	10	38	22	14	0
1899	49	38	37	0	0
1900	26	27	48	0	0
1901	18	23	68	50	5
1902	16	17	40	0	0
1903	26	7	75	27	0
1904	17	18	64	11	0
1905	20	5	50	5	7
1906	17	42	40	35	4
1907	15	5	25	17	0
1908	11	45	20	17	1
1909	8	20	25	20	4
1910	23	20	25	24	0
1911	26	16	11	30	0
1912	18	5	0	27	3
1913	6	3	3	0	0
1914	7	41	26	7	3

NOTE: We recorded the various nouns (other than proper names) that the journals used to refer to big business; these were then classified as either manifestly pejorative (e.g., "hog") or nonpejorative (e.g., "firm").

[a]Because of mistakes made in scoring some of the data from the early issues of the southern farm journals, we did not use the figures from that group. No issues were available for 1880-81.

THE PROGRESSIVE CYCLE, 1902-1914

the trust problem. For both the minister and the farmer, progressivism was an unsettling force at first generating animosity toward the corporation and then offering governmental policies which made for accommodation and a new equilibrium. The political system affected, to a greater or lesser degree, all of the other occupational groups as well. Ranking next to politics as a potent force was organizational change, followed by economic and social factors; together, they eased relations between the large corporation and middle-class America. After 1914, the war in Europe introduced new conditions, and our task in the following chapter is to determine how America's first experience in a modern, international struggle influenced the public image of big business and the emerging corporate culture.

6

WAR AND THE CORPORATE CULTURE, 1915-1919

The long-run process of accommodation between the corporation and middle-class America, a process that had begun in the nineties and continued in a different form through the progressive years, entered a third phase in 1915 when the war in Europe made itself felt in the United States. By this time war had become one of the decisive forces shaping the development of societies. Its impact had been more limited in pre-industrial economies, when armies were smaller and weapons less devastating, when the durable patterns of agrarian life had protected the major interests of a large part of society against everything except the immediate presence of soldiers, friendly or hostile. Such protection had been lost when improved communications and transportation systems made industry, commerce, and even agriculture interdependent and increasingly sensitive to changes in international relations. The advent of total war, advanced weaponry, and propaganda campaigns completed this transformation, assuring that all would share in some way the dubious experiences of modern warfare.

For the United States, World War I was the first foreign struggle of modern proportions, and long before America entered the war it impinged on national politics. Questions of neutrality and preparedness shoved reform into the background; in the presidential election of 1916, for instance, the war and American relations with the belligerents were central issues of the campaign.[1] As historians later observed, the progressive movement was on the wane before August, 1914, but the hostilities in Europe made the decline in reform activity all the more rapid.[2] Woodrow Wilson explained in 1917: "When a war got going, it was just a war and there weren't two kinds of it. It required illiberalism at home to reinforce the men at the front."[3]

Once the United States abandoned neutrality, the political repercussions were immediate and significant. Power flowed from the individual to the government, from the state capitals to Washington, from the legislative and judicial branches to the office of the president. The chief executive had at his command all of the potent symbols of nationalism. With national security at stake, he could wield power in ways that would have been unthinkable before 1917.[4] Wilson mobilized the national economy even though he had no clearly legislated authority to do so. The entire system of priorities worked out to ensure that the country's war needs would be met rested on a questionable legal foundation.[5] Throughout the war, the federal executive branch methodically encroached upon civil liberties without arousing the serious resistance of either the judiciary or the national legislature.[6]

The economic repercussions of the war were of similar import, and they too were evident long before April, 1917. In 1913 and 1914 the national economy had slumped into a recession, with many manufacturing industries on reduced schedules. Unemployment was higher; the stock market lower.[7] President Wilson and his advisers were necessarily concerned, and they were searching for a solution to the nation's economic problems when the war provided an answer. After some months of hesitation, the economy began to respond to a rush of war orders and to the new markets opened for American producers when European suppliers abandoned their overseas outlets. In 1916 exports of American merchandise went up by 16 percent and in the following year by 100 percent.[8] By the fall of 1915 recovery was complete. The economy boomed as orders poured in for both agricultural commodities and manufactured goods. These favorable conditions continued through 1916 and the first part of 1917, as Americans discovered (as they had many times before) that neutrality could be a very profitable business.

After April, 1917, business conditions in America remained good, despite the fact that inflation and new taxes soaked up a significant portion of the profits and higher personal incomes of the war economy. Gross farm income in the Midwest and the South soared to record highs in 1918 and 1919 respectively, and even discounting for inflation, both farmers and munitions makers clearly found that war offered even greater economic opportunities than had neutrality.[9] With four million men in uniform and labor in short supply, workers in manufacturing and construction, in transportation and in mining, also received fatter paychecks in 1918. While they suffered more from inflation than did the farmers, laborers could hardly complain that the war imposed hardships upon them.[10]

Changes in the government and economy called for new patterns of organized behavior in America. Before April, 1917, the prewar trends in organizational development continued largely undisturbed. While labor unions and some businesses grew stronger, the fundamental structure of the primary and secondary bureaucracies and their relative degrees of power remained unchanged until the United States entered the war. At that point, however, the need to mobilize the economy as well as the armed services created a wild flurry of experiments in organization on a national scale.[11] In its early stages, the centralization of control was more apparent than real. As enthusiastic mobilizers gathered in the capital, they formed a variety of overlapping and often conflicting committees—groups that had more energy

SECOND GENERATION

than information, more patriotism than power. The government added to the confusion by forming its own haphazard network of agencies, committees, and councils without adopting any overall plan to match authority with responsibility and keep these several organizations from competing for the money, men, and materials they all needed to achieve their goals. To a considerable extent the executive branch staffed its new array of agencies by recruiting business leaders, and this too impeded the centralization of power. The corporation executives frequently found it difficult to adjust to their new situation, accustomed as they were to private, not public, decision making. They instinctively respected the prerogatives of the primary, corporate bureaucracies, even though they were now working on behalf of central, coordinating organizations. They talked about productivity for the public good, but private profits seemed to loom very large in their plans. This system was ripe with opportunities for conflicts of interest, and there was every reason for the public to be uneasy about what was happening in the wartime economic program.

It was some months before the mobilization plan became less chaotic and power began to collect in the War Industries Board (WIB). Even then, thoroughgoing centralization was not achieved. What emerged under Bernard Baruch's leadership was de facto decentralization, a system that helped to coordinate the activities of the primary organizations without actually depriving them of much of their power. The Emergency Fleet Corporation achieved a similar *modus operandi*, and while some of the wartime bureaucracies were apparently more effective in bringing private organizations to heel, the most common pattern was the one followed by the WIB.

When the government introduced these innovations in Washington, it allowed the antitrust policy to lapse. The Wilson administration sought to promote production, not to prevent concentration.[12] The relaxation of federal restraints, combined with favorable conditions in the stock market, brought about a new wave of industrial mergers. This particular cycle in the concentration movement was not nearly as impressive as the one at the turn of the century, but in 1917-19 over 400 separate firms disappeared by way of mergers. Some of the largest consolidations since the formation of U.S. Steel were consummated. These mergers included the creation of Union Carbide and Carbon and the Allied Chemical and Dye Company (both capitalized at 283 million dollars).[13] Like the mobilization program, the merger movement provided cause for renewed concern about big business.

In the view of some historians, the war represented a cultural as well as an organizational watershed in the American past. Most scholars have agreed that an extensive effort was made to mobilize national emotions. To American political leaders it seemed necessary to justify participation in the struggle and to encourage sacrifices for the war effort. They systematically invoked the ideology and symbols of nationalism in order to instill discipline and suppress dissent. They had barely achieved their goal of a nationalistic mood or temper, however, by the time of the Armistice; and in the aftermath of war Americans became disillusioned with peacemaking. The result—according to some historians—was a significant cultural transition; in their opinion, the social trauma produced by the war and the postwar settlement created a watershed between the cultures of nineteenth-century and modern America.[14]

The years 1915–19 were, it would seem, filled with far-reaching changes in American society—changes that must surely have influenced middle-class attitudes toward the large firm. The task here is to measure the shifts that took place in group images and to sort out the relative effects of those organizational, political, social, and economic forces shaping middle-class concepts of the corporation.

II.   In the midst of a national emergency, many are likely to forget that war in its modern form is preeminently an economic phenomenon. One can take this position without acceding to the analysts who have pictured war as a product of greedy munitions makers or accepting the conclusions of the far more sophisticated Marxists who see imperialistic struggles as a necessary by-product of a maturing capitalistic system. I only wish to suggest that the power to wage war is directly proportional to the level of a nation's economic development and that a major war influences every sector of a modern economy. Thus, the middle-class groups that were primarily interest-oriented in the progressive years were most likely to develop new opinions of the large firm after 1914, and the major factors producing this change were almost certain to be economic.

The cotton farmer occupied a prominent position in this wing of the middle cultures. On the eve of the war he was already convinced that big business provided him with needed products and services at a reasonable price.[15] Prosperity had killed the antitrust movement in his part of the country. While the war at first left the market for his staple in disarray, conditions soon improved, and he saw little reason to attack the trusts for their sometimes suspicious financial manipulations or their tendency to give some customers better prices than others (figure 6–1). Instead, he talked about the contribution of the railroads to the developing regional economy, about the quality of corporate products, about the manner in which big business opened new opportunities for him.[16] The railroads hired "highly trained specialists," some of whom spent all of their time helping southern farmers diversify their crops.[17] Even top management came in for some kind words as the farmer praised the "men with sufficient force and initiative to operate such great enterprises."[18]

SECOND GENERATION

By this time the cotton planter seldom had an unkind word for the trusts, and both qualitative and quantitative data point to income as the chief determinant of the new agrarian mood. The correlation between real income (gross) and unfavorable opinions was even higher (-.68) for the war years than it had been before 1915.[19] Furthermore, the farmer kept his eyes fixed on subjects of immediate economic concern (see table 6-1). He was particularly interested in four industries: railroads, fertilizers (chemicals), automobiles, and meat packing (food processing). The two specific firms he mentioned most often were Swift and Company, which bought his livestock, and the Ford Motor Company, which sold him his car and his tractor. He

TABLE 6-1. The southern farmer's image of big business, 1915-1919

Aspects of big business mentioned[a]	High year	1915-1919 Low year	Mean[b]
Economic	100%	94%	99%
Political	18	0	6
Social	0	0	0

Leading characteristics of big business	1) Products or services 2) Prices 3) Management or ownership
Leading industries mentioned	1) Railroad transportation (40)[c] 2) Chemicals (28); Transportation equipment (37)
Leading firms mentioned	1) Swift 2) Ford 3) Central of Georgia Railroad
Leading sources of items on big business	1) Letters to the editor 2) Meetings and conventions; Action taken by big business
Leading solutions or reponses	1) Private collective action (60%) 2) Individual action (30%) 3) Federal action[d] (10%)

SOURCE: *Southern Cultivator*. For an explanation of my methodology, see chapter 2. Similar data for the previous periods are in tables 3-3, 4-2, and 5-3.
NOTE: If multiple entries follow one number, the categories were tied.
[a]These figures show what percentage of the articles mentioned each aspect; the columns can total more than 100% because a single article could mention one, two, or all three.
[b]Mean of the annual percentages.
[c]The number appearing after each industry indicates its two-digit group in the *Standard Industrial Classification Manual*.
[d]Also includes general references to an unspecified governmental response or solution.

WAR AND THE CORPORATE CULTURE, 1915-1919

FIGURE 6-1. **The southern farmer's evaluation of big business, 1879–1919.** The annual percentages represent the proportion of items in *Southern Cultivator* reflecting each attitude. For an explanation of my methodology, see chapter 2.

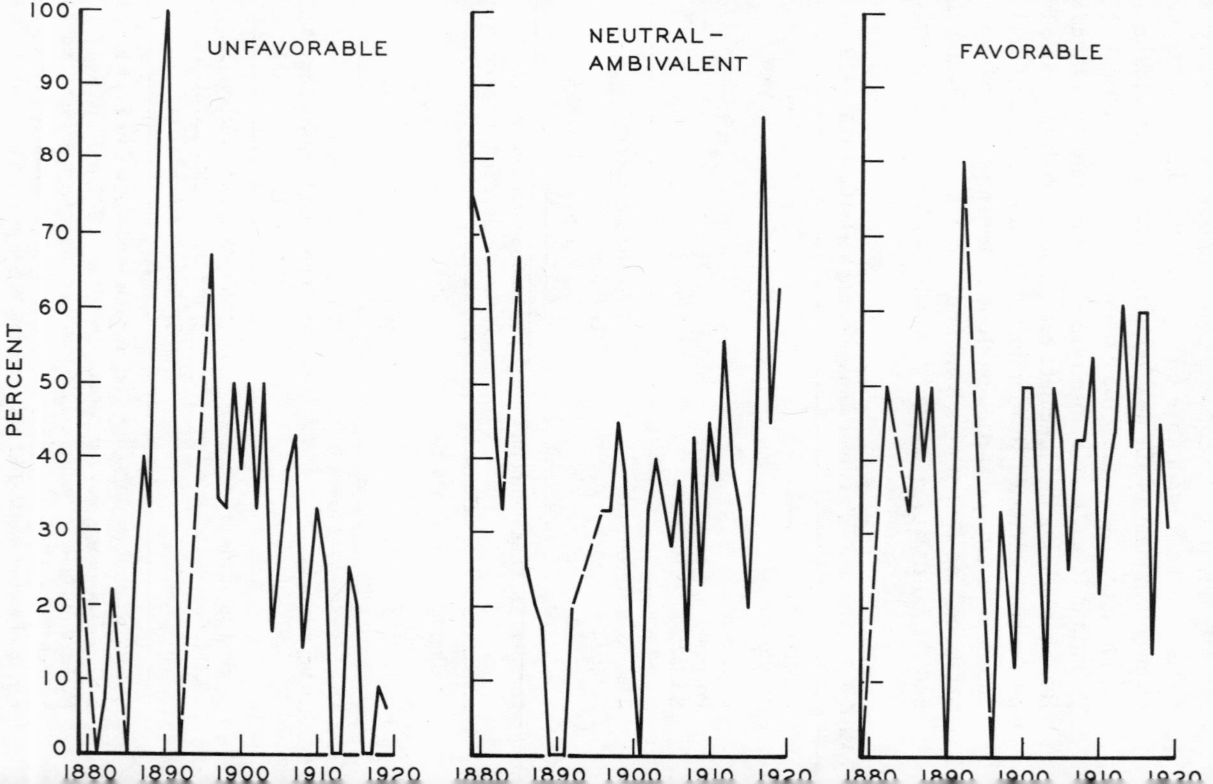

approved of these companies and of big business in general, and his outlook was stabilized by the millions of dollars of additional income flowing into the southern farm country as a result of the war (see Appendix).

In 1915-16 the skilled laborer's view of the trusts also mellowed as his economic situation improved. Those readers who habitually remember batting averages should have tucked in their minds the fact that the correlations between income and attitude were not significant for this group during the progressive era.[20] For the years 1915-19, however, the correlation between income (in both current and constant dollars) and negative attitudes toward the giant firm was unusually high.[21] Our content analysis data on the major characteristics of the skilled worker's image of the corporation lend further support to the conclusion these statistics suggest. Wages and hours (table 6-2) in particular aroused the craftsman's approval in 1915 and 1916. While he witnessed some examples of companies granting the "union shop . . . without a strike," he found many more instances in which large firms yielded quickly to requests for "an increase in wages."[22] Even Standard Oil (of California) garnered his affection when the combine "raised wages 10 per cent without any request from its employees."[23] By 1916, in fact, the worker was so pleased with his paychecks that he actually had more praise than criticism to bestow on the large corporation for the first time since 1894 (figure 6-2).

The laborer's new perspective on the trusts had not filtered down to him from the top leaders of the union. In 1915 and 1916, the editorials in *American Federationist* continued to lash out at the "ruthless, exploiting corporations," but a contradictory view of corporate wages and hours, labor-management relations, and new jobs came from the lower echelons of the union, from the organizer in the field.[24] He saw firsthand the favorable results of the war economy and passed the news back to union headquarters. He had little to say about subjects such as business-government relations; but in 1915-16 he was favorably impressed with the jobs union men were offered and the wages they received, and he continued to laud these aspects of the corporation after America entered the war.

Though not as directly and decisively influenced by economic factors, midwestern farmers clearly responded to the changes taking place in their own wartime balance sheets. When the war began, the midwestern farm region was already prosperous; so much so, in fact, that the editor of *Wallaces' Farmer* urged the corn and hog man to combat the recession confronting the rest of the country with a farm spending program. Difficult as it is for us to imagine, the farmer felt that he was better off than most people: "If every farm family in the United States [he was told] would buy even ten dollars worth of household articles, outside of their immediate necessities, . . . and would pay cash for the purchase, it would stimulate business over the entire country."[25] In the following months, war-induced

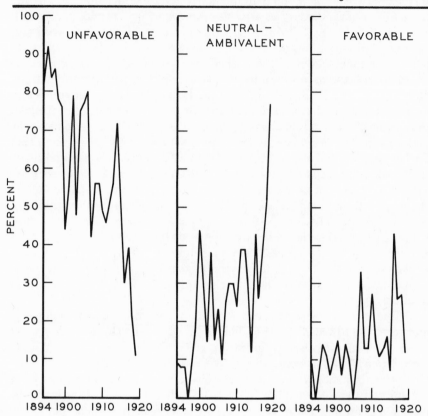

economic recovery alleviated any need for an agrarian spending program, and the corn and hog farmer, along with others, found his favorable situation growing even better. He began to worry less about the trusts and to propose fewer solutions to the problems stemming from the concentration movement.[26] When he did think about big business, it was in increasingly positive terms. Railroads encouraged truck farming, he noted, and thus boosted the price of his land.[27] Even the big packers came in for some praise: "What . . . would happen to the price of hogs," he asked, "if we did not have great packing plants, which were able to take the heavy runs which come during the fall and winter season, cure the meat and hold it, to be used during the time of scant marketing?"[28] Matched against these friendly observations were a variety of criticisms: he felt, for example, that "the motive that led Germany to break her treaty with other nations in behalf of poor Belgium is the same spirit as that which leads trusts to wipe out

SECOND GENERATION

rivals."[29] But by 1916 his evaluation of the prices, financial operations, and management of big business had all changed for the better. Income was not the major variable shaping his attitudes through the entire war period, but it was an important factor making for accommodation between the farmer and the giant firm.[30]

Among farmers and skilled craftsmen the profits of war thus eased relations with the large firm. In each case opinions changed in much the same way as they had prior to 1915. Southern farmers reacted to higher income, pure and simple. In the Midwest, income was of secondary importance, but its influence could nonetheless be recognized in 1915 and 1916, when it worked in tandem with political developments—just as it had before the war. Among organized laborers, too, higher real wages reduced animosity toward the trusts. For these middle-class Americans the patterns and the processes of attitudinal change were much the same in the prewar and war years, but of course the economic forces at work were substantially more potent in 1915-16 than they had been in the progressive era.

TABLE 6-2. The AFL's image of big business, 1915-1919

Aspects of big business mentioned	1915-1919 High year	1915-1919 Low year	Mean
Economic	100%	100%	100%
Political	28	8	14
Social	0	0	0

Leading characteristics of big business	1) Labor relations 2) Wages and hours 3) Existence or expansion
Leading industries mentioned	1) Railroad transportation (40) 2) Coal mining (11-12); Petroleum refining (29); Primary metals (33); Transportation equipment (37)
Leading firms mentioned	1) Standard Oil 2) Wabash Railroad; Pennsylvania Railroad
Leading sources of items on big business	1) Letters to the editor 2) Action taken by labor 3) Federal executive action
Leading solutions or responses	1) Private collective action (77%) 2) Federal action (15%) 3) State action (5%)

SOURCE: *American Federationist*. Similar data for the previous periods are in tables 4-6, and 5-6.

WAR AND THE CORPORATE CULTURE, 1915-1919

III. The first middle-class Americans to feel the political impact of the conflict in Europe were those most attuned to progressive reform, the clergy and midwestern farmers. War across the Atlantic diverted the attention of their national leaders from domestic to foreign affairs, as debates over antitrust and regulatory measures yielded the floor to questions of neutrality. Since President Wilson was preoccupied with foreign relations, progressivism was deprived of its foremost symbol at the crucial point when the liberal movement had already begun to sag. Many reformers, including Wilson, had convinced themselves that the major objectives of reform had been accomplished, and the war, along with the unusual economic conditions it created, gave them further reason to believe that their plans for a good society in America had been realized.[31]

These ideas appealed to the Congregational minister. As his church paper expressed it: "The constructively critical spirit of the Church has grasped all the heathen and supposedly worldly institutions of Society and gradually got an underhold on them until we can all see big business before our eyes—railroads and trusts and department stores—not exactly singing hymns and saying their prayers but acting quietly as if they could sing hymns or as if they were going to ask their prayers the moment they could get their hands washed."[32] Convinced that J. P. Morgan was about to scrub his hands, and deprived of inspirational leadership, the clergy simply lost interest in antitrust. In the five years before the war, there had been twenty-one editorials in the *Congregationalist* which mentioned the large corporation, and more than half of them had been critical of their subject; there were only five in the years 1915–19, and none of these drew a negative portrait of big business. In the eyes of the minister, the mission of the social gospel had been accomplished and the trusts brought to heel by 1916, when he could no longer see any aspects of the corporation which called for correction (figure 6–3).

Surprisingly, in 1917 and 1918 business-government relations did not attract the clergyman's attention. If there was a "mess" in Washington involving big business, he did not seem perturbed; if Bernard Baruch was the hero who spruced up the War Industries Board and revitalized the mobilization plan, the minister was unimpressed.[33] No longer did the federal executive branch stir him to consider the questions raised by business activity, whether in Washington or Wall Street (see "Leading sources" in table 6–3).[34] The firms mentioned most often did not owe that prominence to involvement in government programs, and insofar as the minister felt a need for a response, he stressed private, not public, action (again, see table 6–3). To a substantial degree his view of the giant corporation had been depoliticized.[35] When he did touch upon business-government relations during the war years, he found no occasion to criticize corporate executives. The war itself was an all-encompassing political event that absorbed his mind, much to the benefit of big business.

The corn-belt farmer was similarly vulnerable to political forces, but the effects of American entry into the war differed in his case. The farmer had a direct stake in the mobilization program, and his interests guided his attitudes toward the giant firm. When the war began in Europe, the farmer was less certain than the minister that he had an "underhold" on J. P. Morgan and the trusts, but he was nevertheless satisfied that some progress had been made, particularly in the field of railroad regulation. The large packing firms, he felt, were in need of the same sort of controls that had been imposed on the railroads. When he devoted more and more of his attention to the difficulties created for him by the "big four" in the meat-packing industry, he was indirectly acknowledging his confidence in the revitalized Interstate Commerce Commission (table 6–4). His faith in the commission and the nation-wide decline in enthusiasm for the progressive movement dampened his opposition to the trusts in 1915 and 1916 (figure 6–4). In his case the effects can be clearly seen in his loss of interest in the political activities of the large corporation. Before the war he had often lashed out at business's role in state and national politics, but now he was less worried about this facet of the trust problem.[36] In 1916 he completely neglected the negative dimension of business-government relations for the first time since the early 1890s.

After the United States became a belligerent, the midwestern farmer began once more to worry about corporate politics (table 6–4). He speculated on the possibility that the prices of his livestock were the subject of "an understanding between the packers and the officials at Washington."[37] He saw the railroad rate case being reopened "under pressure from certain powers in Washington," and he lamented the fact that the railroad unions had been able to force "the president and congress to enact a law which gave them a large increase in wages."[38] What would happen to the farmer, he wondered, "when the administration for food control is organized?"[39]

He soon received an answer to that question. During the following months the government erected a formidable structure of controls, including the Food Administration and an agency to centralize the operations of the railroads. As a result, there was some tendency for the farmer to shift the blame for his problems from business "greed" or "mismanagement" to the special conditions resulting from the war and the "Prussians."[40] But he remained suspicious of big business and kept his guard up throughout the following months. Early in 1918, *Wallaces' Farmer* eyed the situation in Washington and concluded that farmers would not object to "whatever it seems wise to do as a matter of national policy. . . . They do not, however, want to be turned over wholly to the mercy of big business. They recognize

FIGURE 6-3. The Congregational clergy's evaluation of big business, 1880–1919. The annual percentages represent the proportion of items in *Congregationalist* reflecting each attitude.

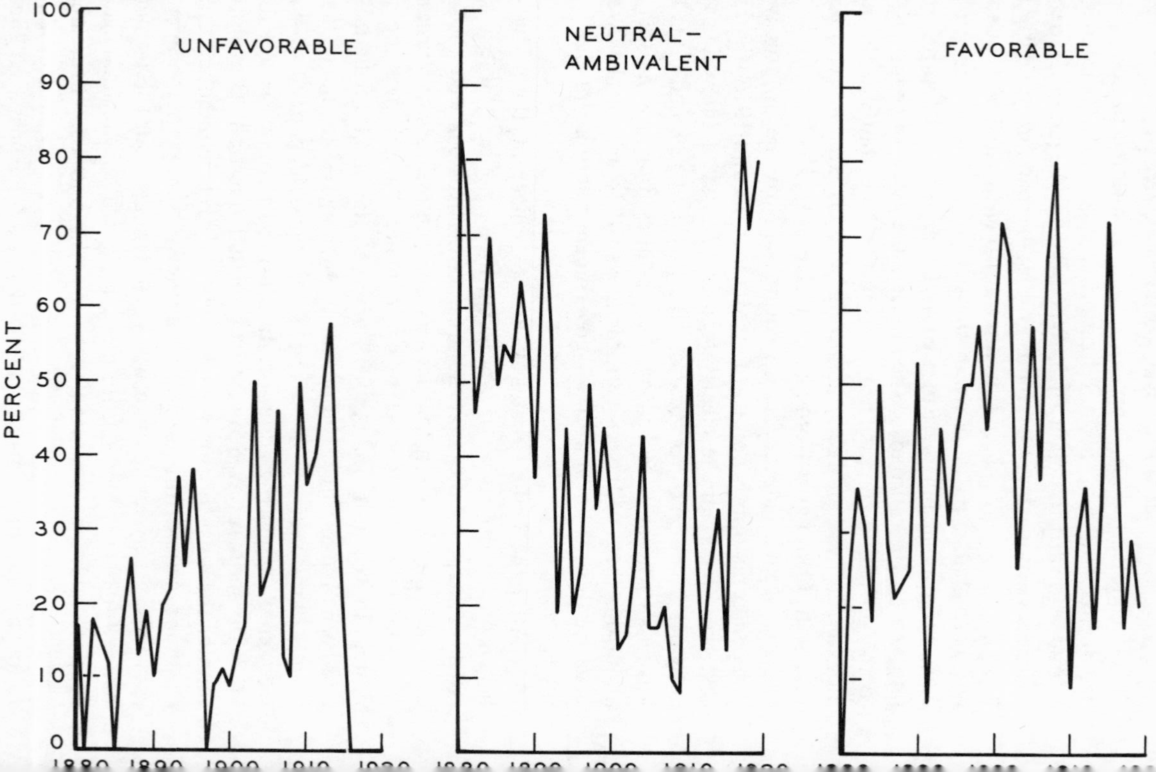

the patriotic spirit of the men of big business who are helping the government to work out these matters of great importance; but they recognize also the ignorance of some of these men on farm matters, and they can see how, thru this ignorance, our agriculture may be tremendously handicapped and in some respects crippled for years to come."[41]

Business leaders from some large firms—particularly the meat packers —had been to the tree of knowledge in agrarian affairs and were held accountable for their sins. Swift and Company "quietly" tried to circumvent government regulations and, along with the other Chicago firms, "doctored" their account books in order to show smaller profits than they actually earned. Looking back on the war experience from the vantage point of 1919, the farmer saw that in reality the regulators had been regulated: "The Food Administration was packed with packer representatives."[42] While the midwestern farmer himself did not do poorly during the war, higher income could not erase the resentment stemming from the central role big business had played in the mobilization program.

Nor was the midwestern farmer pacified when the government began to improve the efficiency of the wartime agencies. Other Americans might

TABLE 6-3. The Congregational clergy's image of big business, 1915-1919

Aspects of big business mentioned	1915-1919		
	High year	Low year	Mean
Economic	100%	100%	100%
Political	30	0	18
Social	20	0	7
Leading characteristics of big business	1) Products or services 2) Management or ownership 3) Prices; Miscellaneous political activities		
Leading industries mentioned	1) Railroad transportation (40) 2) Transportation equipment (37) 3) Retail trade-general merchandise (53)		
Leading firms mentioned	1) Ford 2) Chicago, Burlington and Quincy Railroad 3) Delaware, Lackawanna and Western Railroad		
Leading sources of items on big business	1) Meetings and conventions 2) Action taken by big business 3) Four others tied		
Leading solutions or responses	1) Private collective action (67%) 2) Federal action (33%)		

SOURCE: *Congregationalist*. Data for previous periods are in tables 3-2, 4-1, and 5-1.

FIGURE 6-4. The midwestern farmer's evaluation of big business, 1879-1919. The annual percentages represent the proportion of items in *Farmers' Review* and *Wallaces' Farmer* reflecting each attitude.

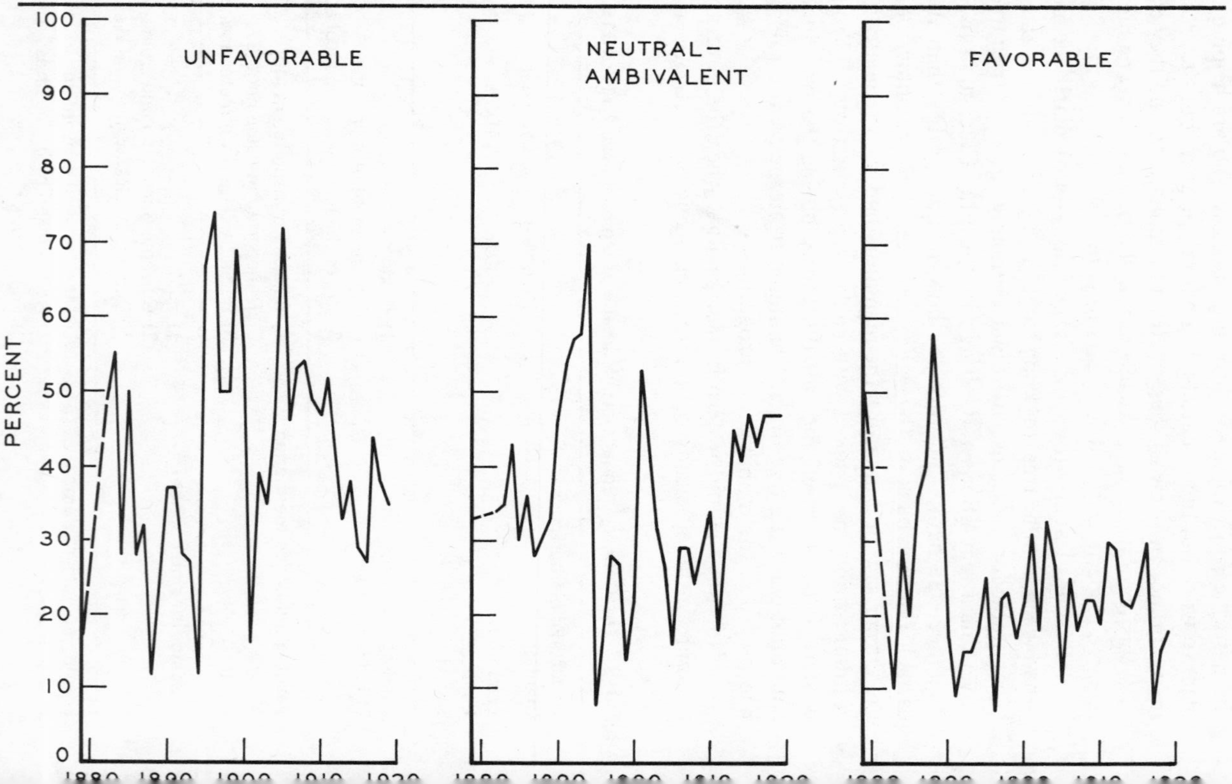

have found comfort in Baruch's success with the WIB, but the farmer said that big business was "in the saddle" and still able to exploit price controls to its own benefit. In the summer of 1918, he felt that "rules and regulations have been put in force without a word to the farmer, the man who is most concerned. The prices of his products have been fixed, directly or indirectly . . . . Freight rates on his products have been advanced to exorbitant figures. Freight service has compelled him at times to hold his products and thereby suffer extremely heavy losses."[43] So powerful were the "interests" standing against him that they might soon, he warned, drive the farmer "to extremes in political action."[44]

If, in fact, a new wave of agrarian radicalism had arisen in response to wartime conditions, corn and cotton growers would not have joined hands as they had in the 1890s. Unperturbed by the national system of controls, southern farmers found few opportunities to comment upon the situation in Washington. When they did, they had no harsh words for either big business or the businessmen who occupied prominent positions in the economic program. They could not ignore the fact that the war impinged on their interests, when, for example, a shortage of railroad cars endangered their

TABLE 6-4. The midwestern farmer's image of big business, 1915-1919

Aspects of big business mentioned	1915-1919		
	High year	Low year	Mean
Economic	96%	80%	88%
Political	50	14	35
Social	6	0	1
Leading characteristics of big business	1) Products or services 2) Miscellaneous political activities 3) Prices		
Leading industries mentioned	1) Railroad transportation (40) 2) Food processing (20) 3) Primary metals (33)		
Leading firms mentioned	1) Armour; Swift 2) Chicago, Burlington and Quincy Railroad; Pullman; Nelson Morris		
Leading sources of items on big business	1) Letters to the editor 2) Meetings and conventions 3) Federal executive action		
Leading solutions or responses	1) Federal action (38%) 2) Private collective action (24%) 3) Individual action (19%)		

SOURCE: *Wallaces' Farmer*. Similar data for previous periods are in tables 3-4, 4-3, and 5-2.

WAR AND THE CORPORATE CULTURE, 1915-1919

supply of fertilizer. But the roads themselves were not blamed for these difficulties, and *Southern Cultivator* called on its readers to help solve the problem by shipping early and by unloading cars at once so that they could be used elsewhere.[45] Controls, in effect, diverted from the large corporation any hostility the southern farmer might otherwise have experienced due to wartime shortages and related problems.

The midwestern farmer also had little opportunity to forge a farm-labor alliance to fight the corporate interests. The AFL member was almost as indifferent as southern farmers were to the political role of business in mobilization. The union had traditionally attempted to solve labor problems in the marketplace instead of in Washington. Shortly before America declared war, the AFL had reiterated its opposition to "compulsory benevolence": "Governmental power grows by what it feeds upon. Give an agency any political power and it at once tries to reach out after more."[46] When wartime controls were introduced, however, they actually worked to labor's advantage and the craftsman found little reason to complain about a regulatory system yielding such obvious benefits as an increase of more than one million in union membership. Although he grumbled about false reports on high labor turnover, the worker actually ignored most of the events centering around Washington.[47] Neither the War Labor Board nor the War Industries Board stirred up any substantial discussion on his part, and he continued to stress private collective action through the union as the proper means of dealing with big business.[48]

While trade unionists were harvesting the fruits of a wartime economy and a congenial regulatory system, the IWW member found himself under fierce attack from a government apparently determined to make the world safe for democracy every place but at home. The resulting changes in his image of the large firm were slight, as his ideology continued to maintain a stable hold on most facets of his attitude toward business (table 6–5 and figure 6–5). Those changes that did take place were largely a product of his new and more threatening political environment. From the vantage point of the radical worker, the federal government, in league with "Big Business," was determined to control the news and to "strangle the truth about itself."[49] These charges became credible when *Solidarity* itself was suppressed.[50] While the paper was in print, however, it provided union members with a rich supply of information on business-government collusion. The defense boards that set prices for copper and steel were composed of the steel and copper "magnates," who naturally set prices so high that even the Secretary of the Navy was unwilling to pay them. These same patriotic businessmen were "tyrannizing workingmen" in Colorado, refusing to pay "living wages," while they called for government help to break a strike that was keeping them from making "profits out of war orders."[51] To the radical worker it was foolish to expect that a capitalist like Julius Rosenwald of Sears, Roebuck and Company would suddenly forget the interests of his own firm simply because he had accepted a post as chairman of a wartime agency.[52]

Any lingering doubts he might have had about the role of government in a capitalistic society were cleared up when most of the union leadership was sent to federal prison. In one such case, the worker found Standard Oil to be "in a gigantic conspiracy against those who are the champions of the workers—who are trying to free the Standards' wage slaves."[53] In another case the copper trust directed the trial. In every instance it was evident that the government was a weapon in the hands of the ruling class, a conclusion reaffirmed when the United States intervened in Russia in an apparent effort to protect trust investments.[54] By 1919, in fact, the radical worker was so hard pressed that he could no longer afford to attack his trade union opponents; he was already losing on every front to his enemies in the Wall Street and Washington branches of the trusts.

Even the placid engineer found that the political overtones of the war deserved consideration. Experiencing none of the repression that was the lot of the radical worker, the engineer worried instead about the overall ability of mobilized industry to meet the demands of the war. In the summer of 1917 he had cause for concern, since the railroad industry was confronted by an "unprecedented business."[55] The resulting crisis in rail transportation was, however, not debited on the side of private enterprise; the engineer was critical of the slow-moving regulatory system and concerned about "the general problem of industrial unrest," but he refused to reverse his earlier decision about the efficacy of corporate management.[56] Even when the government was forced to take over the operation of the nation's railroad system, he retained his "faith in the ability of the railroad officials of the country to operate their properties efficiently." They had made "vigorous efforts . . . to cope with the situation," he said, but "there were obstacles that the railroad managers neither made nor were permitted to remove."[57]

Confident as he was of the efficiency of big business, the engineer saw no cause for alarm when business leaders took a prominent part in the mobilization program. On the contrary, he applauded when men from International Harvester and General Electric helped the army expand its supply system by 2,250 percent.[58] Businessmen might not have experience with the specific problems at hand, but their "intensive knowledge of organization" was even more valuable.[59] The wartime program needed this skill, he felt, even in those industries which had come under direct public control. So long as the problems of production and distribution were being solved, he was unconcerned about the potential for conflicts of interest.[60]

Business-government relations during the war were not, for the engineer, a source of scandal, but they did cause some significant and lasting changes in his attitude toward large enterprise. Before 1914, he had frequently looked to individual and private action as the best means of coping

FIGURE 6-5. **The radical worker's evaluation of big business, 1910-1920.** The annual percentages represent the proportion of items in *Solidarity* reflecting each attitude.

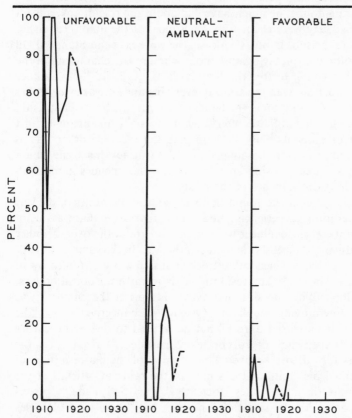

with the problems associated with big business. During the war period, however, that was no longer true. He began to stress the role of the federal government in coping with these situations (table 6–6), and in subsequent years he continued to look to Washington for help when difficulties arose from the activities of giant enterprise.[61] In the period 1915–19, he also became slightly more sensitive to the news emanating from Washington (table 6–6). In this sense the war had the effect of nationalizing and politicizing the engineer's point of view. The degree of change in his concept of the corporation was almost as slight as it was in the case of the radical worker, but the fact that political developments of any sort could crack the hard shell of his professional ideology was significant.

The political aspects of the First World War thus had a variety of effects on the attitudes of different groups in the middle cultures. The war neutralized the clergy's fears about the trusts and left the engineer even more

SECOND GENERATION

174

pleased with the corporation than he had been in 1914. Midwestern farmers and radical workers, by contrast, found in the government's actions new cause to worry about collusion between the trusts and the country's political leaders. Only the cotton farmer and the skilled laborer found it possible to ignore almost entirely the role of the large corporation in economic mobilization. The Great War as a political experience thus produced results which in part cut across class and occupational lines. While war as an economic phenomenon tended toward consensus insofar as big business was concerned, the politics of belligerency pulled groups in the middle cultures farther apart.

IV. Of the various organizational phenomena associated with the war, the resurgence of the merger movement would seem to have been the most likely to produce significant changes in opinions about big business, but this development was almost totally ignored. Among skilled craftsmen the

TABLE 6-5. The radical worker's image of big business, 1915-1919

Aspects of big business mentioned	High year	1915-1919 Low year	Mean
Economic	100%	80%	92%
Political	47	16	27
Social	0	0	0

Leading characteristics of big business	1) Labor relations 2) Wages and hours 3) Management or ownership
Leading industries mentioned	1) Railroad transportation (40) 2) Primary metals (33) 3) Lumber and wood products, except furniture (24)
Leading firms mentioned	1) Chicago, Rock Island and Pacific Railroad 2) A number of other firms tied for second place
Leading sources of items on big business	1) Letters to the editor 2) Action taken by labor 3) Other publications
Leading solutions or responses	1) Private collective action (84%) 2) Federal action (12%) 3) Individual action (4%)

SOURCE: *Solidarity*. This table does not include data for 1918 when the journal was suppressed by the government. Similar data for the previous period are in table 5-7.

expansion (or existence) of the nation's giant firms was a salient subject (see table 6-2), but none of the unionist's comments were in fact directed at the current wave of mergers. Occasionally he noted the existence of the trusts or of a particular combine; he commented on the formation of the steel trust at the turn of the century, for example. But he had nothing to say about the more than four hundred companies that disappeared in mergers between 1917 and 1919.[62] Nor did any of the other occupational groups evince any substantial interest in this development, despite its long-term significance for the American economy. In the years 1897-1901 prosperity had defused middle-class reactions to the first major wave of the concentration movement, and during the period 1917-19, war and the war economy similarly diverted attention from the second cycle of industrial mergers.[63]

More influential than changes in the object perceived, i.e., big business, were organizational developments among the occupational groups themselves. For the engineer, whose durable associations had long proclaimed their support for systematization, for cooperation, and for large-scale undertakings, the war experience confirmed the fundamental values of the profession and its ideology. It appeared to the engineer that all of America was at last coming to appreciate the ideas to which his profession had been dedicated for at least two generations. He applauded when the principles of the Ford assembly line were extended to new industries and applied "on a tremendous scale."[64] He looked forward to the creation of a new railroad system in the postwar era, one in which a "regional plan of private operation" would replace the old patterns of competition.[65] He could now truly appreciate the manner in which, several years before, U.S. Steel's "great leader, Judge Gary, took an important step when he started his steelmaker's dinners, and brought those who had been intent chiefly on cutting each others' throats into aiding each other [i.e., through price fixing]."[66]

The war experience confirmed the engineer's values, supported his sense of his own role in society, and strengthened the associations which were the most important bulwarks for those values and that role concept. This virtually assured that his outlook on big business would remain extremely stable (figure 6-6), as indeed it did (see Appendix). Those few changes that took place could be traced to the mobilization program, as we have seen, and in particular to the efforts of the United States Railroad Administration to improve the efficiency of America's rail network. Hence, the leading representatives of big business were, in his view, all railroad companies. He gave slightly more consideration than he had before to the political facets of the corporation, and he had less faith in self-reform and more in federal regulation than he had displayed before 1915 (table 6-6). Otherwise, his attitude toward the large firm remained as stable as his image of the professional engineer.

War-related organizational developments caused more decisive changes in the opinions of the skilled worker. After April, 1917, he found

SECOND GENERATION

conditions in America highly favorable to the expansion of his trade unions. Jobs were plentiful, and neither employers nor government officials wanted labor-management struggles to slow down production. In addition, the federal government insisted on dealing with formal organizations instead of individuals. There was simply not time, government spokesmen explained, to reach the individual directly; he must be organized in order to play an effective role in the war effort. This general charge to work through strong, national organizations encouraged workers—as well as their employers—to unite for political and economic action. One of the results of the new environment was a tremendous growth in trade union membership.[67]

While this increase was not accomplished without conflict, the government's demands for cooperation muted the tension between labor and management. The number of strikes (many of them spontaneous, unorganized affairs) in America had tripled between 1915 and 1917, and the number increased again after the United States declared war. But most of these strikes were unlike the prolonged and bitter fights waged in previous years; most were brief and many were terminated voluntarily. In several industries government agencies, including the War Labor Board, adjusted disputes,

TABLE 6-6. The engineer's image of big business, 1915-1919

Aspects of big business mentioned	1915-1919		
	High year	Low year	Mean
Economic	100%	96%	98%
Political	31	16	21
Social	0	0	0

Leading characteristics of big business	1) Products or services 2) Management or ownership 3) Miscellaneous political activities
Leading industries mentioned	1) Railroad transportation (40) 2) Primary metals (33) 3) Transportation equipment (37)
Leading firms mentioned	1) Pennsylvania Railroad 2) Baltimore & Ohio Railroad; New York Central Railroad
Leading sources of items on big business	1) Action taken by big business 2) Meetings and conventions 3) Federal executive action
Leading solutions or responses	1) Federal action (69%) 2) Private collective action (27%) 3) State action (4%)

SOURCE: *Engineering News*. Data from previous periods are in tables 3-1, 4-4, and 5-4.

WAR AND THE CORPORATE CULTURE, 1915-1919

FIGURE 6-6. The engineer's evaluation of big business, 1880–1919. The annual percentages represent the proportion of items in *Engineering News* reflecting each attitude.

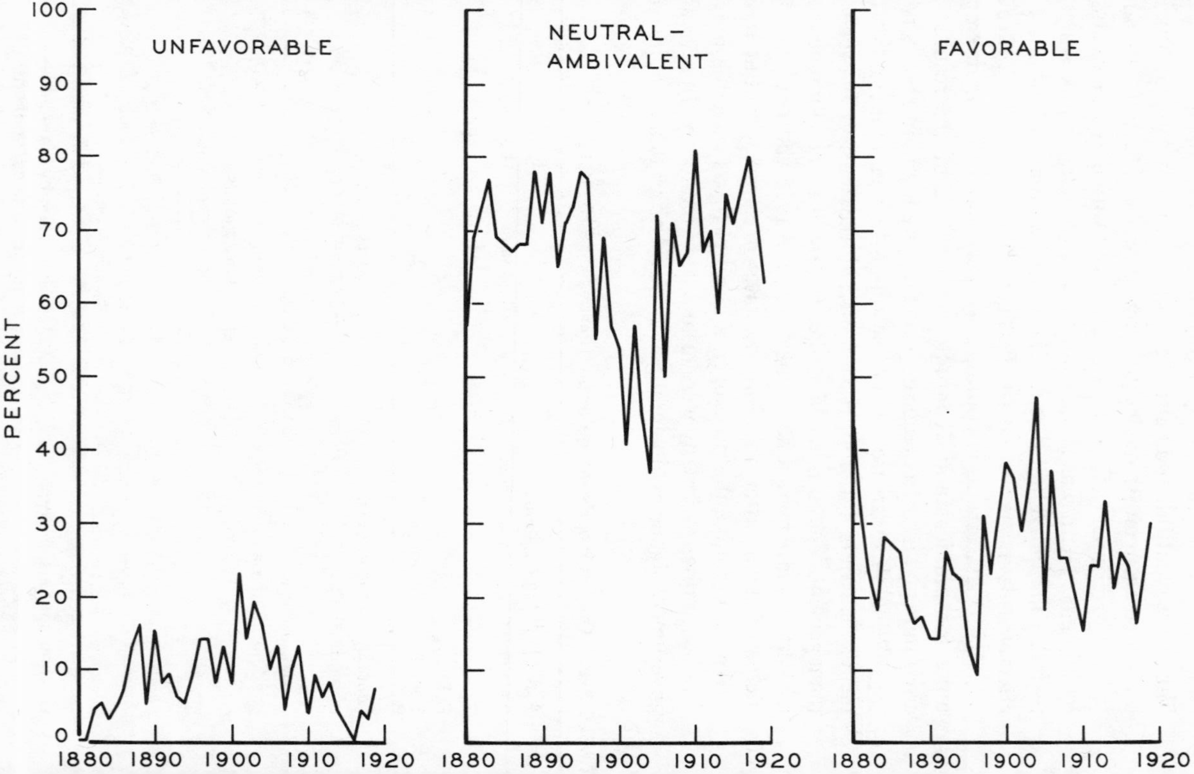

and the result was substantial pressure to prevent strikes and, in effect, to allow workers to organize with less resistance from their employers.[68]

The influence of these new organizational relationships could be seen in the craftsman's changing evaluation of the giant corporation. In 1918 and again in 1919 the unionized worker found less cause to criticize the trusts. His animosity toward big business had been declining before 1917, but the chief causal factor at that time had been his new view of business wage and hour policies. By 1918 his higher wages were being eaten up by inflation, but he could still be satisfied that his trade unions were gaining in strength and his employers becoming more compliant. This development accounted for most of the union man's change in attitude after the United States entered the war. In 1915–16, over 40 percent of the references to corporate labor relations in *American Federationist* had been negative; in the years 1917–19, only 17 percent were unfavorable and three-quarters were either neutral or ambivalent. While much of this news about labor relations came from the lower level of the union, the organizers scattered about the country, the editorials in *American Federationist* also projected less hostility toward the corporation. From top to bottom, the AFL by early 1919 seemed prepared to declare an armistice in its struggle against the trusts.

This pattern of responses to a changing environment duplicated almost exactly the transition in union attitudes which had occurred in the years before the war. At that time, the skilled worker first altered his view of the wage and hour policies of the large corporation, then decided that corporate labor relations also deserved less criticism. The same sequence occurred in the years 1915–19. Although such a pattern could be merely a coincidence arising from unique conditions, it seems more likely that this sequence was an important characteristic of the accommodation process for this particular group. Higher income could ease the craftsman toward a new position vis-à-vis the trusts, but income alone could not have the impact that it had among southern farmers, for instance. The laborer's fatter paychecks merely opened the way for his reevaluation of the more important question: how effectively could his organizations and crafts deal with the giant firm? Organizational and economic phenomena were as closely interrelated for this group as political and economic developments were for midwestern farmers. In both cases, higher income was a necessary, but clearly not a sufficient cause—was indeed, an explicitly secondary or supportive cause—of the changes in attitudes which took place.

Although among corn-belt farmers organizational factors related to the war were clearly less potent than political and economic forces, they still deserve careful attention. For one thing, the new organizations that had begun to arise in the latter part of the progressive era and that grew stronger during the war were fated to play a central role in the agrarian culture during the twenties. Not all of the important institutions were new: the Corn Belt Meat Producers' Association, the National Livestock Association, and others had been around for a number of years. In their record of success and failure the farmer now saw a lesson: he needed strong representatives with permanent, technically skilled staff members who could keep in touch with rapidly changing situations in the private and the public sectors.[69] Local farm clubs might, he felt, provide a foundation for this sort of organization, but a new institution was needed: "Only the farmer continues to play a lone hand. As long as he does this, he must expect to work at a great disadvantage in his dealings with other classes. . . . An organization of farmers brought together mainly to redress some wrong, usually flattens out when the heat of the fight is over, because its members have not beforehand learned the real principles underlying cooperative effort. . . . The day of the individual is rapidly passing. The day of organization, of collective effort, is here. And the corn belt farmer must get in line, or get worse."[70]

Two of the several types of organizations helping the farmer "get in line" were the cooperatives and the burgeoning farm bureaus. The cooperatives (in packing, for instance), purged of political objectives and filled with good business sense, enabled the farmer to solve some of his most pressing economic problems. They provided him with a feeling of countervailing power in his dealings with large enterprise.[71] The Farm Bureau lent assistance, not by forcing big business to change, but by emulating the "organized interests." The farmers needed "formal organization, especially for the purpose of looking after their business interests."[72] Postwar reconstruction was going to be filled with opportunities as well as risks; it was time, the farmer saw, to work through the Farm Bureau, "to follow the example of big business men of every sort, and employ men who know the game. Instead of wearing themselves out complaining because big business men are smart enough to play the game to their own advantage, farmers should make up their minds that they are going to learn how to play it to their advantage."[73] The farm institutions that promulgated this point of view had acquired a foothold in the Midwest before 1915; they grew stronger during the war; they were to exert a substantial influence on agrarian attitudes in the years to come.

Farm associations of this bent were not so much in evidence in the South as they were in the Midwest, but there were certain organizational developments making themselves felt among cotton farmers. For one thing, there was a mounting interest in private collective action through cooperatives as the proper response to big business; the southern farmer began to give less emphasis to such individual responses as better farming.[74] The southerner was also responsive to the efforts large firms made to woo his support. He cheered when the railroads encouraged better general farming, helped improve the quality of southern livestock, and employed specialists to assist Georgia farmers who were diversifying into melon or tobacco production.[75] Even the large industrial corporation—Republic Iron and Steel, for example—could win praise for the interest it took in its employees' gardens; and the Du Pont Powder Company was credited with "a wonderful plan of development" when it formed an agricultural company in the South.[76] Policies of this sort may have been largely symbolic in nature, but they nonetheless curried favor in Georgia and Alabama, where the farmer no longer saw the large corporation threatening his economic or political interests. In that setting even minor public relations efforts yielded a high return in favorable attitudes.

Among farmers in the South and Midwest, engineers, and trade unionists, organizational developments impinged in these several ways upon group concepts of the large corporation. Like the economic phenomena discussed above, and unlike the wartime political environment, the organizational factors drew men in the middle cultures together, molding by 1919 a notable consensus about big business. Just as they had during the progressive era, these factors made for accommodation, for a decline in antitrust sentiment.

V. Social variables had a less significant influence upon middle-class opinions than did economic, political, and organizational developments. During the war, class concepts faded as prosperity and the campaign to mobilize support for the nation homogenized middle-culture opinions.[77] Only the radical worker continued to express a strong sense of class antagonism. As we have seen, the nationalistic fervor that drew middle-class citizens together was used as a weapon against the IWW and its members, driving them into isolation and confirming their analysis of the ruling classes in America. Among the other occupational groups, however, the war experience eased tensions and eroded class lines.

One basic shift in values—itself closely tied to organizational change —seems to have had a significant and lasting effect upon the public image of the large firm. This transition involved the American brand of individualism, a norm that had already begun to change in several groups during the prewar years. Between 1915 and 1919 more and more Americans came to judge organized behavior in impersonal terms, stressing collective over individual responsibility. Just as the language of antitrust had been denatured in the years 1902–14, the large-scale organization was depersonalized in the war years. Another important element was thus added to the corporate culture, since both achievement and failure were increasingly looked upon as organizational, not individual, matters.

This transition is reflected in the data on those business leaders whom the public associated with the giant firm. For years middle-class Americans had singled out certain tycoons to represent all that was good and bad about the concentration movement. In the 1880s and early 1890s, Jay Gould and the Vanderbilts (see table 6–7) had been the major symbols of corporate business, and both names bore a heavy legacy of negative connotations.

TABLE 6-7. Leading businessmen associated with the large corporation, 1880-1919

Period	Clergy	Engineers	Midwestern farmers	Southern farmers	Skilled workers: National Labor Tribune	Organized workers: American Federationist	Radical workers: Solidarity
1880–1892	1) Depew 2) Vanderbilt 3) Astor	1) Gould; Vanderbilt	1) Vanderbilt 2) Gould 3) Huntington; McCormick	1) Vanderbilt; Phinizy	1) Gould 2) Vanderbilt; Carnegie		
1892–1901	1) Rockefeller 2) Vanderbilt 3) Carnegie	1) Westinghouse 2) Vanderbilt 3) Gould	1) Armour; Morgan; Havemeyer	None appeared more than once	1) Carnegie 2) Schwab 3) Morgan	1) Gould 2) Rockefeller	
1902–1914	1) Carnegie 2) Rockefeller 3) Gould	1) Westinghouse 2) Harriman 3) Seddon	1) Morgan 2) Rockefeller; Carnegie	1) Rockefeller; Carnegie; Hill	1) Morgan 2) Rockefeller; Carnegie	1) Rockefeller 2) Carnegie; Harriman; Baer	1) Rockefeller; Morgan
1915–1919	None appeared more than once	None appeared more than twice	1) Swift	1) Armour		1) Rockefeller	1) Rockefeller 2) Rosenwald; Gary; Ford

During the years 1893-1901, Gould and Vanderbilt had given way to Andrew Carnegie, John D. Rockefeller, and J. P. Morgan, all of whom were to maintain their leading positions in the public mind through the progressive era. Interestingly, after 1901 two of the three were no longer actively engaged in business, but the public was slow to respond, preferring to invest the corporation with a personality that was familiar even though the businessman in question was no longer particularly relevant to the country's economic fate. At any rate, through 1914 the giant firm did have a personal dimension about which there was a considerable degree of consensus in the middle cultures.

During the First World War, however, most middle-class Americans forgot about the moguls of yesteryear and began to talk about corporate enterprise in largely impersonal terms.[78] By 1919 the corporation was not providing Americans with a collection of flesh and blood villains upon whom they could focus their anger about big business' performance. This new perception of the large firm reflected the fact that bureaucratic consolidation (along lines discussed in chapter 1) was replacing the titans with less colorful leaders. In U.S. Steel a newsworthy Morgan gave way to Elbert Gary; in General Motors the dynamic William Durant was followed by the meticulous administrator Alfred P. Sloan, Jr. While the public's new image of big business was thus grounded in the reality of an evolving business system, the timing and degree of the change indicate that new norms were being applied to corporate enterprise. Although less important than the other major variables we have discussed, the new social values and their related culture contributed to the long term process of accommodation between the large firm and middle-class America.

VI. What emerges from our study of the various groups and their concepts of corporate enterprise is, I think, a conclusion that stresses the continuity between the progressive era and the war. If we have been searching for some kind of sharp break with the past, for a significant cultural watershed, we have so far failed to find it. Instead, we have found that most of the groups examined reacted to the war along lines closely resembling their responses to the shifting prewar environment; in some cases the resemblance was so close that the groups—in particular organized labor—duplicated the sequence of attitudinal changes characteristic of the progressive years.

The figures on equilibrium in the Appendix and the aggregate data presented in figure 6-7 also stress the continuity between the war and prewar years. For only one of the groups, organized labor, did the war produce a substantial degree of disequilibrium; the clergy's opinions shifted rather sharply in the early years but then stabilized with negative attitudes at a very low level. Change was gradual in the other occupational categories, and in

WAR AND THE CORPORATE CULTURE, 1915-1919

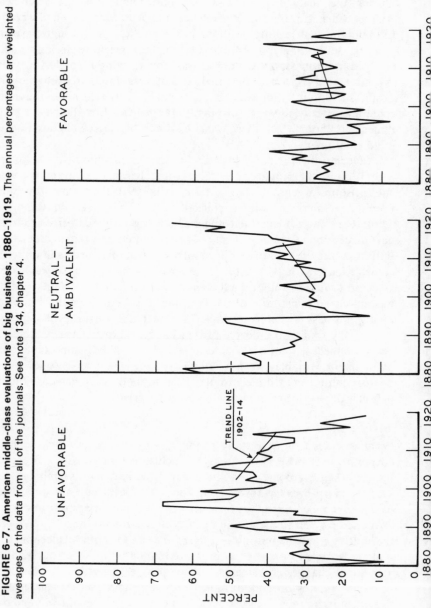

FIGURE 6-7. American middle-class evaluations of big business, 1880-1919. The annual percentages are weighted averages of the data from all of the journals. See note 134, chapter 4.

the aggregate data the years 1915–19 emerge as a period in which middle-class concepts of the corporation were evolving rather slowly. The figures on equilibrium (i.e., the mean deviation) indicate that for the middle cultures as a whole the war did not produce any more instability than had the progressive era. When we inspect the aggregate figures closely, we find that the direction of change was much the same for both periods. The prewar trends in attitude (embodied in the regression lines) were toward a lower degree of hostility and a higher degree of neutrality about the giant firm. Only in the case of favorable viewpoints can we conclude that the prewar trend changed decisively; here there is evidence that the mobilization program had a substantial impact on middle-class opinions, reversing a long-run trend toward a more positive concept of the corporation.

Surprisingly, however, this large segment of the American public was not really upset about the role of big business in mobilization. I had expected to find a sharp increase in negative viewpoints when corporate moguls became entangled in the confused process of developing wartime controls. Judging from the figures on attitudes within the groups, only midwestern farmers responded in this way to the *entente cordiale* between the trusts and the government, and the impact of their reaction barely surfaces in the aggregate data. Perhaps the most important effect of mobilization was to reverse the trend toward a more positive image of the large firm by neutralizing favorable opinions. This was not a negligible result, but it was surely less dramatic than the traditional version of Bernard Baruch rescuing the reputation of American industry by calming the fears of an outraged public.

The war did not decisively alter the direction in which attitudes toward the giant firm were evolving, but the international conflict did increase the rate of change. The slope of the trend lines in figure 6–7 illustrates this point. Posing a counterfactual situation, we can ask what would most likely have happened to middle-culture attitudes had the war not taken place: the answer my data suggest is that by 1919 there would have been more opposition to the trusts but a higher level of favorable opinions as well. Even if we assume that the national economy would shortly have recovered from the 1913–14 downturn, the level of antitrust sentiment in the middle cultures would probably have been higher if the war had not occurred.

The First World War had a more significant influence on the process than it did on the pattern of attitudinal change. After 1914, economic variables replaced politics as the leading causal factor, and both were more influential than either organizational or social determinants of opinion. While the break was a matter of degree, the changes in the rank order of causal variables impose a significant qualification on my conclusion that the war did more to extend prewar trends than to create a sharp break with the progressive experience.

WAR AND THE CORPORATE CULTURE, 1915-1919

VII. The vision of large enterprise this generation developed between 1902 and 1919 deserves careful comparison with the image held by the previous generation of Americans. While the first generation provided a study in the sources of conflict, disequilibrium, and mounting hostility, the second offered an example of accommodation and a long term trend toward a more stable view of corporate business. With the exception of the war period, politics emerged in the second generation as the major independent variable shaping opinions in the middle cultures. Although the progressive view of this process can only be used after serious revisions in its treatment of causation, the central premise of liberal history—that is, its emphasis upon the political system as an agency of change in America—is substantiated by our data. During the war period, economic forces loomed larger than politics (especially in 1915-16), but for the entire generation, 1902-19, and for all of the groups combined, the major determinants of opinion resembled those highlighted by the progressive synthesis. On balance, organizational factors ranked next to politics as a causal force. The organizations of this generation put a more secure foundation under the new perception of big business, sustaining in this way a unique set of values, ideologies, and related role concepts that became important ingredients in the corporate culture. Income and other economic phenomena had a similar effect, especially during the years 1910 through 1919 when they eased America's fears about the trusts and transportation combines. Social variables were less influential, but they too fostered accommodation between big business and the middle class.

By 1918-19 the corporate culture seemed to be firmly planted in America's urban, industrial society. People now discussed big business in largely impersonal terms. Middle-class citizens like the Protestant minister sensed that the times had changed and that some traditional values had to be abandoned. Taking the railroads for an example, he said that in the past, government regulations and antitrust measures had helped to give the country the type of railroad system it needed; but now it was clear to him that "the inevitable drift of the situation is toward some system of unity which will shut out waste."[79] This "drift" toward "unity" was reflected in the language of antitrust. By 1915 new modes of expression had developed, as affective language yielded to more neutral styles of discourse. Among skilled craftsmen, the prewar trend was briefly but decisively reversed in the years 1915-19; among the other groups studied, however, the trend set in the progressive era continued through the war.[80] The clergyman and the corn-belt farmer saw an economy populated with "firms," not "octopuses," with "big businesses" instead of "trusts." Whether they were expressing anger or pleasure with big business, they spoke the language of the impersonal corporate culture.

SECOND GENERATION

By the end of the war, the antitrust movement in America had apparently run out of gas. In 1919 the level of negative opinions about big business was at its lowest point since the panic of 1893. To judge the stability of this new perspective and its cultural context, we must now look at the attitudes characteristic of the 1920s and of a new postwar generation.

PART FOUR. THIRD GENERATION: A STUDY IN THE ANATOMY OF EQUILIBRIUM

7

CONTINUITY AND CHANGE, 1920-1929

The craftsman saw himself trapped between radicals on his left and giant business combines on his right. In America, he said, left-wing unions such as the IWW were the counterpart of the Bolsheviks in Russia.[1] The Industrial Workers of the World were fighting for changes in postwar America even more drastic than those sought by the "powerful interests" of incorporated industry. Big business was, nevertheless, far more likely to achieve its goals, and the skilled worker recognized this. The IWW could sting him and his trade union, but such combines as U.S. Steel, with its "brutal, archaic policy" of crushing unions, presented an immediate danger to him and his trade organization. He concluded that antitrust had "failed completely to protect the people against the outrageous machinations of combinations and monopolies." Under an "autocratic control of industry," management ignored the public interest and treated its employees like "machines."[2]

On midwestern farms there was a similar air of crisis. In the immediate postwar period the government was investigating the big packing companies, and there were new proposals for federal regulation of that industry.[3] A Federal Trade Commission report in 1919 gave the farmer indisputable evidence that the packers were "allied with the powerful interests at the sources of credit," that they dominated the markets in which the farmer sold his products and manipulated the prices consumers paid. The leading packers had, in fact, "long been so big that they have been able to bargain on practically even terms with the leading nations of the world. From the standpoint of bargaining power and price-fixing ability the five big packers have long been far more powerful than the five million American farmers."[4] In words that echoed the 1890s, the farmer charged that his enemies possessed "secret information concerning the nature of demand" and used this information and their market power to beat "down the price of live stock."[5] If a solution could not be achieved through some government agency, the farmer warned, he might be forced to seek "a very radical reorganization of our packing system."[6]

Farmers and skilled laborers were also upset about the railroads. To the midwesterner there was no problem more vital to his interests than deciding what would be done when, and if, the government relinquished supervision of the national rail system. For his part he sought a return to state and federal regulation, with the roads in the hands of their private owners. Government operation invited "officious meddling," entangling the companies in "rules and red tape."[7] He found much to approve in Sen. Albert B. Cummins' bill to restore rate-making power to the ICC; this bill would, he felt, give the shipper "proper protection."[8] The skilled laborer was less optimistic about regulation. He felt that the "government has tried to control and regulate great combinations and failed"; what was needed, he thought, was a new remedy, a peacetime experiment with a nationalized rail system.[9]

These complex questions were discussed in an atmosphere clouded with unreasoned fears. Many Americans seemed to feel the Russian revolution threatened the United States, the fortress of capitalism; for some, the enemies at home were as dangerous as those abroad. During the "red scare" of 1919–20, the IWW, already weakened by wartime suppression, suffered further defeats in the courts and gutters of America. For the radical worker these assaults strengthened the conviction that in a capitalistic society the trusts dictated to the government, manipulated public opinion through a "kept press," and controlled the working class with private armies of "gunmen."[10] Seen on the other hand from a bourgeois vantage point, the incidents "served notice on the reds that we will have no part with them." But even the remote possibility that events might follow a different course was unsettling.[11]

The sense of conflict and crisis was reinforced by wild fluctuations in prices, wages, and profits. In 1919 and 1920 prices shot upward, and the farmer began to wonder when the country was going "to start climbing down the high-price ladder."[12] Inflation disturbed the engineer, who complained about the low salaries paid by railroads, and the farmer nervously asked whether "there will be a disturbance of some kind and someone will get pushed off the ladder to land with a thud at the bottom."[13] The answer came shortly. The "disturbance" started in the fall of 1920 with a severe deflation; by early 1921, the farmer and many others found themselves landing "with a thud at the bottom." In the Midwest the farmer saw the prices of his products fall to prewar levels while freight rates remained high; the skilled worker complained that coal prices held steady while the mining companies cut their employee's wages; the engineer worried about the lack of construction projects and the corresponding decline in engineering jobs. Even the clergyman was agitated. A contributor to the *Congregationalist* suggested that a minister could not help but be influenced when he discovered that he earned less than a girl just out of high school. "In a land where all values are measured in terms of money, what will be the effect on the girl in her respect for her minister when she finds she is making more than he? And if in a church which pays $2,500 per year, the parishioners say, 'We pay our minister a little less than $50 per week,' they will see at once how small that is in comparison with what heads of departments in business are receiving."[14] The clergyman, the engineer, the farmer, the laborer—all found cause for distress in the immediate aftermath of the First World War.

II. Widespread economic problems, conflict, and fear coalesced to produce a sudden and substantial change in the public image of big business (figure 7-1). Attitudes fluctuated more widely in the postwar years than they had at any time other than the 1890s (see Appendix). Neutral opinions in the middle cultures abruptly gave way to verbal assaults on the large firm. While middle-class Americans continued in 1920 to recognize the corporation's accomplishments, they saw far more that irritated than pleased them in the performance of giant enterprise. This third cycle of antitrust sentiment was less severe and less prolonged than those of the mid-nineties and the progressive era; it was in fact roughly comparable to the reaction centering around 1890, when Congress had passed the Sherman Antitrust Act. But in 1920 and 1921 the opposition to big business seemed all the more potent because it followed a long period in which the middle classes had adopted a largely neutral stance toward the corporation.

This sudden reversal in public attitudes fits well in the historical tradition that emphasizes the uniqueness of the 1920s. Historians have long stressed the discontinuity between the prewar and postwar decades, giving to the latter a very special place in their hearts as well as their heads.[15] Merely mentioning the twenties triggers a rush of word pictures that are in part a product of this view of the American past. We think of jazz. Zelda. St. Valentine's Day. Coolidge. Paris. Gin. And Lindy. These ideas cluster around a central assumption about the mood of a unique culture. It was an alienated, even a "lost," generation.[16] This was a generation that prohibited liquor and then eagerly sought it, that rejected Europe and then embraced it, that laughed at the "booboisie" while building an aggressively middle-class "business civilization."[17] These Americans renounced the prewar interest in reform and turned their backs against their own wartime experiences—at the very least, this was a different, a special generation, and the central theme of the twenties in our history has been change, not continuity.

While the postwar fluctuations in middle-class opinions support this interpretation, a careful appraisal of the data for the entire decade suggests that when one is dealing with the pattern (as opposed to the process) of change, the most outstanding feature of the twenties is the degree of continuity between that period and the years 1902–14. The continuity stands out even more clearly if one puts out of mind for a moment developments during the war and the first two years of the postwar era. Through 1920 and 1921 conditions in America were unusual, largely as a result of situations related to the First World War. By 1922, however, the country was through

CONTINUITY AND CHANGE, 1920-1929

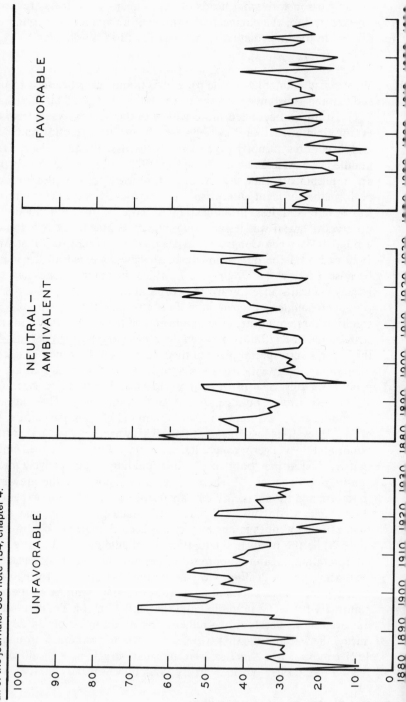

FIGURE 7-1. American middle-class evaluations of big business, 1880–1929. The annual percentages are weighted averages of the data from all of the journals. See note 134, chapter 4.

the postwar crisis and was settling into what might be called the twenties proper. It is here that we must search for the long-run effects of the war, and it is here, I think, that we find little evidence of a major transition or watershed in the middle cultures. Instead, we discover trends similar to the secular developments of the prewar era. Figure 7-2 offers graphic support for this conclusion: if one erases the war experience and postwar reactions, the trend (regression) lines from 1902–14 can be extended through the years 1922–29 to provide a reasonable approximation of the data for the latter period. The poorest fit is with the favorable attitudes, which, as we saw in the last chapter, were most influenced by the war.[18] The long-run patterns of change in negative imagery were much the same. This alone tells us nothing about causation, but it does indicate that we should launch our investigation of the process of change with the initial assumption that this generation of middle-class Americans responded to big business along lines very similar to those of their immediate predecessors in the prewar era of reform.

III. The unionized worker's opinion of the large firm remained overwhelmingly negative and relatively stable in the years following the postwar economic crisis (see figure 7-3 and the Appendix). He evaluated the corporation's performance, in fact, much as he had in the antebellum years. More than half of the times he mentioned the large firm he did so in critical tones, and

FIGURE 7-2. American middle-class evaluations of big business, 1902–1914, 1922–1929. The annual percentages are weighted averages of the data from all of the journals. See note 134, chapter 4.

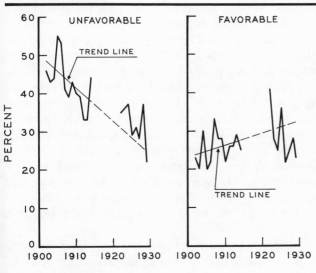

he bestowed on this subject only slightly more praise than had been the case before the wartime economy dulled the edge of his anger.[19] Through the twenties he continued to express these ideas in the bland language of the corporate culture, a style of discourse that had become popular in the progressive era.[20] Even when most upset—as he was, for example, in 1924—he labeled his opponents as "concerns" instead of "the battering rams of monopoly," as "corporations" and not "trusts." Certainly for this group there was substantial evidence of continuity between the two decades divided by the First World War.

Beneath the surface of these trend lines, however, there are contradictory data that point toward significant changes in the way the organized laborer thought about the large corporation. Increasingly, the trade unionist of this generation was concerned with a new kind of problem, a new type of industry, a different sort of firm. He directed much of his attention at the New York Central and the B & O railroads, as well as Ford, International Paper, and General Electric—none of which had attracted much interest in the progressive era (table 7-1). The previous generation had identified big business primarily with older industries that were technologically less progressive; a number of these processed the products of field and forest —that is, the products of the older, agrarian-commercial economy.[21] In relation to these industries a member of the AFL had been able to feel relatively secure on two grounds: he was confident of the importance of his craft as an economic and social institution, and he was equally convinced that his conservative trade union was capable of helping him when he marketed his skills. The latter judgment had seemed well-founded after the Federation multiplied its membership and its bargaining power at the turn of the century. A sense of security also seemed justified when the trade unionist was concerned with public utilities, although in this case the government protected the worker and his trade organization.

In the twenties, however, the skilled laborer began to recognize that his craft was no longer the durable fortress it had been and that his trade union was now a less reliable weapon to use against his corporate opponents. He worried more about the modern, mass-production industries in which he and his union were proving to be extremely vulnerable. These industries were best able to do without skilled workers of the sort protected by the unions in the American Federation of Labor. These were the industries in which firms had been most successful in rooting out existing craft unions and in preventing new labor organizations from establishing a foothold. Against the automobile manufacturers, for example, the unions were virtually powerless, and traditional craft skills provided little security in an industry which had followed Henry Ford's lead in pushing the assembly-line principle to new extremes.

The worker was far more worried about opportunities for employment than he had been in the reform era (see "Leading characteristics" in table

7–1).[22] From around the country, the AFL's organizers filed reports on the job situation. In 1922 the worker learned that the Phelps Dodge Corporation had laid off men in Arizona, while the Georgia railroads were rehiring the workers they had released some months ago. In Cairo, Illinois, the Singer Manufacturing Company and Sears, Roebuck took on additional employees, but in Pittsfield, Massachusetts, General Electric cut back its work force. Happily, the steel mills in northern New York increased their work force, as did the Ford plant at Des Moines, Iowa; but this good news was tarnished by a report that American Shipbuilding in Lorain, Ohio, had released fifty of its craftsmen.[23] The readers of *American Federationist* probably found these riptides of conflicting information as difficult to chart as the historian does now, but fortunately two landmarks stand out: first, the craftsman was much more interested in job opportunities than he had been before the war; and second, his trade union had at best a tenuous influence on this situation. The organizers could urge unionization as the answer to wage cuts, but there was nothing they could do when companies hired or fired—except to pass the word along. Their quandary—and that of the craftsman himself—was reflected in a declining interest in solving the problems stemming from big business. Before 1915, over three-quarters of the items in the *American Federationist* had explained what should be done about the trusts and combines, with the emphasis resting heavily on private collective action through an AFL union. After 1919 the paper continued to favor unionization over other possible responses (e.g., federal legislation), but less than half of the articles mentioned any solution whatsoever.

Adding to the worker's sense of insecurity was the successful open-shop campaign that employers tagged as the "American Plan."[24] When the National Association of Manufacturers launched the American Plan in 1920, labor did not at first identify the program with the large corporation. Within a few years, however, the skilled worker saw that the anti-union movement was closely linked with the "Big Interests," with giant firms like International Paper; he watched his unions being defeated by a powerful politico-economic combine in "that unholy, un-American drive which was led by the porch climbers of Wall Street, assisted by some of our national officers in Washington together with a number of federal courts which fell in line and became willing tools of the big interests. . . . In this pernicious un-American drive by the kaisers of industry, . . . their chief aim and object was the dollar, to gain which, they endeavored to enslave the workers."[25] No longer were the largest companies working through the National Civic Federation to achieve conciliation with organized labor; "the largest capitalistic combines of the entire Universe" were spreading "poisonous propaganda" in an effort to destroy the labor movement.[26]

In the late twenties new dangers arose. Many large firms established company unions designed to forestall the formation of trade unions actually representing the workers. Management normally controlled the company (or

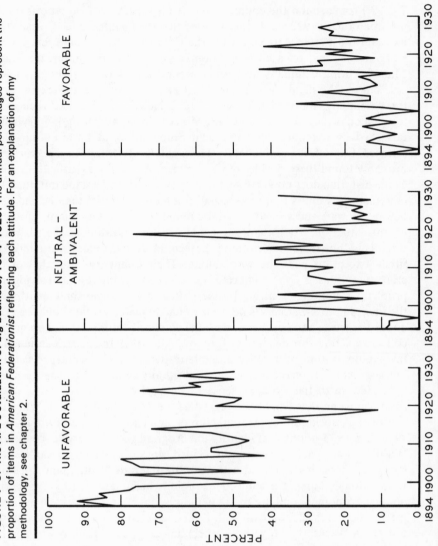

FIGURE 7-3. **The AFL's evaluation of big business, 1894–1929.** The annual percentages represent the proportion of items in *American Federationist* reflecting each attitude. For an explanation of my methodology, see chapter 2.

TABLE 7-1. The AFL's image of big business, 1920-1929

Aspects of big business mentioned[a]	1920-1924			1925-1929		
	High year	Low year	Mean[b]	High year	Low year	Mean
Economic	95%	84%	90%	100%	93%	98%
Political	45	9	25	21	6	13
Social	2	0	less than 1	9	0	2

Leading characteristics of big business	1) Labor relations 2) Diminishes individual's opportunities 3) Enhances individual's opportunities	1) Labor relations 2) Diminishes individual's opportunities; Wages and hours
Leading industries mentioned	1) Railroad transportation (40)[c] 2) Primary metals (33) 3) Petroleum refining (29); Transportation equipment (37)	1) Railroad transportation (40) 2) Transportation equipment (37) 3) Electric-gas-sanitary services (49)
Leading firms mentioned	1) Pennsylvania Railroad 2) New York Central Railroad 3) Baltimore & Ohio Railroad; U.S. Steel; Ford; International Paper; General Electric	1) Baltimore & Ohio Railroad 2) Pennsylvania Railroad; Ford

Leading sources of items on big business	1920-1929
	1) Letters to the editor 2) Other publications; Action taken by labor

Leading solutions or responses	1920-1924	1925-1929
	1) Private collective action (60%) 2) Federal action[d] (29%) 3) State action (4%)	1) Private collective action (77%) 2) Federal action (21%)

SOURCE: *American Federationist*. For an explanation of my methodology, see chapter 2. Similar data for the previous periods are in tables 4-6, 5-6, and 6-2.

NOTE: If multiple entries follow one number, the categories were tied.

[a]These figures show what percentage of the articles mentioned each aspect; the columns can total more than 100% because a single article could mention one, two, or all three.

[b]Mean of the annual percentages.

[c]The number appearing after each industry indicates its two-digit group in the *Standard Industrial Classification Manual*.

[d]Also includes general references to an unspecified governmental response or solution.

CONTINUITY AND CHANGE, 1920-1929

"scab") unions—organizations that were in most cases unions in name only.[27] Hand in hand with these organizations came the so-called yellow dog contract, an agreement requiring a worker not to belong to or join a trade union as a condition of his employment.[28] These weapons proved deadly in the hands of large, already powerful corporations; one measure of their effectiveness was the serious decline in membership that the trade unions, including those affiliated with the AFL, suffered in the twenties.[29]

The employers' offensive against the unions also included some positive programs that influenced the skilled worker's opinion of the corporation. In the early twenties he thought that creating opportunities for employment was the large firm's most laudable role; jobs, he felt, were far more important than benefit plans. In subsequent years, however, the unionist gave more attention to programs such as the one instituted by the Baltimore and Ohio Railroad. The B & O's plan for union-management cooperation gave "unqualified recognition to the place of organized labor in industry"; it provided "economies in operating and maintenance expenses"; it improved service at the same time that it regularized employment for the railroad shop crafts.[30] Company benefit plans earned the worker's praise. Although he remained skeptical about stock purchase programs, he usually looked with favor on the group insurance and pension plans offered by the larger companies.[31]

During the latter part of the decade, the skilled laborer also became less concerned about big business's political power. Before the war this had been important to the members of the AFL; for a time, the trust and the injunction had been practically synonymous terms to the craftsman. After 1919, he still found opportunities to condemn the use of injunctions and the "ruthless service" of the state police against strikers. In the early twenties, too, the activities of the Railway Labor Board aroused numerous bitter thoughts, as did the political features of the American Plan.[32] But despite the hostile Republican administrations in Washington, the worker gradually came to ignore the political power of the corporation and could no longer see any particular form of political activity that deserved special condemnation. By the end of the twenties he felt his problems with big business were no longer political in nature.

In these several ways, the trade unionist's image of the giant firm changed decisively during the 1920s. As the craftsmen sensed, the basic institutions that had protected him (as well as those that attacked him) were evolving along lines weakening his position; these changes were, furthermore, beyond his or his union's control. Neither he nor the AFL leadership had answers to the questions forced upon them by the new economic and organizational environment of the 1920s. One of the results was a new sense of insecurity that sustained the worker's animosity toward the large corporation throughout the prosperous twenties. Higher income was for him no antidote for the feeling of powerlessness engendered by the weakness of his craft and union.[33] While the general outlines of his attitude toward big business thus resembled those of the prewar generation, the process of attitude formation and the specific content of his image of corporate enterprise were significantly different. For the skilled craftsman the twenties were a study in change, not continuity.

IV.   Unlike the craftsman, the corn-belt farmer reacted to the postwar crisis with a brief burst of antibusiness sentiment and then quickly adopted a more placid view of the corporation (figure 7–4). In 1920–22, at the peak of this cycle, his opposition to big business was almost as intense as it had been at the high-water mark of the progressive movement. He was angry about the poor service he received from the railroads—in particular the "disastrous" car shortage that kept him from obtaining supplies or marketing his crops. Prices also upset him, whether they were the freight rates he had to pay or the charges the big packing firms levied on their customers. He also denounced the favors that giant corporations seemed to receive continually from the government.[34] Most of this anger focused on the railroads and on the meat packers, especially on the largest of the Chicago-based firms (table 7–2).

The federal government subjected both of these industries to new regulatory legislation in the early twenties, and the farmer took a strong interest in the Transportation Act of 1920 and the Packers and Stockyards Act of the following year. He favored controls on the packers, and while he opposed government ownership of the railroads, he wanted "strict government supervision" of the lines.[35] He was thus pleased when the Esch-Cummins Act and the law regulating the meat packers ostensibly achieved his two goals; he applauded these policies even though it was 1922 before he could be certain that the courts would not overturn the latter measure.[36]

Both the pattern of attitudinal changes and the variables shaping farm opinion in the early twenties were much the same as they had been before the war. The midwestern farmer was very specific about the sources of his economic and political difficulties; he wasted little animosity on opponents who did not purchase his commodities or supply him with goods or services. In the progressive tradition, he sought to curb his enemies' power through federal legislation. When Congress passed appropriate measures and his economic position improved, the farmer's hostility gave way to a more neutral outlook on the giant firm.[37] Short-term politico-economic interest was, as before, the master of his thought on the trust question.

In the years following 1922, however, farm thought in the corn belt took a new turn. The farmer's outlook gradually mellowed (see Appendix). By the end of the twenties he had hardly any criticisms of big business,

CONTINUITY AND CHANGE, 1920–1929

FIGURE 7-4. The midwestern farmer's evaluation of big business, 1879-1929. The annual percentages represent the proportion of items in *Farmers' Review* and *Wallaces' Farmer* reflecting each attitude.

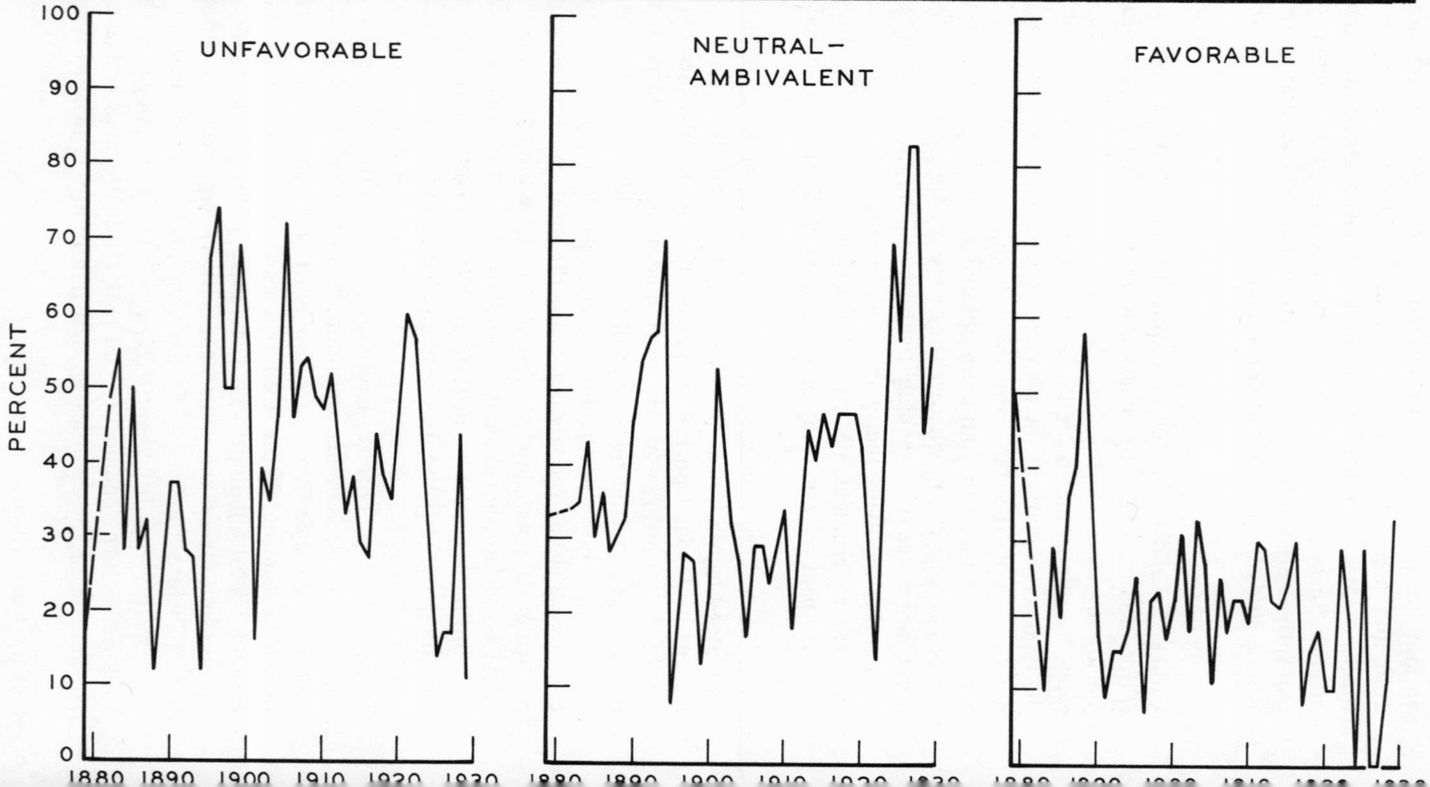

favorable opinions far outweighed negative attitudes, and both were less prevalent than neutral viewpoints. In 1929, in fact, the midwestern farmer expressed less antagonism toward the large corporation than he had at any time since 1879. This ebb tide in antitrust sentiment was not a product of political measures or of politics working in tandem with economic forces. The prime determinant now was income, pure and simple. During this

TABLE 7-2. The midwestern farmer's image of big business, 1920-1929

Aspects of big business mentioned	1920-1924 High year	Low year	Mean	1925-1929 High year	Low year	Mean
Economic	100%	70%	85%	100%	67%	88%
Political	60	14	33	33	0	18
Social	10	0	2	17	0	3

Leading characteristics of big business	1) Products or services 2) Prices 3) Miscellaneous political activities	1) Products or services 2) Prices 3) Wages and hours[a] 4) Dependence upon political assistance
Leading industries[b] mentioned	1) Railroad transportation (40) 2) Food processing (20) 3) Primary metals (33)	1) Railroad transportation (40) 2) Food processing (20) 3) A number of other industries tied for third place
Leading firms mentioned	1920-1929 1) Southern Pacific Railroad; U.S. Steel; Sears Roebuck	
Leading sources of items on big business	1) Letters to the editor 2) Economic conditions 3) Meetings and conventions	
Leading solutions or responses	1) Federal action (44%) 2) Private collective action (33%) 3) Individual action (10%)	

SOURCE: *Wallaces' Farmer.* Similar data for previous periods are in tables 3-4, 4-3, 5-2, and 6-4.

[a]This particular characteristic entered the list under dubious circumstances and should, I think, be discounted to a considerable extent. The paper began to publish a table which showed the relationship between farm prices and other economic measures, including wages and hours. This was almost the only time the subject came up in *Wallaces' Farmer.*

[b]At this point we changed our sample size, and the data on separate industries and firms became relatively thin; this explains the large number of ties which prompted me to omit the third-place industry in 1925-29.

CONTINUITY AND CHANGE, 1920-1929

decade income exerted a far more powerful effect upon attitudes than had been the case prior to the First World War. The correlation between gross income (in constant dollars) and negative opinions was extremely high (r = −.65) and the same was true for the relationship between neutral-ambivalent attitudes (r = .55) and income. Even without the help of political reform measures or of liberal leadership in the White House, higher income washed away the corn-belt farmer's remaining concerns about corporate enterprise.[38]

Organizational developments in the twenties placed the farmer's new outlook on big business on a firm institutional foundation. The crucial organization was the Farm Bureau, with its supporting cast of county agents. By the end of the First World War, there were 2,600 county agents working to organize and maintain county-level farm bureaus—these in turn were joined together in the national Farm Bureau Federation (1919).[39] This formidable network of organizations proclaimed a new gospel in the corn belt, calling upon the farmer to forget about destroying big business and concentrate on emulating the large firm. If the farmers would only organize properly, they would be able to control "the price [of their commodities] themselves, just like the United States Steel Corporation sets its price." The Armour Grain Company had "its own statistical department for collecting the most accurate market news, and acts on this news to its own advantage."[40] Now farmers could do the same thing: "The individual hog producer is helpless. . . . [and] if American . . . producers are going to make their influence felt, it must be thru organization[s] which will take in a very substantial part of the hog producing country. Fortunately," the farmer recognized, "there is such an organization growing up now in the Farm Bureau." Through this body, he felt he could obtain the services of "trained men who will at once begin the study of the probable demand for live stock products during the next year and a half. . . . Then they will turn their attention to the supply, the number of hogs that will be coming to market during the next nine or ten months. . . . They will then be in a position to talk to the packers and to the buyers of the foreign countries."[41] Further armed with selling and shipping cooperatives, the organized farmer would be able to battle his opponents as an equal, not as a member of an oppressed class.[42]

The Farm Bureau philosophy stressed values similar in many ways to the norms characteristic of the engineering profession. The emphasis in both value systems was on collective, not individual, action. The goals of that activity were spelled out in highly specific, measurable terms. To the extent that the achievement of those goals meant involvement, and often conflict, with other parties, farmers were viewed as participants in a normal social process in which agriculture's opponents sought their best interests just as the farmer sought his. When power was distributed unequally, it was the farmer's responsibility to change the balance of power through collective action. Once that was done, he could neutralize or overcome his opponents without seeking to destroy them (as might have been the case if the conflict had been seen as a class struggle).[43] These new values coexisted with an older point of view that stressed individualism, highly diffuse relationships among men, and a vision of the farmer as part of a chosen class. In the twenties, however, the modern, corporate values grew ever stronger, and the Farm Bureau and its related organizations were the leading spokesmen for the modern version of agrarianism.[44] These institutions and values reinforced a relatively narrow, interest-oriented point of view and strengthened the farmer's tendency to see big business in overwhelmingly neutral terms.

On balance, the midwestern farmer's encounter with the twenties was primarily a study in change, not continuity. Particularly significant was the new interrelationship between economic, organizational, and social variables. Missing after 1922 were the reform measures that had played such an important role in the prewar years. While a long-run trend toward less hostility was common to both periods, the process of attitude formation was different. By the end of the decade the midwestern farmer was talking the language and proclaiming the values of the corporate culture. In his viewpoint the great combines in transportation and industry no longer posed a threat to the interests of agriculture or the nation as a whole.

V. The Congregational clergyman found the early twenties almost as trying as did the farmer. The conflict-ridden postwar crisis stirred the minister to question anew the merits of giant enterprise (figure 7-5). Labor-management strife, seen against the backdrop of the communist revolution in Russia, left him worried about America's future. He tried to reassure himself: "Beyond a doubt, the mind of the European furnishes more fertile soil for Soviet doctrine than that of the American."[45] But it was obvious that he would have been more confident about the future if unions and corporations had settled their differences peacefully, and he blamed business leaders like Judge Elbert Gary of U.S. Steel for contributing to the loss of harmony in American life. The clergyman suggested in 1920 that Gary would do well to frame a New Year's resolution to "consider anew the wisdom of larger concessions to organized labor."[46] The minister's sympathies were not really with organized labor or with the laboring class, a strata of society he clearly differentiated from his own; instead, he sought—as he had before 1920—peaceful relations grounded in mutual respect, and he was willing to blame either party when conflict arose.[47] In 1921, he concluded that "Big Business is going out to try to smash Labor Unionism. Labor has had the whip hand for two or three years and has become arbitrary and domineering. It has been an apt pupil of capitalism."[48]

CONTINUITY AND CHANGE, 1920-1929

FIGURE 7-5. The Congregational clergy's evaluation of big business, 1880–1929. The annual percentages represent the proportion of items in *Congregationalist* reflecting each attitude.

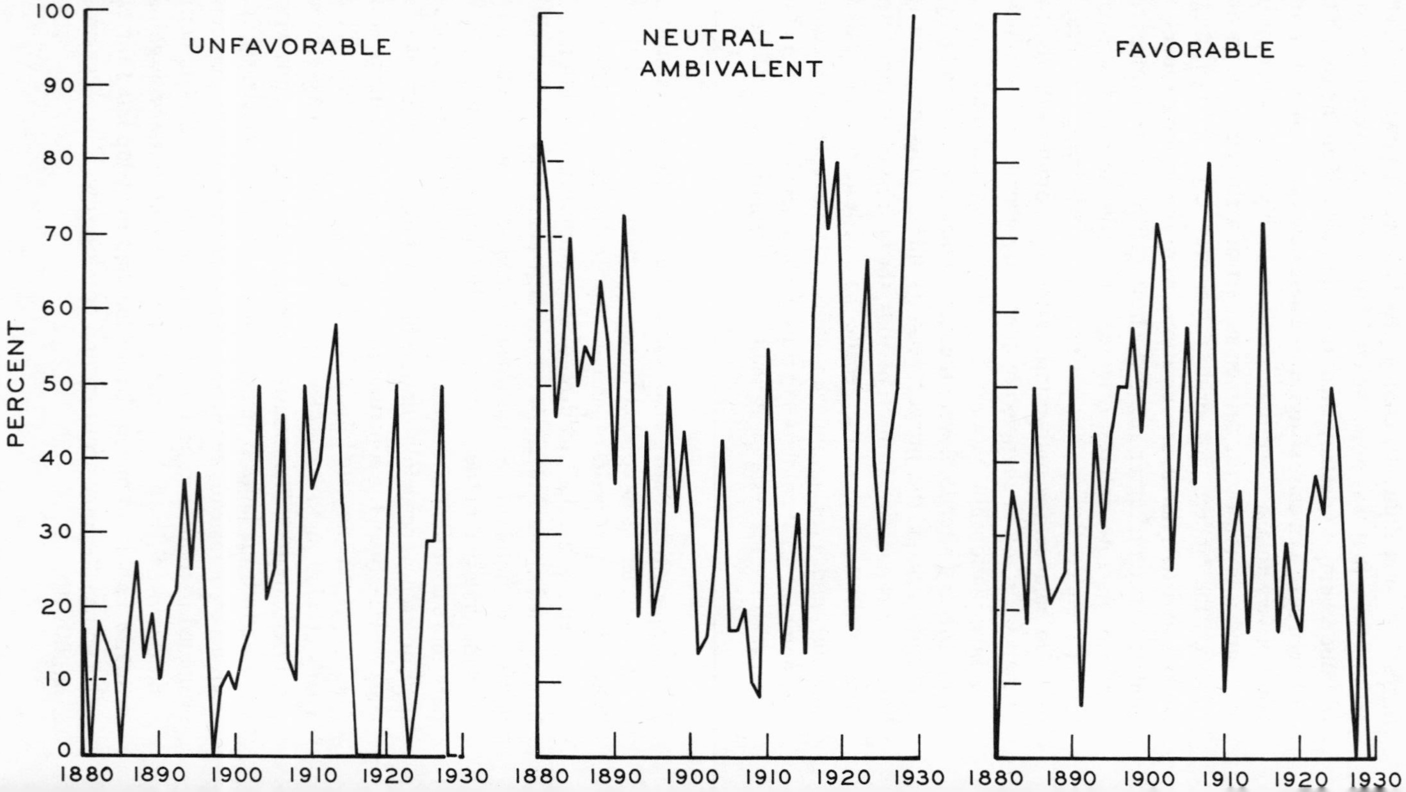

When the economy recovered from the postwar deflation, and prosperity eased tensions between labor and management, the minister's hostility toward big business quickly subsided. His cycle of antitrust sentiment was thus brief, and by 1922 the clergyman was bestowing more praise than blame on corporate enterprise. Social variables, including the minister's sense of class alignment and his personalized view of social relations, had a significant impact on his opinions. Even in the midst of the postwar crisis, he had been certain that when the older capitalists saw things in their proper light or when they were replaced by younger men, conditions would improve. "In the things fundamental to a right relationship of capital and labor there is a good deal of agreement at home and abroad. Here the eight-hour day, decent working conditions, a living wage and *collective bargaining* are coming to be universally accepted as the right of labor. It is significant that the younger men trained in the colleges and universities to the newer ideals of industry are coming into leadership in business; their influence makes for better understanding between capital and labor."[49] Just as immoral men caused problems, new leaders could provide solutions without disturbing the underlying structure of society—that is, the relationships of men to power and property.

When the storm front passed, leaving behind a prosperous and ostensibly peaceful America, the clergyman quickly found much to compliment in the behavior of big business and its leaders. Philanthropy attracted his accolades, as did profit-sharing plans and the superior products of large-scale producers.[50] None ranked above the Ford Motor Company (see table 7-3), whose cars played a large role in the minister's day-to-day life. He considered "his trusty Ford" nothing less than "a valuable assistant," which enabled him to carry the "gospel truth into many an isolated and neglected place."[51] Big businesses like the Ford Company were, he thought, interested in "building up" the country and stimulating commerce.[52] In the mid-twenties he was certain that these positive contributions far outweighed the liabilities of monopoly.

After the Teapot Dome scandal filled the headlines, however, the Congregational minister renewed his attack on the trusts.[53] He lashed out at both the businesses that depended on political assistance and illegal corporate activities.[54] The country, he thought, needed a "national housecleaning" to get rid of the "corrupt officials" who labored on behalf of corporations instead of the public.[55] The Harding administration scandals blended with such issues as the American government's efforts to help the oil companies operating in Mexico, and the result was a second cycle of antitrust fervor which lasted through 1927.[56] Then, abruptly, the clergyman lapsed into a neutral stance vis-à-vis the corporation. Lacking effective, reform-oriented political leadership and deprived of eye-catching scandals or intense battles between labor and management, the Congregational minister saw no need to

TABLE 7-3. The Congregational clergy's image of big business, 1920-1929

Aspects of big business mentioned	1920-1924			1925-1929		
	High year	Low year	Mean	High year	Low year	Mean
Economic	100%	90%	98%	100%	86%	97%
Political	20	0	7	50	0	20
Social	16	0	3	14	0	7

Leading characteristics of big business	1) Products or services 2) Management or owner-ship 3) Existence or expansion; Labor relations	1) Products or services 2) Existence or expansion 3) Dependence upon politi-cal assistance
Leading industries mentioned	1) Railroad trans-portation (40) 2) Transportation equip-ment (37) 3) A number of other indus-tries tied for third place	1) Railroad trans-portation (40) 2) Petroleum refining (29) 3) Transportation equip-ment (37)

Leading firms mentioned	1920-1929
	1) Ford 2) Standard Oil

Leading sources of items on big business	1) Meetings and conventions 2) Other publications

Leading solutions or responses	1) Federal action (75%) 2) Private collective action (25%)

SOURCE: *Congregationalist*. Similar data for previous periods are in tables 3-2, 4-1, 5-1, and 6-3.

attack big business. On the eve of the Great Depression, he had nothing that was critical or favorable to say on the subject. In fact, he rarely discussed corporate enterprise at all.

In certain regards, the process of attitude formation among clergymen closely resembled that of the previous generation. Then, as in the twenties, particular kinds of conflicts aroused his animosity, as did major political events that suggested corporate leaders had too much influence on govern-ment and too little concern for the public weal. Many of the minister's basic values were unchanged, and along with his sense of class alignment, they continued to shape his perception of the country's largest business firms.

Other features of the clergy's thought on the trust issue differed markedly, however, before and after the First World War. In the twenties the minister sorely missed inspirational, reform leadership of the sort that

THIRD GENERATION

Theodore Roosevelt and others had provided. No longer did the federal executive frequently arouse discussion of big business (table 7-3); the only important exception was provided by the Harding scandals that briefly stirred the minister's wrath. In general, political factors were far less influential than they had been in the previous generation. The clergyman's evaluation of big business bobbed about, as neither his sense of class alignment nor his dedication to reform was sufficient to ballast his opinions and hold him on a true course as a friend or enemy of the giant firm.[57] This third generation of Congregational clergymen was thus a study in both continuity and change. The pattern of the clergyman's ideas and the forces ordering his thoughts had changed enough to suggest that the First World War was for him a significant break with the past; the equally compelling similarities of process and pattern indicate that his accommodation with large-scale enterprise was tenuous, his ties with reform tradition still strong, and his acceptance of corporate norms less than complete. The Congregational minister of 1929 was intrigued by organization but was not yet an organization man.

VI.   Like most middle-class Americans, the third generation southern farmer reacted swiftly and emotionally to the postwar crisis. Deflation cut the price of cotton in half between 1919 and 1921.[58] As his income plummeted, he quickly rethought his relationship with big business and found in 1920 that there was much to be said against the giant firm and very little to be said in its behalf (figure 7-6). He was particularly upset about the railroads that were "combining and planning to further their own interest" through a system of government controls.[59] When the roads pushed rate advances and could not provide sufficient cars to move his products, the southern farmer complained bitterly; while his own income was being halved, his corporate opponents, he said, were insisting on a "billion dollars increase in freight rates."[60] Also concerned with the packing industry (see "Leading industries" in table 7-4), he was upset when the government settled its antitrust suit against the packers (1920) with a consent decree instead of pushing for a victory in court.[61]

   The hostility fired by depression was just as quickly dampened when, in the next few years, the cotton grower's income started back up. There is little evidence that government measures were any more decisive in reshaping his opinions now than they had been in the progressive era. On the contrary, he was still far more interested in private than in public solutions to his problems. He was less inclined than he had been before 1915 to believe that if he only had a good pasture for his stock he could be "more independent of . . . the fertilizer trust," but he still gave greater emphasis to this kind of individual action than he did to antitrust or regulatory

FIGURE 7-6. The southern farmer's evaluation of big business, 1879–1929. The annual percentages represent the proportion of items in *Southern Cultivator* reflecting each attitude.

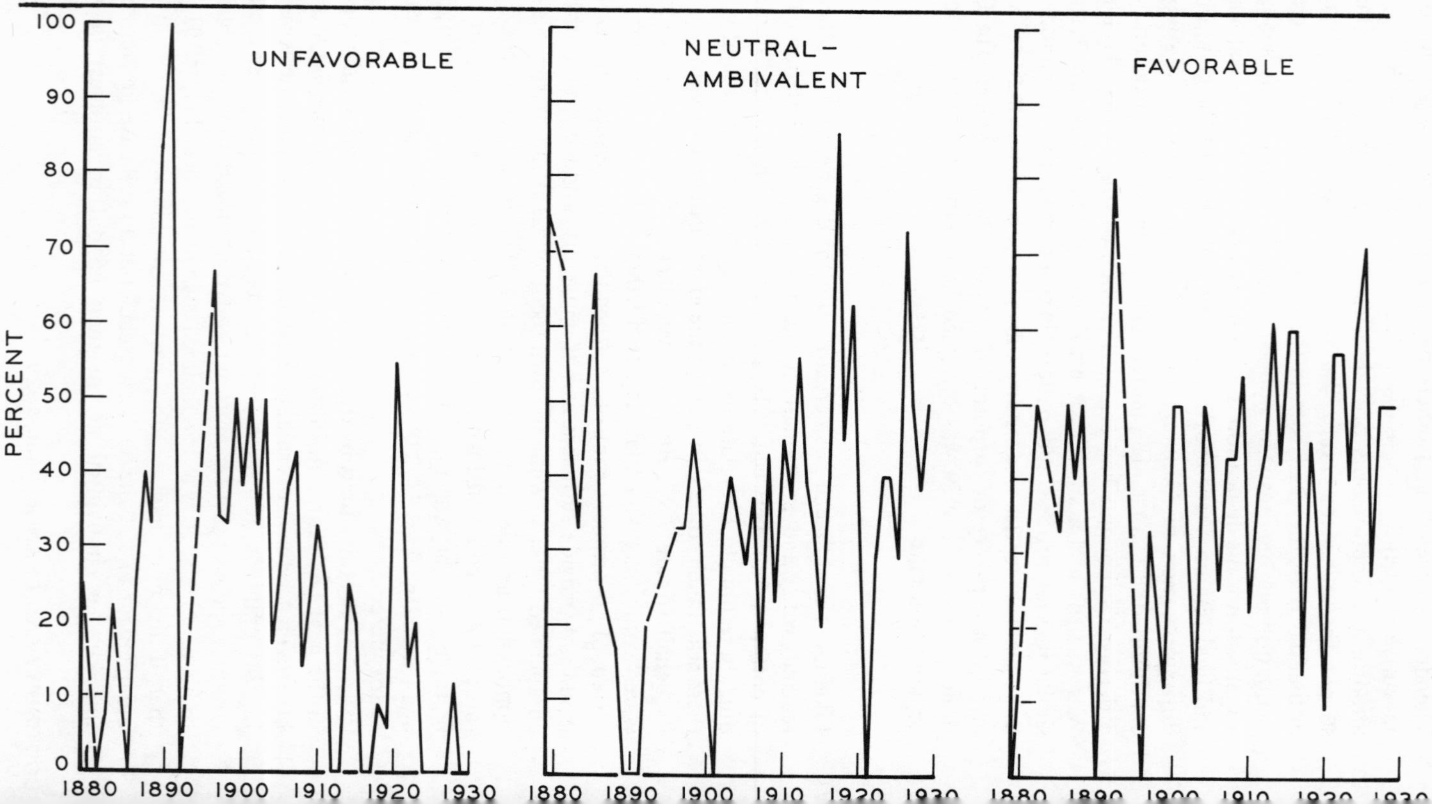

measures.[62] The high correlation between southern farm income and attitudes toward the large firm lends further support to this conclusion: before, during, and after the war, as the cotton farmer's income went, so went his opinion of the corporation.[63] By 1924, he was earning so much money that he could no longer find anything in the realm of big business to criticize.

Both the pattern of his attitudes and the social process forming them represented a continuation of prewar trends. He kept his eyes fixed on a few major industries that were of direct economic interest to him; his major concern was with their products and services, and with the manner in which they contributed to the economic development of his state, region, and the

TABLE 7-4. The southern farmer's image of big business, 1920-1929

Aspects of big business mentioned	1920-1924			1925-1929		
	High year	Low year	Mean	High year	Low year	Mean
Economic	100%	90%	96%	100%	71%	92%
Political	36	0	12	25	0	8
Social	10	0	2	14	0	3

Leading characteristics of big business	1) Products or services 2) Purchasing policies 3) Enhances the general wealth; Prices	1) Products or services 2) Enhances the general wealth 3) Purchasing policies

Leading industries mentioned	1) Railroad transportation (40) 2) Food processing (20) 3) Transportation equipment (37)	1) Railroad transportation (40) 2) Food processing (20); Machinery—nonelectrical (35)

Leading firms mentioned	1920-1929 1) Swift 2) Ford 3) Armour

Leading sources of items on big business	1) Meetings and conventions 2) Action taken by big business 3) Letters to the editor

Leading solutions or responses	1) Individual action (38%) 2) Federal action (32%) 3) Private collective action (29%)

SOURCE: *Southern Cultivator*. Similar data for previous periods are in tables 3-3, 4-2, 5-3, and 6-1.

CONTINUITY AND CHANGE, 1920-1929

nation as a whole. He saw, for instance, that "the Central of Georgia [Railroad] has always recognized that its own interest lay in the advancement and progress of the section it serves."[64] He applauded when Swift and Company built a packing house in Georgia and thus kept southern dollars at home instead of in Chicago.[65] The most significant new dimension to his concept of the corporation was a direct product of this sort of innovation, as the southern farmer, heretofore wedded to cotton, became more interested in livestock and therefore in the purchasing policies of the large packers. In the twenties he found little to criticize in their performance as customers; instead, he discovered that they were highly cooperative with their farm suppliers and with various agrarian organizations.[66] From the mid-twenties on, his evaluation of these and other characteristics of big business was stable and highly favorable (see Appendix).

Farm organizations appear to have had a less significant influence on opinions in the South than in the corn belt. While county agents were in evidence in the South, the Farm Bureau was not the catalyst there that it was in the Midwest.[67] More influential was the general cooperative movement, which had growing appeal as an appropriate means of dealing with the large firm.[68] Of even greater importance were the conscious efforts large firms made to solicit agrarian support. As long as prices were right, the cotton farmer reacted enthusiastically when the Georgia Railroad collaborated with the Extension Division of the State College of Agriculture to put in special demonstration pastures; the farmer was also pleased when the Southern Cotton Oil Company joined the fight against the boll weevil. He was ecstatic when the A. B. and C. Railroad sent a special train around the state in an effort to upgrade Georgia livestock and he noted how much "adding even 100 pure bred dairy sires to one section of a state at one time will mean . . . to the early future prosperity of that section."[69]

The cotton farmer had been equally enthusiastic about the publicity campaigns of big business before 1915, and in this and most other regards, his response to the corporation in the twenties followed lines well established in the late 1890s and the era of reform. His was a study in continuity, not change. Clearly, the primary determinant of his attitudes was his economic situation, and by the second half of the decade his income was high enough to convince him that he could safely hold up "the great captains of industry" as models for his children to emulate: "[They] have set a definite goal and have stuck doggedly to the task until the goal was reached." Neither the business titan nor the young farmer should find any appeal in the line of least resistance.[70] Similarly, the cotton grower saw in the reforestation plans of large lumber companies an object lesson for "small timber land owners."[71] Instead of being a subject for attack, a lightning rod for social discontent, the giant corporation had become the benefactor of the farmer, the South, and the entire nation.

THIRD GENERATION

VII.   The professional engineer had come to a similar conclusion long before the twenties. By 1910 he had resolved the debate over efficiency in favor of the giant firm and after the First World War he did not find it necessary to reopen the question. Nor did he see in the public service corporations a subject that called for reevaluation. Even in the immediate aftermath of the war, with the contest over railroad regulation at its peak, the engineer discussed big business in largely neutral terms. When compelled to judge, the engineer always found more that pleased than displeased him in the performance of the giant firm (figure 7–7). His ideas thus remained stable through the postwar crisis and indeed through the entire decade.[72]

Although in 1920 he was far less agitated about political or economic problems than most middle-class Americans, he was not entirely impervious to the conflict which surrounded him.[73] He worried, for example, about what would happen to the railroads when the Railroad Administration expired in 1920: "The future of the railways and the welfare and prosperity of the country are so inextricably bound together," he said, "that whatever be the fate of the former must be the fate of the latter. It is confidently expected that the great common sense of the American public will assert itself and insist upon a square deal for the railways."[74] Alarmed by proposals for nationalization, he asserted that direct government operation had proven to be inefficient.[75] What was needed, he said, was private ownership combined with intelligent federal regulation and positive support for the companies.[76] The Transportation Act of 1920 struck him as a reasonable measure, particularly as it specifically provided for further consolidation of competing lines.[77] With the passage of this crucial law and a decline in labor-management conflict in 1921 and 1922, he felt reassured, certain that "a prosperous railway system will contribute much to general prosperity." One of the reasons this goal could be achieved was that the companies had been able to eliminate "wasteful working agreements" with organized labor.[78]

Through the rest of the decade, his image of the corporation remained stable—varying little in fact from its prewar outlines (compare table 7–5 with table 6–4). The engineer was concerned above all with the services the railroads provided to the public and with the products of such companies as the Baldwin Locomotive Works and the Bethlehem Steel Company.[79] He frequently discussed the quality of management in big business, and in the latter part of the decade, he hardly ever noticed anything that the leaders of big business needed to correct.[80] Instead, he praised the officers of the Middle West Utilities Company for their effective efforts to achieve "simplified construction and reduced fabricating cost"; he applauded the extensive improvements Chief Engineer John B. Berry introduced on the Union Pacific Railroad.[81] Both before and after the war, superior management of this sort was one of the advantages he thought larger firms had over their smaller rivals.

CONTINUITY AND CHANGE, 1920-1929

FIGURE 7-7. The engineer's evaluation of big business, 1880-1929. The annual percentages represent the proportion of items in *Engineering News* reflecting each attitude.

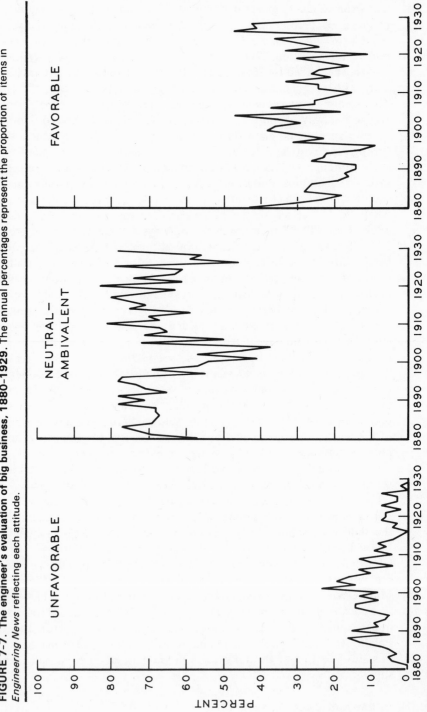

His attention remained fixed, as well, on much the same industries and individual companies. After the war as before, the activities of business itself and the meetings of his professional associations were the chief stimulants to discussion of corporate affairs. Clearly, the most outstanding characteristic of his attitudes in the twenties was their close resemblance to those of the prewar years.

There were, to be sure, some minor changes, including a distinct upward trend in favorable concepts of the large company (figure 7–7). Above all, he found new reasons to be pleased with the products and services

TABLE 7-5. The engineer's image of big business, 1920–1929

Aspects of big business mentioned	1920–1924			1925–1929		
	High year	Low year	Mean	High year	Low year	Mean
Economic	98%	92%	95%	100%	98%	99%
Political	30	16	23	24	11	18
Social	2	0	less than 1	0	0	0

Leading characteristics of big business	1) Products or services 2) Miscellaneous political activities 3) Management or ownership	1) Products or services 2) Existence or expansion 3) Management or ownership
Leading industries mentioned	1) Railroad transportation (40) 2) Electric-gas-sanitary services (49) 3) Primary metals (33)	1) Railroad transportation (40) 2) Electric-gas-sanitary services (49) 3) Primary metals (33)
Leading firms mentioned	1) Pennsylvania Railroad 2) New York Central Railroad 3) San Joaquin Light and Power	1) Pennsylvania Railroad 2) Southern Pacific Railroad 3) Great Northern Railroad

Leading sources of items on big business	1920–1929 1) Action taken by big business 2) Meetings and conventions 3) Economic conditions
Leading solutions or responses	1) Federal action (70%) 2) Private collective action (14%) 3) Individual action (9%)

SOURCE: *Engineering News.* Similar data from previous periods are in tables 3–1, 4–4, 5–4, and 6–6.

CONTINUITY AND CHANGE, 1920–1929

of big business and with its overall efficiency. At the same time, he had become far more likely to expect the federal government to deal with giant enterprise when something had to be done. No longer was he confident that the individual, whether a businessman or an engineer, could cope with the problems associated with large-scale organizations. In the late twenties, the engineer also paid increasing attention to the renewal of the concentration movement, but he saw in this wave of mergers no cause for anxiety: "The trend during recent years toward large combinations of industrial corporations has resulted," he said, "in the elimination of many factors which tended to limit the value of a certain project and hence to require more capital to attain a certain result. For instance, in the electric light and power field the trend toward interconnection and toward reduction of production costs by larger units, by elimination of small plants and by reduction of idle emergency equipment has had the result of enabling the electric-construction dollar to go farther than formerly."[82] So much for competition as a goal of the professional engineer.

The factors guiding his attitudes were those economic and organizational developments stressed by his professional ideology. The associations sustaining this belief system were, if anything, stronger and more vocal than they had been in the progressive era. Their values and their concept of the engineer's role were virtually unchanged, ensuring that the engineer's image of the large firm would remain impervious to most of the unique events which historians have emphasized in their study of American culture in the 1920s. For the engineer there was little that was changed and even less that was unique in the decade following the First World War. His was no lost or alienated generation; it was a generation of middle-class professionals who could by 1929 see no flaws in the highly concentrated industrial system they were helping to build.

VIII. The giant combines the engineer praised were to the radical worker a target for his bitterest words. Instead of seeing how a merger leads to an efficient business, the IWW saw how the "trust gobbles up a shoal of small competitors."[83] The police in steel towns were "cossacks" in service of the trust, and the newspapers which reported their activities were a "kept press" that included "the Standard Oil Company's daily paper, the *Toledo News*."[84] The managers of the combines were "snarling beasts in human form," who like the "pot-bellied president of the Baldwin locomotive works" would never understand why their workers could not live on $6.40 a week.[85]

Harsh invective was common to both the prewar and postwar versions of *Solidarity*, but even the IWW could not entirely avoid the winds of change. In the twenties, that general cultural transformation which had altered the language of antitrust among the middle cultures appears at last to have influenced the radical worker as well.[86] He was less inclined to talk about "beasts" and more likely to discuss "big business"; he gradually substituted "company" for "trust," "corporation" for "monster," and "manufacturer" for "Moloch."[87] While he could apparently hate a "concern" as much as he had a "Moloch," the transition in language indicated that his commitment to socialist ideology did not leave him entirely insensitive to changes in his cultural setting.

The radical worker's outlook changed in other ways during the postwar years. He became more attentive to action taken directly by big business, as did some conservative, middle-class citizens (compare "Leading sources" in table 7-6 with the same category in table 5-7). He also took cognizance of the inflated corporate profits and the closely related boom that occurred in the stock market during the latter part of the decade. To him, however, the profits that symbolized success for most Americans were merely additional evidence that big business had a stranglehold on the working class. "Monopoly means profits," as he saw it, and that was all the trusts cared about; in peace as in war, at home and abroad, big business always sought new means to sacrifice its employees "on the altar of profit."[88] "Remarkably rich returns on investment" were proof "that the slaves are being exploited to the limit."[89] Not content with robbing their employees, the corporations watered their stock to deceive the public and feed the great bull market of the late twenties.[90] The radical worker was attentive to these features of the economy, and as new targets of opportunity presented themselves, he shifted his attention from the lumber industry to petroleum, from American Tobacco to Anaconda Copper and the Ford Motor Company.

While changes of this sort took place, the most outstanding characteristic of the radical worker's image of big business was obviously its stability (figure 7-8). This was equilibrium with a vengeance, a basically invariant set of opinions capable of withstanding major shocks from within and without the IWW.[91] The radical worker's outlook was almost as stable as that of the engineer, in spite of the serious economic, political, and organizational setbacks the laborer suffered after the war. During the postwar crisis, the major outlines of his image of the trusts hardly quivered. Although his own union was under severe political attack, he gave little more consideration to the entente between big business and the government than he had during or before the First World War. Others might find in the swift cycle of inflation and suddenly falling prices new cause to worry about the trusts, but such ephemeral developments did not sway the radical worker. He knew that food prices were relatively high in 1921 "not because there is a shortage of it, but because the food monopolies, 'big business,' have it under control."[92] When the railroads were unable to meet the demand for cars and nevertheless taxed the public with high rates, this flaw in the "private ownership system" did not

CONTINUITY AND CHANGE, 1920-1929

FIGURE 7-8. The radical worker's evaluation of big business, 1910-1930. The annual percentages represent the proportion of items in *Solidarity* reflecting each attitude.

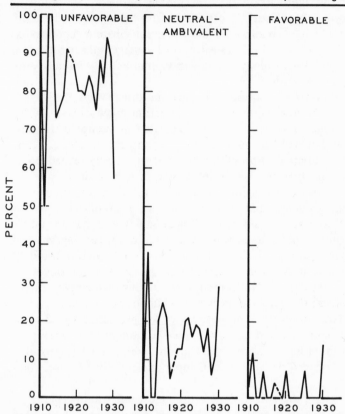

surprise him.[93] Strikes and depressions were all one could expect in a capitalistic society on the brink of collapse.

As the economy recovered, the IWW member had to confront the challenge of prosperity, but as it turned out, this presented no more of a threat to his ideology than did depression. Others heralded the big Christmas sales of the department stores in 1922 as a sign of prosperity, but he reminded them that Marshall Field catered "mostly to [the] so-called better, i.e., wealthy class trade" and not to the underpaid employees of the Pullman Company. Pullman gave its workers Christmas presents, but that was a ruse to hide the firm's year-long exploitation of labor and a weapon to destroy the workers' self-respect.[94] Nor was he deceived when the Ford Motor Company raised its wages. He knew that Henry Ford simultaneously speeded up his assembly line to squeeze more surplus labor out of his workers.[95]

THIRD GENERATION

218

Even the veritable collapse of the IWW did not visibly alter the radical's image of corporate enterprise. The union was divided against itself and in 1924 split into two factions. In the next few years its support dwindled until by the end of the decade it probably had fewer than ten thousand members (although still claiming three times that number). Beset from within and assaulted from without, the Industrial Workers of the World was virtually defunct on the eve of the Great Depression.[96] This cataclysmic decline produced, however, no reappraisal of the role of big business in America, and the durability of the worker's attitudes attests to the powerful

TABLE 7-6. The radical worker's image of big business, 1920-1930

Aspects of big business mentioned	1920-1924			1925-1930		
	High year	Low year	Mean	High year	Low year	Mean
Economic	100%	80%	92%	96%	78%	88%
Political	33	24	29	39	27	32
Social	7	0	2	4	9	1

Leading characteristics of big business	1) Labor relations 2) Wages and hours 3) Management or ownership	1) Labor relations 2) Wages and hours 3) Financial practices
Leading industries mentioned	1) Railroad transportation (40) 2) Primary metals (33) 3) Petroleum refining (29)	1) Railroad transportation (40) 2) Primary metals (33) 3) Transportation equipment (37)
Leading firms mentioned	1) Standard Oil 2) Pennsylvania Railroad; Chicago, Milwaukee and St. Paul Railroad; New York Central Railroad	1) Standard Oil; U.S. Steel 2) Ford; General Electric; Anaconda

Leading sources of items on big business	1920-1930
	1) Action taken by big business; Action taken by labor 2) Letters to the editor 3) Other publications

Leading solutions or responses	1920-1924	1925-1930
	1) Private collective action (97%) 2) Federal action (3%)	1) Private collective action (92%) 2) Individual action (3%); Federal action (3%)

SOURCE: *Solidarity*. Similar data for previous periods are in tables 5-7 and 6-5.

CONTINUITY AND CHANGE, 1920-1929

hold that a socialist ideology could maintain.[97] If the engineering associations had been in similar disarray, one suspects that drastic changes in opinion would have been one of the consequences of organizational decline. This was not the case with the socialist worker, who saw in the demise of his own union nothing more than another temporary setback in the inevitable progression toward a society that would cap the concentration movement by bringing all industry under one public trust. His faith in that outcome remained unshaken, and his experience during the twenties was, like that of the engineer, a study in continuity.

IX. By 1929, the radical worker stood alone. Most middle-class Americans had come to accept the giant corporation as a permanent feature of their society. For the most part, they had not learned to love big business but they had decided they could live with it. Neither progressive nor Marxist frameworks seem suitable to the data at hand, and we can discard them along with the gin-jazz portrait of a lost generation. In place of them we can offer nothing as colorful. Instead, we can only describe a substantial shift in opinions that represented a continuation of prewar trends in the middle cultures: a pattern of accommodation that began in the late nineties, was carried forward under different circumstances in the progressive era, and was completed during the latter part of the twenties.

While the pattern of change before and after the war was similar, the process was different in several ways. In the twenties economic variables were manifestly the most powerful determinants of opinion in the middle classes. In the immediate postwar years, an economic crisis triggered a formidable cycle of antitrust sentiment. After 1921, prosperity eased the tensions that existed between most Americans and big business. Meanwhile, economic developments of a different sort left the trade unionist uncertain about his future and unable to see how his craft organizations could shore up his declining position. For the skilled laborer and others, the interaction between economic and organizational factors was important. On balance, organizational developments ranked next to economic variables in the process of attitude formation. Politics was—especially after 1921—substantially less influential than it had been in the progressive era; and during the 1920s, as in the first generation, the political system actually had less impact on opinions about big business than did social variables. In some instances these were traditional values and class concepts, in others new values attuned to a corporate purview that was threatening by 1929 to become the dominant culture of urban, industrial America.

This new cultural setting was reflected in our data on the language of antitrust and on the businessmen associated with giant enterprise. When middle Americans talked about big business in the twenties, they drew

TABLE 7-7.   Leading businessmen associated with the large corporation, 1920-1929

Clergy	Engineers	Midwestern farmers	Southern farmers	Organized labor	Radical workers
1) Ford; Rosenwald	1) Ford; Loree	None appeared more than twice	1) Ford; Tacone	1) Ford 2) Gary 3) Willard	1) Rockefeller 2) Ford 3) Morgan

heavily on neutral symbols, the pale language of the organization man.[98] Similarly, they no longer invested the corporation with a personality drawn from the ranks of the robber barons (table 7-7). Henry Ford was the only business leader about whom most of middle America could agree, and Detroit's flivver king stood in sharp contrast to the moguls stressed before the war.[99] Ford symbolized the self-made man. He had built his fortune by providing the middle class with a relatively inexpensive product of superior quality. While Ford had his quirks, he had not acquired his industrial empire by mergers; nor could he be associated with Wall Street or the international bankers. The tycoons who had (and who were thus more representative of big business as a whole) were no longer subjects of major concern in the middle cultures. By 1929 the robber barons had been buried and, even more important, forgotten.[100] Personality thus yielded to bureaucracy, as new values and a new order of large-scale organizations achieved a strong position in the United States.

The corporate culture of the late twenties provided new norms by which to judge big business and other American institutions. The emphasis in this value system was on organizational achievement instead of individual responsibility, on specific, unemotional decision-making in place of affective, diffuse judgements. The new consensus blurred class and occupational lines, drawing Americans together around a culture tailored to the needs of a highly organized society. Seemingly, this bureaucratic order was firmly planted, but events of the next few years were to impose a severe trial for the equilibrium of 1929.

8

TOWARD A STABLE EQUILIBRIUM, 1930-1940

The Great Depression of the thirties struck hard at middle-class America, destroying the balance of forces that by 1929 had neutralized most of its antipathy toward big business. The effects were not immediate. At first a number of commentators expressed the opinion that the depression would be short-lived and not too serious, something on the order of the downturn in 1927—merely a temporary chastisement for the financial excesses of the late twenties.[1] Panics in the stock market had taken place before and they would doubtless occur again, men assured themselves; following the downturn one could always expect recovery and a new surge of economic growth. As the months passed and conditions steadily worsened, however, even the most optimistic friends of capitalism despaired of the news reports. By 1931, over eight million persons were unemployed, and during the following year they were joined by another four million. As profits dwindled and bankruptcies multiplied, state and local governments found their revenues slashed just when the demands for relief were greatest. By the winter of 1932, many public as well as private institutions had failed or were on the brink of total collapse.[2]

The Great Depression was the fifth in a sequence of major politico-economic crises faced since 1880 by the modern order of large-scale organizations. The first had taken place in the late eighties and early nineties, when agrarian discontent centered on the industrial and transportation combines apparently threatening the farmer's interests. The second followed the panic of 1893, when depression had robbed many Americans of their confidence and focused their anxieties on the trusts; this second wave of antitrust sentiment carried over into the progressive era and received further impetus from the forces of reform in the years prior to the First World War. A painful postwar readjustment, both economic and political, had generated a fourth cycle of anticorporate opinion in the years 1920 and 1921. Now came a depression dwarfing the previous economic setbacks and bringing to power a political leader who captured and held the affection of the American people (and their historians) as no previous president had.

In this combination of economic distress and powerful political leadership there was the potential for a tidal wave of antitrust opinion in the middle cultures. Coming as it did on the heels of the merger movement of the late twenties, the depression was tailor-made to arouse middle-class resentment toward big business. After all, the larger corporations were the culprits whose stocks traded on Wall Street and whose shares plummeted in value after the 1929 crash—a panic that unhappily heralded, if it did not cause, the ensuing depression. For the clergy the panic and depression furnished lessons in the evils of financial chicanery, offered numerous examples of social conflict, and provided a new experience with liberal reform—a combination of circumstances that in previous years had always fueled clerical animosity toward big business. To the members of the AFL the thirties were even more trying; laborers watched helplessly as the status and market values of their crafts suffered, as their trade unions clashed first with employers and then with the CIO, as the opportunities to find employment of any sort, in a craft or not, dwindled and disappeared. In the Midwest the farmer found himself caught between unyielding mortgage payments and falling income, and things were no better in the rural South, where cotton that had sold for eighteen cents a pound in 1928 was going for less than six cents a pound three years later. While the engineer had less to worry about, the Great Depression also touched his profession. As construction projects stopped, the demand for his services declined. With the national economy faltering, he had cause to reconsider the efficiency of those large-scale organizations that played a central role in America's capitalistic system. This was particularly true for public utilities, and the collapse of the Insull empire was especially suited to provoke the professional engineer.

There was every reason to expect a burst of antitrust opinion, a traumatic period of instability in public attitudes toward big business. Considering the combination of depression problems and liberal politics —something comparable to overlapping the hard times of the nineties and the vigorous reforms of the progressive era—one would expect to find a prolonged and profoundly bitter attack on the giant industrial firm. The experiences of the thirties should, it seems, have caused a decisive breakdown in the corporate culture.

II. This is exactly what happened among the clergy, for whom the New Deal years were the climax of the antitrust movement. The Protestant minister reconsidered the performance of large-scale enterprise, reversed his earlier position, and pronounced big business harmful in terms that became overwhelmingly negative in the mid-thirties (figure 8–1). While in the 1890s and the early phase of progressivism the minister's critique of industrial

FIGURE 8-1. The Congregational clergy's evaluation of big business, 1880–1940. The annual percentages represent the proportion of items in *Congregationalist* and *Advance* reflecting each attitude. For an explanation of my methodology, see chapter 2.

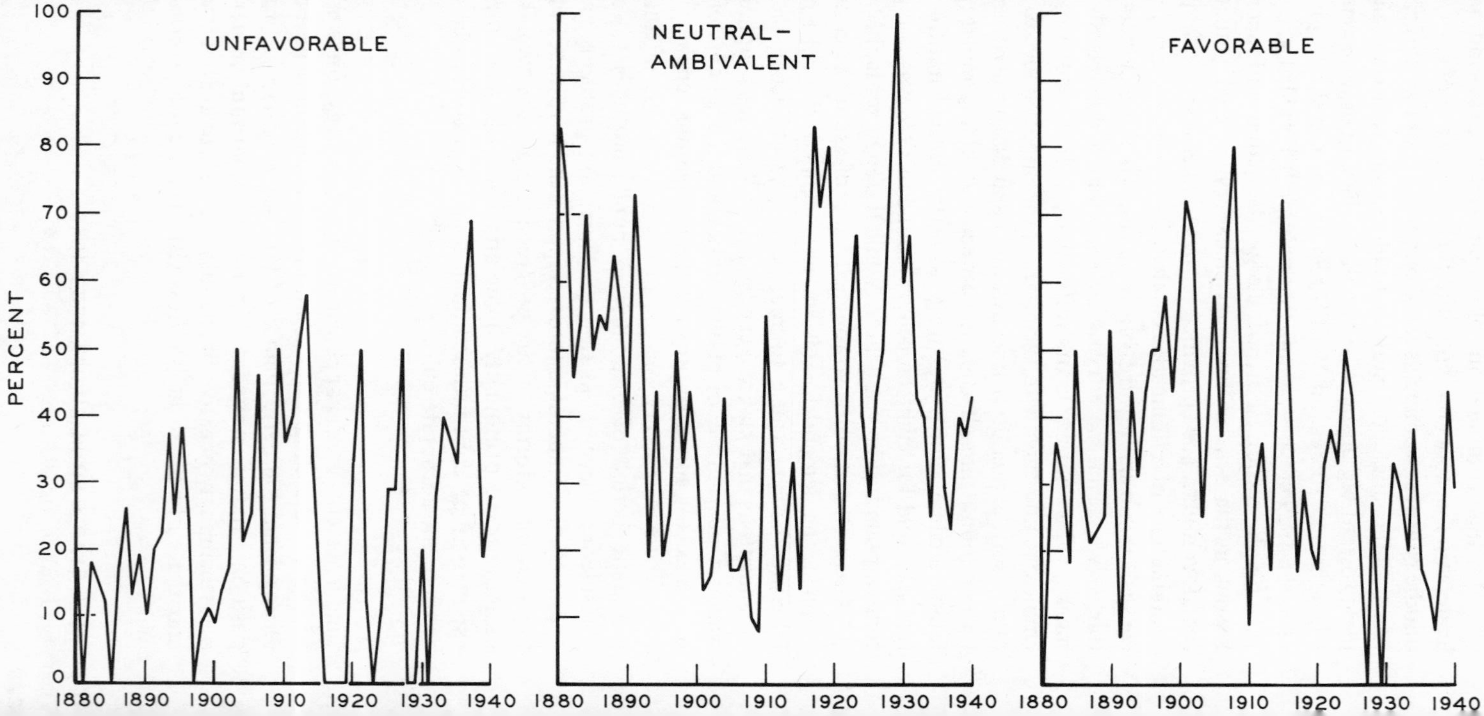

combines had been accompanied by a growing appreciation of the positive aspects of the large firm (figure 8-1), the clergyman was less ambivalent in the thirties. He now saw little in the business world that deserved his kind words. Thereafter, he never really regained confidence in big business (as he had after the 1920–21 cycle), never became again a strong proponent of the large corporation.[3]

Clearly, corporate values and pro-business opinions had not been firmly anchored in this part of the middle classes by the end of the twenties. During the depression the clergyman's ideas changed rapidly, so much so that this decade ranks behind only the progressive and immediate postwar years in terms of attitudinal instability (see Appendix). Looking at the Protestant minister's search for a sense of order in the new age of bureaucracies over a period of three generations, we can see that his perception of big business was primarily characterized not by consensus, comity, or accommodation, but by a sense of mounting conflict.

The depression exposed a variety of unsavory corporate financial practices that provoked the clergyman in the years 1930 through 1935.[4] He felt betrayed by the business elite, men of his social class. Characteristically, in the early thirties the minister was worried more about this problem, which touched the interests of the upper and upper-middle classes, than about unemployment or the declining wages of industrial workers. As he saw it, "High finance invaded the whole field of industry with what was little short of piracy. Through the formation of subsidiary companies, interlocking directorates, and by all the devices of dishonest schemes, even though they may have been technically legal, for the grabbing of other people's money, concerns that had sufficient business to warrant success were put into the hands of a receiver, while the assets disappeared into the pockets of the schemers and exploiters."[5]

In the early part of the decade, when the clergyman first began to get angry at the corporation, two of the features of large enterprise that most irritated him were business involvement in politics and the political values such activity embodied.[6] He had not forgotten the Teapot Dome scandal of the twenties, and he now saw in the large corporation a fundamental threat to the democratic system. Comparing the United States with Germany and Italy, he concluded that "if the rugged individualists have their way with us, we must prepare to welcome some species of Fascism within a brief period of time." He observed glumly: "The industrialists of the Saar and the Ruhr financed Adolf Hitler. The coal and steel and automobile merchants of Pittsburgh and Detroit will do it here. We can have our Fascist state within five years if Roosevelt fails in achieving his goal."[7] Later, the government investigation of the munitions makers prompted further reflections on corporate political values. While the Du Ponts claimed that in the First World War "their services to the nation and to civilization had been very great [as had their profits]," the minister knew that these manufacturers were the same parties who "have been making other profits by re-arming Germany in defiance of the Versailles Treaty and the fears of the rest of the world."[8] The links between fascism and American big business seemed all too close to the clergyman, whose traditional liberal support for democracy now included global concerns that added a new dimension to the social gospel.

After 1935, conflict between the leaders of big business and labor organizations became the minister's chief complaint about the large firm. He saw in the steel strike of 1937 another example of the "illegal use of thugs and spies who have unquestionably again and again provoked violence on the part of the workers."[9] Ford, whose cars were so vital to the minister's daily tasks, was "the conspicuous standard bearer" for the "large employers who resolutely fight all organizations, or who at the most, will accept carefully chaperoned organizations within their own ranks." Ford was guilty of systematically "robbing" his workers.[10] In another instance, big business warded off unionization by shutting down a plant providing most of the employment for an entire city. The company "retired to its midwest headquarters, thereby leaving a situation of chaos behind. Practically every person who lived or worked in that vicinity suffered more or less from that action." Although the minister admitted he could not judge who was guilty in this labor dispute, he was well "aware that this sort of action, as well as actual war, is precisely what makes men distrust life, and makes them wonder if this can be described as a kindly universe."[11]

When John D. Rockefeller died in 1937, the minister reflected at some length on "the essential iniquity" of a society that permitted "such pyramiding of power in the hands of one man." While Rockefeller had been philanthropic and faithful to God, he had amassed his "great wealth by predatory methods, by evasions and defiance of the law, by the practice of vast extorsions [sic], by getting unfair and generally unlawful advantages . . . by secret agreements and manipulation of railway and government officials, by such violations of law as have been brought to light in the rebate cases, by the use of trust funds for private gain, by manifold acts that tend to corrupt the character and destroy the foundations of the social order."[12] In the eyes of the Protestant minister, the performance of such business leaders as Rockefeller raised serious questions about the highly organized business system of twentieth-century America.

The clergyman was indebted for many of these questions to the intellectuals who first raised them and to the popularizers who transmitted elite concepts to a broader audience. His church paper regularly reviewed books and drew upon articles that had appeared in other papers and magazines. These publications were, in fact, the leading source of items (see table 8–1) on big business in the *Congregationalist*.[13] The books ranged from Upton Sinclair's exposé of Ford, *The Flivver King*, to Porter Sargent's appraisal of *The New Immoralities*.[14] The recovery program of the New Deal prompted the minister to look again at Edward Bellamy's *Looking Backward*, and Frederick Lewis Allen's *The Lords of Creation* made him ponder the "social consequences" of the concentration movement and the economic "catastrophes" resulting from "the pyramiding of power in the hands of fewer and fewer men."[15] In 1936 he wondered whether it was true, "as recent studies by Stuart Chase, the Brookings Institution, Berle and Means, and others seem to indicate, that a great group of American industrial concerns,

TABLE 8-1. The Congregational clergy's image of big business, 1930-1940

Aspects of big business mentioned[a]	1930-1935			1936-1940		
	High year	Low year	Mean[b]	High year	Low year	Mean
Economic	100%	86%	96%	100%	80%	96%
Political	50	0	24	54	14	27
Social	0	0	0	14	0	4

Leading characteristics of big business	1) Products or services 2) Management or ownership 3) Existence or expansion	1) Products or services; Management or ownership 2) Existence or expansion
Leading industries mentioned	1) Railroad transportation (40)[c] 2) Transportation equipment (37) 3) Petroleum refining (29)	1) Railroad transportation (40) 2) Transportation equipment (37) 3) Petroleum refining (29)

Leading firms mentioned	1930-1940
	1) Standard Oil 2) Ford 3) Pullman; Republic Iron & Steel
Leading sources of items on big business	1) Other publications 2) Meetings and conventions 3) Miscellaneous political activities
Leading solutions or responses	1) Federal action[d] (39%) 2) Private collective action (31%) 3) Individual action (16%)

SOURCE: *Congregationalist* and *Advance*. For an explanation of my methodology, see chapter 2. Similar data for the previous periods are in tables 3-2, 4-1, 5-1, 6-3, and 7-3.
NOTE: If multiple entries follow one number, the categories were tied.
[a] These figures show what percentage of the articles mentioned each aspect; the columns can total more than 100% because a single article could mention one, two, or all three.
[b] Mean of the annual percentages.
[c] The number appearing after each industry indicates its two-digit group in the *Standard Industrial Classification Manual*.
[d] Also includes general references to an unspecified governmental response or solution.

TOWARD A STABLE EQUILIBRIUM, 1930-1940

upon which the lives and liberties of between 40 and 50 million of our people depend, are finally controlled by less than 200 men? The choice for the future seems to lie between control of our business machine by an increasingly restricted oligarchy of industrial and banking leaders and a planned national control through governmental action. The alternative, a breaking up of the units of control of agricultural and industrial production so that ownership may be widely diffused and exercised, has been charmingly—if somewhat romantically—set forth by Herbert Agar in his recent book *The Land of the Free*. We might realize the American dream along the lines laid down by Mr. Agar; if we don't, perhaps we must make our choice between the control by a self-appointed *junta* of industrialists and bankers, or control of some sort by a national council, politically determined."[16] The minister found none of these alternatives particularly appealing, but they were all that Agar and others had offered him.

Curiously, FDR, the man who has been the central figure in the historian's version of the New Deal, seems not to have played a leading role in channeling the clergyman's opinions. Since Theodore Roosevelt had exerted a dramatic effect on the ideas of the previous generation, the second Roosevelt's lack of influence is all the more surprising. In the thirties, however, the federal executive was not a leading stimulant to discourse on the trust issue; nor was political activity of any sort more important in this regard than it had been in the twenties.[17] Throughout the decade presidential leadership was not a major force shaping opinions in this stratum of the middle cultures, and to that extent, the Roosevelt-centered liberal synthesis needs to be qualified before we can use it to analyze our data.[18]

Roosevelt's inability to capture the minister's attention helps explain the changes that took place in the clergyman's attitudes in the late thirties. Just as the president was launching his antitrust campaign and the Temporary National Economic Committee was setting to work on its massive investigation of the concentration movement, the Protestant minister abruptly lost interest in the trust question. In 1938 and 1939, he became less critical of the giant corporation and began once again to recognize some of the positive contributions business was making to American society. Now he was pleased (1936–40) with the quality of corporate products and services. By the end of the decade he no longer saw any need to mention solutions to the trust problem, so it could not have mattered too much to him that the TNEC's final report in the following year was "as timid as it was unoriginal."[19] By 1940 the peak phase of antitrust feeling had clearly passed.

The abrupt end of this cycle indicates how shallow the commitment to liberalism was in this corner of middle-class America. During the thirties reform concepts had to a substantial degree overcome the clergyman's class bias, but he had a far more tentative attachment to his ideology than the professional engineer or the socialist worker had to theirs. In the late thirties when the economy began to recover from the recession of 1937, when the number of strikes began to decline, when events in Europe began to tug at his mind (just as they had in 1915–16), the Congregational minister ignored Roosevelt's call to action and stopped worrying about big business.[20]

As the tide of antitrust sentiment ebbed, it left behind a minister who had made a partial (and as yet unstable) adjustment to the new age of large-scale organizations. Some of his attitudes and values were different from those of the first generation included in our study. He was more inclined to frame his complaints in terms of organizations and a system of finance than in terms of individual sin. When he sought reform, he was more likely to stress institutional changes than noblesse oblige; some part of his sense of social class had been sacrificed to his interest in coercive controls. In these regards he was beginning to judge the world about him by reference to values that were compatible with an age of large-scale organizations. By 1940, however, this outlook yielded at best an ambivalent stance toward big business, and that precarious balance was dependent upon war abroad, economic recovery, and evidence of social harmony at home. Temporarily, these phenomena reduced, but did not eliminate, the clergyman's fears about the bureaucratic order in American business.

III. The midwestern farmer had emerged from the twenties feeling complacent about the new order of giant firms, but his experience in the following decade severely strained both his relationship with the corporate economy and his acceptance of bureaucratic values. After the stock market collapsed, prices for major farm products steadily declined, reaching a disastrous low point in 1932. Gross farm income (in constant dollars) followed a similar course; by 1932 corn and hog farmers were earning less than half as much as they had grossed in 1929.[21] One expression of the discontent this economic distress bred was the farm strike movement of 1932–33. Another less violent and more successful response was the drive for a national program of subsidies, production controls, and mortgage relief.[22] Government programs under the New Deal-Farm Bureau coalition boosted the farmer's income significantly, but at no time during the thirties did gross income in the Midwest regain 1929 levels. At the end of this decade, after eight years of experimentation with government programs aimed at bolstering the farmer's economic position, the corn and hog producer made about 25 percent less than he had at the end of the twenties.

The farmer in his anguish lashed out (figure 8–2) at "the big packers, big milk companies and big milling concerns."[23] From the stock market crash through 1932, he had remained surprisingly unconcerned with large enterprise, but under the Roosevelt administration the farmer vigorously assaulted his business foes. Upset about high corporate profits—which were partly a consequence of the government's recovery program—he responded to the revelations of the Nye Committee with an attack on the business

FIGURE 8-2. The midwestern farmer's evaluation of big business, 1879-1940. The annual percentages represent the proportion of items in *Farmers' Review, Wallaces' Farmer,* and *Nebraska Farmer* reflecting each attitude.

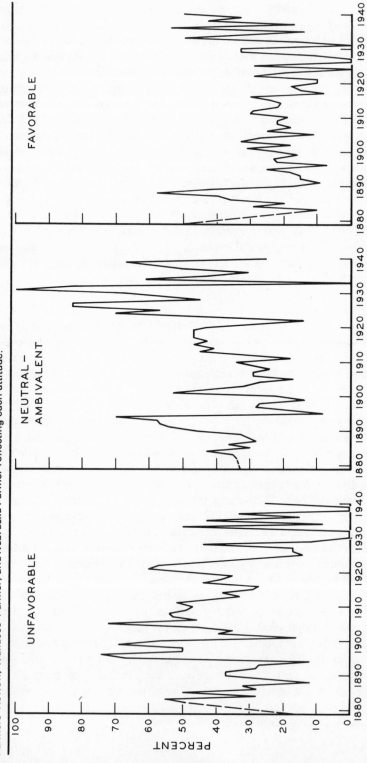

leaders who had become millionaires by exploiting their government positions during the First World War.[24] Obviously, the so-called dollar-a-year men had found some extra dollars for themselves. Worried about business's economic power as well as its profits, the farmer frequently found himself fighting the corporations over New Deal programs.[25]

During this cycle of the antitrust movement, the farmer's attitudes were extremely unstable. By our quantitative measure of disequilibrium, his opinions fluctuated more widely in the thirties than they had at any time since 1879 (see Appendix). His major complaints about corporate behavior were also different from those of previous years, and he was more responsive to political leadership than he had been in the twenties. While the state of the

TABLE 8-2. The midwestern farmer's image of big business, 1930-1940

Aspects of big business mentioned	1930-1935			1936-1940		
	High year	Low year	Mean	High year	Low year	Mean
Economic	100%	77%	95%	100%	67%	93%
Political	50	0	24	83	0	26
Social	0	0	0	17	0	5

Leading characteristics of big business	1) Products or services 2) Financial practices 3) Prices	1) Products or services 2) Management or ownership 3) Existence or expansion; Miscellaneous political activities
Leading industries mentioned	1) Railroad transportation (40) 2) Food processing (20) 3) Communications (48)	1) Railroad transportation (40) 2) Food processing (20) 3) Petroleum refining (29)

Leading firms mentioned	1930-1940
	1) Pullman 2) National Broadcasting 3) Swift
Leading sources of items on big business	1) Economic conditions 2) Federal executive action 3) Meetings and conventions
Leading solutions or responses	1) Federal action (75%) 2) State action (17%) 3) Private collective action (8%)

SOURCE: *Wallaces' Farmer* and *Nebraska Farmer*. Data from previous periods are in tables 3-4, 4-3, 5-2, 6-4, and 7-2.

TOWARD A STABLE EQUILIBRIUM, 1930-1940

economy was the major spur to discussions of big business, FDR had a significant impact upon the agrarian mind (table 8–2). His attacks on "monopolistic and unfair business practices" and on the "economic royalists" who stood in the way of "social progress" found an audience in the corn belt.[26] Under the tutelage of Roosevelt and powerful agrarian organizations, the farmer began to look to the federal government for a solution to the trust problem far more than he had before 1933.[27] During the thirties his confidence in the cooperative movement waned (table 8–2), as did his belief that he might deal effectively with the corporation by simply changing his own behavior. He recognized that the era of individualism had passed and "better farming" no longer appeared to be an appropriate response to the giant corporations that stood arrayed against him in the market place and in Washington, D.C.

While the farmer was inarguably perturbed in the thirties, this cycle of anticorporate opinion was brief, and even at its peak it was less severe than the cycles of the nineties, the progressive era, and the early twenties (figure 8–2). The midwestern farmer's economic situation was dire, but economic adversity no longer turned him against big business to the extent that it had earlier. Hence quantitative measures of correlation do not indicate that there was a close relationship between farm income (or prices) and attitudes toward the corporation, and this in turn points to the considerable change in the agrarian mentality that had taken place in the years since the postwar crisis. In spite of the depression, the farmer now saw a great deal that he liked about the large corporation (figure 8–2), especially its products and services and its management. He applauded the reliability of International Harvester's farm equipment, a quality he traced to the astute leadership of Alexander Legge, who was "one of the nation's foremost industrial and economic leaders, a friend of agriculture and a distinguished public servant."[28] He also enjoyed hearing the NBC Farm and Home Hour on the radio and found railroad services worthy of many more compliments than complaints.[29] There were only two years (1935 and 1937) in which negative opinions of the corporation exceeded favorable viewpoints.

In brief, neither the depression nor Franklin D. Roosevelt reversed the long-run trends in farm attitudes and values. The farmer had not seen big business as a problem central to his (or the nation's) immediate economic or political interests since the twenties. Thus, in his eyes NBC loomed larger than Swift and Company, and in the late thirties he gave more attention to corporate management than he did to the prices big business charged its farm customers. The secular process of accommodation between the farmer and the large firm had depersonalized the corporation and denatured agrarian discourse on this subject. These trends were not reversed in the thirties.[30] While one cannot say that this détente was irrevocable, neither the most severe depression in our history nor the leadership of one of America's most effective presidents disrupted it. This was especially evident in the aftermath of the recession of 1937 when FDR launched his antitrust campaign and the TNEC investigation. Neither had a significant impact upon farm opinion. The farmer was remarkably insensitive to the president's new policies. Corn and hog producers were no longer concerned, no longer worried about solving the trust and railroad problems that had preoccupied two previous generations of midwesterners. The farmer was far more interested in other questions, far more inclined by the late thirties to view antitrust as a dead issue.

Clearly, social and organizational variables now dominated farm opinion, making it increasingly resistant to political and economic factors. In this particular occupational group, organizational values were embedded firmly enough to withstand a major politico-economic crisis. Sustaining the corporate culture were a formidable array of modern agrarian organizations led by the Farm Bureau. In the twenties this organization had been a leading proponent of bureaucratic or corporate values, and its influence had eased relations between big business and the farmer. The Farm Bureau remained a powerful force during the thirties, affecting public policy in Washington and controlling the federal government's commodity programs in the Midwest through its network of agencies.[31] The Bureau was omnipresent. Its impact upon farm opinion in the depression was surely as great or greater than it had been a decade earlier. The organizational values promulgated by the Farm Bureau were also spread by agrarian papers and by government officials: the agents of socialization and social control in the farm community. The new value system—internalized and grounded in effective formal organizations—molded the farmer's response to the depression, ensuring that his reaction against the large corporation would be relatively subdued.

IV. In the 1920s the southern farmer had become a firm friend of large enterprise. When cotton prices and his income slumped after 1929, however, he became more critical of the giant firm, directing his accusations at government policies which gave "unlimited support to big business alone." He also condemned the railroads that maintained their rates in the face of economic collapse (figure 8-3).[32] By 1933 southern farm income (in constant dollars) was about half of what it had been only four years before, and the cotton grower felt that he should no longer be paying exorbitant "wartime freight rates" or suffering the exactions of the jute-bagging trust.[33]

Yet the most noteworthy characteristics of southern farm opinion in the 1930s were its largely favorable view of corporate enterprise (figure 8-3) and its overall stability (Appendix and table 8-3). In depression, as in prosperity, the farmer noticed the special services provided by the southern railroads and praised the efforts of these lines to develop southern livestock;

FIGURE 8-3. **The southern farmer's evaluation of big business, 1879-1940.** The annual percentages represent the proportion of items in *Southern Cultivator* and *Progressive Farmer* reflecting each attitude.

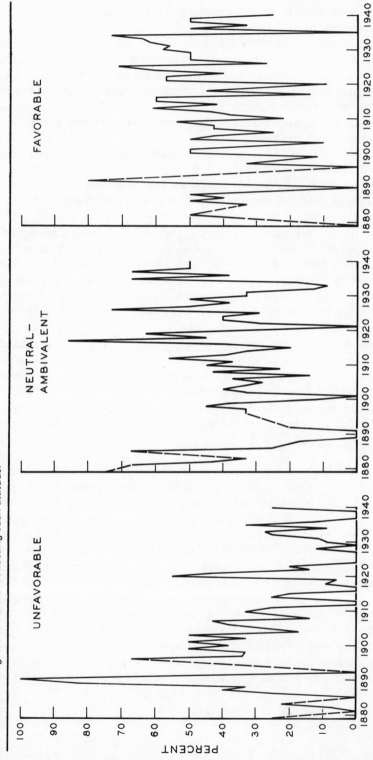

he also warmly greeted the plans of Swift and Company to open a new plant in his home state.[34] Although cotton prices plummeted from seventeen to six cents a pound, he continued to be pleased with the equipment sold by the International Harvester Company and with the markets other large firms provided for his products.[35] Given the adverse conditions the cotton farmer faced, he could easily have focused his anxieties on the trusts, as his predecessors had done in the 1890s; but now he was even less inclined to blame the corporation for his woes than were farmers in the Midwest.

This generation of southern farmers had acquired a different outlook, one centering about a careful economic calculus of the immediate costs and

TABLE 8-3. The southern farmer's image of big business, 1930-1940

Aspects of big business mentioned	1930-1935			1936-1940		
	High year	Low year	Mean	High year	Low year	Mean
Economic	100%	33%	84%	100%	100%	100%
Political	67	9	25	12	0	2
Social	0	0	0	0	0	0

Leading characteristics of big business	1) Products or services 2) Enhances the general wealth 3) Purchasing policies	1) Products or services 2) Enhances the general wealth 3) Purchasing policies; Management or owner-ship; Existence or ex-pansion
Leading industries mentioned	1) Railroad trans-portation (40) 2) Food processing (20) 3) Machinery—nonelec-trical (35)	1) Railroad trans-portation (40) 2) Food processing (20) 3) Communications (48)

Leading firms mentioned	1930-1940 1) Atlantic Coast Line Railroad 2) Armour 3) Swift
Leading sources of items on big business	1) Action taken by big business 2) Meetings and conventions; State execu-tive action
Leading solutions or responses	1) Federal action (37%) 2) State action (26%) 3) Individual action (16%)

SOURCE: *Southern Cultivator* and *Progressive Farmer*. Data from previous periods are in tables 3-3, 4-2, 5-3, 6-1, and 7-4.

TOWARD A STABLE EQUILIBRIUM, 1930-1940

benefits of large-scale organization. Gone were the symbols of social instability and the attitudes characteristic of an oppressed class. No longer was the cotton farmer unnerved by the feeling that his entire universe, from the family to the national government, was about to collapse due to the depredations of the trusts. For better or worse, all that he demanded was equal treatment at the trough of government aid, whether state or federal.[36] He continued to see that there was no advantage in "cussing Wall Street and big business while we ought to be busy adopting some of the methods by which these have become rich and thereby raising our own economic level, rather than trying to tear down the other fellow." The large corporations were "organized and well-managed" and only by following their lessons could the cotton farmer cope with his "highly organized and coordinated society."[37]

In a long-run perspective (see figure 8-3) the thirties emerge as a decade of relative tranquillity in corporate-agrarian relations in this part of the country. Here, even more than in the Midwest, the Great Depression did not disturb the secular process of accommodation. The farmer no longer looked upon the business system as a fiefdom populated with robber barons like the Vanderbilts and Rockefellers; even Henry Ford faded from view in the 1930s. The cotton farmer's image of the large firm was thoroughly depersonalized, and he described business's dealing with his community and region in terms that recall Max Weber's stereotype of the impersonal, modern bureaucracy.[38]

Corporate publicity campaigns had a substantial influence on southern attitudes. Big business provided the southern farmer with ample evidence of its own accomplishments, and for the first time since 1879, the corporation itself was the leading source of discussion on this question (table 8-3). Less of the farmer's information on business filtered down to him through farm organizations and agrarian publications of the sort that had guided his thoughts on the trust question in the days of the Farmers' Alliance.[39] This reinforced a vision of large enterprise that resisted the forces of economic and political change and remained overwhelmingly favorable through years of agricultural distress.

In the latter part of the decade, FDR failed to jar the cotton farmer out of his complaisant attitude. Roosevelt's assistant attorney general in charge of antitrust, Thurman Arnold, "set out to dramatize the issues, manipulate the symbols, and enlist popular support" for the president's policy, but his campaign failed to create an attentive audience on the southern farm.[40] The cotton grower was unresponsive to Arnold and the president, uninterested in the Antitrust Division of the Justice Department and in the inquiries of the TNEC. He was a bit more excited by Gov. Eugene Talmadge of Georgia, who was attacking the giant telephone companies and other "big corporations" that did business in the South.[41] But even the colorful Talmadge could

THIRD GENERATION

not shake the new equilibrium in farm attitudes. By the late thirties the antitrust movement was dead in the South and nothing could rekindle the farmer's animosity toward big business.

The corporate culture was firmly rooted in this corner of the middle class by the beginning of the Second World War. In the South as in the Midwest, organizational values withstood the joint pressures of economic distress and dynamic political leadership. The result was a distinctly minor cycle of antitrust sentiment, ending abruptly in 1936-37, just as the recession created new problems that might well have fueled a burst of anger at the large corporation. The price of cotton fell off 25 percent in the latter year, but the farmer no longer traced his problems to the Wall Street offices of big business. In 1937, 1938, and 1939, in fact, he found nothing to criticize and much to praise in the performance of those giant firms that had once drawn bitter words of condemnation from the cotton country.

V. The depression and New Deal had as little impact on the attitudes of the AFL's skilled craftsman as they had on those of the cotton farmer. In the early thirties the organized laborer's evaluation of big business remained extremely stable in spite of the wage cuts he suffered and the mounting problems he faced in finding a job. If anything, his opinion of the corporation became more favorable (figure 8-4), but the change was slight and the data on equilibrium (see Appendix) indicate that the most outstanding characteristic of the laborer's image was its overall stability. Certainly this was the case from 1930 through the end of 1937. Much of the evidence arrayed in table 8-4 bolsters this conclusion. Most of the worker's attention remained fixed on the transport and oil industries he had focused on before 1930; nor did his concept of the major characteristics of large enterprise change in any substantial way. Despite the rise and fall of the National Recovery Administration and in spite of the passage of the National Labor Relations Act, he did not, for instance, begin to stress the political dimensions of the corporation.

AFL members were, however, sensitive to some of the changes taking place around them. Next to the reports of organizers, the state of the economy most often prompted talk of corporate behavior. By 1931 the skilled worker was looking upon a scene of "World-Wide Unemployment" and was forced to diagnose "The Calamity of Prosperity."[42] As he saw it, the blame was not hard to place: "The evidence that those in control of our industry, commerce and finance are largely responsible for the present depression, is overwhelming. The great majority of the leaders, informed as they are, could not avoid the knowledge that the economically unsound distribution of wealth for which they were responsible, must result in industrial depression and disaster. . . . They had at their command larger

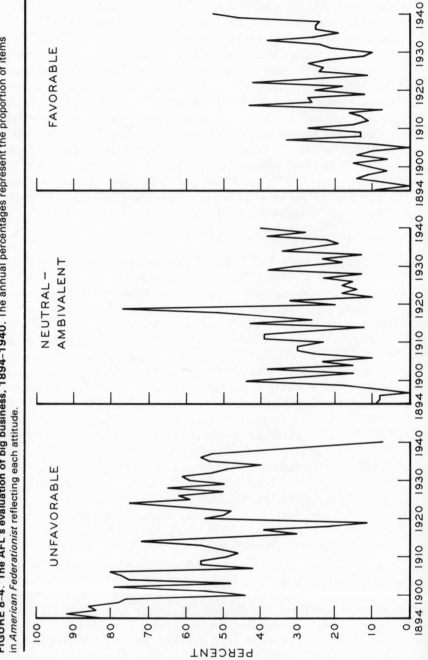

FIGURE 8-4. The AFL's evaluation of big business, 1894-1940. The annual percentages represent the proportion of items in *American Federationist* reflecting each attitude.

staffs of technically trained men than during any previous period; yet, with all of their knowledge and powerful organizations with their far-reaching influence, they created the economic condition which brought about the depression." It was the "captains of industry and finance" who were responsible for America's problems and the craftsman's distress.[43]

The organized worker was not ambivalent about the major problem caused by the corporation: it was unemployment. Neither the political power nor the corrupt financial practices of big business upset him, and for the first time since 1894 his major complaint was not corporate labor practices. More important to him in the early thirties than company unions, or discrimina-

TABLE 8-4. The AFL's image of big business, 1930-1940

Aspects of big business mentioned	1930-1935			1936-1940		
	High year	Low year	Mean	High year	Low year	Mean
Economic	100%	91%	95%	100%	94%	96%
Political	35	0	17	22	0	11
Social	5	0	2	0	0	0
Leading characteristics of big business	1) Labor relations 2) Wages and hours 3) Diminishes individual's opportunities			1) Labor relations 2) Enhances individual's opportunities 3) Wages and hours		
Leading industries mentioned	1) Railroad transportation (40) 2) Transportation equipment (37) 3) Petroleum refining (29)			1) Railroad transportation (40) 2) Primary metals (33) 3) Transportation equipment (37)		
Leading firms mentioned	1) Ford 2) Standard Oil 3) Fisher			1) General Motors 2) International Harvester; Atlantic & Pacific Stores		
Leading sources of items on big business	1930-1940 1) Letters to the editor 2) Economic conditions 3) Action taken by labor					
Leading solutions or responses	1930-1935 1) Private collective action (55%) 2) Federal action (31%) 3) Individual action (11%)			1936-1940 1) Private collective action (69%) 2) Federal action (29%) 3) State action (2%)		

SOURCE: The information in this table is drawn from the *American Federationist*. Data for previous periods are in tables 4-6, 5-6, 6-2, and 7-1.

TOWARD A STABLE EQUILIBRIUM, 1930-1940

tion against trade unionists, or any of the multitude of hostile practices he associated with such large enterprises as the Ford Motor Company or Standard Oil was the vital matter of holding or finding a job. His interest in these and other firms was often aroused by a battle between the companies and an AFL union, but the most favorable labor-management relations could not help him as long as the firms were not doing enough business to keep him employed.[44]

When he thought about this problem and others stemming from the concentration movement, the skilled laborer sometimes looked to the federal government for help (table 8–4). In the summer of 1933, for instance, he found the National Recovery Administration appealing and felt that centralization might be preferable to "allowing every business, big or small, to plan irrespective of other enterprises in the industry."[45] Before many months had passed, however, he realized that big business was "defying the law, the [government Labor] Boards, and . . . working to nullify Labor's rights in the courts."[46] He became somewhat disappointed with the new political order, and even the passage of the Wagner Act in 1935 and the activities of the National Labor Relations Board (1936–40) could not convince him that he should look to Washington instead of his union headquarters for support in dealing with the large corporation. Given the extent of his problems and the increase in governmental activity in the field of labor-management relations, the most surprising aspect of his thought in the late thirties was the absence of interest in or dependence on the Roosevelt administration. In fact, he looked to the federal government for help no more often than he had in the years 1920–24 or during the period just before the First World War.[47]

Thus the worker's opinion of corporate enterprise remained stable through 1937, and the degree of continuity between the depression years and the previous decade suggests that the major determinants of attitude (1930–37) were related neither to politics nor income.[48] Instead, the factors accounting for the skilled laborer's response—rather, his lack of it—were to be found in the nature of his national unions and the secondary organization uniting them, the AFL. By the end of the twenties the craft union movement had been severely weakened, and the experiences of the early thirties left the organizations with even fewer members and less financial support. The quality of trade union leadership in these years was apparently poor—and at the very least we can conclude that the majority of the top men in the AFL were not particularly innovative in their reaction to the depression or to the rare opportunities presented to organized labor by the Roosevelt administration.[49] The emergence of the CIO reflected, in part, the inability of the craft unions to cope with a new, opportunity-filled situation. The AFL and its members were lethargic in their responses to the New Deal, and the same lethargy could be seen in the trade unionist's attitude toward the large firm.

THIRD GENERATION

His was an equilibrium rooted in weakness, in an inability to grapple with change, and in a related necessity to block from view the new conditions in his environment. His situation during these years closely resembled the conditions that had existed among the trade unionists who read the *National Labor Tribune* in the years following the depression of the nineties.[50] Then, as in the 1930s, neither the craft nor the craft union gave the skilled worker the support he needed, and his ideas stabilized in default of effective leadership and union organization.

Even during the years 1935–37, when the craftsman became more upset with big business (figure 8–4), he stopped short of wholesale condemnation. These years were so rife with labor-management conflict, so tense over the activities of the NLRB, and so grave due to the economic downturn in 1937, that one would have expected to see a sudden and sharp increase in anticorporate opinion. Instead, the craftsman became slightly more negative, without surrendering any of his favorable evaluations of big business. Moreover, he soon mellowed toward the corporation, and by 1939 found more in the performance of America's largest firms to merit acclaim than criticism.

When war in Europe brought economic relief at home, the skilled worker reacted much as he had during the progressive era and World War I: he first changed his mind about corporate wages (and hours), and then revised his opinion of the large firm's labor policies.[51] In 1938 real wages started to climb, and in 1939 and 1940 the number of unemployed workers dropped off significantly. Now his craft seemed safer and his trade union stronger. He was pleased with the jobs opening up at companies such as International Harvester, Republic Steel, and Ford; he noticed that the giant Weyerhauser Timber Company was negotiating a union contract; he found himself satisfied with the wages and hours at the Atlantic & Pacific Stores.[52] By 1940 he had more that was favorable and less that was negative to say about big business than at any time since 1894.

The craftsman's new orientation was inherently unstable. It was dependent on special wartime conditions and vulnerable to the problems that always accompanied the return of peace. American business had little cause to feel secure about the trade unionist's affection in 1940. While over a forty-seven-year span the skilled worker had indeed gradually become more friendly toward the corporation, the long-range forecast indicated that he would probably revert to a basically hostile stance.

For a time, however, he agreed with other middle-class citizens that the large corporation no longer endangered the vital interests of America. He also felt big business presented no serious threat to the industrial crafts or the nation's trade unions. Events beyond the control of big business, the unions, or even FDR had temporarily neutralized AFL opposition to the giant corporation.

TOWARD A STABLE EQUILIBRIUM, 1930-1940

VI. While the stability of the craftsman's attitudes between 1930 and 1937 was rooted primarily in the weakness of his unions, strong organizational guidance produced virtually the same result among professional engineers. Looking merely at the information presented in table 8–5 and in figure 8–5, one could hardly conclude that an old order had been overturned or that the country had experienced the worst depression in its history. In the early thirties, while unemployment figures soared and the prices of industrial securities dipped ever lower, the engineer remained aloof from the economic crisis. Before 1930 the state of the economy had been a leading source of discussions touching on big business. In the depression-ridden thirties, such was no longer the case (compare table 8–5 with table 7–5). With over eight million persons unemployed in 1931, the engineer was still preoccupied with the high quality of corporate products and services—for example, the prize-winning structures of the American Bridge Company.[53] By the following year, when unemployment had increased by another four million, he offered praise for the "152 lb. 8-in. rail section" of the Pennsylvania Railroad Company and applauded the efficient shipping facilities of the Lehigh Valley Line.[54] He noted, blandly and regularly, the changes in freight rates affecting the "current prices of construction materials," but he gave little heed to the personal hardships inflicted on even his own class of citizens as the downward spiral of prices and production brought the nation to the edge of economic collapse.[55]

What the engineer did not say was as revealing as what he did. One might have expected him to give serious consideration to labor-management relations, especially after the passage of the Wagner Act and the outbreak of violent strikes in the latter part of the decade. In the nineties the Pullman strike had sufficiently aroused an earlier generation of engineers to discuss its implications; but in the thirties the professional engineer's horizons were narrower, and he found it convenient to overlook the sit-down strikes and other episodes of labor-management strife.[56] Nor did he ever talk much about unemployment and the corporation. When he did consider employment opportunities in the large firm, he was interested in the jobs offered to engineers, and in the latter part of the decade, although the general level of unemployment remained high, he found cause for enthusiasm in the mounting demand for technical services in large companies.[57] In effect he left the rest of the unemployed to fend for themselves, while he applauded his own good fortune.

Holding the engineer on a true course through the thirties were the same professional associations and values and the same basic ideology that had guided his thoughts through the previous decade. The associations included the American Society of Civil Engineers, the American Railway Engineering Association, and the Western Society of Engineers. All of these groups and others reinforced a point of view stressing detachment, scientific objectivity, and material progress; since the 1880s the only significant change in his concept of his social role had been the honing down of his professional self-interest to a narrow knife edge. The class-oriented dimension of his thought had remained largely unaltered. The specific emphasis he gave to certain goals had merely shifted as one organization or another became more active. In the thirties, for example, the American Society for Testing Materials was relatively more influential than it had been before the depression; hence, the adoption of rationalistic standards earned more praise than it had in the previous decade.[58] But the shift in emphasis was slight, and the ideas and values embodied in the engineer's ideology remained fundamentally unchanged—and with it his vision of the great corporation.

Insofar as the engineer did change his mind about big business, his thoughts never wandered far from the concerns of his profession. In the late thirties he became slightly more negative toward big business (figure 8–5). By eliminating neutral-ambivalent items, we can make this cycle stand out more clearly, and the data in the Appendix also suggest that the events of these years did not leave the engineer entirely unscathed.[59] He became critical when he realized that the Aluminum Company of America sought "to obtain control of the entire St. Lawrence power system," because he felt that "private exploitation of Niagara power had been inefficient and extravagant."[60] Next to inefficiency, he reserved his strongest complaints for the corporations that leaned on political aid: "The philosophy that the government is responsible for the condition of our railroads and the asking by the executives for legislation to cure their internal ills is probably the most serious aspect of railway operation today." To the engineer it was axiomatic that "the railway problem will not be solved until railway executives cease seeking a solution through legislation, assuming full responsibility for their difficulties and proceed vigorously to correct these evils through their own efforts."[61] In his eyes federal relief was no substitute for efficient, systematic management.

The professional engineer was sensitive to the growing importance of national economic policies, and in *Engineering News* the activities of the executive branch of the government became a leading source of articles on large enterprise. Characteristically, however, the engineer's view of government was impersonal. FDR attracted little attention. The engineer was impervious to the captivating public personality of the man to whom numerous historians have given the leading role in America's depression drama. Instead, the professional engineer kept his eye on the Public Works Administration, the Federal Power Commission, the Corps of Engineers, and the U.S. Reclamation Office—all of which directly influenced those industries that were uppermost in his mind.[62] If there was any individual in the middle of the stage, it was Secretary of the Interior Harold L. Ickes, who headed the PWA and decided ultimately which railroads were to receive

FIGURE 8-5. The engineer's evaluation of big business, 1880–1940. The annual percentages represent the proportion of items in *Engineering News* reflecting each attitude.

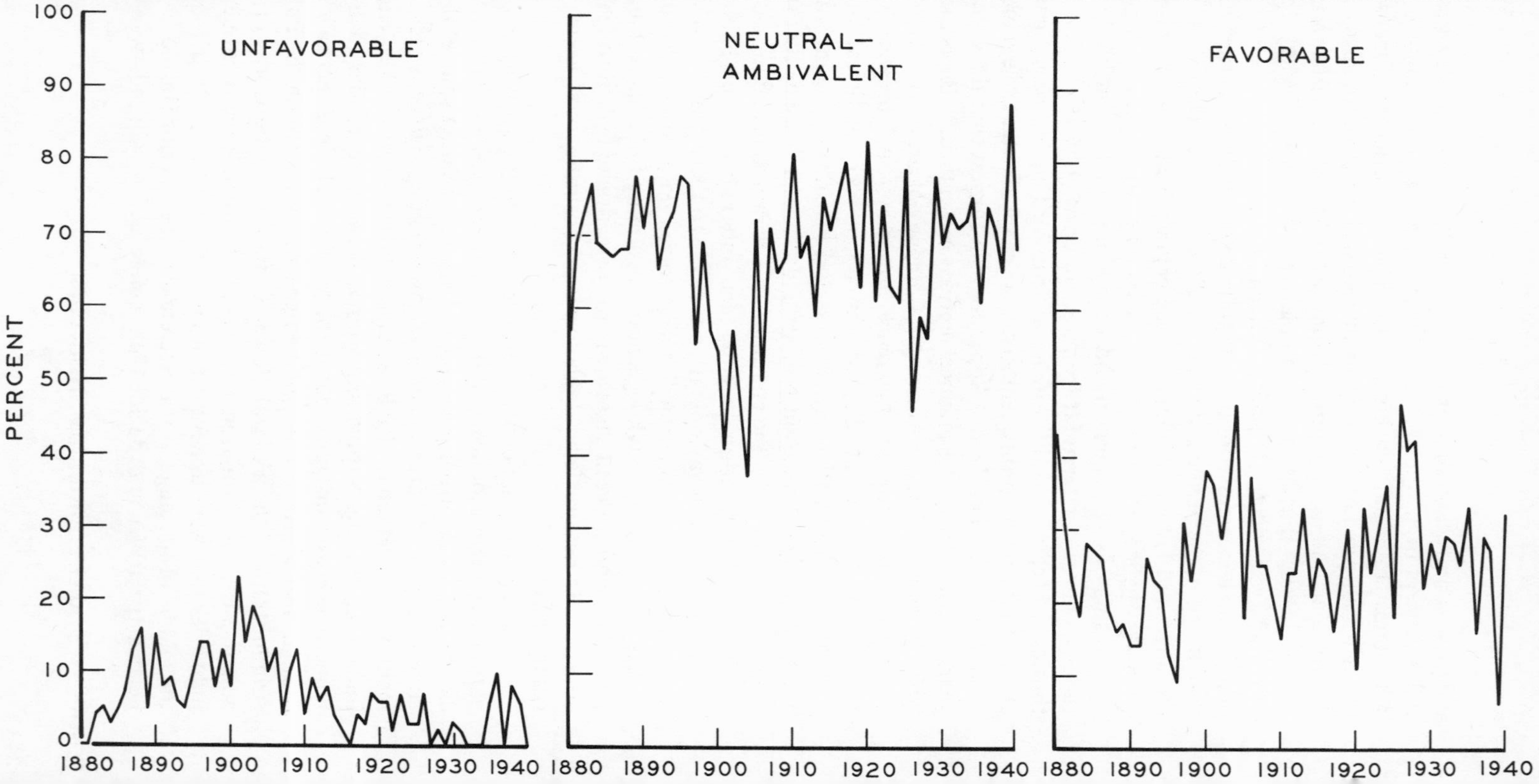

TABLE 8-5. The engineer's image of big business, 1930-1940

Aspects of big business mentioned	1930-1935			1936-1940		
	High year	Low year	Mean	High year	Low year	Mean
Economic	100%	88%	95%	98%	81%	91%
Political	33	11	22	32	15	28
Social	0	0	0	0	0	0

Leading characteristics of big business	1) Products or services 2) Miscellaneous political activities 3) Management or ownership	1) Products or services 2) Miscellaneous political activities 3) Existence or expansion
Leading industries mentioned	1) Railroad transportation (40) 2) Primary metals (33) 3) Electric-gas-sanitary services (49)	1) Railroad transportation (40) 2) Electric-gas-sanitary services (49) 3) Primary metals (33)
Leading firms mentioned	1) Westinghouse 2) Pennsylvania Railroad 3) Baltimore & Ohio Railroad	1) New York Central Railroad 2) Pennsylvania Railroad 3) Union Pacific Railroad; Baltimore & Ohio Railroad; Bethlehem Steel

Leading sources of items on big business	1930-1940 1) Action taken by big business 2) Meetings and conventions 3) Federal executive action
Leading solutions or responses	1) Federal action (63%) 2) Individual action (20%) 3) Private collective action (10%)

SOURCE: *Engineering News*. Data for previous periods are in tables 3-1, 4-4, 5-4, 6-6, and 7-5.

government loans for the purchase of new rails. Even Ickes—whose personality did have a significant influence on this particular program—was less important than the institution he represented and the policies it implemented. To the engineer the New Deal was an organizational phenomenon, not an exercise in political leadership. He was pleased (in the late thirties) when business cooperated with the government—when, for instance, the TVA and a private firm contracted "to furnish each other with stand-by service in cases of emergency, resulting in considerable saving in investment for additional plant and equipment by both parties."[63] But he described this

TOWARD A STABLE EQUILIBRIUM, 1930-1940

relationship in impersonal terms, and in fact he paid less attention to the activities of individual business leaders than he had since 1880 (see "Leading characteristics" in table 8–5).

The dedication of the engineer to organizational values, along with the strength of his professional associations and their ideology, muffled discontent and ensured that this cycle of negative opinions would be as brief as it was restrained. Indeed, by 1940, he again saw nothing to criticize and much to praise (figure 8–5) in the activities of big business. About this subject, as about most things in his universe, he was inclined to withhold judgment. But when forced to evaluate big business, the engineer was a durable advocate of the bureaucratic point of view.

VII. Adding together the responses of the different occupational groups (figure 8–6), one can place the thirties in historical perspective as the fifth cycle of anticorporate opinion between 1880 and 1940. What is apparent is the fact that the peak level of hostility was lower in each successive cycle after the mid-nineties. In the Great Depression, middle-class Americans mounted only a brief and rather feeble attack on big business. The reaction of this third generation seems all the more restrained when one considers how serious and prolonged the depression was. If we take into consideration the entire decade, the public image of the large firm consisted of an almost even mixture of favorable and unfavorable evaluations. Neutral-ambivalent opinions outweighed both.[64] The imagery of the 1880s, the period before most middle-class citizens had become aroused at the "trust octopus," was thus almost exactly duplicated.[65]

Americans of the thirties were not merely reverting to the attitudes of their grandfathers. Much had changed since 1880, and opinions of big business continued to fluctuate through the Great Depression. On the basis of our indicator for stability, the thirties stands out as a phase of disequilibrium ranking behind the nineties and the immediate postwar years (see Appendix). In one of the occupational groups (midwestern farmers) opinions were less stable than they had been at any time before, and in all of the other groups there was evidence of new ideas about big business. As was the case with the level of negative attitudes, however, the degree of disequilibrium was not very great when measured against the politico-economic crisis that the nation had weathered. The only comparable experience in the modern period was the depression of the 1890s, and at that time public attitudes had been far less stable and far more hostile toward the large firm.

The major responsibility for dampening the third generation's animosity rested with social and organizational variables. New values, part of a general corporate culture, ensured that this generation's response to a crisis would be unique. No longer did the middle classes see robber barons of the

Gould ilk as the personification of the giant firm. J. P. Morgan had been forgotten. Even Henry Ford could no longer hold the public's attention.[66] The middle class, from top to bottom, saw modern, large-scale enterprise as a relatively impersonal bureaucracy, a type of organization controlling individuals but itself normally beyond the domination of any one man or family. The third generation described this firm in language that was as colorless as the men who now managed the affairs of big business.[67]

During this third generation a new set of values, part of an intricate corporate culture, had become the rule among middle-class Americans. For some (the clergy in particular) the new norms were not yet entirely stable; for others (especially organized labor) they still played a subordinate role in a value system that was relatively traditional. But by the 1930s organizational values were dominant in the middle class as a whole, and this corporate culture survived the test of the Great Depression. The new bureaucratic norms muffled hostility toward corporate enterprise, and on the eve of the Second World War they helped to ease Americans into an acceptance of big business.[68]

Organizational developments also played a significant role in shaping middle-class opinions. Among midwestern farmers, for example, strong agrarian organizations sustained both the new values and a new outlook on the giant firm. Similarly, the attitudinal stability of the engineers was primarily a function of a strong organizational base, with its related ideology, values, and role concepts. Organizational weakness and a related sense of powerlessness produced a similar result among members of the AFL, although in this instance the equilibrium of the late thirties was far from secure. Whatever their precise effects, organizational variables clearly had more influence on attitudes than economic or political factors during the New Deal.

None of the historical syntheses discussed in chapter 1 provides an entirely satisfactory analysis or description of the changes that occurred in the third generation's image of big business. A Marxian framework, for instance, yields the wrong conclusion, since the Great Depression should have sharpened class differences and brought America one step closer to open conflict between the potentates of business and the proletariat. This did not happen, contra Schumpeter as well as Marx.[69] Class concepts were far more important in the first generation than in the third. In the twenties and thirties, class lines broke down and a new consensus emerged. As social classes became less influential, social values came to be a major determinant of attitudes. Analysis of the inverse relationship between these two social variables would seem to pose for latter-day Marxists a fruitful historical problem to explore.

The consensus and progressive historians can find more support than the Marxists in our figures on third-generation imagery. Revisionists of the

FIGURE 8-6. American middle-class evaluations of big business, 1880–1940. The annual percentages are weighted averages of the data from all of the journals. See note 134, chapter 4.

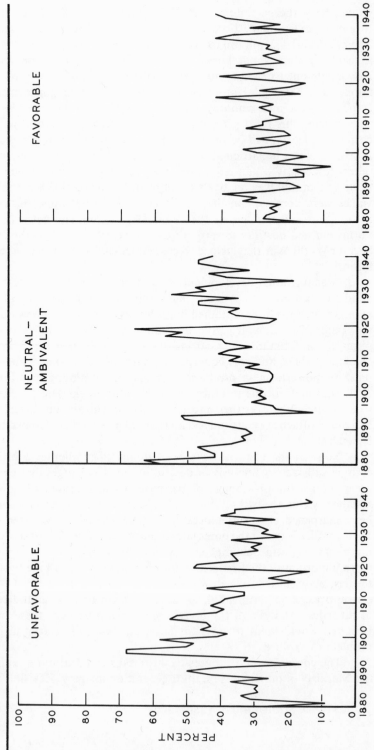

consensus school can take solace in the finding that attitudes and values in the middle classes converged around a new corporate culture, but they must somehow adjust their interpretation to the facts that the long-run process of accommodation involved repeated cycles of intense hostility and that conflict played a large role in achieving equilibrium. Progressive historians have even more to be pleased with in our data, especially since the New Deal years stand out as a period of instability and increased hostility to the corporation. Still, progressive historians must also revise their synthesis if they take all of my conclusions into account: this fifth cycle in the antitrust movement was decidedly weaker than the previous four. Furthermore, FDR exerted far less influence on middle-class attitudes than the Roosevelt-centered histories led us to expect. Political reform had some appeal for all of the groups in this study, but only the clergymen were especially responsive to political leadership, and even they failed to follow the president in his 1938 charge against the trusts.[70] While examining liberal leadership and ideology, progressive historians should, I think, give a causal role to the middle class's accommodation to big business and the related corporate outlook; these values and attitudes doubtless helped shape New Deal politics. Their formative role is a subject beyond the purview of this book but one that warrants extensive study.

The examination of cultural influences on the political system will probably be undertaken by New Left, instead of progressive, scholars. My findings for the third generation are perhaps more compatible with the New Left synthesis than with any other, except the organizational approach outlined in chapter 1. The middle-class accommodation to corporate enterprise will probably help New Left historians explain the conservative nature of many New Deal reforms and the frequent inability of the government to provide help for those who were not organized. Broker state politics was well attuned to the norms of middle-class America.[71] The corporate culture was, I believe, a major impediment to radical reform in a nation whose wealth was largely controlled by large-scale private enterprises. This conclusion will create difficulties only for those New Left historians who feel that better, i.e., more radical, leadership might have produced a thoroughgoing reform of the business system. My findings suggest that even determined radical leaders would have been unable to shake the public's fundamental confidence in the existing corporate order.

The values and attitudes of the new culture clearly emerged intact from the 1930s. By that time most Americans saw antitrust as a dead or dying issue. They were coming to accept—in varying degrees—a different outlook embodying modern, organizational norms and a new image of the large corporation. Gone was the deep hostility of the 1890s, the progressive era, and the postwar crisis. By 1940 the corporate culture had largely supplanted the individualistic-egalitarian outlook characteristic of the nineteenth century. The era of the organization man had begun.

TOWARD A STABLE EQUILIBRIUM, 1930-1940

PART FIVE. CONCLUSIONS, SPECULATIONS, AND AFTERWORD

9

THE MIDDLE CULTURES AND
THE ORGANIZATIONAL REVOLUTION

Among historians, Isaiah Berlin says, some think like the hedgehog and others like the fox. The hedgehogs are those thinkers "who relate everything to a single central vision, one system less or more coherent or articulate, in terms of which they understand, think and feel—a single, universal, organizing principle in terms of which alone all that they are and say has significance." Karl Marx. Joseph Schumpeter. Men with a "single central vision." On the other hand, the foxes are "those who pursue many ends often unrelated and even contradictory, connected, if at all, only in some *de facto* way, for some psychological or physiological cause, related by no moral or aesthetic principle."[1] The revisionists of the 1950s and 1960s—all of those scholars who cracked the clear lines of progressive history. Richard Hofstadter, above all, the master fox who found complexity in every subject he touched.

Ours is an age of foxes, and quantitative history, by its nature, belongs to them. Quantitative studies seem almost always to demonstrate that past human behavior was more complex and its meaning more ambiguous than an earlier generation thought. When historians start to count things, they usually discover that society changed unevenly and rather slowly even during those transitional periods that are called revolutions. It is in this sense that quantification is the natural weapon of the fox.

To my mind, however, the best history draws upon both of these traditions, proclaiming a "single central vision" while it incorporates within that vision the complexity of man's past. The central vision of this book was set forth in the first sentence of chapter 1: "The single most significant phenomenon in modern American history is the emergence of giant, complex organizations." From the subsequent chapters, the reader should have acquired a sufficient acquaintance with the complexities of the public response to one feature of the organizational revolution—that is, the rise of the modern corporation. Attitudes about this phenomenon varied from one group to another, from year to year, sometimes following class or occupational lines and sometimes not. The patterns of changing imagery were exceedingly complex, as were the historical processes shaping middle-class opinions. Here our purpose is to build upon these details some general conclusions about the direction and causes of attitudinal change in an American society experiencing rapid bureaucratization.

II. We can launch this effort by reviewing our findings from the vantage point offered by the Marxian synthesis, one of the great accomplishments of an age of hedgehogs. Socioeconomic classes and their conflict are crucial to this vision, and among the groups examined in this study the sense of class alignment was initially very strong. This was particularly clear in the first generation's response to the trusts, but there was evidence of class consciousness in the second and third generations as well. We can employ as a measure of central tendency the mean value of the annual percentage of favorable, unfavorable, and neutral-ambivalent attitudes; when we do this the data for the three occupational groups—that is, the laborers, farmers, and professional men—fall into order along class lines thoroughly compatible with the Marxian concept of history (table 9-1). The professional men, most bourgeois of the three groups, were least upset about the trusts. Next in this ranking were the farmers, whom Marx condemned as petit bourgeois.[2] The group most concerned with the concentration movement and least likely to see anything praiseworthy in the growth of capitalistic combines were the laborers, whom we placed in the lower middle class but whom Marx would insist upon including in the proletariat.[3]

The data are less congenial to a Marxian analysis, however, when presented in the form of trend lines (figure 9-1) for the period 1895 through 1940. Over the years following the crisis of the mid-nineties, attitudes among farmers and professional men tended to converge, and even the gulf between the laborers and the professionals narrowed during these several decades. From a Marxist perspective, one would not have anticipated this result, predicting instead that the relentless process of capital concentration would have sharpened class antagonisms. This outcome was all the more likely since our study terminated with America mired in the worst depression in its history. Instead of class warfare, the middle cultures were fated to approach a consensus about the corporation. At the beginning of the Second World War, not all middle-class citizens were in agreement about big business nor were their attitudes completely stable, but as our qualitative and quantitative data both suggest, by 1940 class lines were fading as a new consensus emerged.[4]

Even for the first generation (1880–1901), class analysis could not explain most of the shifts taking place in middle-culture images of the trusts. The most significant change was a mounting sense of discontent and conflict with the largest firms in transportation, mining, and manufacturing. All of the middle classes were alert to the spread of the concentration movement

CONCLUSIONS, SPECULATIONS, AND AFTERWORD

and most were increasingly antagonistic to the trusts. Opinions fluctuated sharply and the degree of disequilibrium was greater in the nineties than it had been during the previous decade or would be during the next forty years (figure 9–2). Neither the idea of continuity nor that of consensus, as commonly used by revisionist historians, provided an interpretation consistent with these developments.

Conflict, antagonism, instability: these central themes of the first generation's response to big business accorded with Robert H. Wiebe's analysis of a nation searching for order. My data on equilibrium indicated that for the middle classes and for this one issue, the eighties were not characterized by a high degree of instability. In the nineties, however, a social crisis erupted, a crisis involving values as well as interests, culture as well as politics. For some (southern farmers in particular) there was a sense of fundamental social disorganization; for others (the clergymen), a clash between the new institutions and traditional values; for skilled workers and corn-belt farmers, bitter struggles over political, economic, and organizational issues. Whatever the sources of tension, the nineties stood out as a decade when attitudes were in flux and middle-class America was uniquely unsettled by the tides of social change.

Americans of this generation expressed their opposition in colorful, emotion-laden terms and vested the corporation with the personalities of such tycoons as Gould and Vanderbilt. The leading complaints varied from group to group. To some (midwestern farmers), prices were the crux of the matter, and to others (southern farmers), the overwhelming economic power of the trusts was the chief issue at stake. To the craftsman nothing deserved more criticism than big business's labor policies, and, at times, the Protestant clergyman agreed. In contrast, the engineer was willing to overlook minor disturbances like the Pullman strike if only the railroads would stop ignoring their technicians and install the safety devices called for by good engineering practice.

For the first generation, economic variables were the most important determinant of middle-class opinions, and the peak phase of the antitrust movement (for the years 1880–1901 and for the entire period 1880–1940) occurred during the severe depression of the mid-nineties. Both Marx and Schumpeter would have predicted this result. Contra Schumpeter, however, the intellectual elite was not responsible for focusing on big business the discontent bred by economic distress. Only the Protestant clergyman was sensitive to elite criticisms of the corporation, and he was not suffering from the depression. Others who were not so fortunate did not need intellectuals to tell them that the trusts were the source of their problems. Interests molded opinions, but the concept of economic man, pure and simple, was an analytical device of limited applicability. Statistical tests of the relationships

THE MIDDLE CULTURES AND THE ORGANIZATIONAL REVOLUTION

FIGURE 9-1. Trend lines for unfavorable evaluations of big business, 1895-1940, by organized laborers, farmers, and professional men. See note 134, chapter 4. Trend lines were calculated by using the least-squares method.

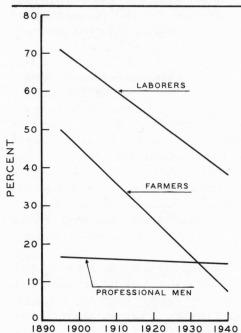

between opinions and income supported this conclusion. To understand middle-culture ideas, economic interests had to be seen in their particular social, political, and organizational settings.

The organizational context, with its related ideologies and role concepts, had a significant impact on opinions. Among engineers a strong foundation of professional organizations with a stable ideology was a decisive factor controlling the group's image of the corporation. Among skilled laborers the trade union was in a similar position but, in this case, the organizational base was far less stable, as was the group's image of big business. Farmers of this generation faced an even more confusing situation: they were wooed by dozens of organizations, each promoting a different concept of the farmer's role in society. In the nineties the farmer's organizational setting became especially complicated when the agrarian movement was diverted into third-party politics and then rudely defeated in the election of 1896.

Closely linked with these organizational developments were the social variables that ranked third as a causal force influencing middle-class opinions. Ascriptive, class concepts guided the responses of many Americans

CONCLUSIONS, SPECULATIONS, AND AFTERWORD

to the concentration movement. To the clergyman, social values were all-important; the events that perturbed him were those in which big business violated his concept of what the good society should be. The southern farmer had more serious problems and he struck out in anger at the trusts, blaming his incorporated enemies for all of the ill fortune besetting him and his family. Only among farmers—and especially those in the South—did a general sense of social disorganization have a substantial effect on attitudes toward large enterprise.

Political factors also helped form middle-class concepts of the large corporation, but for this generation politics was less important than economic, organizational, and social variables. During these years, political leaders were not very effective in guiding discourse on the trust question, nor did most Americans look primarily to reform legislation as the best response to big business. The Interstate Commerce Act of 1887 did not ride through Congress on a deep ground swell of public discontent; and while the middle class was more hostile toward the corporation three years later, even the Sherman Antitrust Act (1890) was not a product of intense public antipathy. Thus, the progressive synthesis was not very useful in analyzing this generation's reaction to the trust movement. Indeed, the evidence was more consistent with a New Left view of the past. If the ICC was not a product of public outrage at the railroads, it seems all the more likely that men with specific material interests in regulation saw to its creation and operation; if the Sherman Antitrust Act was merely a symbolic gesture, then its origins were something less than a study in progress; and if, at the turn of the century, when the merger movement was at its peak, public animosity toward big business sharply declined, the historian might be excused a touch of New Left cynicism about the true course of liberal reform.

The causal relationships posited by placing these four variables in rank order of importance lend themselves to expression as a simple regression equation. For the first generation, middle-class attitudes (A_1) about big

TABLE 9-1. Mean values of the annual percentages for the labor, farm, and professional men's time series, 1880-1940

Mean of the annual percentages	Combined labor series	Combined farm series	Combined professional men's series
Unfavorable items	51%	29%	15%
Favorable items	19	32	30
Neutral-ambivalent items	30	39	55

NOTE: The three time series upon which these means are based are those used to produce the aggregate, weighted series presented in chapters 4 through 8. The calculations used to derive these series are explained in note 134, chapter 4.

THE MIDDLE CULTURES AND THE ORGANIZATIONAL REVOLUTION

business were equal to the effect of economic variables (E), of organizational factors (O), of social variables (S), and finally of politics (P):

$$A_1 = b_1 (E) + b_2 (O) + b_3 (S) + b_4 (P).$$

The data will not allow us to assign even approximate figures to the beta weights (b_1, b_2, b_3, and b_4), but we have at least determined an order of importance and expressed the relationships in a manner that will facilitate comparisons with the second and third generations.[5] By way of explanation, what this equation says is that we can roughly predict (or post-dict) the attitudes (A) of a group (I) using a linear combination of four variables: economic (E), organizational (O), social (S), and political (P). No other method of explanation offers a preferable alternative, although one might arrive at exactly the same conclusions using more intuitive forms of analysis.

III. In the second generation (1902 through 1919) public attitudes toward business began to stabilize and the antitrust movement clearly entered a new phase. The secular trend in the middle cultures was toward accommodation, an easing of tensions between the trusts and the people. The middle class found new things to praise in business's performance and saw much less to criticize. By the end of the First World War, neutral-ambivalent opinions far outweighed either favorable or negative attitudes.

FIGURE 9-2. Indicators of disequilibrium based on the percentage of unfavorable evaluations of big business (figure 8-6) by the American middle class, 1880-1940 (see Appendix). The three periods of maximum disequilibrium are marked and numbered according to their rank order.

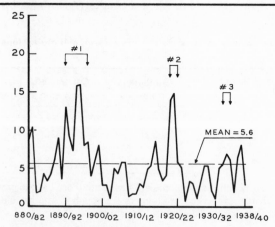

CONCLUSIONS, SPECULATIONS, AND AFTERWORD

Marxian analysis was almost as useless as the Schumpeterian model in our effort to explain these changes. During the second generation, the political system became a major agent of change, focusing and handling middle-culture animosity, relieving discontent through actions sometimes substantial and more often symbolic in nature. Next in importance were organizational developments, followed by economic and social variables. The appropriate equation for this generation was:

$$A_{II} = b_1 (P) + b_2 (O) + b_3 (E) + b_4 (S).[6]$$

The politics of reform (P) had a crucial effect on middle-culture viewpoints, and many of the traditional interpretations offered by progressive historians were helpful in analyzing the shifts taking place in public opinion. Presidential leadership was a far more potent force during these years than it had been in the late nineteenth century. Theodore Roosevelt, William Howard Taft, and Woodrow Wilson focused the public's attention on the trust question; certain Americans (midwestern farmers and the clergy) were unusually attentive to these leaders, and the presidents and public policy influenced all of the middle classes to some degree. On occasion, antitrust decisions convinced the people that their government was curbing the power of big business. Railroad regulation pleased corn-belt farmers, and even the professional engineer acknowledged that government controls were necessary in certain industries. Gradually, reform eased the public into a less hostile mood toward the corporation.

The progressive synthesis could not be used, however, without some revisions. The intellectual elite was a potent force in only one group (the clergy), and by and large one could ignore serious intellectuals and even popularizers like the muckrakers without doing serious damage to the history of the middle cultures. Furthermore, while presidential leadership was important, national elections did not stand out as decisive turning points. The election of 1912 may have seemed to the candidates to be the crossroads of freedom, but it was not a pivotal event for public opinion about big business.

A more fundamental revision was called for in the long-range context of progressive history. Judged from the vantage point of my data, the progressive era was merely one phase in a secular process of accommodation that began before 1900 and lasted through the 1920s. Opinion on the trust issue had started to shift in the late nineties, before Congress had begun passing reform measures and before the presidents had begun to guide public discourse on this question. Among southern farmers, the most crucial transition took place towards the end of the nineties and was essentially unrelated to the politics of reform. During and after the First World War, the public's evaluation of big business continued to evolve along lines similar to the trends of the progressive era. Liberal reform was important, but it was only one phase in an even more significant transition in middle-class relationships to the modern large-scale organization.

One revisionist theme that could be rejected was Richard Hofstadter's concept of status anxiety. Although there was evidence that certain Americans were anxious about their status, and although they occasionally directed these concerns at the large corporation, status anxiety did not reach significant proportions in any strata of the middle class. We could adequately explain the increase in negative opinions of big business and the subsequent decline in antitrust sentiment without reference to status. My findings were thus similar to those of other scholars who have tested Hofstadter's hypothesis and have been unable to find evidence supporting the idea that status anxiety explains either the origins or development of the progressive movement.[7]

Similarly, we uncovered little evidence consistent with Gabriel Kolko's version of New Left history. Whereas legislation before 1900 had seemed to arise out of sources other than public opposition to big business, this was not true after 1901, when there was substantial public interest in reform measures. The middle class felt strong animosity toward big business, and for many Americans, a close relationship developed between public policy and their evaluation of the large firm. I did not, in the style of Kolko, examine the origins of government regulations and cannot suggest which interests were most intimately involved in their development. But I did find evidence of formidable middle-class opposition to the trusts, opposition that accords with the progressive view that public officials were acting with an eye cocked on public opinion—if only to assure their own reelection. President Roosevelt may have launched his antitrust suit against Standard Oil for exactly those self-serving reasons that Kolko elucidates; but to most middle-class Americans, Roosevelt's action appeared to be a perfectly rational and praiseworthy attack on a company symbolizing the worst of the concentration movement.

During the second generation, organizational variables (O) ranked next to politics as a force shaping opinions in the middle cultures. Among skilled laborers, for example, the growing strength of trade unionism helped convince the craftsman that he had less to fear from the large corporation. Although he did not become a friend of big business, increased bargaining power neutralized part of his hostility. In peace and war, the engineer's associations and professional ideology were the gyroscope that held his viewpoints on a settled, neutral course. In the midwestern farm country, new agrarian organizations promulgated values similar to those of the engineer. In tandem with political reform, these organizations fostered a new approach to the large corporation, one that stressed emulation over antitrust, cooperation over class conflict.

CONCLUSIONS, SPECULATIONS, AND AFTERWORD

Economic factors (E) also acted to neutralize middle-culture antipathy to big business. In the cotton country, higher income after 1901 was clearly the most significant ingredient in the process of accommodation. Other Americans, too, felt the soothing effects of prosperity, especially during the First World War. Between 1914 and 1919, in fact, income had a more decisive effect on opinions than political developments, particularly among farmers and laborers.

Changes in social values (S) had a similar (although less substantial) impact, as middle-class Americans found new ways to talk and think about corporate enterprise. Increasingly, they bought goods from companies, not octopuses; they worked for firms, not trusts. By 1919 they viewed these businesses in a relatively impersonal light. In the previous generation many citizens had been upset not just with big business but with Gould and Vanderbilt. After 1902, they focused on J. P. Morgan, Andrew Carnegie, and John D. Rockefeller, but they still felt that behind the office doors of the largest companies there were real, live men who were, for better or worse, deciding what should be produced, where it should be manufactured, and how much it should be sold for. If Americans were upset with the trusts, they could locate their enemy and perhaps (via the Clayton Act) even punish him for his wrongdoing. During the First World War, however, public attention drifted away from the plutocrats and empire builders who had personalized the corporation. Henry Ford was the only businessman who received much attention after the war, and in the thirties even Ford was a less popular subject of discussion. From the First World War on, Americans increasingly looked upon the corporation as an impersonal bureaucracy beyond the control of any one man.

More than the public's evaluation of big business was changing: a new set of values was supplanting traditional norms. Americans were giving less emphasis to individualism than they had in the previous century; they were thinking more in terms of group activity and becoming more tolerant of coercive controls, especially those imposed by the government. It was not just the language of antitrust that was being neutralized, robbed of emotion, personality, and color. The transition in language was part of the emergence of a bureaucratic or corporate culture that by 1919 was becoming the dominant value system throughout middle-class America—on the farm and in the factory, behind the pulpit as well as the drawing board.

IV. In the immediate aftermath of the First World War, it appeared for a time that new circumstances would reverse these long-run trends in the middle cultures. An economic crisis, labor strife, and international problems produced a sudden burst of hostility toward big business. Public opinion was extremely unstable, as Americans lashed out at the giant corporations that

THE MIDDLE CULTURES AND THE ORGANIZATIONAL REVOLUTION

seemed to be responsible for many of their difficulties. Soon, however, political and economic developments brought the postwar reaction to an end. Reform measures—regulation of the railroads and of the packers—convinced interested Americans that the government had solved the problems created by the large corporations in these industries. Higher income persuaded others that the trusts were no longer a threat. After 1922 the process of accommodation continued until, by the end of the decade, favorable and unfavorable opinions were evenly balanced and both were exceeded by neutral attitudes toward the giant industrial firm.

The Great Depression severely tested this new equilibrium in middle-culture attitudes. If the array of forces shaping opinions in these years had resembled that of the first or second generations, the New Deal would have witnessed a tidal wave of anticorporate sentiment, a climax to the antitrust movement in America. But only the Congregational clergy reacted to the depression in this way. For the rest of the middle classes, this cycle of antitrust feeling was feeble by the standards of the 1890s or the progressive era. In spite of Roosevelt's attempt in the late thirties to make big business a viable political issue, the public remained calm about the highly concentrated American economy. Neither a popular president nor a severe economic crisis was able to destroy the new equilibrium and its related culture.

As the experience of the thirties demonstrated, the most important determinants of middle-class opinion were no longer economic or political variables. The appropriate formula for the third generation is:

$$A_{III} = b_1 (S) + b_2 (O) + b_3 (E) + b_4 (P).$$

The social values (S) of the corporate culture militated against a revival of the antitrust movement. Class consciousness had given way to organizational norms that left most Americans looking upon the corporation with detachment and judging its performance in impersonal terms. Sustaining these values were modern organizations (O) like the Farm Bureau and the engineering associations. In general, social and organizational factors exerted more influence than the pressures of economic change (E) or the politics of reform (P). Consequently, the new middle-class consensus about corporate enterprise emerged intact from the Great Depression.

In analyzing third-generation images of big business, the only historical synthesis that was particularly useful was Robert H. Wiebe's concept of a nation finding a new sense of order in bureaucratic values. My findings confirmed Wiebe's conclusion that the new order came to full fruition in the 1920s and represented in substantial degree a continuation of prewar trends. To Wiebe's description of the overall pattern of cultural change I added an analysis of process, some correctives and refinements, and a study of how the new equilibrium fared in the Great Depression. On balance, however, the third generation's changing image of big business fits comfortably in an extended version of Wiebe's historical framework. As both our studies conclude, the new cultural context that emerged in the twentieth century provided Americans with values tailored to fit an age of large-scale, complex organizations. By 1940 bureaucratic norms were relatively stable, and they were a subject of substantial consensus in the middle class.[8]

Historians of the New Left will find these conclusions about the third generation more appealing than will scholars of the progressive school. The corporate culture and the middle class's tolerance of giant enterprise help explain the conservatism of New Deal reform and the public's easy acceptance of a form of broker-state politics that favored well-organized groups. Less attractive to the New Left might be the implication that the corporate culture imposed a constraint on reform that would have resisted even effective radical leadership, since this exonerates the New Dealers for failing to achieve more drastic changes in our society. Clearly, the record of FDR's abortive antitrust campaign substantiates this conclusion. While most Americans wanted the government to cure the nation's economic ills, they did not want to use harsh medicine that would attack the major centers of power and wealth in the business system. Big business was shielded from reform politics by the third generation's acceptance of the corporate culture—a conclusion that poses problems for both a New Left and progressive interpretation of New Deal reform.

V. Each of the three generations thus responded to the concentration movement in distinctive ways for different reasons. The differences are in part reflected in our three equations:

$$\text{Attitude}_I \ (1880-1901) = b_1 \ (E) + b_2 \ (O) + b_3 \ (S) + b_4 \ (P).$$

$$\text{Attitude}_{II} \ (1902-1919) = b_1 \ (P) + b_2 \ (O) + b_3 \ (E) + b_4 \ (S).$$

$$\text{Attitude}_{III} \ (1920-1940) = b_1 \ (S) + b_2 \ (O) + b_3 \ (E) + b_4 \ (P).$$

The leading determinant of public opinion changed in each successive time period, but during all three generations, organizational factors (O) ranked second as a causal force. In some instances formal organizations provided Americans with either the reality or the semblance of countervailing power. Strong associations anchored ideologies and role concepts, stabilizing perceptions of the large firm. Paradoxically, a very weak organizational base sometimes achieved the same result; skilled laborers who were unable to build strong craft unions either looked to their employers for support or simply foundered, as did members of the AFL in the 1930s. In these ways and others, the organizational context influenced middle-class images of large enterprise and, for each generation except the second, played a more prominent causal role than politics. Historians of modern America would do well, this suggests, to shift some of the energy spent on studying political leaders and legislation to the analysis of those basic social organizations that had a crucial effect on middle-class perceptions of their society.

These organizations changed dramatically in the years 1880 through 1940, as we saw in chapter 1, and we can now add a cultural component to the outline of organizational history with which we began this book. In the years 1880–1930, primary bureaucracies of great power and wealth emerged and consolidated their positions in American society. Through the mid-nineties, these organizations developed in an increasingly hostile cultural setting. After the depression of the nineties, however, the middle classes slowly and unevenly came to accept giant enterprise as a necessary element in their urban, industrial system. The people gradually adopted organizational values, and by the late 1920s these norms were dominant in the middle class. From that point on, it seems likely that the cultural setting influenced the development of the primary organizations themselves, but that subject is beyond our purview, as is the effect of the new values on the evolution of government bureaucracies in the years after 1930. One can only guess that the impact was substantial and has grown even more important over time.

These conclusions point to some other general propositions about the study of social change in modern America. For one thing, historians analyzing causation should probably give more attention than they have in the past to cultural factors. All too often, historians (the author included) have focused on power, wealth, and formal organizations, leaving values and belief systems in the hands of the sociologists and anthropologists. My study indicates, however, that values, role concepts, and culture demand more consideration as causes, not just as effects. Social variables are inherently more difficult to specify and analyze than the behavior of a leader or an organization. But this limitation should be seen as a challenge to further examination, not an excuse for ignoring the social dimensions of change.

In the analysis of social change, one of the casualties of a behavioral approach is likely to be what might best be labeled "binary history." Several of the syntheses discussed here and in chapter 1 were innately binary in that they set up only two possibilities for evaluation: men were good or bad; men were capitalists or proletarians; men were liberals or conservatives. Perhaps because of man's ingrained desire to find a moral order in the universe, many historical syntheses have this characteristic. The foxlike revisionists of Hofstadter's generation attacked this feature of progressive history, and behavioral analysis will carry this assault even further, producing data that cannot be forced into a simple binary framework. The patterns and processes that we have studied could best be analyzed in scalar terms: more or less; changing faster or slower; becoming gradually or swiftly, in greater or lesser degree, something new. In our analysis the rate of change was as crucial as the direction, and we found that both changed in different ways for different groups over time. Although we could translate these developments into patterns and central tendencies, we neither could nor should have squeezed them into a binary historical system.[9]

Nor could we isolate a brief period or event that was decisive in the long-run process of social change. Between 1880 and 1940, middle-class Americans first became very angry with the large corporation and then slowly came to tolerate it. They acquired new norms for judging other organizations and themselves, gradually adopting what we have identified as a corporate set of values. The basic nature of the second process of social change, the process of accommodation, is what deserves our attention here. Accommodation began in the 1890s, continued through the progressive era and the First World War, and lasted well into the 1920s. As late as 1940, the new values and the new outlook on big business were still not entirely stable. In each decade between 1890 and 1940, different but related aspects of middle-class culture changed in distinctive ways. If historians are going to study this type of social process, they must be prepared to use long time periods—longer periods than have normally been the case in the highly specialized field of American history. They must stop looking for crucial events or turning points in history. Much energy has been expended on this problem, and I suppose that in my data, the 1890s could be identified as a watershed. In this case, however, we can see why the analogy is dangerously misleading. The changes which followed the 1890s were not prefigured in the events of the nineties; they were not axiomatic or automatic, as is the movement of water down a hillside. There is no counterpart to gravity in man's social behavior, and historians who seek to understand social change would do well to abandon the search for brief transitions in the past.

VI.   The long-run process of accommodation left middle-class Americans of 1940 with a new set of attitudes toward big business and a new set of organizational norms, and one can hardly avoid asking what has happened to these opinions and their supporting culture in the years since the beginning of the Second World War. Lacking content analysis data, I can offer only an impressionistic survey of developments since 1940, basing my conclusions on secondary studies and the available research on public opinion. Fortunately, Burton R. Fisher and Stephen B. Withey conducted a survey on this question in 1950 and published their results in *Big Business As The People See It*.[10] According to Fisher and Withey, most Americans felt that the favorable aspects of big business outweighed the bad. While there was some criticism of particular corporate practices, only 10 percent of the people they

THE MIDDLE CULTURES AND THE ORGANIZATIONAL REVOLUTION

questioned thought the negative features of the large firm were more important than its positive contributions to the economy. Big business garnered special praise as an employer, a creator of jobs, a producer of valuable goods and services, and as a contributor to the general wealth. Apparently neither the Second World War nor the experiences of the immediate postwar years disrupted the corporate culture of 1940 and the middle class's acceptance of large enterprise.

This conclusion seems reasonable in light of our analysis of attitudinal changes between 1880 and 1940. During the Second World War (as during the First), high income and employment opportunities undoubtedly dampened antagonism toward industrial combines. The war ended the longest and deepest depression the nation had ever encountered. Farmers, heretofore beset by enormous surpluses, suddenly found themselves called upon to produce larger crops. The pressure of wartime demand induced innovations that caused a major revolution in agricultural productivity and resulted in great profits for many farmers.[11] With aggregate demand high and unemployment low, skilled workers were able to organize effectively and to win concessions from their employers and the government. Union membership soared and organized labor emerged from the war in a strong economic position.[12] War also pulled public attention away from domestic problems. Thus, a generation of Americans already disposed to accept large enterprise with relative equanimity had little cause to change its viewpoint during the Second World War.

In the immediate aftermath of the war, however, there was a crisis that resembled in some ways the events of 1920–21. Bitter strife between labor and management engulfed the nation's leading industries. The coal mines, the oil companies, and the steel producers resisted the demands of organized labor, and the resulting strikes refueled the skilled worker's hostility toward the corporation. These battles apparently forced many other Americans to worry about their own stakes in the conflict between big unions and big business. A brief postwar recession multiplied these fears and built up the animosity of those who linked the corporation with the nation's economic welfare. The result was a new phase of increased hostility toward the giant firm.[13]

Long before 1950, however, this cycle ended, as the country entered a period of prosperity unmarred for a decade by even serious economic recession. Labor-management relations improved and major strikes became less frequent. Both farmers and most urban Americans enjoyed relatively high and stable incomes, and the beginning of the cold war diverted middle-class attention from domestic to foreign affairs. This protracted global struggle stimulated the economy and also apparently helped to convince many Americans that the productivity, efficiency, and technological expertise of the large firm were essential to the country's well being.[14] The

CONCLUSIONS, SPECULATIONS, AND AFTERWORD

resulting complacency about corporate enterprise was reflected in the politics of the Eisenhower era, when America's leaders began to abandon the traditional symbolic bow to antitrust.

Even during the placid fifties, big business was not entirely free from attack. A new threat to the corporate culture emerged as the contrast between private and public bureaucracies began to blur at the edges. In the area of national defense in particular, one could hardly see the distinction between the government and private enterprise, and as he left office, Dwight D. Eisenhower warned Americans about the growing military-industrial complex.[15] During these same years, bureaucracy and modern American culture became popular targets for intellectual assaults. C. Wright Mills lashed out at *The Power Elite*; William H. Whyte wrote a caustic comment on the life style of the men who worked for corporations; David Riesman et al., published a gentler, but nonetheless telling, critique of the other-directed man.[16] On the far right of the political spectrum as well as on its left, new antagonisms arose. Usually the radical right reserved its invective for government bureaucracies, but occasionally ultra-conservatives saw communism actually penetrating the top echelons of big business in order to hasten America's decline.[17] On balance, however, these assaults seem to have had little impact upon the middle cultures, and through the fifties students of the American scene still worried more about complacency than conflict.

In the sixties the college and university campuses produced a more formidable challenge to the new culture, a movement that spread through the cities and spilled over into national politics. Central to the New Left movement and its opposition to big business were the close ties that appeared to exist between American foreign policy and the large corporation. Young Americans in particular were concerned about the military-industrial complex and the war in Vietnam. They protested against both the public officials who sent American troops into that Asian country and the giant firms that profited from manufacturing the weapons of war. Woven into this new critique of the corporation were other, more subtle charges. Students rejected the bureaucratic life style, and tie-dyed jeans expressed the contempt that many felt for a society in which successful business executives supposedly never wore white socks. The counter-culture was braced against bureaucracy. In music, dress, and political action, young Americans fought a highly organized, impersonal system that seemed to control their future without regard for their feelings, goals, or even their lives.[18]

When America withdrew from the war in Vietnam, however, the New Left protest lost its vigor, and today, big business and the corporate culture are as firmly entrenched as they were in 1940 or the Eisenhower years. From our present perspective, the changes in attitudes and in social values that took place in the third generation (1920–40) appear to have been decisive; the resulting amalgam of powerful, wealthy bureaucracies and a compatible

THE MIDDLE CULTURES AND THE ORGANIZATIONAL REVOLUTION

corporate culture has proven to be a resilient system, vulnerable neither to its own often frightening blunders nor the fiercest attacks of its New Left opponents. Middle-class Americans may eventually become agitated about consumerism, business influence on politics, or the ecological movement. Ralph Nader and his cohorts may actually win out over General Motors. The gray bureaucratic culture may suddenly turn green. But at present the opponents of big business are unable to stir up anticorporate sentiment comparable to that of the 1890s, the progressive era, or even the 1930s. The people seem content with organizational values and giant bureaucracies.[19] For most Americans, antitrust exists only as a chapter in history, an episode they study while preparing themselves for a bureaucratic career in a society steeped in the values of the corporate culture.

CONCLUSIONS, SPECULATIONS, AND AFTERWORD

APPENDIX

The concept of equilibrium plays an important role in this book, and it was necessary to spell out a working definition of this idea—a definition which was applicable to my data and would enable me to test some of the hypotheses set forth in chapter 1. My interest was in identifying situations in which opinions were relatively stable though not entirely devoid of change. I decided to base this part of my analysis on the time series for the percentage of unfavorable items in the respective journals, and to use as my statistical measure of variance the mean deviation from the mean (M.D.). This measure is seldom used because it lacks the mathematical properties of more sophisticated indicators, but since I intended only to compare these figures and not to manipulate them in any complex way, I selected the M.D. on the grounds that it was the simplest to calculate and to understand. In the following tables, I used a three-year moving average based in each case on the percentage of unfavorable items. The M.D. for the first figure in the series on southern farm journals was calculated as follows:

Year	Percentage of unfavorable items	Deviation from the mean
1879	25	14.3
1881	0	10.7
1882	7	3.7
	3)32	3)28.7
	10.7 = M	9.6 = M.D. for the period 1879/82

I identified periods of high instability or disequilibrium as those in which the M.D. was equal to or greater than the mean for the entire series (from 1879 or 1880 through 1940) for three or more years in a row. This enabled me to isolate periods of disequilibrium and also to rank them according to their length and the total amount of variance that occurred. In each of the following series I have marked such periods with asterisks and indicated the top three in rank order.

SERIES FOR *ENGINEERING NEWS*; M = 2.3

Years	Mean deviation	Years	Mean deviation	Years	Mean deviation	Years	Mean deviation
1880/82	1.8	1895/97	2.2	1910/12	1.8	1925/27	2.4
1881/83	2.0	1896/98	2.7	1911/13	1.1	1926/28	2.7
1882/84	.7	1897/99	2.4	1912/14	1.3	1927/29	.9
1883/85	.9	1898/1900	2.2	1913/15	2.2	1928/30	1.1
1884/86	1.3	1899/1901	5.6*	1914/16	1.3	1929/31	1.1
1885/87	3.1*	1900/02	5.3*	1915/17	1.4	1930/32	1.1
1886/88	3.3*	1901/03	3.1*	1916/18	1.6	1931/33	.9
1887/89	4.2* }1	1902/04	1.8	1917/19	1.6	1932/34	0.0
1888/90	4.7*	1903/05	3.3	1918/20	1.6	1933/35	2.7*
1889/91	3.8*	1904/06	2.0	1919/21	.4	1934/36	3.6*
1890/92	2.9*	1905/07	3.3*	1920/22	1.8	1935/37	3.6* }2
1891/93	1.1	1906/08	3.3*	1921/23	2.0	1936/38	5.3*
1892/94	1.6	1907/09	3.3* }3	1922/24	2.0	1937/39	3.1*
1893/95	1.6	1908/10	3.3*	1923/25	1.8	1938/40	3.1*
1894/96	3.1	1909/11	3.1*	1924/26	1.8		

SERIES FOR *CONGREGATIONALIST* AND *ADVANCE*; M = 9.1

Years	Mean deviation	Years	Mean deviation	Years	Mean deviation	Years	Mean deviation
1880/82	7.8	1895/97	13.8	1910/12	5.3	1925/27	9.3*
1881/83	7.3	1896/98	9.1	1911/13	6.2	1926/28	17.6*
1882/84	2.0	1897/99	4.4	1912/14	8.9	1927/29	22.2*
1883/85	6.0	1898/1900	.9	1913/15	15.1	1928/30	8.9
1884/86	6.4	1899/1901	1.8	1914/16	12.0	1929/31	8.9
1885/87	9.6	1900/02	2.9	1915/17	6.2	1930/32	10.7
1886/88	4.9	1901/03	15.3*	1916/18	0.0	1931/33	15.1
1887/89	4.4	1902/04	13.8*	1917/19	0.0	1932/34	4.7
1888/90	3.3	1903/05	12.0*	1918/20	14.7*	1933/35	2.4
1889/91	3.1	1904/06	10.2* }1	1919/21	18.4* }2	1934/36	9.8*
1890/92	4.4	1905/07	12.0*	1920/22	13.1*	1935/37	13.3* }3
1891/93	8.4	1906/08	15.3*	1921/23	19.6*	1936/38	10.2*
1892/94	6.0	1907/09	17.1*	1922/24	4.9	1937/39	17.6*
1893/95	5.3	1908/10	14.7*	1923/25	10.7	1938/40	7.3
1894/96	5.3	1909/11	5.3	1924/26	8.4		

APPENDIX

SERIES FOR SOUTHERN FARM JOURNALS; M = 10.2

Years	Mean deviation	Years	Mean deviation	Years	Mean deviation	Years	Mean deviation
1879/82	9.6	1899/1901	5.3	1914/16	10.0	1929/31	4.4
1881/83	8.2	1900/02	6.4	1915/17	8.9	1930/32	6.7
1882/85	8.2	1901/03	7.6	1916/18	4.0	1931/33	6.7
1883/86	10.4	1902/04	11.1	1917/19	3.3	1932/34	7.6
1885/87	14.4	1903/05	12.0	1918/20	21.1*⎫	1933/35	9.3
1886/88	5.1	1904/06	7.3	1919/21	19.1*⎬ 2	1934/36	10.0
1887/89	20.7*⎫	1905/07	5.1	1920/22	15.6*⎪	1935/37	12.0
1888/90	26.0*⎪	1906/08	11.8	1921/23	11.6*⎭	1936/38	5.3
1889/91	12.2*⎪	1907/09	10.9	1922/24	.6	1937/39	0.0
1890/92	36.4*⎬ 1	1908/10	6.4	1923/25	8.9	1938/40	11.1
1891/96	29.1*⎪	1909/11	4.0	1924/26	0.0		
1892/97	22.4*⎪	1910/12	12.9*⎫	1925/27	0.0		
1896/98	14.9*⎭	1911/13	11.1*⎬ 3	1926/28	5.3		
1897/99	7.3	1912/14	11.1*⎭	1927/29	5.3		
1898/1900	6.4	1913/15	10.0	1928/30	4.7		

SERIES FOR MIDWESTERN FARM JOURNALS; M = 9.2

Years	Mean deviation	Years	Mean deviation	Years	Mean deviation	Years	Mean deviation
1879/83	15.6*⎫	1897/99	8.4	1913/15	3.1	1929/31	4.9
1882/84	10.7*⎬ 3	1898/1900	7.1	1914/16	4.4	1930/32	0.0
1883/85	10.9*⎪	1899/1901	20.7*	1915/17	7.6	1931/33	22.2*⎫
1884/86	9.8*⎭	1900/02	14.0*	1916/18	6.4	1932/34	20.4*
1885/87	8.9	1901/03	9.3*	1917/19	3.8	1933/35	17.1*
1886/88	8.0	1902/04	4.0	1918/20	4.7	1934/36	14.0*⎬ 1
1887/89	7.3	1903/05	14.0*	1919/21	8.4	1935/37	10.2*
1888/90	8.4	1904/06	11.6*	1920/22	5.1	1936/38	11.3*
1889/91	5.3	1905/07	10.0*	1921/23	8.2	1937/39	14.7*
1890/92	4.0	1906/08	3.3	1922/24	9.8	1938/40	11.1*⎭
1891/93	4.2	1907/09	2.0	1923/25	9.3		
1892/94	6.9	1908/10	2.7	1924/26	6.4		
1893/95	21.1*⎫	1909/11	1.8	1925/27	1.3		
1894/96	26.0*⎬ 2	1910/12	3.3	1926/28	12.0*		
1895/97	9.1*⎪	1911/13	6.4	1927/29	13.3*		
1896/98	10.7*⎭	1912/14	3.1	1928/30	17.1*		

APPENDIX

SERIES FOR *NATIONAL LABOR TRIBUNE*; M = 6.0

Years	Mean deviation	Years	Mean deviation	Years	Mean deviation	Years	Mean deviation
1880/82	5.1	1890/92	5.1	1900/02	3.8	1910/12	8.9* ⎫
1881/83	5.1	1891/93	11.1* ⎫	1901/03	4.2	1911/13	6.0* ⎬ 2
1882/84	5.1	1892/94	11.3* ⎬ 3	1902/04	2.4	1912/14	6.0* ⎪
1883/85	8.0	1893/95	7.3* ⎭	1903/05	2.4	1913/15	7.3* ⎭
1884/86	6.0	1894/96	5.3	1904/06	5.3		
1885/87	5.1	1895/97	5.8	1905/07	5.6		
1886/88	2.0	1896/98	6.7* ⎫	1906/08	5.3		
1887/89	5.3	1897/99	8.7* ⎬ 1	1907/09	5.3		
1888/90	6.0	1898/1900	10.0* ⎪	1908/10	7.1		
1889/91	4.4	1899/1901	8.2* ⎭	1909/11	4.4		

SERIES FOR *AMERICAN FEDERATIONIST*; M = 7.9

Years	Mean deviation	Years	Mean deviation	Years	Mean deviation	Years	Mean deviation
1894/96	4.0	1906/08	13.6	1917/19	10.2* ⎫	1928/30	5.3
1895/97	3.1	1907/09	6.7	1918/20	17.3* ⎬ 2	1929/31	4.4
1896/98	3.1	1908/10	3.6	1919/21	18.4* ⎭	1930/32	3.1
1897/99	4.0	1909/11	4.2	1920/22	2.7	1931/33	4.4
1898/1900	14.7* ⎫	1910/12	15.7	1921/23	3.6	1932/34	4.9
1899/1901	11.8* ⎪	1911/13	3.6	1922/24	10.0	1933/35	5.1
1900/02	13.1* ⎬ 1	1912/14	8.4* ⎫	1923/25	7.6	1934/36	6.7
1901/03	12.2* ⎪	1913/15	8.4* ⎬ 3	1924/26	6.4	1935/37	1.1
1902/04	12.9* ⎪	1914/16	14.2* ⎭	1925/27	4.7	1936/38	7.3
1903/05	12.4* ⎭	1915/17	6.9	1926/28	6.0	1937/39	9.3
1904/06	1.8	1916/18	6.0	1927/29	6.7	1938/40	11.1
1905/07	16.2						

SERIES FOR *SOLIDARITY*; M = 7.0

Years	Mean deviation	Years	Mean deviation	Years	Mean deviation	Years	Mean deviation
1910/12	20.0* ⎫	1915/17	6.2	1921/23	2.0	1926/28	4.0
1911/13	22.2* ⎬ 1	1916/19	4.4	1922/24	1.8	1927/29	4.2
1912/14	12.2* ⎪	1917/20	4.0	1923/25	3.3	1928/30	15.3
1913/15	11.6* ⎭	1919/21	3.1	1924/26	4.4		
1914/16	2.2	1920/22	.4	1925/27	4.4		

APPENDIX

AGGREGATE, WEIGHTED SERIES FOR ALL JOURNALS; M = 5.6

Years	Mean deviation	Years	Mean deviation	Years	Mean deviation	Years	Mean deviation
1880/82	8.7	1897/99	4.0	1914/16	8.7	1931/33	5.1
1881/83	10.4	1898/1900	6.0	1915/17	4.7	1932/34	5.6* ⎫
1882/84	1.8	1899/1901	8.2	1916/18	3.3	1933/35	6.9* ⎬ 3
1883/85	2.0	1900/02	2.9	1917/19	4.2	1934/36	6.2* ⎭
1884/86	4.3	1901/03	2.9	1918/20	14.0* ⎫	1935/37	1.8
1885/87	3.3	1902/04	1.1	1919/21	14.9* ⎬ 2	1936/38	6.7
1886/88	4.2	1903/05	5.1	1920/22	5.6* ⎭	1937/39	8.2
1887/89	6.2	1904/06	4.4	1921/23	5.1	1938/40	2.9
1888/90	9.1	1905/07	5.8	1922/24	.7		
1889/91	3.6	1906/08	5.8	1923/25	3.3		
1890/92	13.1* ⎫	1907/09	1.3	1924/26	3.1		
1891/93	9.3*	1908/10	1.6	1925/27	1.1		
1892/94	7.3*	1909/11	1.6	1926/28	3.3		
1893/95	15.8* ⎬ 1	1910/12	2.9	1927/29	5.3		
1894/96	16.0*	1911/13	2.7	1928/30	5.3		
1895/97	8.0*	1912/14	4.9	1929/31	2.2		
1896/98	8.4* ⎭	1913/15	5.3	1930/32	1.1		

APPENDIX

NOTES

1. THE LARGE-SCALE ORGANIZATION IN MODERN AMERICA

1. William H. Whyte, Jr., popularized this idea with *The Organization Man* (Garden City, N.Y.: Doubleday, 1956).

2. The expression is drawn from John Kenneth Galbraith, *American Capitalism* (Boston: Houghton Mifflin Co., 1952), pp. 108–23.

3. U.S. Bureau of the Census, *Statistical Abstract of the United States: 1971* (Washington, D.C.: 92d edition, 1971), pp. 373, 388, 389; U.S. Bureau of the Census, *Historical Statistics of the United States, Colonial Times to 1957* (Washington, D.C., 1960), p. 710. The reference is to civilian employees.

4. U.S. Bureau of the Census, *Statistical Abstract: 1971*, pp. 306, 407, 421.

5. Clark Kerr, *The Uses of the University* (Cambridge: Harvard University Press, 1963), pp. 6–45.

6. Gibson Winter, "Religious Organizations," in W. Lloyd Warner et al., *The Emergent American Society* (New Haven: Yale University Press, 1961), pp. 408–91.

7. Ibid., pp. 276–313; Roy Lubove, *The Professional Altruist: The Emergence of Social Work as a Career, 1880–1930* (Cambridge: Harvard University Press, 1965).

8. Max Weber, *The Theory of Social and Economic Organization* (Glencoe, Ill.: The Free Press, 1947), pp. 329–34.

9. Ibid., p. 337.

10. Gresham M. Sykes, "The Corruption of Authority and Rehabilitation," *Social Forces* 34 (1956): 257–62; reprinted in part in Amitai Etzioni, *Complex Organizations* (New York: Holt, Rinehart, and Winston, 1961), pp. 191–97.

11. Richard H. McCleery, "Policy Change in Prison Management," in Etzioni, *Complex Organizations*, pp. 376–400; see also R. K. Merton et al., eds., *Reader in Bureaucracy* (Glencoe, Ill.: The Free Press, 1952), and Alvin W. Gouldner, "Organizational Analysis," in Robert K. Merton et al., eds., *Sociology Today*, 2 vols. (New York: Harper Torchbooks, 1965), 2: 400–428.

12. This statement is likely to be misunderstood. I am not saying that all of American history in, for example, the last century can be best comprehended from this vantage point. What I *am* saying is that organizational change along the lines discussed here had a more decisive impact upon our history than any other single factor. My position—after substituting the organization for the frontier—is the one that Richard Hofstadter graciously attributes to Frederick Jackson Turner; see *The Progressive Historians* (New York: Vintage Books, 1970), pp. 118–25.

13. Some of the literature is reviewed in Louis Galambos, "The Emerging Organizational Synthesis in Modern American History," *Business History Review* 44 (Autumn 1970): 279–90. See also Robert D. Cuff, "American Historians and the 'Organizational Factor,' " *The Canadian Review of American Studies* 4 (Spring 1973): 19–31; and Jerry Israel, ed., *Building the Organizational Society* (New York: The Free Press, 1972).

14. Kenneth Boulding, *The Organizational Revolution* (New York: Harper & Brothers, 1953).

15. Here and throughout the book I am using the concept of a generation in a special and restricted sense. I employ the term as merely a convenient tool for aggregating data and ranking causal factors for time periods of approximately twenty years. Demographers and social historians use other, more complex definitions, especially when they are studying family history.

16. My statement is true only if one is searching out the beginnings of an interrelated sequence of events, a continuous developmental process which resulted in the rise of modern bureaucracies. For a different opinion, see Lynn L. Marshall, "The Strange Still-birth of the Whig Party," *American Historical Review* 72 (January 1967): 445–68.

17. Bernard Bailyn, *The New England Merchants in the Seventeenth Century* (Cambridge: Harvard University Press, 1955), especially pp. 1–111. See also Charles M. Andrews, *The Colonial Period of American History*, 4 vols. (New Haven: Yale University Press, 1934), 1: 165–79, 320–74, 462–95; W. F. Craven, *The Dissolution of the Virginia Company* (New York: Oxford University Press, 1932). On plantations, see Lewis Cecil Gray, *History of Agriculture in the Southern United States to 1860*, 2 vols. (Washington, D.C.: Carnegie Institute of Washington, 1933), 1: 301–41, 437–61; on commercial organizations, W. T. Baxter, *The House of Hancock* (Cambridge: Harvard University Press, 1945) is informative, as is Bailyn's book cited above.

18. This theme and the related sources are discussed, from a different angle of vision, in Jack P. Greene, "An Uneasy Connection: An Analysis of the Preconditions of the American Revolution," in Stephen G. Kurtz and James Hutson, eds., *Essays on the American Revolution* (Chapel Hill: University of North Carolina Press, 1973), pp. 32–80. See also Jack P. Greene, ed., *Great Britain and the American Colonies, 1606–1763* (Columbia: University of South Carolina Press, 1970), pp. x–xlvii.

19. Bray Hammond, *Banks and Politics in America, from the Revolution to the Civil War* (Princeton: Princeton University Press, 1957), pp. 251–325. One private banking firm which became rather large and complex was Brown Brothers; but the company remained a partnership, and when, in the 1850s and 1860s, one of the branch offices forced the partners to decide between the family and the firm, it was the family that won. See Edward Perkins, "The House of Brown: America's Foremost International Bankers: 1800–1880" (Ph.D. diss.: Johns Hopkins University, 1972), pp. 100–117, 138–55.

20. On canal administration, see Louis Hartz, *Economic Policy and Democratic Thought: Pennsylvania, 1776–1860* (Cambridge: Harvard University Press, 1948), pp. 148–60. The cotton textile mills are discussed in Caroline F. Ware, *The Early New England Cotton Manufacture* (Boston: Houghton Mifflin Co., 1931), and in Evelyn H. Knowlton, *Pepperell's Progress* (Cambridge: Harvard University Press, 1948).

21. Alfred D. Chandler, Jr., ed., *The Railroads: The Nation's First Big Business* (New York: Harcourt, Brace & World, 1965), p. 16.

22. Alfred D. Chandler, Jr., has analyzed this subject in a number of publications, including the following: "The Railroads: Pioneers in Modern Corporate Management," *Business History Review* 39 (Spring 1965): 16–40; and "The Coming of Big Business," in C. Vann Woodward, ed., *The Comparative Approach to American History* (New York: Basic Books, Inc., 1968), pp. 220–37.

23. Alfred D. Chandler, Jr., and Louis Galambos, "The Development of Large-Scale Economic Organizations in Modern America," *The Journal of Economic History* 30 (March 1970): 201–17.

24. On the freight pools, see Julius Grodinsky, *The Iowa Pool: A Study in Railroad Competition 1870–1884* (Chicago: University of Chicago Press, 1950); Edward C. Kirkland, *Industry Comes of Age* (New York: Holt, Rinehart, and Winston, 1961), pp. 81–88; and David T. Gilchrist, "Albert Fink and the Pooling System," *Business History Review* 34 (Spring 1960): 24–49. The National Labor Union is discussed in Norman J. Ware, *The Labor Movement in the United States, 1860–1890* (New York: Vintage Books, 1964), pp. 6–11, and in

Gerald N. Grob, *Workers and Utopia* (Evanston: Northwestern University Press, 1961), pp. 11–33.

25. Ralph W. and Muriel Hidy, *Pioneering in Big Business: History of Standard Oil Company (New Jersey), 1882–1911* (New York: Harper & Brothers, 1955), pp. 14–75.

26. Joseph F. Wall, *Andrew Carnegie* (Oxford: Oxford University Press, 1970), pp. 307–60. As late as 1900, the Carnegie interests were still using the partnership form of organization (p. 763).

27. The national craft unions are analyzed in Lloyd Ulman, *The Rise of the National Trade Union* (Cambridge: Harvard University Press, 1955); the early years of the AMA are treated in James G. Burrow, *AMA: Voice of American Medicine* (Baltimore: Johns Hopkins Press, 1963), pp. 1–151. For the civil engineers the reader should see Daniel H. Calhoun, *The American Civil Engineer: Origins and Conflict* (Cambridge, Mass.: The Technology Press, 1960); Monte A. Calvert treats *The Mechanical Engineer in America, 1830–1910* (Baltimore: Johns Hopkins Press, 1967), pp. 109, 197–213, 221–24.

28. See, for example, Michael B. Katz, *The Irony of Early School Reform: Educational Innovation in Mid-Nineteenth Century Massachusetts* (Cambridge: Harvard University Press, 1968), especially pp. 145–53, 160, 206–7, 215; also, the same author's *Class, Bureaucracy and Schools: The Illusion of Educational Change in America* (New York: Praeger, 1971), pp. 28–48, 56–104. See also Gerald N. Grob, *Mental Institutions In America: Social Policy to 1875* (New York: The Free Press, 1973), pp. 84–131, 174–220, 257–342; Kirkland, *Industry Comes of Age*, pp. 114–26; and the same author's *Men, Cities and Transportation*, 2 vols. (Cambridge: Harvard University Press, 1948), 2: 230–67.

29. This general phenomenon is discussed in Robert H. Wiebe, *The Search for Order, 1877–1920* (New York: Hill and Wang, 1967), pp. 111–32. For purposes of illustration, Wiebe describes the professional groups in medicine, law, education, and social work.

30. Calvert, *The Mechanical Engineer*, pp. 107–38; Kirkland, *Industry Comes of Age*, p. 178. See also *Scientific and Technical Societies of the United States and Canada*, 6th ed. (Washington, D.C.: National Academy of Sciences—National Research Council, 1955), p. 244.

31. *Scientific and Technical Societies*, pp. 29, 63–66, 85, 88–89, 91–92, 94, 96–97, 101, 104–5, 121–23, 192–93, 198–201, 244, 255, 318–19, 323–24, 339–40.

32. Ulman, *The Rise of the National Trade Union*, pp. 425–566. See also Leo Wolman, *The Growth of American Trade Unions, 1880–1923* (New York: National Bureau of Economic Research, 1924), pp. 19–66.

33. Grant McConnell, *The Decline of Agrarian Democracy* (Berkeley: University of California Press, 1953), provides an excellent analysis of this transition, although, as his title indicates, he evaluates the results in a way different from mine.

34. We prepared a list of such companies, using *Moody's Industrials, 1929*.

35. Ralph L. Nelson, *Merger Movements in American Industry* (Princeton: Princeton University Press, 1959), pp. 3–5; Alfred S. Eichner, *The Emergence of Oligopoly: Sugar Refining as a Case Study* (Baltimore: Johns Hopkins Press, 1969), pp. 1–25; Alfred D. Chandler, Jr., "The Beginnings of 'Big Business' in American Industry," *Business History Review* 33 (Spring 1959): 1–31.

36. Nelson, *Merger Movements*, pp. 33–70.

37. The classic exposition of this point is found in Adolf A. Berle, Jr., and Gardiner C. Means, *The Modern Corporation and Private Property* (New York: Macmillan, 1933).

38. Two examples which readily come to mind are the Fords and the Du Ponts; see Allan Nevins and Frank Ernest Hill, *Ford: Decline and Rebirth, 1933–1962* (New York: Charles Scribner's Sons, 1962); and Alfred D. Chandler, Jr., and Stephen Salsbury, *Pierre S. Du Pont and the Making of the Modern Corporation* (New York: Harper & Row, 1971).

39. I am indebted here to David M. Potter's reinterpretation of the frontier thesis, as explained in *People of Plenty* (Chicago: University of Chicago Press, 1954), pp. 142–65.

40. See, for instance, W. Lloyd Warner, "The Corporation Man" in Edward S. Mason, ed., *The Corporation in Modern Society* (Cambridge: Harvard University Press, 1959), pp. 106–21.

41. Hidy and Hidy, *Pioneering in Big Business*, especially pp. 14–23, 32–75, 219–32, 305–38.

42. Ulman, *The Rise of the National Trade Union*, pp. 68–200; the quotations are from pp. 124–25.

43. Hidy and Hidy, *Pioneering in Big Business*, pp. 76–200, 233–302.

44. *Scientific and Technical Societies of the United States and Canada*, pp. 104, 244. See also Edwin T. Layton, Jr., *The Revolt of the Engineers: Social Responsibility and the American Engineering Profession* (Cleveland: The Press of Case Western Reserve University, 1971), pp. 29–46.

45. Gabriel Kolko, *The Triumph of Conservatism* (New York: The Free Press, 1963), pp. 98–112.

46. Philip Taft, *The A.F. of L. in the Time of Gompers* (New York: Harper & Brothers, 1957), pp. 163–83, 185–210.

47. This is a major theme in Louis Galambos, *Competition and Cooperation: The Emergence of a National Trade Association* (Baltimore: Johns Hopkins Press, 1966), pp. 1–138.

48. Kolko, *The Triumph of Conservatism*, pp. 217–54.

49. Marver H. Bernstein, *Regulating Business by Independent Commission* (Princeton: Princeton University Press, 1955), p. 294.

50. Ellis Hawley, *The New Deal and the Problem of Monopoly* (Princeton: Princeton University Press, 1966).

51. Walter Galenson, *The CIO Challenge to the AFL* (Cambridge: Harvard University Press, 1960).

52. Alfred D. Chandler, Jr., *Strategy and Structure* (Cambridge: The M.I.T. Press, 1962).

53. Henrietta M. Larson, Evelyn H. Knowlton, and Charles L. Popple, *New Horizons, 1927–1950* (New York: Harper & Row, 1971), pp. 435–42, 580–81; the prior administrative changes are discussed on pp. 1–36.

54. Chandler, *Strategy and Structure*, pp. 324–82.

55. *The Lonely Crowd* (New Haven: Yale University Press, 1961), pp. 13–25. While they relate the other-directed character to "contemporary, highly industrialized, and bureaucratic America," the authors nonetheless adopt a causal analysis that stresses demographic change (perhaps because it enables them to stretch their generalizations from ancient Athens to contemporary America). Ibid., pp. 7–17.

56. Here and throughout the book, I am using the Parsonian pattern variables to analyze changes in values. See Talcott Parsons et al., *Toward a General Theory of Action* (New York: Harper & Row, 1962), pp. 76–91.

57. Karl Marx, *Capital*, 3 vols. (Moscow: Foreign Languages Publishing House, 1961), 1: 624–40.

58. *Capital*, 3: 259. Karl Marx and Friedrich Engels, "Manifesto of the Communist Party," in Lewis S. Feuer, ed., *Basic Writings on Politics and Philosophy: Karl Marx and Friedrich Engels* (Garden City: Anchor Books, 1959), pp. 1–41, analyzes the varieties of reformers, including conservative, or bourgeois, socialists who are "desirous of redressing social grievances, in order to secure the continued existence of bourgeois society." Marx and Engels conclude: "The socialist bourgeois want all the advantages of modern social conditions without the struggles and dangers necessarily resulting therefrom. . . . The socialism of the bourgeoisie simply consists of the assertion that the bourgeois are bourgeois—for the benefit of the working class" (pp. 35–36).

59. Joseph A. Schumpeter, *Capitalism, Socialism, and Democracy* (New York: Harper & Brothers, 1950), pp. 61–163.

60. For general analyses of the progressive synthesis see the following: John Higham et al., *History* (Englewood Cliffs, N.J.: Prentice Hall, 1965), pp. 221–30; Samuel P. Hays, "The Social

Analysis of American Political History," *Political Science Quarterly* 80 (September 1965): 373–94; Hofstadter, *The Progressive Historians.*

61. For examples, see John D. Hicks, *The Populist Revolt* (Lincoln: University of Nebraska Press, 1961), especially pp. 404–23; Arthur S. Link, *Woodrow Wilson and the Progressive Era, 1910–1917* (New York: Harper & Brothers, 1954); Arthur S. Link, *Wilson: Campaigns for Progressivism and Peace, 1916–1917* (Princeton: Princeton University Press, 1965); Arthur M. Schlesinger, Jr., *The Coming of the New Deal* (Boston: Houghton Mifflin Co., 1958).

62. Thus, Eric F. Goldman, in *Rendezvous with Destiny* (New York: Vintage Books, 1956), pp. 66–81, found that the reform Darwinists "developed ideological acids capable of dissolving every link in conservatism's steel chain of ideas." George E. Mowry, *The Era of Theodore Roosevelt, 1900–1912* (New York: Harper & Brothers, 1958), p. 37, discovered that around 1900, "varying streams of thought formed a flood beating against the damlike structure of old ideas and conventions."

63. Arthur S. Link, *American Epoch* (New York: Alfred A. Knopf, 1959), p. 114, said that "by the end of the Taft administration the primary objectives of the antitrust movement had been fairly accomplished. There was no longer any constitutional doubt that the federal government possessed ample power to prevent monopoly and suppress unfair trade practices in the day to day operations of businessmen. Because of Roosevelt's and Taft's vigorous prosecutions, moreover, the age of monopoly was over. Great corporations remained and dominated certain industries, but these oligopolies existed by the sufferance of public opinion and a government that jealously guarded their smaller competitors."

64. See Robert H. Wiebe, *Businessmen and Reform* (Cambridge: Harvard University Press, 1962); Samuel P. Hays, *Conservation and the Gospel of Efficiency* (Cambridge: Harvard University Press, 1959), pp. 1–2, 20, 29–35, 51–52, 73, 126, 264–66; Lee Benson, *Merchants, Farmers, and Railroads* (Cambridge: Harvard University Press, 1955).

65. Kolko, *The Triumph of Conservatism*; Melvin I. Urofsky, *Big Steel and the Wilson Administration* (Columbus: Ohio State University Press, 1969).

66. Richard Hofstadter in *The Age of Reform* (New York: Vintage Books, 1955) launched this phase of revisionism. In regard to the recent literature on status anxiety, David P. Thelen, "Social Tensions and the Origins of Progressivism," *Journal of American History* 56 (September 1969): 323–41, is useful. See also Wiebe, *The Search for Order*, for a somewhat different analysis of cultural politics.

67. Louis Hartz, *The Liberal Tradition in America* (New York: Harcourt, Brace & World, 1955), pp. 232–43; John Higham, "The Cult of the 'American Consensus': Homogenizing our History," *Commentary* 27 (February 1959): 93–100; and the same author's "Beyond Consensus: The Historian as Moral Critic," *American Historical Review* 67 (April 1962): 609–25.

68. Richard Hofstadter, "What Happened to the Antitrust Movement?" in *The Paranoid Style in American Politics and Other Essays* (New York: Alfred A. Knopf, 1965), pp. 188–237.

69. *The Search for Order*, p. 18.

70. Ibid., pp. 301–2.

71. Louis Galambos, "Parsonian Sociology and Post-Progressive History," *Social Science Quarterly* 50 (June 1969): 31–34.

72. Critics of this social model have charged that equilibrium analysis has a built in bias toward conservative values. Obviously, I disagree. The only way the reader can decide whether I am correct is to keep on reading. Those who are interested in the question of implicit values should consult Edward C. Devereux, Jr., "Parsons' Sociological Theory," in Max Black, ed., *The Social Theories of Talcott Parsons: A Critical Examination* (Englewood Cliffs, N.J.: Prentice-Hall, 1961), pp. 33–34; and Gabriel Kolko, "The Premises of Business Revisionism," *Business History Review* 33 (Autumn 1959): 335–37.

73. The assumption here was that values had to be grounded in effective and lasting organizations, built into their structure of roles and sanctions, to be of major significance.

2. RESEARCH TECHNIQUE: CONTENT ANALYSIS DESCRIBED AND DEBATED

1. For a convenient guide to some of the philosophical questions, see Robert F. Berkhofer, Jr., *A Behavioral Approach to Historical Analysis* (New York: The Free Press, 1969). For a typical response (by a distinctly atypical scholar) see David Herbert Donald, "Between Science and Art," *American Historical Review* 77 (April 1972): 445–52.

2. The so-called new economic history is by now middle-aged, but the reader who is unfamiliar with the work which falls under this rubric can consult Albert Fishlow and Robert W. Fogel, "Quantitative Economic History: An Interim Evaluation," *Journal of Economic History* 31 (March 1971): 15–42; Ralph L. Andreano, ed., *The New Economic History: Recent Papers on Methodology* (New York: John Wiley & Sons, Inc., 1970); and, for a less favorable evaluation, Thomas C. Cochran, "Economic History, Old and New," *American Historical Review* 74 (June 1969): 1561–72.

3. An important exception is provided by Irma Adelman and Cynthia T. Morris, "An Econometric Model of Socio-Economic and Political Change in Underdeveloped Countries," *American Economic Review* 58 (December 1968): 1184–1218.

4. William N. Parker, "From Old to New to Old in Economic History," *Journal of Economic History* 31 (March 1971): 3–14. Recent institutional studies are reviewed in James H. Soltow, "American Institutional Studies: Present Knowledge and Past Trends," ibid., pp. 87–105.

5. Lance E. Davis and Douglass C. North, "Institutional Change and American Economic Growth: A First Step Towards a Theory of Institutional Innovation," *Journal of Economic History* 30 (March 1970): 131–49; and, by the same authors, *Institutional Change and American Economic Growth* (Cambridge: At the University Press, 1971).

6. Robert W. Fogel, *Railroads and American Economic Growth: Essays in Econometric History* (Baltimore: Johns Hopkins Press, 1964), pp. 4–6.

7. *Public Opinion Quarterly* 31 (Winter 1967): 522–67.

8. Ernest R. May, "American Imperialism: A Reinterpretation," *Perspectives in American History* 1 (1967), especially pp. 135–53 and 280–83.

9. Richard L. Merritt, *Symbols of American Community, 1735–1775* (New Haven: Yale University Press, 1966).

10. For guides to the literature as well as the techniques, see the following: Bernard Berelson, *Content Analysis in Communications Research* (Glencoe, Ill.: The Free Press, 1952); Ithiel de Sola Pool, ed., *Trends in Content Analysis* (Urbana: University of Illinois Press, 1959); the RADIR (Revolution and Development of International Relations) studies, especially Harold Lasswell et al., *The Comparative Study of Symbols*, and Ithiel de Sola Pool et al., *The "Prestige Papers"* (both published at Stanford, Calif.: Hoover Institute Studies, 1952). See also Ole R. Holsti, *Content Analysis for the Social Sciences and Humanities* (Reading, Mass.: Addison-Wesley Publishing Co., 1969), especially pp. 1–41, 195–221; Richard L. Merritt, *Systematic Approaches to Comparative Politics* (Chicago: Rand McNally & Co., 1970), pp. 64–103. Historian Paul Kleppner, *The Cross of Culture* (New York: The Free Press, 1970), pp. 151 ff, uses content analysis but provides the reader with little explanation of his technique.

11. David C. McClelland, *The Achieving Society* (New York: The Free Press, 1967); Richard de Charms and Gerald H. Moeller, "Values Expressed in American Children's Readers, 1800–1950," *Journal of Abnormal and Social Psychology* 64 (1962): 136–42. For other references see Holsti, *Content Analysis*, pp. 42–93.

12. Here I am consciously placing one foot at least part way into the historicist camp, as staked out by R. G. Collingwood in *The Idea of History* (New York: Oxford University Press, 1956), especially pp. 54–55, 179–80.

13. The philosophical position might well be labeled "Mandelbaum's Middleground"; see Maurice Mandelbaum, "Historical Explanation: The Problem of 'Covering Laws,'" *History*

and *Theory* 1 (1961): 229–42. A similar conclusion—stated in a different way—can be found in Berkhofer, *A Behavioral Approach to Historical Analysis*, pp. 270–91.

14. My research assistant and I tested our ability to reproduce our results, working as a team. In order to check our reliability in deciding what opinion an item expressed, we reexamined four issues, picked at random, after all of the materials had been read and the results tabulated. The results of the first and second readings were compared, using a percentage agreement index: the index $= \dfrac{2\,\mathrm{Pab}}{\mathrm{Pa} + \mathrm{Pb}}$. In this formula, Pa is the number of items scored in the initial reading; Pb is the number scored in the second reading; Pab is the number scored both times. The index for our decisions about the opinion reflected by the material was 0.96. (We derived this index from Merritt, *Symbols of American Community*, pp. 200–201.) We did *not* do a similar test using two other readers, in large part because we felt that both readers would need about a month's experience with the materials and the rather complex score sheet we were using before they could reproduce our results. This, I decided, made the test cost more than it was worth. Had I looked upon myself as a scientist, I would doubtless have concluded that the cost was commensurate with the benefits. Richard L. Merritt has ardently proposed that I erred in this decision, and I would like to acknowledge his earnest advice, even though I ignored it.

15. The definition was drawn from Talcott Parsons et al., *Toward a General Theory of Action* (New York: Harper and Row, 1962), pp. 7–8; and Talcott Parsons, *The Social System* (New York: The Free Press, 1964), pp. 5–6, 10–11. The distinction here is the same one made in Henry F. May, *The End of American Innocence: A Study of the First Years of Our Own Time, 1912–1917* (New York: Alfred A. Knopf, 1959), p. 30, but May concentrates on the type of culture which "meant a particular part of the heritage from the European past, including polite manners, respect for traditional learning, appreciation of the arts, and above all an informed and devoted love of standard literature."

16. These two areas included a substantial number of the nation's farmers. In 1880, 64.4 percent of the country's farms were concentrated in the north central and south central regions; in 1900 the figure was 67.2 percent. U.S. Census Office, *Twelfth Census of the United States, 1900, Agriculture,* 5 (Washington, D.C., 1902), p. xxxiii.

17. This paper appeared under various names: *Southern Cultivator; The Southern Cultivator and Dixie Farmer*; and *The Southern Cultivator and Industrial Journal*. In this case and others, I have used only one name throughout. All of the circulation figures for *Southern Cultivator* and for the other papers were taken from N. W. Ayer & Son's *American Newspaper Annual*. These figures are not above suspicion, and in several instances there is good reason to believe that the subscription rates were inflated to enhance the image of the paper or an affiliated organization; thus, the *Journal of the Knights of Labor* claimed a circulation of 100,000 in 1905, long after the union had entered a period of significant decline. For an intelligent discussion of circulation data, see Daniel A. Pope, "The Development of National Advertising, 1865–1920" (Ph.D. diss., Columbia University, 1973), pp. 263–72.

18. This and other comments upon the readers are based in part upon the published letters to the editor.

19. We analyzed one overlapping year for both journals in order to test this conclusion.

20. In January 1895 the name of this publication was *The Farm and Dairy*; this was changed to *Wallaces' Farm and Dairy*, and then to *Wallaces' Farmer*. In 1901, *Wallaces' Farmer* had a circulation of 23,769; by 1910 the figure had reached 54,006, and by 1920 it was 65,200.

21. To be consistent, I should not have used *Wallaces' Farmer* for the years 1921–24, when Henry C. Wallace was secretary of agriculture.

22. The *National Labor Tribune* claimed a circulation of 13,000 in 1890 and 18,000 in 1905.

23. The circulation of the *American Federationist* was officially listed as 43,389 in 1905 and 100,000 in 1920.

NOTES TO PAGES 26-29

24. *Solidarity*, July 3, 1915; July 1, 1922. *Solidarity*, which also appeared under the names *Industrial Solidarity* and the *New Solidarity*, wandered from New Castle, Pennsylvania, to Cleveland, Ohio, and finally to Chicago, Illinois.

25. Ibid., Jan. 7, 1925.

26. This publication was also entitled *Engineering News and American Contract Journal*, *Engineering News and American Railway Journal*, and *Engineering News-Record*. Its circulation was 6,000 in 1890 and 31,327 in 1920.

27. This issue was discussed in 1934 when *Congregationalist* went out of business (March 29, 1934, p. 211). In 1938, an editorial in its successor, *Advance*, noted that "perhaps the most persistent false notion concerning *Advance*, the one that most deeply affects the paper, and the one that is hardest to overcome, is the idea that '*Advance* is a minister's paper.' Often it is expressed as if it were a clearly-recognized assumption, or a commonly-established fact. It is cited by ministers in extenuation of their failure to interest laymen in the paper, and by laymen as an excuse for an attitude in which they have not even taken the trouble to test the matter for themselves." The editorial denied that this was the case. *Advance* 130, no. 4 (April 1938): 145.

28. Henry F. May, *Protestant Churches and Industrial America* (New York: Octagon Books, 1963), pp. 187–88.

29. The *Congregationalist*, which was published in Boston, did not survive the Great Depression and its place was taken in 1934 by the *Advance*. The circulation of the *Congregationalist* was 21,000 in 1880, 24,000 in 1901, and 20,000 in 1915.

30. The shift at this point from the singular to the plural pronoun is deliberate. The plural indicates that two persons, myself and my research assistant, Barbara B. Spence, were directly involved in this part of the research. After some initial trials and a period of floundering, we settled into the following routine: Ms. Spence made the preliminary selection of items to be scored and prepared a score sheet on each such article or editorial; I then read each of these items (as well as any marginal choices) and checked the score sheets; we then discussed and resolved any differences of interpretation. When, for a time, we exchanged duties and I did the initial reading, Ms. Spence raised most of the same objections to my decisions that I had to hers, which suggested that our different opinions were more closely related to the content analysis procedure than to personal bias or previous training.

31. As it turned out, this was an error. There were a large number of very small railroad companies which could well have been eliminated.

32. In a few instances simple addition produced a result which contradicted our intuitive impressions of the article. If our intuitive impressions agreed, we broke the rule.

33. In Pool, *The "Prestige Papers,"* p. 41, only explicit judgments were counted; thus, an editorial associating communism with slave labor camps was considered neutral unless the editor said that slave labor camps were bad.

34. Future scholars will doubtless improve on our technique and introduce more sophisticated measures of attitude. One might, for instance, use a scale ranging from plus three to minus three to measure the intensity of feeling. See Charles E. Osgood, "The Representational Model and Relevant Research Methods," in Pool, *Trends*, pp. 48–49.

35. In this case we simply wrote down a description of what caused the item to appear and categorized the answers after we had read most of the journals.

36. Executive Office of the President, Bureau of the Budget, *Standard Industrial Classification Manual* (Washington, D.C., 1957).

37. We discarded this part of the data from the southern farm journals because when we first read the early issues of these papers we were still experimenting with the technique and later changed our rules for this part of the study.

38. Since the information in these categories was used in order to reach conclusions about patterns of attention, I introduced a systematic bias by providing two slots for some aspects (e.g., 13 and 14) and one for others (e.g., 23). It would also have been better if I had been able to

design categories with the same level of generalization; but, for example, price policy (23) was highly specific, while the large firm's contribution to the general welfare (17) was not. In this sense the two types of information were not completely comparable, but I compared them nevertheless by ranking them in order of importance.

39. *Engineering News*, January 14, 1926, p. 50.

40. In order to check the difference between a two-month and a four-month sample, we compared the total number of items in two samples, one for January and July, and the other for April and October. The samples were taken from yearly issues, picked at random, of *Southern Cultivator* and *Wallaces' Farmer*. At the 5 percent level of significance, we could not reject the hypothesis that there were no differences between the populations from which the two samples were drawn. For practical purposes, what this means is that 95 times out of 100 there would be no statistically significant difference between matched samples drawn from these publications. On sampling, see Alexander Mintz, "The Feasibility of the Use of Samples in Content Analysis," in Harold D. Lasswell et al., *The Language of Politics* (Cambridge: The M.I.T. Press, 1965), pp. 127–52. For a different technique, see Merritt, *Symbols of American Community*, pp. 199–201.

41. We actually tested our sample for several of the different journals, including *American Federationist*. In the latter case we compared our regular sample with a six-month sample for one year, picked at random. Changing the sample size increased the number of items scored from ten to twelve per issue and altered the percentage of unfavorable items by 10 percent, for this particular year. This was the least favorable of our results and should perhaps be regarded as an outside limit. The choice of July as one of the two months selected probably introduced an upward bias into the data on corporate political activities, because the Fourth of July usually stirred up some special commentary on the state of American democracy; since, however, the same bias existed for all of the years studied, the figures from any two (or more) years could still be compared without discounting for this bias.

42. My work was funded in part by the Advanced Research Projects Agency under ARPA Order No. 738 and monitored by the Office of Naval Research, Group Psychology Branch, under Contract Number N00014-67-A-0145-0001, NR 177-909. To those of a patriotic bent, this can be seen as a contribution to the national defense effort; those who are critical of university involvement in the military-industrial complex can take solace in the fact that money spent for content analysis could not be used to buy napalm.

3. AN UNEASY EQUILIBRIUM, 1879–1892

1. Alfred H. Conrad, "Income Growth and Structural Change," in Seymour E. Harris, ed., *American Economic History* (New York: McGraw-Hill, 1961), pp. 46–54; Robert Higgs, *The Transformation of the American Economy, 1865–1915* (New York: John Wiley & Sons, 1971), pp. 18–49, 107–25.

2. Until recently, the least understood of the changes has been the development of the distribution system. Fortunately, we can now turn to Glenn Porter and Harold C. Livesay's study of *Merchants and Manufacturers* (Baltimore: Johns Hopkins Press, 1971).

3. Robert P. Swierenga, *Pioneers and Profits* (Ames: Iowa State University Press, 1968); Allan G. Bogue, *Money at Interest* (Lincoln: University of Nebraska Press, 1969).

4. Gerald N. Grob, *Workers and Utopia* (Evanston: Northwestern University Press, 1961), focuses on these conflicts; see also Philip Taft, *The A.F. of L. in the Time of Gompers* (New York: Harper & Brothers, 1957), pp. 21–62; and Lloyd Ulman, *The Rise of the National Trade Union* (Cambridge: Harvard University Press, 1955).

5. Robert H. Wiebe, *The Search for Order* (New York: Hill and Wang, 1967), pp. 11–75.

6. *Congregationalist*, Jan. 3, 1884, p. 8.

7. I use singular nouns and pronouns throughout the book when I am discussing the various groups and their perceptions of big business; this is merely a literary device, and I do not mean

to imply that I am studying either an individual or personality as a system. My focus is upon social phenomena which characterize relatively large groups such as engineers and professional men in general.

Those readers who are interested in the annual percentages depicted in figure 3-1 (and in all of the subsequent graphs) can write directly to the author for a mimeographed copy of the data.

8. Annual data on salaries in engineering and on the demand for engineers are not available for the eighties, but with employment opportunities on the railroads obviously increasing and with the national economy recovering from the recession, it is highly unlikely that engineers were motivated at this time by economic distress.

9. This was the theme of Veblen's collection of essays on *The Engineers and the Price System* (New York: Viking Press, 1921).

10. *Engineering News*, July 2, 1887, p. 8. Quotations cannot, in any strict sense, be representative; each has its own individual qualities and that is generally why we employ them. In my case I considered each quotation to be representative of a general category of thought, but I made no effort to ensure that the selections were drawn from the central range of statements within that category. In fact, there was an inherent bias toward the unusual comment, a bias which may not be recognizable in this case because of the rather bland verbal recipes that the engineers used when they wrote.

11. Ibid., Jan. 7, 1888, p. 1.

12. Ibid., July 7, 1888, p. 11.

13. Ibid., July 4, 1891, pp. 14–15.

14. My working definition of ideology is taken from Talcott Parsons, *The Social System* (New York: The Free Press, 1964), p. 349: "An ideology . . . is a system of beliefs, held in common by the members of a collectivity, i.e., a society, or a sub-collectivity of one—including a movement deviant from the main culture of the society—a system of ideas which is oriented to the evaluative integration of the collectivity, by interpretation of the empirical nature of the collectivity and of the situation in which it is placed, the processes by which it has developed to its given state, the goals to which its members are collectively oriented, and their relation to the future course of events."

15. This distinction is between what Parsons calls "existential" and "evaluative" belief systems. Ibid., pp. 326–32.

16. Their ideology was thus an empirical, existential belief system rooted in a role structure that was characterized by a high degree of achievement orientation (as opposed to ascriptive norms), by very specific (as opposed to diffuse) relationships, by an emphasis on the collectivity and on the maintenance of affective neutrality and relatively universal standards.

17. On the organizations, see chapter 1, section III, and Monte A. Calvert, *The Mechanical Engineer in America, 1830–1910* (Baltimore: Johns Hopkins Press, 1967), especially part 2, "Internal Development," pp. 43–186.

18. *Engineering News*, Jan. 4, 1890, pp. 9–10, 13–14.

19. Ralph W. and Muriel E. Hidy describe the various attacks on the Standard Oil combine in *Pioneering in Big Business: History of Standard Oil Company (New Jersey), 1882–1911* (New York: Harper & Brothers, 1955), pp. 201–19. The reader should recall that the figure presented here is based on a two-issue sample; the number is only useful in a relative sense, when compared, for instance, to the thirty-five times that the Pennsylvania Railroad Company was mentioned during these same years.

20. *Engineering News*, July 7, 1888, pp. 1, 12.

21. Even in the period 1887–92, favorable comments outweighed negative remarks about management (11 to 8).

22. *Engineering News* was not opposed to regulation as such; when it could be shown to be necessary, as for instance, in assuring the construction of safe iron bridges, the paper approved

of "mandatory legislation." *Engineering News*, July 2, 1887, pp. 8, 10–11. But, on the other hand, the engineer recognized that "anti-railway legislation puts a check on railway extension" (Jan. 5, 1889, p. 10).

23. Ibid., July 4, 1891, pp. 14–15; Jan. 2, 1892, pp. 14–15; see also July 6, 1893, pp. 10–11, 17–18; and Jan. 4, 1894, p. 15, for later comments. U.S. Interstate Commerce Commission, *Seventh Annual Report* (Washington, 1893), pp. 74–76, 261–66. The Safety Appliance Act introduced federal controls in 1893.

24. *Engineering News*, Jan. 2, 1892, pp. 1, 14–15.

25. Ibid., p. 22; July 7, 1892, pp. 10, 12. My conclusion is based in large part on the decline in negative remarks about this problem. For the annual number of deaths and injuries, see U.S. Interstate Commerce Commission, *Sixth Annual Report, Statistics of Railways* (Washington, 1894), pp. 65–80; and U.S. Bureau of the Census, *Historical Statistics of the United States, Colonial Times to 1957* (Washington, D.C., 1960), p. 437.

26. Henry F. May, *Protestant Churches and Industrial America* (New York: Octagon Books, 1963), provides an excellent analysis of the movement through the 1890s.

27. Ibid., pp. 91–135, 163–81. On p. 182, May says that "it is . . . difficult to estimate the effect of these new teachings [that is, the social gospel] on the large, solid homogeneous mass of American Protestant opinion." This, I think, is one of the problems that data of the sort I am using can help us solve. An important question to which I am not addressing myself is why this denomination or any part of it was more or less open to these ideas than were other denominations.

28. Buried here are some important distinctions. One is between two kinds of belief systems—those which are ideological and thus empirical, and those which are nonempirical and are philosophical or religious in nature (hence not subject in any final sense to what Talcott Parsons calls "the canons of empirical knowledge"). (*The Social System*, pp. 328–32.) The other distinction is between a belief system and a value. The latter is in this usage "*a conception, explicit or implicit, distinctive of an individual or characteristic of a group, of the desirable which influences the selection from available modes, means, and ends of action*" (Clyde Kluckhohn et al., "Values and Value-Orientations in the Theory of Action," in Talcott Parsons et al., *Toward a General Theory of Action* [New York: Harper and Row, 1962], p. 395). A belief system is a cultural pattern which incorporates a number of such values, lends order to them, and performs an integrative function in the social system.

29. Throughout, I am using the pattern variables introduced in chapter 1, section IV.

30. *Congregationalist*, July 7, 1892, p. 216.

31. Ibid., Jan. 10, 1889, p. 14.

32. Ibid., Jan. 2, 1890, p. 8.

33. Ibid., July 7, 1887, p. 231.

34. Ibid., July 3, 1890, p. 234.

35. Ibid., Jan. 13, 1887, p. 12.

36. Ibid., Jan. 14, 1886, p. 16.

37. Ibid., July 3, 1890, p. 230.

38. Ibid., July 2, 1891, p. 221.

39. Ibid., Jan. 10, 1883, p. 11.

40. Ibid., Jan. 2, 1890, p. 4.

41. Ibid., Jan. 14, 1892, p. 12.

42. This pattern of trade union development was not broken until the 1920s. See Ulman, *The Rise of the National Trade Union*, pp. 42–43; Irving Bernstein, *The Lean Years* (Boston: Houghton Mifflin Co., 1960), pp. 84–90.

43. *Congregationalist*, Jan. 13, 1887, p. 12.

44. Ibid., Jan. 13, 1887, p. 11.

45. *Southern Cultivator* 40, no. 1 (January 1882): 7, 13; 44, no. 7 (July 1886): 279.

46. Ibid., 41, no. 4 (April 1883): 5. Albert Fishlow stresses this aspect of the railroad's economic impact in *American Railroads and the Transformation of the Ante-Bellum Economy* (Cambridge: Harvard University Press, 1965), pp. 154–55.

47. *Southern Cultivator* 40, no. 3 (March 1882): 2; 41, no. 4 (April 1883): 3.

48. This happened so frequently and was the occasion for so many favorable remarks in both the southern and midwestern papers that I felt it distorted my data on the agrarian view of corporate price policies. Very often the same issue of the paper that attacked monopoly prices and price discrimination would follow up these remarks with a friendly comment on the most recent convention rate—itself a form of discrimination in the farmer's behalf. See, for instance, ibid., 47, no. 7 (July 1889). With this in mind, I have partially discounted the large number of favorable references to price policies.

49. Ibid., 38, no. 1 (January 1880), quoting remarks made at an Alabama Grange meeting, with editorial comment; and W. L. Jones's article in 44, no. 7 (July 1886).

50. See the letter from J. B. Hunnicutt in ibid., 49, no. 4 (April 1891); also the letter from Thomas D. Baird in 50, no. 10 (October 1892).

51. Ibid., 46, no. 1 (January 1888): 16; 47, no. 1 (January 1889): 26; 48, no. 7 (July 1890): 308, 320.

52. Ibid., 45, no. 7 (July 1887): 300–301.

53. The figure of 40% refers, of course, only to those articles that mentioned big business. The annual percentages were: 1887, 30%; 1888, 25%; 1889, 17%; and 1890, 40%.

54. Ibid., 49, no. 1 (January 1891): 23.

55. Ibid., 48, no. 7 (July 1890): 321.

56. Ibid. As table 3-3 indicates, almost all of the items mentioned the firm's economic functions, and the four leading characteristics of the corporation, 1887–92, were all economic in nature.

57. Ibid., p. 324; 47, no. 7 (July 1889): 360–61. The leading *negative* characteristics, 1887–92, were: 1) general economic power; 2) prices, which was tied with the existence or expansion of the firm.

58. Ibid., 47, no. 7 (July 1889): 356.

59. Ibid., 46, no. 1 (January 1888): 16.

60. Frederick Strauss and Louis H. Bean, *Gross Farm Income and Indices of Farm Production and Prices in the United States, 1869–1937* (Washington, D.C., 1940), p. 64. See also Richard A. Easterlin, "Regional Income Trends, 1840–1950," in Harris, *American Economic History*, pp. 537–39.

61. U.S. Bureau of the Census, *Eleventh Census, 1890, Report on the Statistics of Agriculture* (Washington, D.C., 1895), p. 51. In Alabama, for instance, the effects of this change could be seen in the steady increase in the number of bales grown per acre. James L. Watkins, *King Cotton* (New York: James L. Watkins & Sons, 1908), pp. 152–55.

62. Fred A. Shannon, *The Farmer's Last Frontier* (New York: Rinehart & Co., 1945), pp. 112–15.

63. This subject came up one or more times every year from 1882 through 1888.

64. *Southern Cultivator* 48, no. 1 (January 1890): 26, and no. 7 (July 1890): 289–99.

65. The Pearsonian coefficient of correlation (used here and in all subsequent calculations) between cotton prices and the percentage of neutral-ambivalent items was $+.58$. The coefficient for prices against unfavorable attitudes was only $-.14$. All prices and income data were taken from Strauss and Bean, *Gross Farm Income*, pp. 63–67. Lacking information on net income (which would measure the cost-price squeeze), I prepared an index of annual gross income from cotton and cottonseed (in constant dollars). Correlations between this index and the figures on unfavorable attitudes indicated, however, that for the years 1879–92 there was a significant positive relationship ($+.86$). Forced either to concede that during these years the income statistics did not accurately reflect economic distress or, on the other hand, to explain why lower income made farmers less hostile toward the trusts, I chose the first alternative.

66. It was not irrational to be concerned about one's status, about the family, or about the declining moral condition of the country. At best, however, these problems had a tenuous connection—if any at all—to the rise of the large firm. Doing away with big business entirely would not have altered the farmer's status or shored up the family farm, and the farmer's tendency to see a causal relationship between these problems was, in my view, irrational.

67. *Southern Cultivator* 45, no. 7 (July 1887): 300–301.

68. Ibid., 47, no. 7 (July 1889); 49, no. 1 (January 1891); and 47, no. 7 (July 1889): 320.

69. Ibid., pp. 360–61.

70. *The Age of Reform* (New York: Vintage Books, 1955), pp. 60–93. This publication stirred up a lively academic debate; for some of the more prominent rejoinders see: Norman Pollack, "Hofstadter on Populism," *Journal of Southern History* 26 (November 1960): 478–500; and three other selections by the same author, "The Myth of Populist Anti-Semitism," *American Historical Review* 68 (October 1962): 76–80; "Fear of Man: Populism, Authoritarianism, and the Historian," *Agricultural History* 39 (April 1965): 59–67; and *The Populist Response to Industrial America* (Cambridge: Harvard University Press, 1962). Also relevant are C. Vann Woodward, *The Burden of Southern History* (New York: Vintage Books, 1960), pp. 141–66; and Walter T. K. Nugent, *The Tolerant Populists* (Chicago: University of Chicago Press, 1963).

71. *The Search for Order*, pp. 49–50, 71–75.

72. Of course, Hofstadter and his opponents have concentrated primarily on those farmers who were actively engaged in reform, and in that sense my sources are different from theirs. I am not meeting the question head on, as does Nugent, for example. Since, however, fine distinctions have not been made in this debate and since the farm mentality in general has been brought into question, I feel justified in contributing to the discussion.

73. *Southern Cultivator* 48, no. 10 (October 1890). See also ibid., 45, no. 7 (July 1887), where the secretary of the East Tennessee Farmers' Convention says (pp. 300–301) that "the scum of European population is coming here as never before, but few of them have any ideas or appreciation of our system of government." Cf. *Engineering News*, Jan. 4, 1890, p. 2, which comments "unhappily" on the recent increase in immigration; and *Congregationalist*, Jan. 14, 1892, p. 12. See also ibid., July 1, 1886, p. 217. After 1900 the attitudes expressed in *Congregationalist* suggest that nativism was on the decline, but as late as 1901 the paper quoted a letter from a prominent minister in the interior (that is, the Midwest) that said: "To think that the man who shot the President [McKinley] was American born fills me with horror. If he had been a Russian or Italian, it would not have been half so bad" (Oct. 5, 1901, p. 486).

74. *Farmers' Review* 17, no. 3 (July 1886): 40; *National Labor Tribune*, July 2, 1881, p. 2.

75. *National Labor Tribune*, Jan. 3, 1891, p. 8; *Congregationalist*, Jan. 3, 1895, p. 16. See also John Higham, "Anti-Semitism in the Gilded Age," *Mississippi Valley Historical Review* 43 (March 1957): 559–78; and *American Agriculturist* 50 (October 1891): 566.

76. Solon Justus Buck, *The Granger Movement* (Cambridge: Harvard University Press, 1913). For editorial discussion of the organizational side of farm life, see *Southern Cultivator* 48, no. 1 (January 1886); 44, no. 7 (July 1886); 45, no. 7 (July 1887); 49, no. 1 (January 1891).

77. John D. Hicks, *The Populist Revolt* (Lincoln: University of Nebraska Press, 1961), pp. 96–185; C. Vann Woodward, *Origins of the New South, 1877–1913* (Baton Rouge: Louisiana State University Press, 1951), pp. 188–245. In 1888, *Southern Cultivator* was in "full sympathy" with only the "legitimate purposes of the Alliances," but by 1890 the paper was less cautious. See 46, no. 8 (August 1888): 372; 48, no. 7 (July 1890): 319.

78. Hans B. Thorelli, *The Federal Antitrust Policy* (Baltimore: Johns Hopkins Press, 1955), pp. 369–80. The impact of the Sherman Antitrust Act can be seen in the change that took place in the number of industries the farmers associated with the concentration movement. In the late eighties, the number increased sharply, while the (relative) amount of attention devoted to the railroad declined; after the law was passed, the number of industries dropped off and railroads assumed their customary position as the leading subject of concern.

NOTES TO PAGES 63-64

79. *Farmers' Review*, Jan. 26, 1882, p. 59; Jan. 2, 1889, p. 10.

80. Ibid., July 7, 1886, p. 1.

81. Ibid., July 6, 1882, especially the article on "Farming at the Front," pp. 424–25. For similar statements, see ibid., Jan. 6, 1886, p. 12; July 7, 1886, p. 13; Jan. 16, 1889, p. 34; July 8, 1891, p. 433; July 22, 1891, p. 468; Jan. 27, 1891, p. 58.

82. Ibid., April 16, 1890, p. 265; July 2, 1890, p. 448; Jan. 21, 1891, p. 34; Jan. 28, 1891, p. 59; July 8, 1891, p. 427; and July 22, 1891, pp. 458–59.

83. Ibid., Jan. 14, 1891, pp. 18, 30.

84. Ibid., July 29, 1891, p. 475. In both the South and Midwest there was thus evidence of lightning rod effects and of a sense of general social crisis. When one takes the entire period into consideration, however, these patterns of thought were a major aspect of farm thought in the South and only a minor element in the Midwest.

85. Ibid., Jan. 26, 1887, p. 56.

86. Ibid., Jan. 3, 1884, p. 8; Jan. 30, 1889, p. 65. In a discussion of the United States Senate, one article said: "In all matters relating to or affecting either nearly or remotely the questions of methods of accumulating money, and the safety, security, and profitableness of investments, the granting of privileges to corporations, by which fortunes may be made, and the thousand and one ways in which men with fortunes seek to add to them still other fortunes, they act for the interest of their class" (July 7, 1886, p. 8).

87. For examples, ʳᵉe the following selections: *Farmers' Review* January 1879, p. 8; July 22, 1885, p. 53; July 29, 1885, p. 72; Jan. 6, 1886, p. 12; July 7, 1886, p. 5; Jan. 26, 1887, p. 60; Jan. 11, 1888, p. 442; April 30, 1890, p. 309; July 16, 1890, p. 480; Jan. 7, 1891, pp. 3, 6.

88. In the Midwest (and not in the South), the railroads had exerted an important influence on patterns of settlement. Additionally, the close link between railroads and elevator companies left the wheat and corn farmers convinced that the prices they received for their products were controlled by the roads. The southern farmer did not face this situation; his closest relationships were with the local merchants who were the southern counterpart of the elevator companies. (I am here using *northern* and *midwestern* as synonymous terms.)

89. *Farmers' Review*, Jan. 4, 1883, p. 8.

90. Ibid., Jan. 15, 1885, p. 52; Jan. 29, 1885, p. 73.

91. Ibid., Jan. 18, 1883, p. 33.

92. Ibid., Jan. 15, 1885, p. 47. This particular missive aroused a rejoinder from a correspondent who felt that the Northwestern's rates were "as low as any other" and that "their agents here . . . would rough . . . it to accommodate any one of the settlers along the line" (Jan. 29, 1885, p. 84).

93. In the period 1879–86, the leading negative aspects were (in rank order): prices; dependence upon political assistance; and the existence or expansion of big business.

94. Ibid., July 20, 1882, p. 33; Jan. 1, 1885, p. 16; July 5, 1883, p. 8.

95. Ibid., Jan. 15, 1885, p. 54.

96. I tested these relationships using index numbers for gross income (in constant dollars) from corn and hogs; the data on income came from Strauss and Bean, *Gross Farm Income*, pp. 39, 119. Here and throughout the book, I converted income to constant dollars by using a consumer price index. See Ethel D. Hoover, "Retail Prices after 1850," in *Trends in the American Economy in the Nineteenth Century* (Princeton: Princeton University Press, 1960), p. 162. For later periods, I spliced the Hoover index into the consumer price index of the Bureau of Labor Statistics, which is available in *Historical Statistics*, p. 126. In the instance at hand the results were as follows (1918 = 100):

1879	24.3	1883	40.0	1887	30.9	1890	30.8
1880	39.3	1884	39.3	1888	36.6	1891	30.5
1881	35.4	1885	32.9	1889	32.8	1892	30.8
1882	40.9	1886	28.8				

The wheat farmer had similar problems; the price per bushel (yearly average) and the annual gross income from wheat both stayed below the 1882 level during the following ten years.

97. On the rate wars and declining charges, see Julius Grodinsky, *The Iowa Pool: A Study in Railroad Competition, 1870–1884* (Chicago: University of Chicago Press, 1950), pp. 136–67; *Poor's Manual of Railroads, 1885* (New York: J. J. Little and Co., 1885), pp. vii–viii; and William Z. Ripley, *Railroads: Rates and Regulation* (New York: Longmans, Green and Co., 1913), pp. 411–32.

98. The coefficient of correlation (r) between the percentage of favorable items and an index for freight rates, 1879–89, was -.66. For the percentage of unfavorable items, r =+.59. The index (1882 = 100) was based upon revenue per ton mile. See Ripley, *Railroads*, pp. 411–25; and *Historical Statistics*, p. 428.

99. *Farmers' Review*, Jan. 12, 1887, p. 17; Jan. 19, 1887, p. 40; Jan. 4, 1888, p. 9.

100. Ibid., April 23, 1890; Jan. 7, 1891, p. 3; July 22, 1891, pp. 458–59. The paper quoted with approval Supreme Court Justice Barrett's remark: "This question of trust is, I think, almost of as much consequence as slavery" (July 2, 1890, p. 448).

101. Ibid., Jan. 27, 1892, p. 55; July 27, 1892, pp. 467–68.

102. These figures are the respective means of the annual percentages.

103. Between 1880 and 1886, the leading negative aspects (as opposed to the leading aspects given in table 3–5) were as follows: labor relations; dependence upon political assistance; wages and hours.

104. *National Labor Tribune*, July 2, 1881, p. 2. This was the Frick Coke Co., which, as mentioned above, "vomited" strikebreaking "hungry Hungarians" on Pennsylvania.

105. Ibid., p. 5.

106. Ibid., July 1, 1882, p. 1.

107. Ibid., Jan. 1, 1881, p. 1; July 1, 1882, p. 2.

108. Thorelli, *The Federal Antitrust Policy*, pp. 37–38, 52–53, 110–17, discusses the older version of monopoly.

109. *National Labor Tribune*, Jan. 1, 1881, p. 8; and July 1, 1882, p. 2.

110. Ibid., Jan. 3, 1880, p. 2.

111. Ibid., Jan. 6, 1883, p. 1; Jan. 5, 1884, p. 1; July 7, 1883, p. 1; July 4, 1885, p. 1.

112. Ibid., Jan. 14, 1888, p. 3; July 7, 1888, p. 4; Jan. 4, 1890, p. 1.

113. I correlated the figures on attitudes for the period 1880–92 with an index (1890 = 100) of average hourly wages in manufacturing, adjusted for changes in living cost. The wage data came from Clarence D. Long, *Wages and Earnings in the United States, 1860–1890* (Princeton: Princeton University Press, 1960), p. 153. I estimated the figures for 1891 and 1892 on the basis of the indices of real hourly earnings (all manufacturing) in Albert Rees, *Real Wages in Manufacturing, 1890–1914* (Princeton: Princeton University Press, 1961), p. 120. For wages against favorable opinions, r = +.65; for wages against the percentage of unfavorable items, r = -.51. Similar correlations using daily wages in current dollars did not yield significant results.

114. David Brody, *The Steel Workers in America: The Nonunion Era* (Cambridge: Harvard University Press, 1960), pp. 50–55.

115. Grob, *Workers and Utopia*, pp. 119–37; Taft, *The A.F. of L. in the Time of Gompers*, pp. 31–59.

116. For examples, see the following: *National Labor Tribune*, July 1, 1882, pp. 1, 3, and 4; Jan. 6, 1883, p. 5; Jan. 5, 1884, p. 1; July 13, 1889, p. 1.

117. Ibid., Jan. 3, 1891, p. 1.

118. From Harrisburg, Pennsylvania, came a letter offering an optimistic report and a wonderfully mixed metaphor: "We have now got this district in proper shape in unionism. . . . It is moved from center to circumference, and the tower of monopoly that has been predominant is no more as such. A break has been made, the clouds are scattered, and a firmness of purpose is exhibited by the men that the power of monopoly cannot break" (ibid. July 4, 1891, p. 4).

119. Ibid., July 2, 1892, pp. 1, 4.

120. The literature on this first value set is discussed quite cogently in Theodore P. Greene, *America's Heroes: The Changing Models of Success in American Magazines* (New York: Oxford University Press, 1970), pp. 3–15; on the particular nature of individualism in the nineties, see pp. 110–65.

Achievement orientation has been the special province of David C. McClelland, but for his nineteenth-century American sample, *The Achieving Society* (New York: The Free Press, 1967), pp. 149–51, he depends exclusively upon Richard de Charms and G. H. Moeller, "Values Expressed in American Children's Readers, 1800–1950," *Journal of Abnormal and Social Psychology* 64 (February 1962): 136–42.

121. Historians have given little attention to these two value sets. My own rather casual generalizations about diffuse relationships and affectivity (see Parsons, *The Social System,* pp. 59–67) are based largely upon the data presented in chapter 5, section XII above, and upon a nonsystematic study of the journals included in this project.

122. Seymour Martin Lipset, *The First New Nation* (Garden City, New York: Doubleday & Co., 1967), pp. 115–233.

123. Gabriel Kolko, *Railroads and Regulation, 1877–1966* (Princeton: Princeton University Press, 1965), offers a popular variant of this interpretation, but the position outlined above is actually closer to that of Lee Benson, *Merchants, Farmers & Railroads: Railroad Regulation and New York Politics, 1850–1887* (Cambridge: Harvard University Press, 1955).

124. The problem and the relevant literature are discussed in great detail in Thorelli, *The Federal Antitrust Policy,* pp. 79–162. See also William Letwin, *Law and Economic Policy in America: The Evolution of the Sherman Antitrust Act* (New York: Random House, 1965), pp. 54–59; John Tipple, "The Robber Baron in the Gilded Age," in H. Wayne Morgan, ed., *The Gilded Age, a Reappraisal* (New York: Syracuse University Press, 1963), pp. 16–34; and Richard Hofstadter, "What Happened to the Antitrust Movement?" in *The Paranoid Style in American Politics, and Other Essays* (New York: Alfred A. Knopf, 1965), pp. 205–6, for interpretations which are substantially different from mine.

125. My data of course provide no information about the motives of the legislators, a subject that others (especially Hans B. Thorelli) have examined with great care.

4. CRISIS, 1893–1901

1. Charles Hoffmann, *The Depression of the Nineties: An Economic History* (Westport, Conn.: Greenwood Publishing Co., 1970).

2. The data on income for these groups are presented in the subsequent pages of this chapter. For information on railroad construction and on unemployment, see Hoffmann, *The Depression of the Nineties,* pp. xxx, 97–112, 128; and Stanley Lebergott, *Manpower in Economic Growth* (New York: McGraw-Hill, 1964), pp. 180–84, 187–90.

3. Paul Kleppner, *The Cross of Culture* (New York: The Free Press, 1970), pp. 179–268.

4. *Congregationalist,* Jan. 4, 1900, pp. 7–8. While the range of organizations generating discussion was wide, most of the groups involved were church-related and most of these were Congregational.

5. The first was a collection of essays by Washington Gladden and the second a book by Professor David Macgregor Means. Ibid., Jan. 6, 1898, pp. 21–22.

6. His scope was broad in comparison to that of the engineers, who are discussed in section V of this chapter.

7. *Congregationalist,* Jan. 4, 1894, pp. 6–7; see also ibid., p. 8.

8. Ibid., July 5, 1894, p. 7.

9. Ibid., July 6, 1893, p. 15.

10. Ibid., Jan. 4, 1894, p. 33.

11. Ibid., July 4, 1895, pp. 15–16, 33.

12. Ibid., July 5, 1894, pp. 7–8.

13. Ibid., pp. 9–10; Jan. 3, 1895, p. 34. See also July 4, 1895, p. 33, where "the tyranny of labor" is labeled one of the nation's "new problems"; and July 2, 1896, pp. 10–11.

14. Ibid., July 5, 1894, pp. 9–10.

15. Ibid., Jan. 2, 1896, p. 33, contains approval of a gentle variety of noblesse oblige.

16. This statement may appear to contradict the information under "Leading characteristics" in table 4–1, but the data in that table are based on the total number of times "Labor relations" and "Financial practices" were mentioned, regardless of whether they were presented in a favorable, unfavorable, or neutral way. The statement above refers to the number of times these characteristics were considered in a negative fashion between 1893 and 1896.

17. Ibid., Jan. 4, 1894, pp. 10–11. See also July 6, 1899, pp. 12–14.

18. Ibid., Jan. 3, 1895, p. 34; July 4, 1895, pp. 8, 36.

19. Ibid., Jan. 14, 1897, p. 38; July 1, 1897, p. 34; July 7, 1898, p. 29; Jan. 5, 1899, pp. 2, 6–7; July 5, 1900, p. 2; Jan. 5, 1901, p. 46; April 6, 1901, p. 567.

20. Ibid., July 6, 1899, p. 8.

21. Ibid., July 6, 1901, p. 42.

22. Ibid., July 1, 1897, p. 9; Jan. 4, 1900, p. 16; July 5, 1900, pp. 2, 26; Jan. 5, 1901, p. 17; April 6, 1901, pp. 513–14, 524, 556; July 6, 1901, pp. 7, 18, 26–31, 33, 51; Oct. 5, 1901, pp. 497–501.

23. Ibid., July 6, 1901, p. 7.

24. I prepared a rough index of real annual income, 1890–1926, based on the average earnings listed in *Historical Statistics of the United States, Colonial Times to 1957* (Washington, D.C., 1960), pp. 91–92; I converted these average earnings to constant dollars by using the consumer price index that was discussed in note 96, chapter 3. The resulting index figures for income (1926 = 100) are:

1890	84	1893	87	1896	88	1899	84
1891	83	1894	93	1897	87	1900	84
1892	84	1895	90	1898	86	1901	83

25. The coefficient of correlation for favorable attitudes against real income = .12; for unfavorable opinions against real income, r = .52; *Congregationalist*, Jan. 5, 1899, p. 9.

26. Ibid., Jan. 5, 1901, p. 6.

27. *Southern Cultivator* 54, no. 1 (January 1896): 17; July 15, 1897, p. 16; Aug. 1, 1897, p. 30. The price of cotton fell from 8.0 cents a pound in 1893 to 6.0 cents in 1894, went back up to 7.4 cents in 1895 and 1896, and then fell to 6.1 cents and finally to 5.1 cents in 1897 and 1898 respectively. The price in 1898 was lower than it had been at any time in the previous twenty years. Frederick Strauss and Louis H. Bean, *Gross Farm Income and Indices of Farm Production and Prices in the United States, 1869–1937* (Washington, D.C., 1940), p. 64. The figures presented here are farm prices for the calendar year.

28. The period of greatest disequilibrium was from 1887/89 through 1896/98. Hereafter, the reader should look to the Appendix for data in support of any references to equilibrium or disequilibrium, stability or instability.

29. *Southern Cultivator*, July 15, 1899, p. 8.

30. The July 15, 1897, issue of *Southern Cultivator* is sprinkled with articles in this vein.

31. Ibid.

32. Ibid., Jan. 1, 1897; see also similar comments in 54, no. 1 (January 1896); August 1, 1897; and Jan. 15, 1898.

33. See tables 3–3 and 5–3.

34. My hypothesis about the relative importance of these two factors is grounded in the assumption that negative sanctions are generally less effective in the learning process than positive sanctions; hence, I concluded that the removal of those organizations which either rewarded or seemed to hold out the promise of positive rewards to the farmer would be more likely to influence his behavior than would the negative experience of Bryan's defeat.

35. *Southern Cultivator*, Jan. 1, 1898, p. 16.

36. Ibid., July 1, 1900, p. 4.

37. Ibid., July, 1889, pp. 360–61.

38. Hoffmann, *The Depression of the Nineties*, pp. 84–89. Strauss and Bean, *Gross Farm Income*, p. 64.

39. Strauss and Bean, *Gross Farm Income*, p. 64.

40. *Southern Cultivator*, Jan. 15, 1901, pp. 18–19. There were more favorable references to products and services than to any other aspect of the large firm, 1897–1901.

41. Ibid., Jan. 1, 1900, p. 10.

42. Ibid., July 15, 1900, pp. 9, 16; Jan. 1, 1901, p. 20. In 1900, 50% of the references to the economic dimensions of the large firm were favorable and 38% unfavorable; in 1901, the figures were 60% and 40%.

43. In 1900 the percentage of favorable items in *Southern Cultivator* was greater than the percentage of negative articles for the first time since 1892.

44. This transition has received substantially less attention from historians than have the origins of the several periods of intense agrarian political activity—in particular the Populist phase in the mid-nineties. In general, historians have been more concerned about where agrarian discontent came from than they have been about how, when, and why it waned. For exceptions to this rule, see the following studies, each of which offers an explanation which differs in some regards from the one given above: Fred A. Shannon, *The Farmer's Last Frontier* (New York: Rinehart & Co., 1945), p. 327; Richard Hofstadter, *The Age of Reform* (New York: Vintage Books, 1955), pp. 109–30; Harold U. Faulkner, *Politics, Reform and Expansion, 1890–1900* (New York: Harper & Row, 1963), pp. 268–70; Eric F. Goldman, *Rendezvous with Destiny* (New York: Vintage Books, 1956), pp. 55–56; C. Vann Woodward, *Origins of the New South, 1877–1913* (Baton Rouge: Louisiana State University Press, 1951), pp. 369–70; Sheldon Hackney, *Populism to Progressivism in Alabama* (Princeton: Princeton University Press, 1969), pp. 107, 112–16.

45. *Wallaces' Farmer*, June 21, 1895, pp. 6, 12; Jan. 3, 1896, p. 5.

46. The highest figure (M.D.) for any single three-year period, 1879 to 1940 inclusive, fell in the middle of this decade (1894/96); the nineties still rank below the thirties, however, in terms of the total amount of variation and the length of the phase of disequilibrium.

47. To a considerable extent, the shift from *Farmers' Review* to *Wallaces' Farmer* was responsible for the high degree of disequilibrium in the period 1893/95 to 1894/96. Because of the discontinuity in this instance, we analyzed *Farmers' Review* for 1895–96 and compared these figures with the data from *Wallaces' Farmer*. In both journals there was evidence that a cycle of heightened antitrust opinion was taking place, but there were substantial differences between the two papers. In part the differences stemmed from the *Farmers' Review* policy of printing a large number of small news items which were almost always neutral toward big business; even if the neutral-ambivalent items were ignored, however, the contrast between the two journals was extreme (the percentage of unfavorable items was thirty-five points higher in *Wallaces' Farmer*). The editor of *Farmers' Review* had apparently become rather heavily involved in businesses which were not related to agriculture, and I had the impression that in the early nineties he was increasingly out of touch with farm opinion. In retrospect I can see that it would have been wise to have shifted journals before 1895. By contrast, Henry Wallace was an avowed antimonopolist who said (in 1895) that he had left his previous job with the *Iowa Homestead* because the paper's business manager had objected to Wallace's policy of maintain-

ing the publication's "position as the leading western exponent of anti-monopoly principles. Failing in this . . . ," Wallace moved to a paper "over the editorial policy of which he [had] full control" (*Wallaces' Farmer*, March 1, 1895, p. 2).

48. Ibid., Jan. 10, 1896, p. 2.

49. Ibid., July 31, 1896, p. 6. The only things that would apparently not be sucked in were "the beef trust, the coal trust, the Standard Oil trust and one or two others."

50. Ibid., Jan. 10, 1896, p. 2.

51. Ibid., July 16, 1897, p. 2.

52. Ibid., July 3, 1896, p. 3.

53. Ibid., Jan. 6, 1899, p. 4.

54. Ibid. In 1899 there were an unusual number of comments on the social aspects of big business, with 17% of the items mentioning this subject; see table 4-4. In 1900 this dimension of the trust movement did not arouse any discussion, but it came up again in 1901 and in every year thereafter, until 1911.

55. Ibid., Jan. 13, 1899, p. 22; Jan. 27, 1899, p. 63; July 7, 1899, p. 564.

56. Ibid., Jan. 6, 1899, p. 4.

57. Ibid., Jan. 20, 1899, p. 42.

58. Ibid., Jan. 3, 1896, p. 1; Jan. 10, 1896, p. 6; Jan. 24, 1896, p. 6; Jan. 13, 1899, p. 27.

59. Ibid., July 3, 1896, p. 3. In the years 1893–1901, political technique was the third-ranked negative aspect of big business; it attracted more criticism than anything except prices and the expansion (or existence) of the trusts.

60. Ibid., p. 6.

61. Ibid., Jan. 10, 1896, p. 2.

62. In 1895, 17% of the items in *Wallaces' Farmer* mentioned political facets of the corporation and half of these were negative; in 1896, 35% of the items touched on this subject and 92% of the articles were unfavorable. During the following year, political functions came up in only 8% of the items, but by 1899 the figure was back up to 48% (with 88% of the selections unfavorable).

63. The second half of this statement is based on figures not presented in table 4-4; these data indicate that during the years 1893–1901, 5% of the items appeared in response to some form of political activity at the national level, while 7% could be traced to state governments.

64. One could mount an argument against both my evidence and my conclusion on this point. First, the information under "Leading sources" does not go back to an original or primary source; if an article appeared as a result of a meeting of the livestock association, we scored the category "Meetings and conventions," even though the discussion at this particular gathering might in part have been prompted by a political campaign. Furthermore, if one adds together all of the various forms of political activities—national, state, and local—for all branches of government, this category would rank higher than "Meetings and conventions" as a source of items. Together, political actions accounted for 14% (up from 10% for the years 1879–92) of the items for which a source could be identified; the comparable figure for the "Meetings and conventions" category was 12%. So it goes.

65. They were the leading negative characteristic of the giant firm from 1879 through the end of the First World War in the eyes of the midwestern farmer.

66. Revenue per ton-mile was .898 cents in 1892 and only .750 cents in 1901 (*Historical Statistics*, p. 431); *Wallaces' Farmer*, June 21, 1895, p. 12.

67. *Wallaces' Farmer*, Jan. 17, 1896, p. 5.

68. The existence or expansion of the firm was the second-ranking characteristic (table 4-4) in the midwestern paper and was also in second place among the negative characteristics.

69. Ibid., July 10, 1896, p. 4; Jan. 10, 1896, p. 3.

70. Ibid., July 7, 1899, p. 561.

71. The sources for my income and price data (in each case for corn and hogs) are listed in note 96, chapter 3; the index numbers (1918 = 100) are as follows:

Year	Gross income in current dollars	Gross income in constant dollars	Mean index of corn and hog prices	Year	Gross income in current dollars	Gross income in constant dollars	Mean index of corn and hog prices
1893	23	39	29	1898	18	33	21
1894	19	33	24	1899	19	34	22
1895	19	33	27	1900	24	43	27
1896	16	29	18	1901	27	47	33
1897	17	30	18				

72. For current dollar income and favorable attitudes, r = .54; for unfavorable opinions, r = −.56. For constant dollar income and favorable attitudes, r = .61; for unfavorable attitudes, r = −.51. For prices against favorable opinions, r = .60; for negative opinions, r = −.56.

73. The leading favorable aspect was corporate prices, but for reasons advanced in the previous chapter (note 48), I have ignored those figures and focused attention on the second-ranking characteristic, that is, the manner in which business enhanced the general wealth.

74. *Wallaces' Farmer*, July 7, 1899, p. 564; Jan. 25, 1901, p. 104.

75. During the years 1893–1901, *Engineering News'* comments on prices were favorable by a margin of three to one.

76. In the period 1893–96, the engineering journal made no negative remarks about corporate management, and the financial affairs of big business were looked upon with favor (here the margin was four to one).

77. In 1894 only 5% of the items in our sample discussed labor relations. This was the peak period of concern for this issue during the entire decade. In the following year labor relations was not mentioned once.

78. *Engineering News*, July 5, 1894, pp. 1, 12. On p. 22 of the same issue another article analyzed the strike in language that was uncharacteristically strong for this journal: "That the war now being waged against the public—for so has the 'strike' developed—was ill-conceived, criminal of execution and certain of ignominious failure is easily apparent. The genuine cause of the whole uprising—it is rank rebellion against law and order—has long since been lost sight of. It has developed into a determination as to whether owners or employees are to be masters of a property, and to such a struggle there can be but one outcome."

79. Ibid., Jan. 4, 1900, p. 10.

80. In terms of the total amount of fluctuation and the duration of the phase of disequilibrium, the depression years rank below the periods 1885/87 through 1890/92 and 1933/35 through 1938/40.

81. Ibid., Jan. 5, 1893, p. 14; July 2, 1896, p. 7; Jan. 3, 1901, p. 7.

82. On occasion, international bodies aroused comment; during the years 1893–1901, these included the International Railway Commerce Congress, the Paris Exposition, and the International Association for Testing Materials.

83. Ibid., July 5, 1894, p. 5.

84. Ibid., pp. 13–14.

85. These remarks were in a letter from an anonymous civil engineer in Chicago. The editor of *Engineering News* disagreed with the letter writer and said that an engineering education provided "a good foundation on which to build an experience in the railway service which may or may not lead to the highest positions, according to the abilities that a man develops in handling men." The editor's remarks were especially revealing insofar as the only factor that he assumed would influence success was individual ability, an assumption about achievement and individualism that was widely held in nineteenth-century America; on the other hand, the particular ability he specified was that of "handling men," and this acceptance of the primacy of collective orientation seems not to have become normative in most other sectors of the middle

cultures until well into the twentieth century. Both items are in *Engineering News*, Jan. 4, 1900, p. 10.

86. Since I was unable to find any direct estimates of income in engineering for the years before 1929, I used the figures in *Historical Statistics*, pp. 91–92, on the average annual earnings of clerical workers in manufacturing and on steam railroads. I adjusted these figures upward, basing my multiplier on the relationship between these estimates and the 1929 figures (p. 97) on the median base monthly salary rate for engineers. For the period 1929–40, I used the latter data exclusively and estimated the income for the years not included by assuming a linear rate of change. The current dollar figures were converted to constant dollars in the manner outlined in chapter 3, note 96. The results of these calculations (in constant dollars), expressed as index numbers (1940 = 100), are as follows:

1890	52	1899	68	1908	68	1917	64	1925	71	1933	83
1891	54	1900	67	1909	70	1918	63	1926	71	1934	75
1892	54	1901	66	1910	68	1919	62	1927	76	1935	78
1893	57	1902	67	1911	71	1920	60	1928	79	1936	82
1894	60	1903	66	1912	70	1921	67	1929	81	1937	84
1895	63	1904	66	1913	70	1922	69	1930	78	1938	90
1896	64	1905	67	1914	70	1923	70	1931	80	1939	96
1897	65	1906	67	1915	70	1924	72	1932	83	1940	100
1898	68	1907	65	1916	70						

87. For current dollar income against favorable attitudes, 1890–1901, r = .64; for constant dollars, r = .54; when I used the index numbers (which were rounded off), r = .50. None of the correlations between income and negative evaluations produced significant results. This was neither surprising nor disappointing because the important shifts that took place in the respective percentages were due more to changes in the real number of favorable than of unfavorable opinions. Between 1893–94 and 1895–96, for example, the number of negative items increased from 6 to 9, while the number of positive articles dropped from 23 to 8.

88. The number of positive comments on management declined in the mid-nineties, but critical remarks did not in this case supplant the engineer's praise.

89. For a discussion of the increasing importance of urban projects in the main patterns of economic development in America, see Alan D. Anderson, "Urbanization and American Economic Development, 1900–1930: Patterns of Demand in Baltimore and the Nation" (Ph.D. diss., Johns Hopkins University, 1973).

90. Hence, the third leading characteristic of the large firm (table 4-3) became miscellaneous political activities, and the percentage of the items mentioning the political functions of the firm increased slightly. In 1901 (by one of our measures, a peak year for negative comments) all of the critical articles touched in some way upon politics. *Engineering News*, Jan. 3, 1901, pp. 1, 9, 12–13; July 4, 1901, pp. 8–9. Local passenger transportation had been the third-ranking industry in the years 1887–92; see table 3-1.

91. Steffens published his first such article—"Tweed Days in St. Louis"—in *McClure's Magazine* in October 1902; his several muckraking articles on this subject were gathered into a book, *The Shame of the Cities* (New York: Peter Smith, 1948), that first appeared in 1904. The quotation is from *Engineering News*, Jan. 5, 1893, p. 13. See also July 7, 1898, for an appraisal of "the supercilious and insulting tone adopted, in the negotiations with the Rapid Transit Commission, by the young multi-millionaire and the sage dealer in puts and calls who control the destinies of the Manhattan Company."

92. *Engineering News*, July 4, 1901, p. 8.

93. The efficiency of the large corporation was tied with products and services as the leading *favorable* characteristic, 1893–96, and was the second-ranking favorable aspect, 1897–1901.

94. *Engineering News*, Jan. 5, 1893, p. 9.

95. Ibid., Jan. 4, 1900, p. 8; see also Jan. 7, 1897, pp. 8, 11–13; and July 4, 1901, p. 1.

96. Samuel Haber, *Efficiency and Uplift: Scientific Management in the Progressive Era, 1890-1920* (Chicago: University of Chicago Press, 1964); Samuel P. Hays, *Conservation and the Gospel of Efficiency: The Progressive Conservation Movement, 1890-1920* (Cambridge: Harvard University Press, 1959).

97. William Z. Ripley, *Railroads: Rates and Regulation* (New York: Longmans, Green and Co., 1913), pp. 77–86.

98. *National Labor Tribune*, July 2, 1892, pp. 1, 4.

99. Joseph F. Wall, *Andrew Carnegie* (Oxford: Oxford University Press, 1970), pp. 537–82, analyzes the strike in some detail; see also David Brody, *The Steelworkers in America: The Nonunion Era* (Cambridge: Harvard University Press, 1960), pp. 55–57.

100. *National Labor Tribune*, Jan. 5, 1893, p. 4.

101. Ibid., July 6, 1893, p. 1.

102. Ibid., Jan. 4, 1894, p. 1.

103. During the years 1893–96 the Pullman Co. ranked fourth among the firms receiving the most attention.

104. Ibid., July 5, 1894, p. 1.

105. Ibid., Jan. 3, 1895, p. 3; July 4, 1895, p. 5.

106. I correlated the data on attitudes with three separate indices of income: hourly real wages, daily real earnings in all manufacturing (both from Albert Rees, *Real Wages in Manufacturing, 1890-1914* [Princeton: Princeton University Press, 1960], p. 120), and average annual real earnings of employed wage-earners in all industries (from Paul H. Douglas, *Real Wages in the United States, 1890-1926* [Boston: Houghton Mifflin, 1930], p. 391). In this case none of the coefficients of correlation were significant, whereas they had been for the period 1880–92 (see note 124 in chapter 3).

107. Again, let me remind the reader that the list of leading characteristics in table 4-5 is based on all of the references to big business, regardless of their evaluative content; here I am discussing only the negative characteristics (in rank order).

108. This latter characteristic appears in our data as comments on the existence or expansion of the large company. This was the leading overall characteristic in these same years, as table 4-5 illustrates.

109. See, for example, any of the following: *National Labor Tribune*, Jan. 4, 1900, pp. 4, 8; Feb. 1, 1900, pp. 1, 4, 5; April 5, 1900, p. 8; July 5, 1900, pp. 4, 5; Jan. 10, 1901, pp. 1, 2.

110. For some exceptions, see ibid., Jan. 4, 1894, p. 5; Jan 3, 1895, p. 1; and Jan. 2, 1896, p. 5. Failure to talk about mechanization is not necessarily related to a sense of powerlessness; see, for instance, John Higham, "Hanging Together: Divergent Unities in American History," *Journal of American History* 61 (June 1974): 19–23. In the case of the skilled worker, however, the problem of mechanization was so acute, and his willingness to discuss lesser problems so evident, that his omission of this issue can not, I think, be satisfactorily explained without reference to the craftsman's failure to find any solution to his dilemma.

111. There is also the possibility that opposition to these kinds of changes might not have seemed legitimate to some workers, but I am suspicious of this explanation, if only because the workers seemed to approve of other actions—in strikes, for example—which were by general standards equally unacceptable.

112. Brody, *Steelworkers in America*, pp. 85–95.

113. Charles Tilly has made a similar point in a number of recent publications that probe the relationship between collective violence and political supression; as Tilly concludes, the absence of collective violence does not necessarily indicate the presence of consensus or social harmony. See, for example, David Snyder and Charles Tilly, "Hardship and Collective Violence in France, 1830–1960," *American Sociological Review* 37 (October 1972): 520–32; and

Charles Tilly, "How Protest Modernized in France, 1845-1855," in William O. Aydelotte, Allan G. Bogue, and Robert W. Fogel, eds., *The Dimensions of Quantitative Research in History* (Princeton: Princeton University Press, 1972), especially pp. 235-50.

114. Because of the importance of this combine, we did a month-by-month content analysis of the *National Labor Tribune*'s image of big business for the years 1900, 1901, and 1902. *National Labor Tribune*, April 5, 1900, p. 1.

115. Ibid., Sept. 6, 1900, p. 4.

116. Ibid., Feb. 14, 1901, pp. 1, 8.

117. Ibid., March 7, 1901, p. 4; and April 4, 1901, p. 4.

118. Ibid., Aug. 1, 1901, p. 4.

119. Strictly speaking, these two groups of workers overlapped, and if my central assumption about the relationship between attitudes and publications is correct, then the AFL data includes the information from the *National Labor Tribune*. The Amalgamated Association was, for instance, a member of the AFL. There is, however, no way to separate the two sets of information, and as a matter of convenience I have discussed the results as if they were drawn from two separate bodies of skilled workers.

120. In this instance there was so little neutral or favorable data that the aspects under "Leading characteristics" in table 4-6 are the same as the leading negative aspects.

121. *American Federationist* 1, no. 1 (March 1894): 12; 1, no. 5 (July 1894): 98-99; 2, no. 5 (July 1895): 92; 2, no. 11 (January 1896): 201-4, 207.

122. Ibid., 2, no. 11 (January 1896): 201-4; 1, no. 1 (March 1894): 7.

123. The importance of the American Tobacco Company can in part be traced to the fact that the Federation's president, Samuel Gompers, headed the Cigar Makers' International Union. The Rockefeller mining firm was the Bunker Hill & Sullivan Mining Co.

124. *American Federationist* 2, no. 11 (January 1896): 201-4.

125. Ibid., 4, no. 5 (July 1897): 97.

126. Ibid., 1, no. 1 (March 1894): 4, 13.

127. The correlations between unfavorable attitudes and hourly real wages (r = -.79) or daily real earnings (r = -.79) in all manufacturing are significant; the income figures are from Rees, *Real Wages in Manufacturing, 1890-1914*, p. 120. It is suggestive of the Federation's major sources of strength, however, that the highest coefficients are for unfavorable attitudes (r = -.88) and for favorable opinions (r = +.54) against average hourly earnings in the unionized building trades; these figures on earnings are in *Historical Statistics*, p. 91.

128. The third leading source, "Other publications," lagged far behind the first two, but the information collected in this category slightly qualifies my conclusion. The *American Federationist* drew ideas from a number of different papers—including the *New York Journal*, the *Denver Times*, and the *Philadelphia Inquirer*—which were not directly affiliated with organized labor.

129. For specific references to wages, see any of the following: *American Federationist* 7, no. 1 (January 1900): 14, 18, 19, 21; 7, no. 7 (July 1900): 211, 219; 8, no. 1 (January 1901): 21; 8, no. 7 (July 1901): 271, 274.

130. Leo Wolman, *The Growth of American Trade Unions, 1880-1923* (New York: National Bureau of Economic Research, 1924), pp. 32, 122-23.

131. *American Federationist* 7, no. 1 (January 1900): 14, 21; Lloyd Ulman, *The Rise of the National Trade Union* (Cambridge: Harvard University Press, 1955), pp. 37-42, discusses how combinations actually affected the unions.

132. *American Federationist* 6, no. 5 (July 1899): 97-100.

133. Ibid., 8, no. 7 (July 1901): 245-47.

134. I calculated the aggregate, weighted percentages in figure 4-9 (and in all of the subsequent figures presenting aggregate data) in the following manner. First, I combined the southern and midwestern farm series by using the means of the annual percentages; I did the

same with the data from the two classes of professional men. The figures from organized labor presented a different sort of problem, in part because the organizations involved varied so greatly in membership; here I weighted the averages on the basis of the best available figures on union membership, drawing on the following sources: Wolman, *The Growth of American Trade Unions, 1880-1923*, pp. 32, 122-23; and the same author's volume on *Ebb and Flow in Trade Unionism* (New York: National Bureau of Economic Research, 1936), pp. 236-37. In subsequent chapters I also use data from the IWW, and I found it difficult to get reliable membership figures for this organization. I squeezed my rough estimates from the pages of John S. Gambs, *The Decline of the I.W.W.* (New York: Columbia University Press, 1932), pp. 164-69; U.S. Bureau of Labor Statistics, *Bulletin No. 420, Handbook of American Trade-Unions* (October 1926), p. 199, and *Bulletin No. 541, Handbook of Labor Statistics, 1931* (September 1931), p. 396. I used the membership of the Amalgamated Association of Iron, Steel, and Tin Workers to weight the data from the *National Labor Tribune* for the years 1894-1915.

The results of these calculations were time series representing the shifting attitudes about big business among laborers, farmers, and professional men. As a final step in the process of aggregation, I figured the weighted means of the annual percentages in these three sets of time series. The weighting was based on the respective sizes of the three occupational groups (that is, farmers, skilled laborers, and professionals) in the total American population, as determined by the census. Between census years, I assumed that a regular rate of change took place. *Historical Statistics*, pp. 74-78; U.S. Bureau of the Census, *Sixteen Census, Population. Comparative Statistics for the United States, 1870 to 1940* (Washington, D.C., 1943), pp. 104, 111, 187. The rounded off figures (in thousands) for the three groups studied were:

Year	Farmers	Skilled laborers	Professionals	Year	Farmers	Skilled laborers	Professionals
1880	4,301	1,396	550	1920	6,442	5,482	2,283
1890	5,382	2,214	876	1930	6,032	6,246	3,378
1900	5,763	3,062	1,234	1940	5,362	6,203	3,879
1910	6,163	4,315	1,758				

135. For comments on the consensus school, see chapter 1.

136. For example, the arguments Henry Steele Commager advanced in *The American Mind: An Interpretation of American Thought and Character Since the 1880's* (New Haven: Yale University Press, 1950) have been attacked from this angle by John A. Garraty in *The New Commonwealth, 1877-1890* (New York: Harper & Row, 1968), especially pp. xiii-xiv. For other treatments of the nineties as a watershed, see Kleppner, *The Cross of Culture*, pp. 179-279; Theodore P. Greene, *America's Heroes: The Changing Models of Success in American Magazines* (New York: Oxford University Press, 1970), pp. 110-43; and John Higham, "The Reorientation of American Culture in the 1890's" in John Weiss, ed., *The Origins of Modern Consciousness* (Detroit: Wayne State University Press, 1965), pp. 25-48.

5. THE PROGRESSIVE CYCLE, 1902-1914

1. Simon Kuznets, "Notes on the Pattern of U.S. Economic Growth," in Edgar O. Edwards, ed., *The Nation's Economic Objectives* (Chicago: University of Chicago Press, 1964), pp. 16-26; Alfred H. Conrad, "Income Growth and Structural Change," in Seymour E. Harris, ed., *American Economic History* (New York: McGraw-Hill, 1961), pp. 31-32; Harold U. Faulkner, *The Decline of Laissez Faire, 1897-1917* (New York: Rinehart & Co., 1959), pp. 22-35.

2. Conrad, "Income Growth and Structural Change," pp. 48-54.

3. For examples, see Eric F. Goldman, *Rendezvous with Destiny* (New York: Vintage Books, 1956), pp. 66-81, 125-79; George E. Mowry, *The Era of Theodore Roosevelt 1900-1912* (New York: Harper & Brothers, 1958), pp. 16-37, 123-42; Arthur S. Link, *Woodrow Wilson and the Progressive Era 1910-1917* (New York: Harper & Brothers, 1954), pp. 1-80.

4. Richard Hofstadter, *The Age of Reform* (New York: Vintage Books, 1955), pp. 131-73; and "The Pseudo-Conservative Revolt (1955)," and "Pseudo-Conservatism Revisited: A Postscript (1962)," in Daniel Bell, ed., *The Radical Right* (Garden City, N.Y.: Doubleday & Co., 1964), pp. 75-103. In the latter essay Hofstadter refines and revises the concept of status politics.

5. See the references in chapter 1, note 66.

6. C. Vann Woodward, *Origins of the New South, 1877-1913* (Baton Rouge: Louisiana State University Press, 1951), p. 380.

7. Here and in all subsequent references to stability and equilibrium, see the Appendix for the relevant data.

8. *The Search for Order, 1877-1920* (New York: Hill and Wang, 1967), p. 165.

9. *Congregationalist*, July 2, 1904, p. 7.

10. Ibid., July 7, 1906, p. 5; Jan. 7, 1905, pp. 7-8; July 1, 1905, p. 6.

11. The category "Federal executive action" ranks second among the leading sources of items on big business. When all of the various divisions of political activity (i.e., state as well as federal action; legislative as well as executive and judicial behavior) are added together, they account for 20% of the items (1902-14) in which we could identify a source. The comparable figure for 1880-92 is 13%, and for 1893-1901 it is only 8%.

12. "Other publications" was the category ranked third.

13. *Congregationalist*, Jan. 6, 1906, p. 24.

14. Ibid.

15. Ibid., July 4, 1912, p. 22.

16. Ibid., July 7, 1906, p. 10.

17. Ibid., July 4, 1912, p. 11; Jan. 6, 1906, p. 9.

18. Ibid., Jan. 4, 1902, p. 9.

19. Ibid., Jan. 6, 1906, p. 6.

20. See table 5-1.

21. *Congregationalist*, Jan. 2, 1909, p. 7; July 2, 1910, pp. 9, 17.

22. Ibid., July 7, 1906, pp. 7-8. The case involved the murder of architect Stanford White by Henry Thaw, the son of a wealthy Pennsylvania family.

23. Ibid., Jan. 3, 1903, pp. 13-14.

24. Ibid., July 4, 1903, p. 9; see also p. 27.

25. Ibid., Jan. 6, 1906, p. 24; July 1, 1905, p. 6; see also July 7, 1906, p. 10.

26. Hofstadter, "Pseudo-Conservatism Revisited," p. 99.

27. See the note on "Leading solutions" in table 5-1 for data on the years 1880-1901. During the period 1880-92, 14% of the items mentioned some type of solution or response in favorable terms; in the years 1893-1901, the figure was 15% in the progressive era, 26%.

28. *Congregationalist*, July 3, 1914, p. 13.

29. Ibid., July 7, 1906, p. 5. See also Jan. 2, 1904, p. 43; July 2, 1904, p. 7; Jan. 7, 1905, pp. 7-8; July 6, 1907, p. 9; Jan. 2, 1909, p. 7; July 2, 1910, pp. 7, 9; July 1, 1911, p. 6; Jan. 6, 1912, pp. 9, 14, 26, 34; Jan. 2, 1913, p. 11; July 3, 1913, p. 31; July 2, 1914, p. 18.

30. Ibid., July 2, 1910, p. 9.

31. Ibid., July 1, 1905, p. 6; Jan. 2, 1913, pp. 12, 32.

32. The midwestern farmer saw the corporation's tendency to enhance the general wealth as its most positive attribute during the period 1902-8; during the period 1909-14, this aspect ranked second, behind the way big business enhanced the individual's opportunities.

33. In one year, 1903, the percentages of unfavorable and of favorable attitudes were approximately equal (35% and 33% respectively).

34. There was substantially more continuity in the editorials than in the other parts of the paper.

Year	Unfavorable items	Unfavorable editorials	Year	Unfavorable items	Unfavorable editorials
1899	69%	81%	1902	39%	83%
1900	56	86	1903	35	80
1901	16	50	1904	46	67

35. In the years 1902–14, all political activities combined accounted for 23% of the items for which we could determine a source; the comparable figure for 1893–1901 was 14%, and for 1879–92, 10%. In the progressive era, the federal executive and legislative branches were the most important stimulants to discourse, but the farmers were less open to the influence of presidential personalities than was the Congregational clergy.

36. *Wallaces' Farmer*, Jan. 13, 1905, p. 33.

37. Ibid., p. 40; July 6, 1906, p. 851. See also July 21, 1905, p. 891; July 28, 1905, p. 913; July 13, 1906, pp. 871, 890; Jan. 10, 1908, p. 29. In the latter issue, the editor of *Wallaces' Farmer* said that "the old ways of doing business will not be tolerated longer by the American people. . . . We have adopted a new standard of morals, or rather have a clear conception of the everlasting principles of righteousness. . . . When it is once settled that the Roosevelt policies are here to stay and will be continued, if not by a republican then by a democrat, there will be no cloud on the financial sky."

38. Our figures thus understate the impact of politics to the extent that letters to the editor, the leading source of items in the years 1902–14, were themselves inspired by political activity. Frequently this was the case; see, for example, the letter from John G. Osborn, of Rock Island County in Illinois, July 6, 1906, p. 857. Osborn discussed the meat inspection law and its probable impact upon public health and upon the packing industry, but in our procedure for recording data, the source of the item was scored under "Letter."

39. For an exception see *Wallaces' Farmer*, July 15, 1904, p. 902.

40. Ibid., Jan. 15, 1904, p. 68; Jan. 8, 1904, p. 37; Jan. 29, 1904, p. 132.

41. Ibid., Jan. 1, 1904, p. 2; Jan. 8, 1904, p. 40; Jan. 22, 1904, p. 114; Jan. 15, 1904, p. 83.

42. See section IV, chapter 4. Before 1899 and after 1915, the farmer hardly ever mentioned the social dimension of the large firm; between these two dates, however, 6% of the items in *Wallaces' Farmer* touched upon this aspect of the corporation. Compared to the percentage mentioning the economic functions, this is not a very impressive figure, but it is nonetheless a distinctive feature of the progressive years.

43. Ibid., Jan. 30, 1903, pp. 166–67.

44. Ibid., July 3, 1903, p. 921; July 15, 1904, p. 902. For other examples, see Jan. 13, 1905, p. 35; Jan. 27, 1905, p. 98; July 28, 1905, p. 909; Jan. 19, 1906, p. 82; Jan. 11, 1907, p. 34; July 24, 1914, p. 1044.

45. Ibid., Jan. 3, 1902, p. 17; July 4, 1902, p. 911. See also Jan. 31, 1908, p. 148; Jan. 1, 1909, p. 5; Jan. 28, 1910, p. 126; July 21, 1911, p. 1046; July 1, 1913, pp. 11–12.

46. Ibid., Jan. 30, 1903, pp. 166–67.

47. Ibid., July 3, 1903, p. 921.

48. Ibid., Jan. 13, 1905, p. 35.

49. Ibid., Jan. 20, 1905, pp. 72, 78.

50. Ibid., July 13, 1906, p. 871.

51. The efforts to strengthen the ICC were a central concern of *Wallaces' Farmer* in 1904, 1905, and 1906; see the editor's reflections on this and other measures in the issue of July 6, 1906, p. 851. See also Jan. 21, 1910, p. 82; July 29, 1910, p. 1023. The paper appears to have

concentrated more of its attention on this single issue than some of its readers felt was justified; see Jan. 20, 1905, p. 66.

52. Ibid., July 6, 1906, p. 857; Jan. 29, 1904, p. 139; Jan. 27, 1905, p. 99; July 14, 1905, p. 871; Jan. 14, 1910, p. 42.

53. Ibid., Jan. 23, 1903, p. 110; Jan. 30, 1903, pp. 147, 166–67; July 15, 1904, p. 902; Jan. 27, 1905, p. 99; July 14, 1905, p. 871; July 6, 1906, p. 851; Jan. 10, 1908, p. 31.

54. See the data on the mean deviation in the Appendix.

55. K. Austin Kerr, *American Railroad Politics, 1914–1920* (Pittsburgh: University of Pittsburgh Press, 1968), pp. 12–52.

56. *Engineering News*, Jan. 5, 1905, pp. 18–19; Jan. 4, 1906, p. 22.

57. Ibid., Jan. 1, 1903, pp. 16–18; July 5, 1906, pp. 17–18.

58. Ibid., Jan. 4, 1912, pp. 34–36. See also July 6, 1911, p. 26, which discusses "The Duty of Electrical Engineers Toward the Public"; the article concludes that "the public service corporations are the natural outcome of the demand of the civilized world for efficient and rapid transportation and intercommunication." The engineer's role was to stand between these corporations and the public, to ensure that the public did not go too far in its efforts to control the companies, and to help provide the sort of regulation that would prevent the corporations from becoming "despots."

59. *National Labor Tribune*, Jan. 7, 1904, p. 1; Jan. 4, 1906, p. 1. The panic of 1907 provided a good test of his faith on this point, and he appears to have concluded: "If the iron and steel industry were not controlled by a few men, it is probable it would have been demoralized by this time. As it is, production is being adjusted to consumption, and the accumulation of heavy unsold stocks has been, and is still being, prevented. In the end, recovery from the depression will be much more rapid on this account" (ibid., Jan. 2, 1908, p. 1).

60. *Southern Cultivator*, July 1, 1906, p. 27.

61. Ibid., July 1, 1909, pp. 28–29.

62. Ibid., Jan. 1, 1902, pp. 3–4.

63. All of these figures are based on data from Frederick Strauss and Louis H. Bean, *Gross Farm Income and Indices of Farm Production and Prices in the United States, 1869–1937* (Washington, D.C., 1940), pp. 64–65. See note 96 in chapter 3 for an explanation of the conversion from current to constant dollars. I used the following income data:

Year	Gross income (millions of current dollars)	Gross income (millions of constant dollars)	Year	Gross income (millions of current dollars)	Gross income (millions of constant dollars)
1902	454	468	1909	715	694
1903	556	556	1910	880	815
1904	704	697	1911	854	791
1905	572	566	1912	851	774
1906	710	696	1913	968	864
1907	660	622	1914	602	533
1908	649	624			

64. *Southern Cultivator*, Jan. 1, 1903, pp. 1–2, 12–13; July 15, 1903, pp. 8–9.

65. For unfavorable attitudes against gross income in constant dollars, r = −.53.

66. *Southern Cultivator*, Jan. 1, 1912, p. 6.

67. Ibid., Jan. 15, 1913, p. 22.

68. Ibid., Jan. 1, 1904, pp. 13–15.

69. Ibid., July 1, 1914, p. 14; Jan. 15, 1914, p. 22.

70. *Engineering News,* Jan. 1, 1903, p. 14; see also July 5, 1906, p. 19.

71. Ibid., July 2, 1908, p. 20.

72. Ibid., Jan. 2, 1913, p. 37.

73. The coefficient of correlation between the data on income and the percentage of unfavorable attitudes was –.69. I am hesitant to make greater use of this figure because the same coefficient falls below the level of significance when the income data is converted into constant dollars. I used the following estimates of annual income for engineers:

Year	Current dollars	Constant dollars	Year	Current dollars	Constant dollars	Year	Current dollars	Constant dollars
1902	1426	1470	1907	1518	1432	1911	1687	1562
1903	1442	1442	1908	1545	1486	1912	1682	1529
1904	1469	1454	1909	1580	1534	1913	1719	1535
1905	1497	1482	1910	1608	1489	1914	1748	1547
1906	1494	1465						

74. *American Federationist*, January 1904, pp. 40–42; *National Labor Tribune*, Jan. 7, 1904, p. 4.

75. Ibid., July 3, 1902, p. 8.

76. Kerr, *American Railroad Politics*, pp. 12–52.

77. For the changes in rates see *Historical Statistics*, p. 432.

78. The index numbers (1918 = 100) for midwestern farm income were as follows:

Year	Current dollars	Constant dollars	Year	Current dollars	Constant dollars	Year	Current dollars	Constant dollars
1902	28	49	1907	32	52	1911	33	52
1903	27	46	1908	32	51	1912	35	54
1904	25	41	1909	34	56	1913	38	58
1905	27	45	1910	40	63	1914	38	57
1906	31	52						

79. If one adds together all forms of political behavior, politics would rank third in table 5-4 as a source of items. But the federal government attracted no more attention than did the state governments, and even the colorful T. R. was unable to break down the restraints imposed by the engineer's professional ideology.

80. *Engineering News*, Jan. 2, 1902, p. 6; July 3, 1902, pp. 9–11; July 5, 1906, pp. 10–11; July 2, 1908, pp. 21–25.

81. Ibid., July 3, 1902, pp. 21–24; July 2, 1903, pp. 23–24.

82. Efficiency was seen as the leading favorable and unfavorable aspect in the years 1902–8; it was the second ranking aspect (in both categories) in the period from 1909 through 1914. Layton, in *Revolt of the Engineers*, emphasizes, more than I do, the impact of the reform impulse upon the profession. While Layton and I both find a cycle of reform sentiment, we disagree over the breadth and depth of the movement's support.

83. *Engineering News*, Jan. 2, 1902, pp. 8–9.

84. Ibid., July 5, 1906, pp. 17–18.

85. Ibid., Jan. 1, 1903, pp. 5–7.

86. Ibid., July 7, 1910, pp. 11–12, 17, 22–25, 26–28; July 3, 1913, pp. 20–21, 23, 26–28.

87. Ibid., Jan. 5, 1911, pp. 12, 18; see also July 6, 1911, pp. 16–17.

88. *Wallaces' Farmer*, Jan. 17, 1913, p. 96; July 4, 1914, pp. 996–7, 1000; July 18, 1913, p. 1036; July 25, 1913, pp. 1056, 1059; July 3, 1914, p. 985; July 10, 1914, p. 1000.

89. *National Labor Tribune,* Jan. 2, 1902, pp. 1, 2, 4, 8; July 3, 1902, pp. 1, 4, 5, 8.

90. Ibid., July 6, 1905, p. 1; Jan. 4, 1906, p. 8; July 3, 1902, pp. 3, 4, 8; July 2, 1903, p. 1.

NOTES TO PAGES 136-143

91. Ibid., July 2, 1908, pp. 1, 4.

92. Ibid., Jan. 2, 1902, p. 8.

93. Ibid., July 1, 1909, p. 4; Jan. 6, 1910, p. 4; July 7, 1910, p. 4.

94. Ibid., Jan. 12, 1911, pp. 1, 5, 8.

95. Ibid., Jan. 12. 1911, p. 4; Jan. 4, 1912, p. 4.

96. Leo Wolman, *The Growth of American Trade Unions 1880-1923* (New York: National Bureau of Economic Research, 1924), pp. 32, 122-23.

97. *American Federationist* 17, no. 1 (January 1910): 35-37, 40-43; 17, no. 7 (July 1910): 615.

98. Ibid., 17, no. 7 (July 1910): 629; 19, no. 1 (January 1912): 70.

99. Albert K. Steigerwalt, *The National Association of Manufacturers, 1895-1914: A Study in Business Leadership* (Ann Arbor: Bureau of Business Research, Graduate School of Business Administration, 1964), pp. 103-49.

100. Philip Taft, *The A.F. of L. in the Time of Gompers* (New York: Harper & Brothers, 1957), p. 226.

101. Ibid., pp. 225-32; Marguerite Green, *The National Civic Federation and the American Labor Movement, 1900-1925* (Washington: Catholic University of America Press, 1956).

102. *American Federationist* 18, no. 7 (July 1911): 551; 20, no. 7 (July 1913): 553; 21, no. 7 (July 1914): 579.

103. Ibid., 21, no. 7 (July, 1914): 559-60.

104. Ibid., 21, no. 1 (January, 1914): 35-40; 20, no. 7 (July 1913): 533-37.

105. *Solidarity*, Jan. 1, 1910, p. 1.

106. Ibid., Jan. 1, 1910, p. 2; July 2, 1910, pp. 1, 4; Jan. 28, 1911, p. 3.

107. The fluctuations in the level of unfavorable opinions in 1911 and in 1914 inflate the M.D. (see Appendix) and place my conclusion about stability on shaky ground. To some considerable extent, I am looking ahead to the war years and the twenties (see chapters 6 and 7) and basing my conclusion on 1) the limited changes which took place in the specific characteristics (see table 5-7, above) stressed by *Solidarity*; 2) the low M.D. for these years; and 3) the fact that the changes in 1911 and in 1914 had a random quality which defied explanation (by the author, at least) and did not seem to constitute a trend.

108. Philip Taft, "A Theory of the American Labor Movement," in Gerald D. Nash, ed., *Issues in American Economic History* (Boston: D. C. Heath & Co., 1964), pp. 395-400.

109. See the discussion in Kenneth McNaught, "American Progressives and the Great Society," *Journal of American History* 53 (December 1966): 504-20.

110. See, for example, Melvin Dubofsky, *We Shall Be All: A History of the Industrial Workers of the World* (Chicago: Quadrangle Books, 1969), pp. 12-13, 146-70, 445-46, 477-89.

111. *Congregationalist*, Jan. 14, 1911, pp. 33, 37.

112. Ibid., July 2, 1914, p. 13. See also James Weinstein, *The Corporate Ideal in the Liberal State: 1900-1918* (Boston: Beacon Press, 1968).

113. Other words in the pejorative category included *conspiracy, kings, magnate, master, monsters, oligarchy, potentate, ring, robbers*, and *syndicate*.

6. WAR AND THE CORPORATE CULTURE, 1915-1919

1. Arthur S. Link, *Wilson: Campaigns for Progressivism and Peace, 1916-1917* (Princeton: Princeton University Press, 1965), pp. 91-164.

2. Arthur S. Link, *Woodrow Wilson and the Progressive Era: 1910-1917* (New York: Harper & Brothers, 1954), pp. 79-80.

3. Eric F. Goldman, *Rendezvous with Destiny* (New York: Vintage Books, 1956), p. 191; also quoted in Link, *Wilson: Campaigns for Progressivism and Peace*, p. 399.

4. Arthur S. Link, *American Epoch* (New York: Alfred A. Knopf, 1959), pp. 214-16.

5. Robert D. Cuff, "Bernard Baruch: Symbol and Myth in Industrial Mobilization," *Business History Review* 43 (Summer 1969): 125-28; and the same author's study of *The War Industries Board* (Baltimore: Johns Hopkins University Press, 1973), pp. 109-22.

6. William Preston, Jr., *Aliens and Dissenters: Federal Suppression of Radicals, 1903–1933* (Cambridge: Harvard University Press, 1963), pp. 88–151.

7. William Howard Shaw, *Value of Commodity Output since 1869* (New York: National Bureau of Economic Research, 1947), p. 3; Harold U. Faulkner, *The Decline of Laissez Faire, 1897–1917* (New York: Rinehart & Co., 1959), pp. 32–35.

8. *Historical Statistics of the United States, Colonial Times to 1957* (Washington, D.C., 1960), p. 537.

9. The index numbers (1918 = 100) for gross farm income from corn and hogs are:

Year	Millions of current dollars	Millions of constant dollars
1915	38.3	56.7
1916	46.7	64.5
1917	72.0	84.4
1918	100.0	100.0
1919	91.9	79.7

For an explanation of the sources of the data and the calculations, see note 96 in chapter 3.

10. Paul Douglas, *Real Wages in the United States, 1890–1926* (Boston: Houghton Mifflin, 1930), pp. 135, 239–41, 325, 350. The four million figure is for Nov. 11, 1918; George Soule, *Prosperity Decade: From War to Depression: 1917–1929* (New York: Rinehart & Co., 1947), p. 81.

11. The following account of economic mobilization is based upon Soule, *Prosperity Decade*, pp. 7–45 and, to a much greater extent, upon Cuff's excellent study of *The War Industries Board*.

12. Melvin I. Urofsky, *Big Steel and the Wilson Administration* (Columbus: Ohio State University Press, 1969), pp. 178–82.

13. Ralph L. Nelson, *Merger Movements in American Industry* (Princeton: Princeton University Press, 1959), pp. 35–37.

14. See, for example, Henry F. May, *The End of American Innocence: A Study of the First Years of Our Own Time, 1912–1917* (New York: Alfred A. Knopf, 1959), p. 386. Robert H. Wiebe offers a different conclusion in *The Search for Order, 1877–1920* (New York: Hill and Wang, 1967), pp. 272–302. On p. 286, he says of the war: "Beneath the trappings, most Americans followed the same old goals for the same old reasons."

15. In 1913–14 only 9% of the references to prices and none of the remarks about products and services were negative.

16. These were three of the four leading favorable characteristics of the large company.

17. *Southern Cultivator*, Jan. 1, 1917, pp. 8–9.

18. Ibid., p. 34.

19. This coefficient is for attitudes against gross income in constant dollars; the income figures for the war period are:

Year	Millions of constant dollars
1915	722
1916	933
1917	1106
1918	1050
1919	1164

20. Those who do not remember details such as Frank Robinson's batting average in 1966 (.316) can look back to section VII in chapter 5.

21. The coefficients are –.64 for unfavorable opinions against average annual real earnings of employed wage-earners in all industries; Douglas, *Real Wages*, p. 391. For unfavorable attitudes against average hourly earnings in the building trades (union), r = –.89; *Historical Statistics*, p. 91.

22. *American Federationist* 22, no. 1 (January 1915): 53; 23, no. 1 (January 1916): 61.

23. Ibid., 23, no. 7 (July 1916): 581. For a different view of this company and of Rockefeller, Jr., see ibid., 22, no. 1 (January 1915): 42–43; and 22, no. 7 (July 1915): 514–15, where it was said that in Colorado "the richest man in the world [i.e., John D. Rockefeller, Jr.] was concerned in the policies and conditions that took from other men industrial and political rights and freedom, and even their lives." This article was a response to the investigations of the U.S. Commission on Industrial Relations, which was probing the coal miners' strike. On the commission and this strike, see Graham Adams, Jr., *Age of Industrial Violence, 1910–15* (New York: Columbia University Press, 1966), especially pp. 146–75.

24. *American Federationist* 22, no. 1 (January 1915): 42–43; see also the editorial on "Sycophancy and Callousness," in 22, no. 7 (July 1915): 515–17. The respective figures on the percentage of unfavorable items were:

Year	Editorials	Entire journal
1915	80%	50%
1916	100	30
1917	100	39
1918	0	21
1919	100	11

25. *Wallaces' Farmer*, Jan. 29, 1915, p. 149.

26. The gross income data are in note 9 in this chapter. The percentage of the items favoring some solution or response was:

1913	40%
1914	40
1915	29
1916	27
1917	53
1918	59
1919	61

27. *Wallaces' Farmer*, Jan. 7, 1916, p. 12.

28. Ibid., Jan. 12, 1917, p. 44.

29. Ibid., July 30, 1915, p. 1025.

30. I might also have included the Congregational ministers in this section, since prosperity dampened conflicts in society and gave the clergyman fewer opportunities to reflect upon the less favorable aspects of the concentration movement. But in fact the minister had been losing interest in this subject before the war. In 1915 his anxiety about the trusts continued to decline, in spite of the fact that the U.S. Commission on Industrial Relations was still pumping out headlines drawing attention to the worst examples of corporate labor relations. Despite this publicity about an aspect of big business which had long aroused his interest, the minister looked on the giant corporation with increasing favor and saw less need to propose solutions to the trust problem. It would appear that the war influenced his attitudes, but that the struggle was not for him primarily an economic phenomenon.

31. Arthus S. Link, *Wilson: The New Freedom* (Princeton: Princeton University Press, 1956), pp. 469–71.

32. *Congregationalist*, Jan. 6, 1916, pp. 14–15.

33. Cuff, "Bernard Baruch," pp. 115–33.

34. When we added together all forms of political activity, they accounted for 20% of the items on which we could identify a source for the years 1902–14; during the war period, this figure dropped to 12%.

35. Only 18% of the items mentioned the political activities of the corporation (table 6–3), compared with 27% in the years 1909–14.

36. This change does not show up in table 6–4, under the mean percentage (35) of the items mentioning political aspects because the figures for 1917–19 were so high (44%, 50%, and 50%). In 1915, *Wallaces' Farmer* had nonetheless found an opportunity to attack "the great firms that are engaged in the manufacture of war material" (Jan. 1, 1915, p. 5). In the following year, the paper was concerned about the possibility of railroad rate increases, but during the debate on this subject the journal did not once condemn the roads for their techniques of influencing politics or for their political power—two negative themes that had been very prominent in previous years. The paper observed that the companies "have their regular force of attorneys, clerks and statisticians. They are on the job all the time, and constantly preparing evidence to show that railroads are not getting as much money for hauling live stock as they should." No longer was the paper attacking the "oily-tongued lobbyists," and the techniques employed by the corporation were seen as a proper model for farm organizations to imitate. See ibid., Jan. 28, 1916, p. 117; July 28, 1916, p. 1012; Jan. 12, 1917, pp. 45, 54.

37. *Wallaces' Farmer*, July 6, 1917, p. 983; see also July 20, 1917, p. 1032; July 27, 1917, pp. 1056–57.

38. Ibid., July 6, 1917, p. 984.

39. Ibid., p. 985.

40. Ibid., Jan. 25, 1918, p. 124. Compare Jan. 18, 1918, p. 76, with Jan. 25, 1918, p. 116, and July 12, 1918, p. 1033. See also July 26, 1918, p. 1081.

41. Ibid., Jan. 4, 1918, p. 4.

42. Ibid., July 5, 1918, p. 1004; July 12, 1918, pp. 1033, 1045; Jan. 24, 1919, p. 185. On the sisal trust, see Jan. 25, 1918, p. 116; on the merchant marine, July 5, 1918, p. 1001.

43. Ibid., July 12, 1918, p. 1033. See also July 5, 1918, p. 1001.

44. Ibid., July 26, 1918, p. 1081.

45. *Southern Cultivator*, Jan. 1, 1918, pp. 10, 29.

46. *American Federationist* 24, no. 1 (January 1917): 47–48.

47. Ibid., 25, no. 1 (January 1918): 41–49.

48. See ibid., 25, no. 7 (July 1918): 594–95. During the years 1915–19, only 6% of the items on big business were inspired by some form of political activity, compared to 10% during the progressive era.

49. *Solidarity*, July 7, 1917, p. 2.

50. Melvin Dubofsky, *We Shall Be All: A History of the Industrial Workers of the World* (Chicago: Quadrangle Books, 1969), pp. 398–444, provides an excellent account of the government's policy toward the union.

51. *Solidarity*, July 7, 1917, pp. 1–2, 4.

52. Ibid., Jan. 4, 1919, p. 2; July 5, 1919, pp. 1, 2.

53. Ibid., July 5, 1919, pp. 1, 3.

54. Ibid., p. 2.

55. *Engineering News*, July 5, 1917, p. 3.

56. Ibid., July 5, 1917, pp. 3, 43–44; Jan. 3, 1918, pp. 1–2.

57. Ibid., Jan. 3, 1918, pp. 1–2, 4–5.

58. Ibid., pp. 25–29.

59. Ibid., pp. 40–42.

60. Ibid., July 4, 1918, pp. 23–25. For example, see the favorable comments on the government's shipbuilding program in ibid., Jan. 3, 1918, pp. 3–4, 12–23; July 4, 1918, pp. 5–12; Jan. 2, 1919, pp. 7–13. On the other hand, the engineer was critical of the "inexperienced heads" of the railroad administration; ibid., July 4, 1918, pp. 3–4.

61. See table 5 in chapter 7.

62. *American Federationist* 22, no. 1 (January 1915): 17–35; 23, no. 7 (July 1916): 542–58; 24, no. 1 (January 1917): 28–36; 26, no. 7 (July 1919): 620–21.

63. The existence or expansion of the giant corporation had been among the top three subjects of discussion during the following years: engineers, 1880–92; clergy, 1880–92, 1909–14; southern farmers, 1887–92, 1896–1901; midwestern farmers, 1879–1901; laborers who read the *National Labor Tribune*, 1880–86, 1897–1901; AFL members, 1894–1914.

64. *Engineering News*, Jan. 3, 1918, pp. 3–4; see also July 4, 1918, pp. 5–12.

65. Ibid., July 4, 1918, pp. 23–25.

66. Ibid., pp. 45–46. The so-called Gary Dinners were a means of bringing together the industry's leaders so that they could agree to stabilize the market by holding prices at a mutually acceptable level.

67. Leo Wolman, *The Growth of American Trade Unions, 1880–1923* (New York: National Bureau of Economic Research, 1924), p. 123. For the AFL, the increase between 1915 and 1917 was 506,700 members; between 1917 and 1919, 882,700.

68. *Historical Statistics*, p. 99; Taft, *The A.F. of L. in the Time of Gompers* (New York: Harper & Brothers, 1957), pp. 344–53, 355–58.

69. *Wallaces' Farmer*, July 6, 1917, p. 985; July 13, 1917, p. 1008; Jan. 10, 1919, pp. 67, 72C.

70. Ibid., Jan. 5, 1917, p. 4. This item called for a brand of "class consciousness which will result in organizations strong enough to prevent the evils and abuses." The local farmers' clubs were seen as a means of "laying the foundation for a real class consciousness through which the farmers of the younger generation can make their influence felt."

71. Ibid., Jan. 7, 1916, p. 8; Jan. 28, 1916, pp. 116, 135–36, 141; July 11, 1919, p. 1353. The midwestern farmer's interest in private collective responses to big business had increased during the progressive period and it increased again during the war; see tables 5–2 and 6–4.

72. Ibid., Jan. 3, 1919, p. 20.

73. Ibid., Jan. 17, 1919, pp. 112, 128; Jan. 31, 1919, pp. 248, 254; July 25, 1919, p. 1424.

74. *Southern Cultivator*, July 5, 1919, p. 28.

75. Ibid., July 1, 1915, p. 9; Jan. 1, 1916, p. 34; July 1, 1916, p. 13; Jan. 1, 1917, pp. 8–9; Jan. 15, 1918, p. 2; July 1, 1918, p. 7.

76. Ibid., Jan. 15, 1919, p. 28. Republic was praised for (among other things) giving "three sets of prizes . . . to Americans, Italians and Negroes" (July 15, 1919, p. 2).

77. For an exception, see note 70, chapter 6.

78. Sigmund Diamond, *The Reputation of the American Businessman* (Cambridge: Harvard University Press, 1955), pp. 120–25, 140–41, notes a similar shift in emphasis from the individual to the social context.

79. *Congregationalist*, Jan. 3, 1918, p. 8.

80. See table 5–8. The percentage of pejoratives for the several groups were as follows:

Year	Farmers, Midwest	Laborers, AFL	Congregational clergy	Engineers
1915	5%	67%	0%	2%
1916	7	28	20	0
1917	2	7	0	0
1918	6	0	0	0
1919	2	50	0	0

7. CONTINUITY AND CHANGE, 1920–1929

1. *American Federationist* 26, no. 7 (July 1919): 620–21. I have included events of 1919 in this chapter because the postwar crisis extended into the twenties and had its major impact on middle-culture opinions at that time. In this instance my choice of a January-July sample obviously affected my results, at least insofar as the data for 1919 were concerned.

2. Ibid., 27, no. 1 (January 1920): 33–40.

3. *Wallaces' Farmer*, Jan. 17, 1919, pp. 112, 128; Jan. 24, 1919, pp. 184–85; July 11, 1919, p. 1353; July 25, 1919, pp. 1438–43, 1451.

4. Ibid., July 30, 1920, p. 1856.

5. Ibid., July 1, 1921, p. 925.

6. Ibid., July 9, 1920, p. 1714.

7. Ibid., Jan. 24, 1919, p. 213; July 2, 1920, p. 1683.

8. Ibid., July 25, 1919, p. 1424; Jan. 2, 1920, p. 6; Jan. 23, 1920, p. 266.

9. *American Federationist* 27, no. 1 (January 1920): 68, 75–79.

10. *Solidarity*, July 3, 1920, p. 2; July 2, 1921, p. 2.

11. *Engineering News*, Jan. 1, 1920, p. 1. The editor noted with satisfaction that "the vast majority of the workers believe in improving the present order of society rather than in upsetting it and experimenting with a soviet regime."

12. *Wallaces' Farmer*, Jan. 17, 1919, p. 112.

13. *Engineering News*, Jan. 1, 1920, p. 60; *Wallaces' Farmer*, Jan. 7, 1921, p. 3.

14. *American Federationist* 28, no. 1 (January 1921): 47–48; *Engineering News*, Jan. 5, 1922, pp. 2, 14, 16–17. One solution to the engineer's problem was to control entry to the profession through licensing; see ibid., July 6, 1922, pp. 8–11. *Congregationalist*, July 7, 1921, p. 16. The author of the letter quoted above was apparently a minister; he also said: "A few years ago, when Mr. Charles Mellen became president of the New Haven Railroad, the publicity agent of that road said to me, 'Mr. Mellen speaks in millions and the directors are coming to think in millions.' That is to say, speaking in large terms tends to lead men to act in a large way. In like manner the habit of speaking in small terms [e.g., about ministers' salaries] would tend to show the smallness of that which is spoken of." David Burner, "1919: Prelude to Normalcy," in John Braeman et al., eds., *Change and Continuity in Twentieth-Century America: The 1920's* (Columbus: Ohio State University Press, 1968), pp. 3–31, also stresses the high degree of conflict and tension in the immediate postwar period.

15. The historical literature on the twenties is reviewed with considerable insight in Henry F. May, "Shifting Perspectives on the 1920's," *Mississippi Valley History Review* 43 (December 1956): 405–27; and Burl Noggle, "The Twenties: A New Historiographical Frontier," *The Journal of American History* 53 (September 1966): 299–314.

16. Paul A. Carter, *The Twenties in America* (New York: Thomas Y. Crowell, 1968), pp. 5, 12–13.

17. Edgar Kemler, *The Irreverent Mr. Mencken* (Boston: Little, Brown and Co., 1950), p. 159; James Truslow Adams, *Our Business Civilization* (New York: Albert & Charles Boni, 1939).

18. See section VI, chapter 6.

19. The means for the annual percentages of unfavorable items in *American Federationist*, 1907–14 and 1920–29, were 54% and 57%, respectively.

20. The annual percentages for pejorative nouns were:

1920	9%	1924	12%	1927	0%
1921	0	1925	2	1928	27
1922	2	1926	26	1929	18
1923	16				

21. An exception is provided by petroleum refining in general and the Standard Oil Co. in particular; both were subjects of substantial concern before the war. The shift from the old to

the new industries is particularly clear when one compares the data for 1902–8 (table 5–6) with those for 1920–29.

22. This issue actually began to emerge in the prewar years, but it was 1921–22 before job opportunities became, from the union point of view, the leading question associated with large enterprise. The precise timing of the transition is concealed because I lumped the figures together for a five-year period, but from that time on the corporation's influence on job opportunities remained one of the three leading characteristics of big business.

23. *American Federationist* 29, no. 1 (January 1922): 74–78; 29, no. 7 (July 1922): 520.

24. Irving Bernstein, *The Lean Years* (Boston: Houghton Mifflin Co., 1960), pp. 146–89; Selig Perlman and Philip Taft, *History of Labor in the United States, 1896–1932* (New York: The Macmillan Co., 1935), pp. 489–91, 499–500, 507–8.

25. *American Federationist* 29, no. 7 (July 1922): 503; 29, no. 1 (January 1922): 38–39; 30, no. 1 (January 1923): 39–41, 44–45, 47, 48–49.

26. Ibid., 30, no. 1 (January 1923): 54–55, 57–58; 31, no. 1 (January 1924): 61; 31, no. 7 (July 1924): 570–71.

27. The company unions became a major theme in 1924 and remained important in the years that followed. See ibid., 21, no. 7 (July 1924): 590–91, for the reference to "scab" unions.

28. While the yellow dog contract was discussed frequently after 1925, the AFL seems to have been more worried about company unions.

29. Bernstein, *The Lean Years*, pp. 83–90.

30. *American Federationist* 30, no. 7 (July 1923): 577; 31, no. 7 (July 1924): 574–75; 32, no. 7 (July 1925): 525–33; 33, no. 1 (January 1926): 113; 35, no. 1 (January 1928): 32–44; 36, no. 1 (January 1929): 21–35.

31. Ibid., 33, no. 1 (January 1926): 111–13; 33, no. 7 (July 1926): 858–61; 878; 34, no. 7 (July 1927): 794–96.

32. Ibid., 29, no. 1 (January 1922): 38–39, 44–48; 29, no. 7 (July 1922): 503; 30, no. 1 (January 1923): 48–49, 53–54, 57–58, 74–76, 79–92; 31, no. 1 (January 1924): 69–76, 96; 31, no. 7 (July 1924): 570–71, 583–88; 35, no. 1 (January 1928): 25–30.

33. While the coefficients of correlation between income and attitudes suggested a significant relationship during the war years, this was no longer true in the twenties. None of the coefficients approached the level of significance for the period 1920–29.

34. *Wallaces' Farmer*, July 2, 1920, pp. 1686, 1690, 1702; July 9, 1920, p. 1716; Jan. 7, 1912, p. 3; July 1, 1921, p. 938; July 9, 1920, p. 1714; Jan. 16, 1920, p. 193; Jan. 23, 1920, p. 259; July 9, 1920, p. 1716. In 1920, almost 20% of the items on big business in this journal touched in some way on the Farm Bureau.

35. Ibid., Jan. 30, 1920, p. 339.

36. Ibid., Jan. 6, 1922, p. 12.

37. As this happened, the farmer lost interest in responses or solutions to the situations associated with big business; the percentage of the items in *Wallaces' Farmer* which favored some solution were as follows:

1920	53%	1924	40%	1927	25%
1921	40	1925	14	1928	44
1922	43	1926	17	1929	22
1923	50				

38. The data on the mean deviation (see Appendix) indicate that the entire decade, including the immediate postwar years, was a period characterized by a relatively high degree of equilibrium. The index numbers (1918 = 100) for gross farm income (constant dollars) from corn and hogs were:

1920	57	1924	49	1927	50
1921	38	1925	54	1928	51
1922	44	1926	56	1929	53
1923	45				

39. Grant McConnell, *The Decline of Agrarian Democracy* (Berkeley: University of California Press, 1953), pp. 46–48.

40. *Wallaces' Farmer*, July 30, 1920, pp. 1842, 1852.

41. Ibid., July 23, 1920, p. 1807.

42. On the cooperatives, see McConnell, *Decline of Agrarian Democracy*, pp. 56–62; Theodore Saloutos and John D. Hicks, *Twentieth-Century Populism: Agricultural Discontent in the Middle West, 1900–1939* (Lincoln: University of Nebraska Press, 1951), pp. 238–52, 255–320. This shift in emphasis is reflected in the data (table 7-2) on leading solutions or responses. In the twenties, 33% of the items mentioning a response favored private collective action (e.g., cooperatives), as compared with 24% in the years 1915–19 and 16% in the years 1902–14.

43. Translated into Parsonian pattern variables, this mode of thinking involved a shift in values from: 1) self- to collective-orientation; 2) particularism to universalism; 3) diffuseness to specificity; and, 4) eventually, affectivity to affective neutrality. See section IV, chapter 1, and Parsons, *The Social System* (New York: The Free Press, 1964), pp. 59–67.

44. For a contrary view of the degree of change, see M. A. Straus and L. J. Houghton, "Achievement, Affiliation and Cooperation Values as Clues to Trends in American Rural Sociology, 1924–1958," *Rural Sociology* 25 (1960): 394–403. If I had studied only the "Boys' Corner" in *Wallaces' Farmer*, my results would probably have been similar to those of Straus and Houghton, who analyzed the *National 4-H Club News*.

45. *Congregationalist*, July 3, 1919, p. 21.

46. Ibid., Jan. 1, 1920, p. 8. See also Paul A. Carter, *The Decline and Revival of the Social Gospel: Social and Political Liberalism in American Protestant Churches, 1920–1940* (Hamden, Conn.: Archon Books, 1971), pp. 18–28.

47. As one article pointed out, a particular church in Illinois included in its congregation "not only college people, but railroad men, business men of all classes, working people, and every element of the population" (ibid., July 3, 1919, p. 23). See also July 1, 1920, p. 29.

48. Ibid., Jan. 6, 1921, p. 10. Labor relations became one of the three leading aspects of the large firm for the first time since the tumultuous nineties. See table 7-2.

49. Ibid., Jan. 6, 1921, p. 10 (italics mine); See also July 5, 1923, p. 8–9.

50. Ibid., July 6, 1922, pp. 14–16; Jan. 1, 1925, p. 17. Two subjects of substantial interest were Julius Rosenwald of Sears, who was a Jew, and Henry Ford, who was a blatant anti-Semite. Of the former, *Congregationalist* said on one occasion: "Though he is a Jew, he is famous for financing Negro Y.M.C.A.'s and Negro schools in the South, most of which are Christian" (ibid., Jan. 3, 1924, p. 8). Under the heading "Mr. Ford Explains," the paper discussed, without adverse comment, Ford's claim that the Jews controlled much of the world's gold and thus had too much power (ibid., Jan. 5, 1922, p. 6).

51. Ibid., Jan. 3, 1924, p. 23; July 3, 1924, pp. 14–15, 27–28.

52. Ibid., July 6, 1922, pp. 2–3; July 3, 1924, p. 23; Jan. 1, 1925, p. 10. In rank order, the three leading favorable aspects of the large firm were: "Management or ownership"; "Enhances the general wealth"; and "Products or services."

53. In the 1920s the *Congregationalist* was generally paying less attention to big business than it had before the war, and as a result, the data were thin; on this account one should be cautious (as I have tried to be) about interpreting even such major fluctuations as this second cycle of unfavorable viewpoints.

54. These were the two leading unfavorable aspects of big business.

55. *Congregationalist*, Jan. 1, 1925, p. 14.

56. Ibid., Jan. 6, 1927, pp. 17–18.

57. As measured by the mean deviation, the years 1918/20-1921/23 ranked second and the years 1925/27-1927/29 ranked fourth in terms of the degree of disequilibrium which existed between 1880 and 1940. See also Carter, *Decline and Revival of the Social Gospel*, pp. 66 ff.

58. Frederick Strauss and Louis H. Bean, *Gross Farm Income and Indices of Farm Production and Prices in the United States, 1869–1937* (Washington, D.C., 1940), pp. 65–66.

NOTES TO PAGES 204–209

59. *Southern Cultivator*, Jan. 15, 1920, p. 2.

60. Ibid., July 1, 1920, p. 19; July 15, 1920, pp. 2, 4; Jan. 1, 1921, p. 7; July 1, 1921, pp. 3–4.

61. Ibid., Jan. 15, 1920, p. 25.

62. Ibid., July 15, 1920, p. 8. Compare the data on leading solutions in table 7-4 with the same information in table 6-3. See also ibid., Jan. 1, 1921, p. 7.

63. For gross income (current dollars) against unfavorable opinions, $r = -.51$; against neutral attitudes, $r = .58$. The same figures for income in constant dollars are $-.60$ and $.38$, respectively.

64. *Southern Cultivator*, Jan. 1, 1928, p. 6.

65. Ibid., Jan. 1, 1924, p. 2.

66. Ibid., July 1, 1923, p. 2; Jan. 1, 1925, p. 13.

67. Ibid., Jan. 1, 1920, p. 9; Jan. 1, 1925, p. 13; Jan. 1, 1926, p. 10.

68. Ibid., July 1, 1921, p. 5; July 1, 1923, p. 5; Jan. 1, 1924, p. 15; Jan. 1, 1929, p. 4. Before 1915, private collective responses to big business had been favored only 7% of the time; the comparable figure in table 7-4 is 29%.

69. Ibid., July 1, 1922, p. 14; Jan. 1, 1923, p. 5; July 1, 1928, pp. 3, 5. See also Jan. 1, 1924, p. 10; and Jan. 1, 1925, p. 15. There were a few instances during the twenties in which material was so favorable to a particular business and its products that there was a strong possibility that we scored a concealed advertisement. See, for example, the article on "A General Purpose Tractor," in ibid., July 1, 1926, pp. 6–7; and a similar item on p. 9.

70. Ibid., July 1, 1925, p. 11; see also Jan. 1, 1924, p. 15.

71. Ibid., July 1, 1927, p. 4.

72. For the data on equilibrium, see the Appendix.

73. Eliminating the neutral-ambivalent items makes a brief postwar cycle of anticorporate sentiment stand out more clearly; the annual percentages of unfavorable items are, in this case, as follows:

1919	18%	1923	19%	1927	0%
1920	33	1924	7	1928	4
1921	15	1925	12	1929	0
1922	8	1926	12		

74. *Engineering News*, Jan. 1, 1920, pp. 1, 7, 12–14.

75. Ibid., Jan. 2, 1919, pp. 18–20; July 3, 1919, pp. 17–18; Jan. 1, 1920, pp. 12–14. In 1919, *Engineering News* concluded: "Government operation has proved an expensive experiment and will cost the country upward of two billions of dollars before the books are closed and accounts settled. It has, however, demonstrated and settled these facts—the inefficiency of the Government operation and the doom of Government ownership of public utilities."

76. Ibid., Jan. 1, 1920, pp. 12–14.

77. Ibid., Jan. 1, 1920, p. 7; Jan. 6, 1921, pp. 1, 7–9, 33–36.

78. Ibid., Jan. 5, 1922, p. 4. For a more tolerant view of organized labor, see the response to the preliminary report of the Industrial Conference: "The plain fact is that the public has long been uneasy about the power of great employers; it is becoming uneasy about the power of great labor organizations. The community must be assured against domination by either" (ibid., Jan. 1, 1920, pp. 49–50).

79. On the railroads, see, for example, ibid., Jan. 6, 1921, pp. 7–9; Jan. 4, 1923, p. 2; Jan. 3, 1924, pp. 14–16; Jan. 14, 1926, pp. 52–53; Jan. 10, 1929, pp. 63–66. In regard to Baldwin and Bethlehem, see Jan. 13, 1927, pp. 58–61; and July 5, 1928, p. 16.

80. The ratio of favorable to unfavorable remarks about management was 9 to 1 in the years 1925–29.

81. Ibid., July 5, 1928, pp. 15–16, 34.

82. Ibid., pp. 17–19.

NOTES TO PAGES 209-216

83. *Solidarity*, Jan. 3, 1920, p. 2.

84. Ibid., Jan. 3, 1920, p. 2; and July 3, 1920, p. 2.

85. Ibid., p. 4; Jan. 1, 1921, p. 1.

86. In a previous publication, I said that "*Solidarity* was insulated by its ideology from the type of cultural change which influenced the *American Federationist*; the series on pejorative words in *Solidarity* clearly reflects this difference." See "AFL's Concept of Big Business," *The Journal of American History* 57 (March 1971): 862. I had in mind the prewar era, but on reflection, I think this statement is misleading insofar as the entire period from 1910 through 1930 is concerned.

87. The mean percentage of pejoratives used in *Solidarity* was 41% for the years 1910–14, 35% for the war period, and only 26% for 1920–30.

88. *Solidarity*, July 1, 1925, p. 2; July 7, 1926, p. 2. See also July 1, 1925, pp. 3, 4, 5; Jan. 6, 1926, pp. 1, 3, 4; July 7, 1926, p. 4; Feb. 2, 1927, pp. 2, 4; July 4, 1928, p. 3; Jan. 2, 1929, p. 2; July 3, 1929, pp. 1, 3.

89. Ibid., July 4, 1928, p. 2.

90. Ibid., July 1, 1925, p. 3; Jan. 6, 1926, pp. 2, 3.

91. See the data on equilibrium in the Appendix.

92. Ibid., July 2, 1921, p. 4.

93. Ibid., Jan. 1, 1921, p. 1.

94. Ibid., Jan. 6, 1923, p. 2.

95. Ibid., July 1, 1925, p. 4.

96. Melvyn Dubofsky, *We Shall Be All: A History of the Industrial Workers of the World* (Chicago: Quadrangle Books, 1969), pp. 465–68, 475–77; John S. Gambs, *The Decline of the I.W.W.* (New York: Columbia University Press, 1932), pp. 165–69.

97. While normally I have avoided analysis of fluctuations in one year, the decline in unfavorable viewpoints in 1930 prompts me to break this rule. The key here is the panic of 1929 and the resulting depression. In this case the situation was so serious that the radical worker could merely note without comment that the prices of stocks were continuing to fall; he was no longer compelled to offer an evaluation because the problems were so obvious. *Solidarity*, July 1, 1930, p. 2.

98. See note 20 in this chapter for the figures from the AFL. The percentages of pejoratives used by the other groups were:

Year	Congregational clergy	Engineers	Farmers, midwestern	Year	Congregational clergy	Engineers	Farmers, midwestern
1920	50%	0%	2%	1925	33%	0%	0%
1921	0	0	0	1926	0	6	0
1922	25	2	14	1927	0	0	0
1923	0	0	0	1928	0	0	40
1924	0	0	0	1929	0	0	0

99. See section V, chapter 6 for the wartime changes. Also see Reynold M. Wik, *Henry Ford and Grass-Roots America* (Ann Arbor: University of Michigan Press, 1972), pp. 103–79.

100. Five years later Matthew Josephson published his famous volume on *The Robber Barons* (New York: Harcourt, Brace and Co., 1934).

8. TOWARD A STABLE EQUILIBRIUM, 1930–1940

1. Arthur M. Schlesinger, Jr., *The Crisis of the Old Order, 1919–1933* (Boston: Houghton Mifflin Co., 1957), pp. 162–65.

2. *Historical Statistics of the United States, Colonial Times to 1957* (Washington, D.C., 1960), p. 73; Harry L. Hopkins, *Spending to Save: The Complete Story of Relief* (New York: W. W. Norton & Co., 1936), pp. 43–96.

3. This statement is qualified by the fact that my study ends with 1940. I do not have the content analysis data that would enable me to extend my generalizations beyond that date. See also Paul A. Carter, *Decline and Revival of the Social Gospel: Social and Political Liberalism in American Protestant Churches, 1920–1940* (Hamden, Conn.: Archon Books, 1971), pp. 141–79; and Robert Moats Miller, *American Protestantism and Social Issues, 1919–1939* (Chapel Hill: University of North Carolina Press, 1958), pp. 63–112, 203–54, 274–87. My data indicate that Carter and Miller could have emphasized the reaction to big business more than they did.

4. Normally, I enumerated the leading negative characteristics in rank order, but in this instance I have described the second-ranking aspect first.

5. *Congregationalist*, Jan. 11, 1934, p. 23.

6. The "Leading characteristics" in table 8–1 include neutral and favorable, as well as negative, evaluations. Here, I am dealing only with the leading unfavorable characteristics.

7. *Congregationalist*, July 5, 1934, pp. 271–72. This article also said: "We have therefore a curious alliance between Mr. Eugene Grace of the Bethlehem Steel Corporation with Mr. William Z. Foster of the Communist Party. They are both gunning for the skin of Mr. Roosevelt and his New Deal. They may get it. And then what?"

8. Ibid., Jan. 3, 1935, p. 17.

9. Ibid., 129, no. 7 (July 1937): 306, 313.

10. Ibid., 130, no. 1 (January 1938): 14, 26, 32.

11. Ibid., 122, no. 1 (January 1940): 6–7.

12. Ibid., 129, no. 7 (July 1937): 302. See also Sigmund Diamond, *The Reputation of the American Businessman* (Cambridge: Harvard University Press, 1955), pp. 107–41.

13. We included accounts of movies and radio broadcasts in this category, and during the thirties they provided some interesting items. One of these was the Paramount production of *The President Vanishes*, which showed "the big bosses of American industry to be the vultures they are" and illustrated "the tie-up between big business and war" (ibid., Jan. 3, 1935, p. 18). In this chapter I have tried to avoid confusion by using the title *Congregationalist* to identify both that journal and its successor, *Advance* (1934–40).

14. Ibid., 130, no. 1 (January 1938): 32; 128, no. 10 (July 1936): 463.

15. Ibid., July 4, 1935, p. 529; 128, no. 4 (January 1936): 178–79.

16. Ibid., 128, no. 4 (January 1936): 164.

17. Even when one discounts the data on the grounds that the Congregational minister was most likely to be a Republican, FDR's lack of influence seems significant. The federal executive branch of the government accounted for only 3% of the items on which we could identify a source. All political activity accounted for 8% of the articles scored, as compared to 20% in the years 1902–14.

18. This theme is analyzed perceptively in Alfred B. Rollins, Jr., "Was There Really a Man Named Roosevelt?" in George A. Billias and Gerald N. Grob, eds., *American History: Retrospect and Prospect* (New York: The Free Press, 1971), pp. 232–70. I am indebted to Rollins for the expression "Roosevelt centrism."

19. Ellis Hawley, *The New Deal and the Problem of Monopoly* (Princeton: Princeton University Press, 1966), p. 465.

20. *Historical Statistics*, pp. 99, 139.

21. The index numbers (1918 = 100) for gross farm income (constant dollars) from corn and hogs were as follows:

1929	53.4	1932	23.3	1935	34.5	1938	43.8
1930	47.2	1933	30.9	1936	51.4	1939	44.5
1931	33.7	1934	29.6	1937	45.1	1940	39.2

Frederick Strauss and Louis H. Bean, *Gross Farm Income and Indices of Farm Production and Prices in the United States, 1869-1937* (Washington, D.C., 1940), pp. 37, 119; *Historical Statistics*, pp. 291, 296.

22. Theodore Saloutos and John D. Hicks, *Twentieth-Century Populism: Agricultural Discontent in the Middle West, 1900-1939* (Lincoln: University of Nebraska Press, 1951), pp. 435-70; Arthur M. Schlesinger, Jr., *The Coming of the New Deal* (Boston: Houghton Mifflin Co., 1958), pp. 27-84; John L. Shover, *Cornbelt Rebellion: The Farmers' Holiday Association* (Urbana: University of Illinois Press, 1965).

23. *Nebraska Farmer*, July 7, 1934, p. 22.

24. Ibid., pp. 21-22.

25. My description here is based on the list of leading unfavorable characteristics of the large firm, 1930-40. For other examples, see ibid., July 7, 1934, p. 22; Jan. 5, 1935, p. 21; Jan. 4, 1936, p. 28; July 4, 1936, p. 21; July 3, 1937, p. 6.

26. Ibid., July 4, 1936, p. 21; July 3, 1937, p. 6.

27. In one year, 1937, the percentage of the items mentioning the corporation's political aspects was at its all-time high (83%) for the period 1879-1940. I am, however, inclined to discount the importance of this figure, in part because most of these items were neutral and not—on the basis of their content—apparently very important. One exception might be the quotation from an AAA official who said that corporations were being helped by the government: "But if I understand the temper of the farmers correctly, they are in no mood to let legalistic barriers and finespun interpretations keep them from having equality with large corporations in meeting nationwide problems of production and prices" (Ibid., Jan. 2, 1937, pp. 9, 29).

28. Ibid., July 4, 1936, pp. 6, 23; Jan. 2, 1937, p. 8; see also July 4, 1936, p. 4; and Jan. 1, 1938, pp. 6, 16. On Legge's chairmanship of Herbert Hoover's Federal Farm Board, see Saloutos and Hicks, *Twentieth-Century Populism*, pp. 409-34. Forrest Crissey, *Alexander Legge, 1866-1933* (Chicago: The Alexander Legge Memorial Committee, 1936), offers some information on its subject but is essentially a eulogy.

29. For NBC, see *Nebraska Farmer*, July 7, 1934, p. 26. The railroads are mentioned in ibid., pp. 6-8; July 6, 1935, p. 6; July 14, 1936, pp. 14, 22; July 14, 1938, pp. 14, 22; July 2, 1938, p. 15. For a contrasting viewpoint see July 3, 1937, p. 21.

30. The midwestern farm journals did not use any pejorative nouns in the years 1930-40. Alexander Legge was the only business leader mentioned more than once.

31. Grant McConnell, *The Decline of Agrarian Democracy* (Berkeley: University of California Press, 1953), pp. 66-83; Christiana McFayden Campbell, *The Farm Bureau: A Study of the Making of National Farm Policy, 1933-40* (Urbana: University of Illinois Press, 1962).

32. *Southern Cultivator*, July 1, 1932, pp. 2, 4.

33. Ibid., Feb. 1, 1933, pp. 5, 9; July 1, 1933, p. 4. The price of cotton was 17 cents a pound in 1929 and only 6 cents in 1932. Gross income (from cotton and cottonseed, in millions of constant dollars) was as follows:

1929	779	1932	297	1935	456	1938	389
1930	436	1933	396	1936	576	1939	408
1931	289	1934	568	1937	530	1940	463

Strauss and Bean, *Gross Farm Income*, pp. 65-66; *Historical Statistics*, p. 301. I used crop year (not calendar year) prices for 1938-40.

34. *Southern Cultivator*, Jan. 1, 1932, p. 7; July 1, 1933, pp. 3, 9, 11.

35. Ibid., July 1, 1931, p. 8; July 1, 1933, p. 4.

36. See, for example, ibid., July 1, 1932, p. 2.

37. Ibid., Jan. 1, 1934, pp. 3, 8; see also *Progressive Farmer* 53, no. 7 (July 1938): 4.

38. The southern farm journals did not mention any corporate manager or owner more than once during the years 1930-40.

39. This shift in the sources of information had, in fact, been taking place gradually over a number of decades. In the years 1879–1901, "Action taken by big business" was not among the top three sources of articles; in 1902–14, it was tied for third place; in the war years, it was tied for second; during the twenties, it was the second ranking source of items.

40. Hawley, *The New Deal and the Problem of Monopoly*, p. 431.

41. Southern farm income declined sharply after the recession of 1937, and as late as 1940 gross income (in constant dollars) was still far below the level which had been reached in 1936. See note 33, above. *Southern Cultivator*, February 1, 1933, p. 9; July 1, 1933, p. 6; Jan. 1, 1934, pp. 4, 6, 10; July 1, 1934, p. 6. The increasing attention paid to state government shows up under "Leading sources" and "Leading solutions" in table 8–3.

42. *American Federationist* 38, no. 1 (January 1931): 85–87.

43. Ibid., 38, no. 7 (July 1931): 809–23. This particular article pointed out that "the period from 1922 was marked by the extension of combinations in finance, industry and commerce. Mergers, trusts and holding corporations not only increased rapidly in number, but in their wide control. Certainly the period was not one in which sound economic policies guided those in control of the nation's activities. What occurred bears much more resemblance to the law of the jungle than to the sane management of business by those responsible for its development."

44. The three leading negative traits in the "Characteristics of big business" category, 1930–35, were: "Diminishes individual's opportunities"; "Labor relations"; and "Wages and hours." In 1936–40, the top three were the same, but "Labor relations" pushed the lack of job opportunities down into second place.

45. *American Federationist* 40, no. 7 (July 1933): 677.

46. Ibid., 42, no. 1 (January 1935): 11–12.

47. Compare the figures in table 8–4 with the same data for 1920–24 (29%) and 1909–14 (27%). Between 1934 and 1940, 55% of the items in *American Federationist* favored some particular response to big business; this figure was higher than it had been (42%) in the years 1921–33, but substantially lower than the percentage (77%) for the progressive years 1902–14.

48. The coefficient of correlation for neutral-ambivalent attitudes (1930–40) against an index of hourly wage rates (in the union building trades) is .51; for unfavorable attitudes against the same index, $r = -.47$. The index is from *Historical Statistics*, p. 93.

49. Irving Bernstein, *Turbulent Years: A History of the American Worker, 1933–1941* (Boston: Houghton Mifflin Co., 1969), pp. 352–98.

50. See section X, chapter 5.

51. See section IV, chapter 6.

52. In reference to jobs see, for example, *American Federationist* 46, no. 1 (January 1939): 92, 104; 47, no. 1 (January 1940): 89. Labor relations are mentioned in 46, no. 1 (January 1939): 91–92, 100–101; 47, no. 1 (January 1940): 90; 48, no. 1 (July 1940): 30. On wages and hours, third-ranked among the favorable characteristics, 1936–40, see 46, no. 7 (July 1939): 727–28; 47, no. 1 (January 1940): 92, 94.

53. *Engineering News*, July 2, 1931, p. 30. All of the figures on unemployment are from *Historical Statistics*, p. 73.

54. *Engineering News*, Jan. 14, 1932, pp. 54–55; July 7, 1932, pp. 1–4.

55. Ibid., pp. 30–32.

56. This statement is qualified, as are all of the others in the book, by the fact that I am using a two-month sample from the journal. I am only asserting that these particular events did not appear in that sample.

57. This became the leading favorable characteristic of the corporation in the years 1936–40.

58. ASTM was the source of fewer items in the period 1930–40 than it had been in the years 1920–29, but ASTM's relative position among the various associations was strengthened as the other groups became less influential (and perhaps less active) during the depression. In the thirties, ASTM accounted for over 40% of those articles on big business which were prompted by associational activities (as compared with 25% before 1930).

59. The figures for negative items as a percentage of negative and positive articles are:

1930	9%	1933	0%	1936	40%	1939	50%
1931	8	1934	0	1937	0	1940	0
1932	0	1935	14	1938	22		

60. *Engineering News*, July 7, 1938, p. 5.

61. Ibid., July 2, 1936, pp. 19–20.

62. See, for instance, ibid., Jan. 4, 1934, pp. 22–23, 24; July 5, 1934, p. 20; July 4, 1935, pp. 16–18; July 7, 1938, p. 1; Jan. 5, 1939, p. 4; July 6, 1939, pp. 61–63; Jan. 4, 1940, pp. 64–66; July 4, 1940, p. 76.

63. Ibid., July 1, 1937, p. 8.

64. The means for the annual percentages, 1930–40, are: unfavorable, 28%; neutral-ambivalent, 40%; favorable, 32%.

65. The means for the annual percentages, 1880–89, are: unfavorable 30%; neutral-ambivalent, 43%; favorable, 27%.

66. Reynold M. Wik, *Henry Ford and Grass-Roots America* (Ann Arbor: University of Michigan Press, 1972), pp. 180–85. Two of the groups in my sample (engineers and southern farmers) failed to mention any business leader more than once, and the other groups did not agree as to which businessmen were most worthy of their attention. The clergyman focused on Rockefeller and Henry Ford; the midwestern farmer on Alexander Legge; the trade unionist on Ford and Owen Young.

67. The data on pejoratives are as follows:

Year	Congregational clergy	Engineers	Farmers, Midwest	Laborers, AFL
1930	0%	0%	0%	0%
1931	0	0	0	3
1932	0	0	0	5
1933	0	0	0	8
1934	0	10	0	2
1935	0	0	0	1
1936	14	0	0	0
1937	7	0	0	18
1938	0	0	0	5
1939	11	0	0	6
1940	0	0	0	33

68. My position throughout the book has been that value changes reflect (rather than cause) transitions in major social systems. See J. Zui Namenwirth, "Some Long- and Short-Term Trends in One American Political Value: A Computer Analysis of Concern with Wealth in 62 Party Platforms," in George Gerbner et al., eds., *The Analysis of Communication Content* (New York: John Wiley & Sons, 1969), pp. 223–41. In the present chapter I am merely adding to my analysis (and Namenwirth's) the proposition that new values, once accepted, can impede further changes. For the opposite position on values and social change, see Talcott Parsons, *Societies: Evolutionary and Comparative Perspectives* (Englewood Cliffs, N.J.: Prentice-Hall, 1966).

69. In support of Schumpeter, one could argue that the depression did in fact arouse intellectual antagonism toward the large firm, but my point here is that intellectual leaders were unable to focus mass discontent on big business as the source of the peoples' difficulties.

70. Hawley, *The New Deal and the Problem of Monopoly*, pp. 383–455. William E. Leuchtenburg, *Franklin D. Roosevelt and the New Deal, 1932–1940* (New York: Harper & Row,

1963), pp. 246–49, 257–60, discusses the origins of the antimonopoly policy, but Leuchtenburg does not consider its relationship to public opinion. See also Paul K. Conkin, *The New Deal* (New York: Thomas Y. Crowell Co., 1967), pp. 64–67, 97.

71. John Braeman, "The New Deal and the 'Broker State:' A Review of the Recent Scholarly Literature," *Business History Review* 46 (Winter 1972): 409–29.

9. THE MIDDLE CULTURES AND THE ORGANIZATIONAL REVOLUTION

1. Isaiah Berlin, *The Hedgehog and the Fox* (New York: Mentor Books, 1957), pp. 7–8. Berlin based his categories on a line from the Greek poet Archilochus: "The fox knows many things, but the hedgehog knows one big thing."

2. See, for instance, Karl Marx and Friedrich Engels, "Manifesto of the Communist Party," in Lewis S. Feurer, ed., *Basic Writings on Politics and Philosophy: Karl Marx and Friedrich Engles* (Garden City: Anchor Books, 1959), pp. 31–32.

3. They could, in the Marxian view, either accept this fact or be guilty of having a false sense of class consciousness. For an informative discussion of this problem in an English setting, see David Lockwood, *The Blackcoated Worker* (London: George Allen & Unwin, Ldt., 1958).

4. The quantitative behavioral studies undertaken in political science have pointed to a similar conclusion about the variability of class attitudes. See Robert A. Dahl, "The Behavioral Approach in Political Science: Epitaph for a Monument to a Successful Protest," *The American Political Science Review* 55 (December 1961): 769.

5. Future historians will, I feel certain, use these equations and similar statements of causal relationships in more sophisticated ways; one can only hope that when they do so, they will keep in mind the limitations of their data and of mine.

6. In this equation (as in the previous one), P stands for political variables, O for organizational factors, E and S for economic and social variables, respectively.

7. Here I am commenting only on Hofstadter's original statement of his thesis. As I made clear in the previous chapters, I found numerous occasions to use the amended form of Hofstadter's concept, that is, the version expanding status anxiety into "cultural politics."

8. As this conclusion suggests, one might see here a variant on consensus history. What I have described, however, is the making of a consensus, a historical process involving substantial conflict and sharp differences of opinion; this, I believe, is not what the consensus school of historians had in mind.

9. Other less desirable losses will probably include the humanistic emphasis upon personality and place. Throughout this book, I constantly referred to individuals: the farmer, the organized laborer, the professional engineer, and the clergyman. But these individuals were as abstract as the statistics they illustrated. None of them sweated. They were not men at all as we see them about us, work with them, like them—are them. Nor were they residents of a particular place, despite the fact that I labeled my farmers as southern and midwestern. The author spent his boyhood in the Midwest and can remember the smells and sounds and feel of farm country, but this land found no place in his history and should be tallied as part of the price of a behavioral approach to the past. I am indebted to Robert J. Brugger and his study, "A Secessionist Persuasion: The Mind and Heart of Beverly Tucker, Virginian" (Ph.D. diss., Johns Hopkins University, 1974), for helping me see these contrasts between behavioral and humanistic history.

10. Burton R. Fisher and Stephen B. Withey, *Big Business As The People See It: A Study Of A Socio-Economic Institution* (Ann Arbor: The Survey Research Center, Institute for Social Research, University of Michigan, 1951).

11. Edward C. Higbee, *Farms and Farmers in an Urban Age* (New York: Twentieth Century Fund, 1963).

12. *Historical Statistics of the United States, Colonial Times to 1957* (Washington, 1960), p. 98. Philip Taft, *The A.F. of L. from the Death of Gompers to the Merger* (New York: Harper & Brothers, 1959), pp. 219–31; Fred H. Joiner, "Developments in Union Agreements," in Colston E. Warne et al., eds., *Labor in Postwar America* (New York: Remsen Press, 1949),

pp. 25–41; Arthur F. McClure, *The Truman Administration and the Problems of Postwar Labor, 1945–1948* (Rutherford, N.J.: Fairleigh Dickinson University Press, 1969), pp. 23–33.

13. Ibid., pp. 45–78. See also Bert G. Hickman, *Growth and Stability of the Postwar Economy* (Washington: The Brookings Institution, 1960), pp. 25, 43–48.

14. Hickman, *Growth and Stability*, pp. 15–33; *Historical Statistics*, p. 283; Harold G. Vatter, *The U.S. Economy in the 1950's: An Economic History* (New York: W. W. Norton & Co., 1963); Elmo Roper, "The Public Looks at Business," *Harvard Business Review* 27 (March 1949): 169–70; Fisher and Withey, *Big Business As The People See It*, pp. 90, 94–95, 141.

15. Dwight David Eisenhower, "Farewell Radio and Television Address to the American People, January 17, 1961," in *Selected Speeches of Dwight David Eisenhower* (House Doc. no. 91-355, 91st Cong., 2d Sess., 1970), p. 148.

16. C. Wright Mills, *The Power Elite* (New York: Oxford University Press, 1956); William H. Whyte, Jr., *The Organization Man* (Garden City, N.Y.: Doubleday, 1956); David Riesman et al., *The Lonely Crowd* (New Haven: Yale University Press, 1961).

17. Alan F. Westin, "The John Birch Society," in Daniel Bell, ed., *The Radical Right* (Garden City, N.Y.: Doubleday & Co., 1964), pp. 241, 246, 249–50.

18. Irwin Unger, *The Movement: A History of the American New Left, 1959–1972* (New York: Dodd, Mead & Company, 1974). Unger stresses (more than I have) the internal problems of the movement.

19. Expressed in the terms used in our three equations, social (S) and organizational (O) factors have, since 1940, continued to exert a more significant influence on attitudes than economic (E) or political (P) variables.

INDEX

References to tables and figures are printed in boldface type

Bricklayers Union, 10
Brookings Institution, 227
Bryan, William Jennings, 8, 79–80, 88–89
Bryce, James, 24
Buffalo Express, 100
Bunker Hill & Sullivan Mining Co., **111**
Bureaucracy, 3–5, 7; culture of, 5, 14–15, 21, 117, 142, 153–56, 181–83, 186–87, 196, 204–5, 209, 216–17, 220–21, 225, 229, 233, 237, 246–47, 249, 261–68; development of, 117, 158–59, 183, 264, 267; problems of, 10–14; theory of, 4–5. *See also* Big business
Bureau of Corporations, 131

Carnegie, Andrew, 7, 73, 108, **182**, 183, 261; and Homestead strike, 85, 103–4; philanthropy of, 85, 104. *See also* Carnegie Iron and Steel Co.
Carnegie Iron and Steel Co., 72, 106, **107**, 137, **145**, **151**; Homestead plant of, 73–74, 103–4
Central of Georgia Railroad, **89**, **161**, 212
Chase, Stuart, 227
Chicago and Northwestern Railroad, **94**, **129**
Chicago, Burlington and Quincy Railroad, **83**, **94**, **99**, **129**, **169**, **171**
Chicago, Great Western Railroad, **94**
Chicago, Milwaukee and St. Paul Railroad, **129**, **219**
Chicago, Rock Island and Pacific Railroad, **94**, **175**
Chicago Tribune, 95
Civil Engineers Club of Cleveland, 99
Clay Frick Co., 70
Clayton Act, 261
Clergymen (Congregational), 31, **34**, 48, 59, 63, 69, 80, 97; economic condition of, 79, 85, 192–93; perceptions of big business of, 53–58, 74–75, 80–86, 113, 120–26, 132–33, 148, 152–56, 166–69, 174, 182, 186, 205–9, 221, 223–29, 247, 249, 255, 257, 259, 262. *See also* Equilibrium, in clergymen's attitudes
Commons, John R., 149–50
Congregationalist, 31, **34**, 54–58, 80–81, **82**, **83**, 84–85, 120, **122–23**, **152**, 153, 166, **168**, **169**, **206**, **208**, **224**, 226, 270
Congress of Industrial Organizations (CIO), 223, 240

Consensus history, 17, 19, 112–13, 149, 225, 247–48, 255
Content analysis: description of, 24–26; evaluation of, 40–43, 149; sources used in, 26–32; technique of, 32–40
Continental Tobacco, **147**
Corn Belt Meat Producers' Association, 179
Corporate culture. *See* Bureaucracy, culture of
Corps of Engineers, 243
"Covering law," theory of, 22–23, 25–26
Croly, Herbert, 126–27
Crop Reporter, 127
Cummins, Albert B., 192

Delaware, Lackawanna and Western Railroad, **169**
Depew, Chauncey, 57, **182**
Des Moines Register, 95
Dewey, John, 21, 127
Duke, James B., 108
Du Pont (family), 225–26
Du Pont Powder Co., 181
Durant, William, 183

East Tennessee Farmers' Convention, 90
East Tennessee, Virginia and Georgia Railroad, **89**
Ehret, George, Co., **111**
Eisenhower, Dwight D., 267
Ely, Richard T., 21, 52, 58, 126
Emergency Fleet Corporation, 159
Engineering Association of the South, 99
Engineering News, 30–31, 37, 49, **50**, **51**, 51–52, 54, **98**, **99**, 102, 136–37, **140**, **141**, **152**, **177**, **178**, **214**, **215**, 243, **244**, **245**, 270
Engineers, 30–31, **34**, 54–55, 59, 63, 69, 100, 117, 154, 176, 216; economic conditions of, 79, 100–103, 136–38, 192, 223, 242; organizations of, 8, 52, 59, 75, 98–100, 138–40, 148–49, 176, 181, 215–16, 220, 242–43, 246, 256, 260, 262; perceptions of big business of, 37–40, 48–53, 74–76, 97–103, 131–32, 136–41, 148, 152–55, 173–77, 181–82, 213–16, 221, 223, 228, 242–47, 255–56, 259–60. *See also* Equilibrium, in engineers' attitudes
Equilibrium, 19, 20–21, 269–73; in clergymen's attitudes, 53, 57–58, 81, 156, 183,

INDEX